"I like that the key terms are given at the beginning of the chapter. It helps to know what is important while reading. I also like that the key definitions are put in the margins. It makes it easier for reviewing and studying."

—Joe Hoff, student at University of Wisconsin–LaCrosse

Online Study Center
Prepare for Class

Online Study Center
Improve Your Grade

Online Study Center
ACE the Test

Do you find the marginal callouts useful?

#	Answer		Number of Responses	Percentage
1	Strongly agree		166	38.16%
2	Agree		207	47.59%
3	Somewhat agree		55	12.64%
4	Disagree		7	1.61%
	TOTAL:		435	100.00%

Mean : 1.777   Mean Percentile : 80.57%   Standard Deviation : 0.723

"It's nice that the book specifically tells you the resources you can use and where you can find them."

—Kristin Chimento, student at Miami University

Do you find the concept checks useful?

#	Answer		Number of Responses	Percentage
1	Strongly agree		117	27.08%
2	Agree		205	47.45%
3	Somewhat agree		86	19.91%
4	Disagree		24	5.56%
	TOTAL:		432	100.00%

Mean : 2.039   Mean Percentile : 74.02%   Standard Deviation : 0.831

CONCEPT CHECK 1.1

Identify the components of communication (stimulus, filter, message, medium, destination, and feedback) in the following situation: Eva glanced up just in time to see the pot of pasta begin boiling over. "Oh, no," she yelled. "Now what's the matter?" said Rosario.

"The test preppers with the chapter seemed to be a hit with the students. That way they could stop and review while the information was still fresh."

—Malika Blakely, Professor at Georgia State University

Do you find the test prepper useful?

#	Answer		Number of Responses	Percentage
1	Strongly agree		163	38.08%
2	Agree		194	45.33%
3	Somewhat agree			15.19%
4	Disagree			1.40%
	TOTAL:			100.00%

Mean : 1.799   Mean Percentile : 80

Data in barcharts from student survey at San Francisco State University.

Fundamentals of Contemporary Business Communication

STUDENT ACHIEVEMENT SERIES

Fundamentals of Contemporary Business Communication

▶
▶
▶

Scot Ober

Ball State University

▶
▶
▶
▶

Houghton Mifflin Company

Boston   New York

Vice President, Publisher: *George Hoffman*

Senior Sponsoring Editor: *Lise Johnson*

Senior Marketing Manager: *Mike Schenk*

Senior Developmental Editor: *Chere Bemelmans*

Cover Design Director: *Tony Saizon*

Senior Photo Editor: *Jennifer Meyer Dare*

Senior Project Editor: *Nancy Blodget*

Editorial Assistant: *John Powers*

Senior Art and Design Coordinator: *Jill Haber*

Composition Buyer: *Chuck Dutton*

▶ TO DIANA, WHO MAKES MY WRITING POSSIBLE—
AND EVERYTHING ELSE, FOR THAT MATTER.

Cover Photo: © Hemer

The model letters provided on authentic company stationery have been included by permission to provide realistic examples of company documents for educational purposes. They do not represent actual business documents created by these companies.

Screen shots reprinted by permission from Microsoft Corporation.

Other credits appear on page 409, which is considered an extension of the copyright page.

Printed in the U.S.A.

Library of Congress Control Number: 2006936066

Instructor's Annotated Edition:
ISBN 13: 978-0-618-90101-2
ISBN 10: 0-618-90101-9

For orders, use student text ISBNs:
ISBN 13: 978-0-618-90093-0
ISBN 10: 0-618-90093-4

1 2 3 4 5 6 7 8 9—CRK— 11 10 09 08 07

Brief Contents

Contents

CHAPTER 7

PERSUASIVE LETTERS, MEMOS, AND E-MAIL MESSAGES   140

CHAPTER 8

BAD-NEWS LETTERS, MEMOS, AND E-MAIL MESSAGES   168

CHAPTER 12

THE JOB SEARCH, RÉSUMÉS, AND JOB-APPLICATION LETTERS 278

CHAPTER 13

EMPLOYMENT INTERVIEWING AND FOLLOW-UP 312

MODULE E

MECHANICS IN BUSINESS WRITING   380

STYLE MANUAL: FORMATTING BUSINESS DOCUMENTS   392

Preface

▶ A TEAM APPROACH: BUILT BY PROFESSORS AND STUDENTS, FOR PROFESSORS AND STUDENTS

Over the past two years Houghton Mifflin has conducted research and focus groups with a diverse cross-section of professors and students from across the country to create the first textbook model that truly reflects what professors and students want and need in an educational product. Everything we have learned has been applied to create and build a brand new educational experience and product model, from the ground up, for our two very important customer bases. *Student Achievement Series: Fundamentals of Contemporary Business Communication* is based on extensive professor and student feedback and is specifically designed to meet the teaching needs of today's instructors as well as the learning, study, and assessment goals of today's students. Professors and students have been involved with every key decision regarding this new product development model and learning system—from content structure, to design, to packaging, and even to marketing and messaging. The result is an educational model that has been specifically designed to meet the teaching needs of today's instructors, as well as the learning, study, and assessment goals of today's students.

It has long been a Houghton Mifflin tradition and honor to partner closely with professors to gain valuable insights and recommendations during the development process. Partnering equally as closely with students through the entire product development and product launch process has proved to also be extremely gratifying and productive.

▶ WHAT STUDENTS TOLD US

Working closely with students has been both rewarding and enlightening. Their honest and candid feedback and their practical and creative ideas have helped us to develop an educational learning model like no other on the market today.

Students have told us many things. While price is important to them, they are just as interested in having a textbook that reflects the way they actually learn and study. As with other consumer purchases and decisions they make, they want a textbook that is of true value to them. The *Student Achievement Series* model accomplishes both of their primary goals: it provides them with a price-conscious textbook, and it presents the concepts in a way that pleases them.

Today's students are busy individuals. They go to school, they work, some have families, they have a wide variety of interests, and they are involved in many activities. They take their education very seriously. Their main goal is to master the materials so they can perform well in class, get a good grade, graduate, land a good job, and be successful.

Different students learn in different ways; some learn best by reading, some are more visually oriented, and some learn best through practice and assessment. Although students learn in different ways, almost all students told us the same things regarding what they want their textbook to "look like." The ideal textbook for students gets to the point quickly; is easy to understand and read;

has fewer and/or shorter chapters; has pedagogical materials designed to reinforce key concepts; has a strong supporting website for quizzing, testing, and assessment of materials; is cost conscious; and provides them with real value for their dollar.

Students want smaller chunks of information rather than the long sections and paragraphs found in traditional textbooks. This format provides them with immediate reinforcement and allows them to assess the concepts they have just studied. They like to read materials in more bulleted formats that are easier to digest than long sections and paragraphs. They almost always pay special attention to key terms and any materials that are boldfaced or highlighted in the text. In general, they spend little time reading or looking at materials that they view as superficial, such as many of the photographs (although they want some photos for visual enhancement) and boxed materials. However, they do want a textbook that is visually interesting; holds their interest; and is designed in an open, friendly, and accessible format. They want integrated study and assessment materials that help them reinforce, master, and test their knowledge of key concepts. They also want integrated Web and technology components that focus on quizzing and provide them with an interactive place to go to for help and assessment. They don't want websites that simply repeat the textual information in the book or that provide superficial information that is not primary to the key concepts in the text.

While students learn and study in a variety of different ways, a number of students told us that they often attend class first to hear their professor lecture and to take notes. Then they go back to read the chapter after (not always before) class. They use their textbook in this fashion to not only get the information they need but to also reinforce what they have learned in class. Students told us that they study primarily by using an index or flashcards that highlight key concepts and terms, by reading lecture notes, and by using the supporting book website for quizzing and testing of key concepts. They also told us that they are far more likely to purchase and use a textbook if their professor actively uses the textbook in class and tells them that they need it.

▶ TAKING WHAT PROFESSORS AND STUDENTS TOLD US TO CREATE THE *Student Achievement Series* MODEL

The *Student Achievement Series* provides exactly what students want and need pedagogically in an educational product. While other textbooks on the market include some of these features, *Student Achievement Series* is the first program model to fully incorporate all of these cornerstones, as well as to introduce innovative new learning methods and study processes that completely meet the wishes of today's students. It does this by:

▌ Being concise and to the point.

▌ Presenting more content in bulleted or more succinct formats.

▌ Highlighting and boldfacing key concepts and information.

▌ Organizing content in more bite-size and chunked-up formats.

▌ Providing a system for immediate reinforcement and assessment throughout the chapter.

▌ Creating a design that is open, user friendly, and interesting for today's students.

▌ Developing a supporting and integrated Web component that focuses on quizzing and assessment of key concepts.

▌ Eliminating or reducing traditional chapter components that students view as superficial.

▌ Creating a product that is easier for students to read and study.

▌ Providing students with a price-conscious product.

▌ Providing students with a product they feel is valuable.

▶ PROFESSORS AND STUDENTS: WE COULDN'T HAVE DONE IT WITHOUT YOU

We are very grateful to all the students across the country who participated in one form or another in helping us to create and build the first educational series designed specifically for them and their learning and educational goals. Working with these students was an honor, as well as a lot of fun, for all of us at Houghton Mifflin. We sincerely appreciate their honesty, candor, creativeness, and interest in helping us to develop a better learning experience. We also appreciate their willingness to meet with us for lengthy periods of time and to allow us to videotape them and use some of their excellent quotes. We wish them much success as they complete their college education, begin their careers, and go about their daily lives.

STUDENT PARTICIPANTS

Katie Aiken, *Miami University*
O'Neil Barrett, *Borough of Manhattan Community College*
Joe Barron, *Providence College*
Laura Beal, *Miami University*
Ryan Bis, *Boston University*
Gerius Brantley, *Florida Atlantic University*
Angie Brewster, *Boston College*
Cyleigh Brez, *Miami University*
Veronica Calvo, *Keiser College*
Kristin Chimento, *Miami University*
Catie Connolly, *Anna Marie College*
Angelique Cooper, *DePaul University*
Adam Delaney-Winn, *Tufts University*
Stephanie DiSerio, *Miami University*
Rita Diz, *Lehman College*
Maggie Dolehide, *Miami University*

Matthew Dripps, *Miami University*
Gabriel Duran, *Florida International University*
Giovanni Espinoza, *Hunter College*
Tanya Fahrenbach, *Benedictine University*
Christina Fischer, *University of Illinois at Chicago*
Danielle Gagnon, *Boston University*
Paulina Glater, *DePaul University*
Donna Gonzalez, *Florida International University*
Barry Greenbaum, *Cooper Union*
Rachel Hall, *Miami University*
Emma Harris, *Miami University*
Erika Hill, *University of Florida*
Joe Hoff, *University of Wisconsin–LaCrosse*
Matt Janko, *University of Massachusetts–Amherst*
Travis Keltner, *Boston College*
Matthew Konigsberg, *Baruch University*
Fritz Kuhnlenz, *Boston University*

Lindsey Lambalot, *Northeastern University*
Cheng Lee, *University of Wisconsin–LaCrosse*
Steven Lippi, *Boston College*
Henry Lopez, *Florida International University*
Jessie Lynch, *Miami University*
Sarah Marith, *Boston University*
Nichelina Mavros, *Fordham University*
Marika Michalos, *City College of New York*
Evan Miller, *Parsons School of Design*
Fernando Monzon, *Miami Dade College*
Matt Nitka, *University of Wisconsin–LaCrosse*
Rehan Noormohammad, *Northeastern Illinois University*
Caitlin Offinger, *Amherst College*
Durrell Queen, *University of New York*
Adrienne Rayski, *Baruch University*

Kevin Ringel, *Northwestern University*
Alison Savery, *Tufts University*
Laura Schaffner, *Miami University*
Jordan Simkovi, *Northwestern University*
Karissa Teekah, *Lehman College*
Patrick Thermitus, *Bentley College*
Gregory Toft, *Baruch University*
Rebecca Tolles, *Miami University*
Sam Trzyzewski, *Boston University*
Vanessa Uribe, *Florida International University*
Kristin Vayda, *Miami University*
Michael Werner, *Baruch University*
Robert White, *DePaul University*
Helen Wong, *Hunter College*
Aliyah Yusuf, *Lehman College*
Students at San Francisco State University

We are equally grateful to all the professors across the country who participated in the development and creation of this new product model through content reviews, advisory boards, and/or focus group work regarding the new pedagogical learning system. As always, professors provided us with invaluable information, ideas, and suggestions that consistently helped to strengthen our final product. We owe them great thanks and wish them much success in and out of their classrooms.

PROFESSOR PARTICIPANTS AND REVIEWERS

Paula E. Brown, *Northern Illinois University*
Bruce Fisher, *Elmhurst College*
Mark Fox, *Indiana University South Bend*
Paula Hladik, *Waubonsie Community College*
Lisa McConnel, *Oklahoma State University*
Suzanne Peterson, *Arizona State University*
Gerald Silver, *Purdue University–Calumet*
Nancy Thannert, *Robert Morris College*
Ron Thomas, *Oakton Community College*
Kenneth Thompson, *DePaul University*
Benjamin Weeks, *St. Xavier University*

▶ FEATURES OF *Student Achievement Series: Fundamentals of Contemporary Business Communication*

By the time students enter the business communication class, they know enough about the business environment to appreciate the critical role communication plays in the contemporary organization. They're also aware of the role communication will play in helping them secure an internship or get a job and be successful at work. Thus, a major objective of *Student Achievement Series: Fundamentals of Contemporary Business Communication* is to present comprehensive coverage of real-world concepts in an interesting, lively, and concise manner.

OBJECTIVE-BASED ORGANIZATION

Student Achievement Series: Fundamentals of Contemporary Business Communication makes it convenient for instructors to easily customize their course to meet their particular needs. Each chapter is organized around learning objectives; they appear at the beginning of the chapter and are identified throughout the text. All content relating to an objective is presented before moving on to the next objective, and a Test Prepper assesses student knowledge of that objective. Further, the Learning Objective Review is organized around each objective, as are the end-of-chapter exercises.

Instructors can easily assign an entire chapter or only components of the chapter and then identify the related end-of-chapter exercises. In addition, all business English coverage has been organized into modules at the back of the text, along with an extensive array of exercises, to provide greater flexibility—and a one-stop reference for students. Finally, in addition to increased emphasis on ethics, e-mail, and audience analysis throughout the text, each of the following topics has been expanded and is now placed in a separate chapter:

▌ Interpersonal Communication Skills

▌ The Writing Process

▌ Revising Your Writing

▌ Persuasive Letters, Memos, and E-Mail Messages

▌ Employment Interviewing and Follow-Up

BUSINESS COMMUNICATION—IN CONTEXT

Business communication problems in the real world do not occur in a vacuum. Events happen before the problem and will happen after the problem, and these affect its resolution. Various learning tools provide long-term situations and a "slice-of-life" reality students will actually face at work.

On the Job. Each chapter begins with an on-the-job interview with managers from multinational companies, small entrepreneurial companies, and nonprofit organizations. These insider perspectives set the stage for the particular concepts presented in that chapter.

Continuing Text Examples and End-of-Chapter Exercises. Continuing examples are often used throughout the chapter in both the text and end-of-chapter exercises. For example, in Chapter 7, students write a persuasive request from a subordinate; in Chapter 8, they assume the role of superior and turn down this well-written persuasive request. Such situations are realistic because they let students follow a problem and they provide a continuing thread through the chapters. They also reinforce the concept of audience analysis because students must first assume the role of sender and second the role of receiver for the same communication task.

Real Company Letterheads. Full-page models of each major writing task appear in the text on real company letterheads, shown in complete, ready-to-send format, so that students become familiar with the appropriate format for every major type of writing assignment. Each model provides marginal step-by-step composition notes as well as grammar and mechanics notes that point out specific illustrations of the grammar and mechanics instruction presented in the business English modules at the back of the text.

Technology-Centered.   Every aspect of contemporary business communication—from determining what information to communicate to processing the information and sharing it with others—depends on technology. In the *Student Achievement Series: Fundamentals of Contemporary Business Communication,* students learn to:

▌ Compose, format, and manage e-mail and conduct productive instant-messaging sessions.

▌ Access the Internet and evaluate the quality of the information they receive.

▌ Format electronic and HTML résumés and search online for a job.

▌ Prepare and deliver electronic presentations.

▌ Cite electronic sources such as webpages, online journals and directories, e-mail, and other Internet sources in business, APA, and MLA formats.

THE 3PS—THINK FIRST; WRITE LATER

As soon as most students are given a writing assignment, they quickly scan the problem and then immediately begin composing what they think is the final draft—without first planning the best strategy to use. The 3Ps teaches students to think first—and write later.

Each 3Ps activity begins with a *problem*—a typical business situation that requires some sort of communication task. The *process* questions force students to concentrate on the critical elements of the situation; that is, they must delay their impulse to begin writing until after they've thought through (and solved) these important issues. The activity ends with the *product*—the final, ready-to-submit formatted document.

STREAMLINED COVERAGE OF ESSENTIAL TOPICS

As the body of knowledge comprising the theory, research, and practice of business communication has grown, textbooks have expanded to include the new coverage. They have become longer and longer, often making it difficult to cover all the material in a typical course. *Student Achievement Series: Fundamentals of Contemporary Business Communication* is true to its name: it presents the fundamental traditional and emerging topics in business communication in about half the length of more traditional textbooks.

BASIC SKILLS EMPHASIS

Students must learn these basic skills at some point, and the collegiate business communication course may be their last opportunity. Five modules at the back of *Student Achievement Series: Fundamentals of Contemporary Business Communication* systematically review and expand on basic English skills, organized as follows:

A. Business Sentence Structure
B. Business-Style Punctuation
C. Verbs and Subject-Verb Agreement
D. Using Pronouns, Adjectives, and Adverbs
E. Mechanics in Business Writing

Also included on the Instructor's website (and available through the Houghton Mifflin Faculty Service Center) are more than 50 handout masters that provide important supplemental reference materials or practice opportunities to help students expand their skills.

STUDENT PORTFOLIOS—FOR PROOF OF COMPETENCE

In the *Student Achievement Series: Fundamentals of Contemporary Business Communication* is a planned progression of eight portfolio projects designed to demonstrate students' communication skills. These can be shown to prospective employers. The eight projects are:

1. Routine informational message
2. Routine adjustment letter
3. Persuasive request
4. Bad-news message
5. Situational business report
6. Videotape of an oral business presentation
7. Résumé and cover letter
8. Videotape of a practice interview

▶ UNPRECEDENTED INSTRUCTOR AND STUDENT SUPPORT

FOR INSTRUCTORS

▌ ***Online Instructor's Resource Manual.*** The Instructor's Resource Manual contains chapter teaching aids for each chapter and end-of-text module, such as a detailed chapter overview (which includes a detailed lecture outline) and suggestions and sample solutions to all chapter exercises. The Online Instructor's Resource Manual is available on the Instructor Website (Online Teaching Center) and course management platforms (BlackBoard/WebCT CD).

▌ ***Online Test Bank.*** The Test Bank contains more than 1,650 items. Each of the questions has been reviewed for clarity, accuracy, appropriateness, and difficulty. Furthermore, each question was designed to test the student's knowledge, understanding, or ability to integrate and apply the subject matter. The Test Bank contains true-false, multiple-choice, and short-answer essay questions. The Test Bank is available through course management platforms (BlackBoard/WebCT CD) and Faculty Services.

▌ ***HMTesting Instructor CD.*** This CD-ROM contains electronic Test Bank items. Through a partnership with the Brownstone Research Group, HM Testing—now powered by *Diploma*®—provides instructors with all the tools they need to

xxiv FUNDAMENTALS OF CONTEMPORARY BUSINESS COMMUNICATION

create, author/edit, customize, and deliver multiple types of tests. Instructors can import questions directly from the Test Bank, create their own questions, or edit existing algorithmic questions, all within *Diploma's* powerful electronic platform.

▌ *Online Teaching Center*. This text-based instructor website offers valuable resources, including basic and premium PowerPoint slides, downloadable Instructor's Resource Manual and Test Bank files, classroom response system content, and classroom handouts. Detailed lecture notes are also provided for each chapter, as well as sample solutions to all in-text exercises. The site also includes a correlation of SCANS competencies to in-text material, grading rubrics (objective forms to help instructors evaluate students' work), and guidelines for helping students develop a writing portfolio. The site is also a forum for exchanging ideas with the author, publisher, and other instructors around the country teaching this course.

▌ *Business Communication Newsletter.* This e-mailed newsletter is available for free to any instructor of business communication. Subscribers receive monthly issues highlighting articles that reinforce teaching concepts and current events illustrating business communication concepts.

▌ *BlackBoard/WebCT.* This online course management system, powered by BlackBoard, contains the Instructor's Resource Manual with Test Bank files, Test Bank pools, classroom response system content, basic and premium PowerPoint slides, audio chapter summaries and quizzes (MP3s), interactive LAB tests, and much more.

FOR STUDENTS

▌ *Online Study Center*. This text-specific student website offers non-passkey protected content such as Ask Ober (e-mail: askober@ober.net), ACE practice tests, outlines, summaries, glossaries (chapter-based and complete), and much more. Content behind "Your Guide to an 'A'" passkey includes ACE+ quizzes, Flashcards, Interactive LAB tests, crossword puzzles, and audio chapter reviews (MP3 chapter summaries and quizzes).

▶ ACKNOWLEDGMENTS

During the development of this textbook series, it has been my great pleasure to work with a dedicated and skillful team of professionals at Houghton Mifflin, and I gratefully acknowledge the major contributions they have made to this text. In addition, I express my sincere appreciation to Carolee Jones of Ball State University, who prepared the Instructor Manual with Test Bank for this text, and to Marian Wood, consultant and writer extraordinaire, for the many elements she created for this edition.

Finally, I wish to thank the following reviewers for their thoughtful contributions:

Carl Bridges, *Arthur Andersen Consulting*
Annette Brisco, *Indian University Southeast*
Mitchel T. Burchfield, *Southwest Texas Junior College*

Janice Burke, *South Suburban College*
Cheryl Byrne, *Washtenaw Community College*
Barbara Cameron, *Embry-Riddle Aeronautical University*
G. Jay Christensen, *California State University, Northridge*
Anna Hutta Colvin, *Montgomery Country Community College*
Brenda Cornell, *Central Texas College*
Doris L. Cost, *Metropolitan State College of Denver*
Ashly Cowden, *Clemson University*
L. Ben Crane, *Temple University*
Ava Cross, *Ryerson Polytechnic University*
Terence P. Curran, *Siena College*
Nancy J. Daugherty, *Indiana University–Purdue University, Indianapolis*
Corla Dawson, *Missouri Western State College*
Rosemarie Dittmer, *Northeastern University*
Graham N. Drake, *State University of New York, Geneseo*
Kay Durden, *The University of Tennessee at Martin*
Karen Gaines, *Johnson County Community College*
Bonnie Grossman, *College of Charleston*
Phillip A. Holcomb, *Angelo State University*
Larry R. Honl, *University of Wisconsin, Eau Claire*
Michael Hricik, *Westmoreland City Community College*
Kimberlie Johnson, *North Idaho College*
Michelle Kirtley Johnston, *Loyola University*
Alice Kinder, *Virginia Polytechnic Institute and State University*
Richard N. Kleeberg, *Solano Community College*
Patricia Laidler, *Massasoit Community College*
Lowell Lamberton, *Central Oregon Community College*
E. Jay Larson, *Lewis and Clark State College*
Michael Liberman, *East Stroudsburg University*
Julie MacDonald, *Northwestern State University*
Marsha C. Markman, *California Lutheran University*
Cynthia Marshall, *Wright State University*
Diana McKowen, *Indiana University, Bloomington*
Maureen McLaughlin, *Highline Community College*
Sylvia A. Miller, *Cameron University*
Wayne Moore, *Indiana University of Pennsylvania*
Gerald W. Morton, *Auburn University of Montgomery*
Paul Murphey, *Southwest Wisconsin Technical College*
James M. O'Donnell, *Huntington College*
Rosemary Olds, *Des Moines Area Community College*
Allene Parker, *Embry-Riddle Aeronautical University*
Catherine Peck, *Chippewa Valley Technical College*
Yamil Perez, *ATI Oakland Park*
Richard O. Pompian, *Boise State University*
Karen Sterkel Powell, *Colorado State University*
Seamus Reilly, *University of Illinois*
Jeanette Ritzenthaler, *New Hampshire College*
Betty Robbins, *University of Oklahoma*
Joan C. Roderick, *Southwest Texas State University*
Lacye Prewitt Schmidt, *State Technical Institute of Memphis*

Phyllis Lee Schulz, *Western Business College*
Sue Seymour, *Cameron University*
Sherry Sherrill, *Forsyth Technical Community*
John R. Sinton, *Finger Lakes Community College*
Curtis J. Smith, *Finger Lakes Community College*
Eunice A. Smith, *Bismarck State College*
Dottie Snider, *Eastern Connecticut State University*
Craig E. Stanley, *California State University, Sacramento*
Marilyn St. Clair, *Weatherford College*
Ted O. Stoddard, *Brigham Young University*
Vincent C. Trofi, *Providence College*
Deborah A. Valentine, *Emory University*
Randall L. Waller, *Baylor University*
Maria W. Warren, *University of West Florida*
Delmar Wilcox, *Western New England College*
Michael R. Wunsch, *Northern Arizona University*
Annette Wyandotte, *Indiana University, Southeast*
Betty Rogers Youngkin, *University of Dayton*

Fundamentals of Contemporary Business Communication

1 Understanding Business Communication

Nissan North America, Inc., works hard to communicate clear and effective messages to its audiences in the United States, Mexico, and Canada. This communication includes everything from e-mail, to television, to advertising on its own building.

1 *Describe the components of communication.*

2 *Identify the common forms of verbal communication.*

3 *Identify the major barriers to verbal communication.*

Chapter Outline

Online Study Center
Prepare for Class
Chapter Outline

Nissan Drives Effective Communication

Steering communication upward, downward, horizontally, and across business and borders—at full throttle—is part of a race that never ends for Debra Sanchez Fair. As vice president of corporate communications for Nissan North America, Inc., she and her 43-person staff drive all communications for the automaker's operations in the United States, Mexico, and Canada.

Fair uses various media to share information within the organization, ranging from e-mail, videoconferencing, and satellite television to more traditional newsletters, meetings, and memos. Before

Online Study Center college.hmco.com/pic/oberSASfund

on the job

DEBRA
SANCHEZ FAIR
Vice President,
Corporate
Communications,
Nissan North
America, Inc.
(Carson, California)

KEY TERMS

abstract word   *p. 12*
audience   *p. 6*
communication   *p. 5*
concrete word   *p. 12*
connotation   *p. 10*
denotation   *p. 10*
euphemism   *p. 12*
feedback   *p. 7*
filter   *p. 6*
jargon   *p. 12*
medium   *p. 7*
message   *p. 6*
slang   *p. 11*
stimulus   *p. 5*

selecting any medium, however, she carefully plans what she wants to achieve. "First, you have to think about your objective, the audience you are targeting, and your communication strategy," Fair says. "Then you think about the tactics. Every situation or initiative may require a different approach."

To find out whether audiences understand Nissan's messages, at least once a year Fair surveys employees, business leaders, and media representatives. Monitoring this feedback helps Fair and her team analyze audience response and keep Nissan's communication on track in the race that never ends. ■

As Debra Sanchez Fair of Nissan North America knows firsthand, effective communication drives successful businesses. Walk through the hallways of any contemporary organization—no matter whether it's a small start-up entrepreneurial firm, a *Fortune* 500 global giant, a state government office, or a not-for-profit organization. What do you see? You see employees:

- Reading documents
- Drafting messages
- Attending meetings
- Conducting interviews
- Talking on the telephone
- Conferring with others
- Reading mail
- Typing on the computer
- Making presentations

In short, you see people *communicating*. An organization is a group of people working together to achieve a common goal. Communication, of course, is a vital part of that process. Indeed, communication must have occurred before a common goal could even be established because communication is the means by which information is shared, activities are coordinated, and decisions are made.

Understanding how communication works in business and how employees communicate competently within an organization will help you participate more effectively in every aspect of business. Good communication skills are crucial to your success in the organization (Figure 1.1). Competent writing and speaking skills will help you get hired, perform well, and earn promotions. If you decide to go into business for yourself, excellent writing and speaking skills will help you obtain start-up funds, promote your product, and manage your employees. The same skills will also help you achieve your personal and social goals.

It is no wonder then that, according to Mark H. McCormack, chairperson of International Management Group and bestselling author of *What They Don't Teach You at Harvard Business School,* "People's written communications are probably more revealing than any other single item in the workplace."[1]

THE COMPONENTS OF COMMUNICATION

1 ▶ *Describe the components of communication.*

Because communication is such a vital part of the organizational structure, our study of communication begins with an analysis of its components

(Figure 1.2). **Communication** is the process of sending and receiving messages—sometimes through spoken or written words and sometimes through nonverbal means such as facial expressions, gestures, and voice qualities.

Thus, if someone communicates the following message to you and you receive it, communication will have taken place. The communication will be successful, however, only if you understand Chinese.*

communication The process of sending and receiving verbal and nonverbal messages.

To illustrate the communication model shown in Figure 1.2, let us follow the case of Dave, a chemist. Several years ago, while working on another project, Dave developed Ultra Light, a flat sheet of luminescent material that serves as a light source. The market for lighting is vast, and Dave was disappointed when his company decided not to manufacture and market this product. As we learn what happened to Dave after this decision, we'll examine the components of communication, one at a time, as listed below:

Incident	*Communication Component*
Dave receives a memorandum from the head of research and development (R & D).	Dave receives a *stimulus*.
He interprets the memo to mean that his company has no interest in his invention.	He *filters* the stimulus.
He decides to relay this information to his brother Marc.	He forms a *message*.
He telephones Marc.	He selects a *medium*.
His brother receives the call.	The message reaches its *destination*.
Marc listens and gives Dave his reaction.	Marc provides *feedback*.

stimulus An event that creates the need to communicate.

FIGURE 1.1

Dissatisfied Employers
The lack of competent written communication skills is the number one source of dissatisfaction that employers have about their employees.

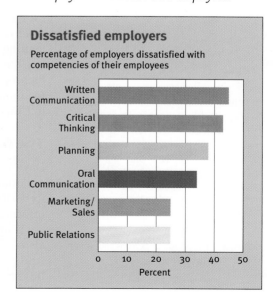

The Stimulus

For communication to take place, there first must be a **stimulus** (plural: *stimuli*), an event that creates within an individual the need to communicate. This stimulus can be internal or external. An internal stimulus is simply an idea that forms in your mind. External stimuli come to you through your sensory organs—your eyes, ears, nose, mouth, and skin. A stimulus for communicating in business might be any of the following:

*Illustrated here is the Chinese word for *crisis*, which is composed of the words *danger* and *opportunity*, perhaps an inspirational reminder to always remain hopeful.

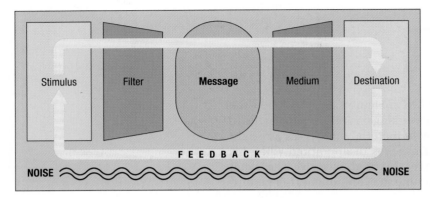

FIGURE 1.2

The Components of Communication

The communication model consists of five components: stimulus, filter, message, medium, and destination. Ideally, the process ends with feedback to the sender, although feedback is not necessary for communication to have taken place.

- An e-mail message you just read

- A presentation you heard at a staff meeting

- A bit of gossip you heard over lunch

- Your perception that the general manager has been acting preoccupied lately

- The hot air generated by an overworked heating system (or colleague!)

You respond to the stimulus by formulating a message: a *verbal message* (written or spoken words), a *nonverbal message* (nonwritten and nonspoken signals), or some combination of the two. For Dave, the stimulus for communication was a memorandum he received informing him that his company was not interested in developing Ultra Light but would, instead, sell the patent to another company that *was* interested in bringing this product to market.

The Filter

filter The mental process of interpreting stimuli based on one's knowledge, experience, and viewpoints.

If everyone had the same perception of events, your job of communicating would be easy. That is, you could assume that your view of what happened was accurate and that others would understand your motives and intent. Instead, each person has a *unique* view of reality, based on his or her individual experiences, culture, emotions at the moment, personality, knowledge, socioeconomic status, and a host of other variables. These variables act as a **filter** in shaping everyone's unique impressions of reality.

The memo Dave received simply reinforced what he had come to expect at his company. The company had become successful by focusing on its own long-range objectives and showed little interest in taking advantage of unexpected discoveries such as Ultra Light. Dave had been intimately involved in the research leading to the discovery of Ultra Light and was quite interested in its future. Besides, after so many years in the lab, he was ready for a new challenge. These factors, then, acted as a filter through which Dave interpreted the memo and formulated his response—a phone call to his brother Marc, a marketing manager in Chicago.

The Message

message The information that is communicated.

audience The person or persons with whom you are communicating.

Dave's message to Marc was simple: "Let's form our own company to manufacture and market Ultra Light." The extent to which any communication effort achieves its desired goal depends directly on how well you construct the **message**—that is, the information to be communicated.

Your success depends not only on the purpose and content of the message but also on how skillful you are at communicating, how well you know your **audience** (the person or persons with whom you are communicating), and how much you hold in common with your audience.

As a scientist, Dave did not have an extensive business vocabulary. Nor did he have much practice at oral business presentations and the careful pacing and reinforcement required in such circumstances. In effect, Dave was attempting to make an oral business proposal, but unfortunately without much technique or skill.

"You're crazy, Dave. You don't know what you're talking about." Marc's initial response made it clear to Dave that his message wasn't getting through. But what Dave lacked in skill, he made up for in knowing his audience (his kid brother) intimately.

"You're chicken, Marc" had always gotten Marc's attention and interest in the past, and it worked again. Dave continued challenging Marc, something he knew his brother couldn't resist, and kept reminding him of their common ground—namely, all the happy adventures they had shared as children and adults.

The Medium

Once the sender has formulated a message, the next step in the process is to transmit that message to the receiver. At this point, the sender must choose the form of message to send, or **medium** (plural: *media*). Oral messages might be transmitted through media such as a staff meeting, personal conference, telephone conversation, voice mail, or informal conversation. Written messages might be transmitted through e-mail, letter, contract, brochure, bulletin-board notice, company newsletter, or an addition to the company's policy and procedures manual. Nonverbal messages might be transmitted through facial expressions, gestures, or body movement. Because Dave is talking with Marc over the phone, his medium is the telephone.

You should be aware, however, that the most common forms of communication may not be the most effective for your purposes (Figure 1.3).

The Destination

The message is transmitted and then enters the sensory environment of the receiver. At this point, control passes from the sender to the receiver. Once the message reaches its destination, there is no guarantee that communication will actually occur. We are constantly bombarded with stimuli, and our sensory organs pick up only some of them. Even assuming the receiver *does* perceive your message, you have no assurance that it will be interpreted (filtered) as you intended. Your transmitted message then becomes the source, or stimulus, for the next communication episode, and the process begins anew.

After Dave's enthusiastic, one-hour phone call, Marc promised to consider the venture seriously. Marc's response provided **feedback** (reaction to a message) to Dave on how accurately his own message had been received. Although feedback is not required for communication to occur, it is, of course, helpful. In time, Marc's feedback led to many more versions of the communication process, both written and oral. The brothers' communications ultimately led to their forming a new company to manufacture the Ultra Light product.

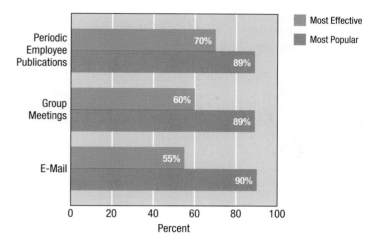

FIGURE 1.3

Effectiveness Versus Popularity of Communication Media

The International Association of Business Communicators recently surveyed nearly 1,000 organizations about their communication practices. The survey revealed that although e-mail was the most frequently used medium of communication, it was not the most effective.[2]

Most Effective — Most Popular

Periodic Employee Publications: 70% / 89%
Group Meetings: 60% / 89%
E-Mail: 55% / 90%

(Percent: 0, 20, 40, 60, 80, 100)

medium   The form of a message.

CONCEPT CHECK 1.1

Identify the components of communication (stimulus, filter, message, medium, destination, and feedback) in the following situation: Eva glanced up just in time to see the pot of pasta begin boiling over. "Oh, no," she yelled. "Now what's the matter?" said Rosario.

feedback   The receiver's reaction or response to a message.

Online Study Center
Improve Your Grade
Audio Chapter Review 1.1

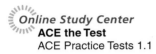

ANSWERS CAN BE FOUND ON P. 410

True or False?

_____ 1. A verbal message consists only of written words.

_____ 2. E-mail is generally considered to be the most effective form of communication.

_____ 3. Every person has a unique view of reality.

_____ 4. It is *not* necessary for feedback to occur for communication to take place.

_____ 5. The *medium* is the information that is communicated.

 Online Study Center
ACE the Test
ACE Practice Tests 1.1

Online Study Center
Improve Your Grade
Audio Chapter Quiz 1.1
PowerPoint Review 1.1

Vocabulary

Define the following terms in your own words and give an original example of each.

6. Audience
7. Communication
8. Feedback
9. Filter
10. Medium
11. Message
12. Stimulus

Critical Thinking

13. Which form of communication (reading, writing, speaking, or listening) do you think is most important in business? Why?

VERBAL COMMUNICATION

2 *Identify the common forms of verbal communication.*

The ability to communicate by using words separates humans from the rest of the animal kingdom. Our verbal ability also enables us to learn from the past—to benefit from the experience of others.

Oral Communication

Oral communication is one of the most common functions in business. Consider, for example, how limiting it would be if a manager or staff person could not attend meetings, ask questions of colleagues, make presentations, appraise performance, handle customer complaints, or give instructions.

Oral communication differs from written communication because it allows more ways to get a message across to others. You can clear up any question immediately; use nonverbal clues; provide additional information; and use pauses, emphasis, and voice tone to stress certain points.

For oral communication to be effective, a second communication skill—listening—is also required. No matter how well crafted the content and delivery of an oral presentation, it cannot achieve its goal if the intended audience does not have effective listening skills. We'll learn more about listening in Chapter 3.

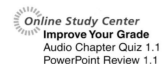 **CONCEPT CHECK 1.2**

What are the four types of verbal communication? Give an example of each.

Written Communication

Writing is more difficult than speaking because you have to get your message correct the first time; you do not have the advantage of immediate feedback and nonverbal clues such as facial expressions to help you achieve your objective. Examples of typical written communication in business include the following:

▌ *E-mail* is a message transmitted electronically over a computer network whose computers are most often connected by cable, telephone lines, or satellites. In the contemporary office, e-mail is replacing traditional memorandums and, in many cases, letters as well.

▌ *Websites* comprise one or more pages of related information that is posted on the World Wide Web and is accessed via the Internet (the main page of a website is called its homepage).

▌ *Memorandums* are written messages sent to people working in the same organization.

▌ *Letters* are written messages sent to people outside the organization.

▌ *Reports* are orderly and objective presentations of information that assists in decision making and problem solving.

▌ Other examples of written communication include contracts, sales literature, newsletters, and bulletin-board notices.

Writing is crucial to the modern organization because it serves as the major source of documentation. A speech may make a striking impression, but a written report leaves a permanent record for others to refer to in the future in case memory fails or a dispute arises.

For written messages to achieve their goal, they must, of course, be read. The skill of efficient reading is becoming more important in today's technological society. The abundance of widespread data and word processing, the Internet, and the growth of convenient and economical photocopying and faxing have all created *more* paperwork, not less.

The typical manager reads about one million words every week.[3] As a consequence, information overload is one of the unfortunate by-products of our times. These and other implications of technology on business communication are discussed throughout this text.

CONCEPT CHECK 1.3

Name five types of written communication.

Online Study Center
Improve Your Grade
Audio Chapter Review 1.2

TEST PREPPER 1.2   ANSWERS CAN BE FOUND ON P. 410

True or False?

_____ 1. The ability to remember separates humans from the rest of the animal kingdom.

_____ 2. Memorandums are written messages sent to people working in the same organization.

_____ 3. As opposed to oral communication, written communication allows more ways to get your message across.

_____ 4. Writing serves as the major source of documentation.

_____ 5. The typical manager reads about one million words per week.

Critical Thinking

6. E-mail is now the most common form of written communication in most businesses. When might e-mail *not* be appropriate to use for communicating needed information? Why?

Online Study Center
ACE the Test
ACE Practice Tests 1.2

Online Study Center
Improve Your Grade
Audio Chapter Quiz 1.2
PowerPoint Review 1.2

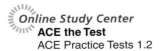
Online Study Center college.hmco.com/pic/oberSASfund

BARRIERS TO VERBAL COMMUNICATION

> **3** ▶ *Identify the major barriers to verbal communication.*

Considering the complex nature of the communication process, your messages may not always be received exactly as you intended. In fact, sometimes your messages will not be received at all; at other times, they will be received incompletely or inaccurately.

Verbal barriers are related to what you write or say. They include inadequate knowledge or vocabulary, differences in interpretation, language differences, inappropriate use of expressions, overabstraction and ambiguity, and polarization.

Inadequate Knowledge or Vocabulary

Before you can even begin to think about how you will communicate an idea, you must first *have* the idea; that is, you must have sufficient knowledge about the topic to know what you want to say. Regardless of your level of technical expertise, developing this knowledge may not be as simple as it sounds. Assume, for example, that your boss has asked you to evaluate the purchase of a new word processing program for your company. You've completed all the necessary research and are now ready to write your report. Or are you?

Have you analyzed your audience? Do you know how much your boss knows about word processing so that you'll know how much background information to include? Do you know how familiar he or she is with word processing terminology? Can you safely use terms like *hanging indent*, *templates*, *decimal tabs*, and *styles*, or will you have to define them first? Do you know whether your boss would prefer to have your conclusions at the beginning of the report, followed by your analysis, or at the end? What tone should the report take? The answers to such questions will be important if you are to achieve your objective in writing the report.

Differences in Interpretation

Sometimes senders and receivers attribute different meanings to the same word or attribute the same meaning to different words. When this mismatch happens, miscommunication can occur.

denotation The literal meaning of a word.

connotation The subjective, emotional meaning associated with a word.

Every word has both a denotative and a connotative meaning. **Denotation** refers to the literal, dictionary meaning of a word. **Connotation** refers to the subjective, emotional meaning that you attach to a word. For example, the denotative meaning of the word *plastic* is "a synthetic material that can be easily molded into different forms." For some people, the word also has a negative connotative meaning—"cheap or artificial substitute."

Most interpretation problems occur because of the personal reactions engendered by the connotative meaning of a word. For example, do you have a positive, neutral, or negative reaction to the terms *broad, bad, profit, aggressive, hard-hitting, workaholic, corporate raider, head-hunter, gay, golden parachute,* and *wasted*? Are your reactions likely to be the same as everyone else's?

Language Differences

In an ideal world, all managers would know the language of each culture with which they deal. Most of the correspondence between U.S. or Canadian firms and foreign firms is in English; in other cases, the services of a qualified interpreter (for oral communication) or translator (for written communication) may be available. Even with such services, problems can occur. Consider, for example, the following blunders:[4]

▌ In Brazil, where Portuguese is spoken, a U.S. airline advertised that its Boeing 747s had "rendezvous lounges," without realizing that *rendez-vous* in Portuguese implies prostitution.

▌ In China, Kentucky Fried Chicken's slogan "Finger-lickin' good" was translated "So good you suck your fingers."

To ensure that the intended meaning is not lost during translation, legal, technical, and all other important documents should first be translated into the second language and then retranslated into English. Be aware, however, that communication difficulties can arise even among English speakers. For example, a British advertisement for Electrolux vacuum cleaners displayed the headline "Nothing Sucks Like an Electrolux." Copywriters in the United States and Canada would never use this wording!

IBM data wrangler Nelson Mattos is a computer scientist in charge of IBM's information integration effort. His job is to help companies make sense of the gigabits of information they create every day. According to Mattos, "Everyone struggles with how to gain value from their investment in information."

Inappropriate Use of Expressions

Expressions are groups of words whose intended meanings are different from their literal interpretations. Examples include slang, jargon, and euphemisms.

Slang

Slang is an expression, often short-lived, that is identified with a specific group of people. Here, for example, are some slang terms (and their meanings) currently popular on college campuses:[5]

slang An expression, often short-lived, that is identified with a specific group of people.

> *As if*—"In your dreams"
> *Bounce*—To leave
> *Crib*—A place of residence
> *Homey*—A friend, usually male
> *My bad*—My fault
> *Ride*—A car
> *Stoked*—Happy or excited
> *Sweet*—Generic positive (also *phat* or *tight*)

Teenagers, construction workers, immigrants, knowledge professionals, and just about every other subgroup you can imagine all have their own sets of slang. Using appropriate slang in everyday speech presents no problem; it conveys precise information and may indicate group membership. Problems arise, however, when the sender uses slang that the receiver doesn't understand. Slang that sends a negative nonverbal message about the sender can also be a source of problems.

Jargon

jargon   The technical vocabulary used within specialized groups.

Jargon is the technical terminology used within specialized groups; it has sometimes been called "the pros' prose." Technology, for example, has spawned a whole new vocabulary. Do you know the meanings of these common computer terms?

applet	flame	patch
blog	hacker	PDA
BRB	HTML	plug 'n' play
BTW	IMO	ROFL
CU	JPEG	spam
e-commerce	killer app	worm
FAQ	locked up	WYSIWYG

As with slang, the problem arises not from using jargon—jargon provides a very precise and efficient way of communicating with those familiar with it. Rather, the problem comes either in using jargon with someone who doesn't understand it or in using jargon in an effort to impress others.

Euphemisms

euphemism   An inoffensive expression used in place of an expression that may offend or suggest something unpleasant.

Euphemisms are inoffensive expressions used in place of words that may offend or suggest something unpleasant. For example, public officials sometimes use the term *collateral damage* to refer to injury to civilians during a military operation, and the Academy Awards spokespeople refer to the award losers as "nonwinners." Sensitive writers and speakers use euphemisms occasionally, especially to describe bodily functions. How many ways, for example, can you think of to say that someone has died?

Overabstraction and Ambiguity

abstract word   A word that identifies an idea or feeling.

concrete word   A word that identifies something that can be seen or touched.

An **abstract word** identifies an idea or a feeling instead of a concrete object. For example, *communication* is an abstract word, whereas *memorandum* is a **concrete word**, a word that identifies something that can be seen or touched. Abstract words are necessary to communicate about things you cannot see or touch. Unfortunately, communication problems result when you use too many abstract words or when you use too high a level of abstraction. The higher the level of abstraction, the more difficult it is for the receiver to visualize exactly what the sender has in mind. For example, which sentence communicates more information: "I acquired an asset at the store" or "I bought a laser printer at ComputerLand"?

Similar communication problems result from the overuse of ambiguous terms such as *a few, some, several,* and *far away,* which have too broad a meaning for use in much business communication.

Polarization

CONCEPT CHECK 1.4

What are six verbal barriers to communication?

At times, some people act as though every situation is divided into two opposite and distinct poles, with no allowance for a middle ground. Of course, some true opposites do exist. You are either male or female, and your company either will or will not make a profit this year. Nevertheless, most aspects of life involve more than two alternatives.

For example, you might assume that a speaker either is telling the truth or is lying. In fact, what the speaker actually says may be true, but by selectively omitting some important information, he or she may be giving an inaccurate impression.

Is the speaker telling the truth or not? Most likely, the answer lies somewhere in between. Likewise, you are not necessarily either tall or short, rich or poor, smart or dumb. Competent communicators avoid inappropriate either/or logic, instead making the effort to search for middle-ground words when such language best describes a situation.

Online Study Center
Improve Your Grade
Audio Chapter Review 1.3
Handouts

TEST PREPPER 1.3

ANSWERS CAN BE FOUND ON P. 410

True or False?

_____ 1. *Jargon* is the technical vocabulary of a particular group.

_____ 2. *Connotation* refers to the literal, dictionary meaning of a word.

_____ 3. Euphemisms are sometimes appropriate in business writing.

_____ 4. It is generally safe to assume that a speaker or writer is either telling the truth or lying.

_____ 5. Just about every subgroup of a population has its own set of slang.

Vocabulary

Define the following terms in your own words and give an original example of each.

6. Abstract word
7. Concrete word
8. Connotation
9. Denotation
10. Euphemism
11. Jargon
12. Slang

Critical Thinking

13. The text argues against the overuse of ambiguity. Can you think of a business situation in which the use of ambiguity might be effective?

Online Study Center
ACE the Test
ACE Practice Tests 1.3

Online Study Center
Improve Your Grade
Audio Chapter Quiz 1.3
PowerPoint Review 1.3

INTRODUCING THE THREE PS: PROBLEM, PROCESS, PRODUCT

Every chapter in this text concludes with a 3Ps model designed to illustrate important communication concepts covered in the chapter (see the feature on page 14). These short case studies of typical communication assignments include the *problem*, the *process*, and the *product* (the 3Ps). The *problem* defines the situation and discusses the need for a particular communication task. The *process* is a series of questions that provides step-by-step guidance for accomplishing the specific communication task. Finally, the *product* is the result—the finished document.

The 3Ps model provides a practical demonstration of a particular type of communication, shown close up so that you can see the *process* of writing, not just the results. This process helps you focus on one aspect of writing at a time. Use the 3Ps steps regularly in your own writing so that your written communications will be easier to produce and will be more effective.

Pay particular attention to the questions in the Process section, and ask yourself similar questions as you compose your own messages. Finally, read through the finished document, and note any changes made from the draft sentences composed in the Process section.

> **THREE Ps**
> **PROBLEM, PROCESS, PRODUCT**

Using Euphemisms Appropriately

Problem

Jane was editing her company newsletter when she came across this paragraph:

> Raisa, an administrative assistant, was perspiring as she read about the involuntary separations at her company. Raisa knew she would soon reach her golden years and was concerned that the recent revenue enhancements enacted by the state government would affect her financial position if she should become physically challenged or get the big C before she died.

Jane realized immediately that this paragraph contained too many euphemisms for the strong, clear, concise tone she strove for in her newsletter.

Process

1. Underline all the possible euphemisms in the paragraph.

   > Raisa, an <u>administrative assistant</u>, was <u>perspiring</u> as she read about the <u>involuntary separations</u> at her company. Raisa knew she would soon reach her <u>golden years</u> and was concerned that the recent <u>revenue enhancements</u> enacted by the state government would affect her financial position if she should become <u>physically challenged</u> or get <u>the big C</u> before she died.

2. Because not all euphemisms are *bad,* consider the appropriateness of each one.

   a. *administrative assistant:* Some people might consider the term a euphemism for *secretary,* but I think it implies a higher level of responsibility. In fact, I think I'll change it to the more contemporary *administrative professional.*

   b. *perspiring:* I'll definitely change this to the more direct *sweating.* (After all, did anyone ever say "perspiring bullets"?)

   c. *involuntary separations:* I'll call it what it is—*layoffs.*

   d. *golden years:* I could use the more direct *old age,* but that seems harsh—and subjective. I'll use *retirement* instead.

   e. *revenue enhancement:* This was a tax increase, and that's what I'll call it.

   f. *physically challenged:* I'll change to *disabled.*

   g. *the big C:* I'll call it what it is—*cancer.*

3. Are there other changes you'd make to the paragraph?

   > While there is nothing wrong with the expression *before she died,* I think I'll use the gentler euphemism *before she passed away.*

Product

> Raisa, an administrative professional, was sweating as she read about the layoffs at her company. Raisa knew she would soon reach retirement and was concerned that the recent tax increases enacted by the state government would affect her financial position if she should become disabled or get cancer before she passed away.

Online Study Center
Improve Your Grade
Crossword Puzzles
Flashcards
LAB Tests

LEARNING OBJECTIVE REVIEW

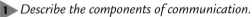

1 ▶ *Describe the components of communication.*

- A stimulus is an event that creates within an individual the need to communicate.
  - It can be internal or external.
  - Individuals respond to the stimulus by formulating a verbal or nonverbal message.
- The filter is the mental process of interpreting stimuli.
  - It is based on one's knowledge, experience, and viewpoints.
  - These variables act as a filter in shaping everyone's unique impressions of reality.
- The message is the information that is communicated.
  - It determines whether the communication is successful.
  - Successful messages consider the needs of the audience.
- The medium is the form a message takes.
  - Messages can be oral or written.
  - Nonverbal messages are expressed through facial expressions, gestures, or body movement.
- The destination is the sensory environment of the receiver of the message.
  - If the communication is successful, the receiver understands the message.
  - Feedback is the receiver's reaction or response to the message.

2 ▶ *Identify the common forms of verbal communication.*

- Oral communication is one of the most common functions in business. It includes:
  - participating in meetings
  - talking with colleagues
  - making presentations
  - appraising performance
  - handling customer complaints
  - giving instructions
- Written communication consists of:
  - e-mail
  - websites
  - memorandums
  - letters
  - reports
  - contracts, sales literature, newsletters, and bulletin-board notices

3 ▶ *Identify the major barriers to verbal communication.*

- Verbal barriers include:
  - inadequate knowledge or vocabulary
  - differences in interpretation
  - language differences
  - inappropriate use of expressions
  - overabstraction and ambiguity
  - polarization

EXERCISES

1. Communication on Television (▶1.1)

Use an incident from a recent television program to illustrate each of the five components of the communication process. Discuss any communication barriers that you observed. (Be sure to identify the television program and describe the incident you're analyzing.)

2. Communication Components (▶1.1)

Working with a partner, identify the five components of communication in the following situation:

> Alice Liston has had a dream of going to State College. She has worked hard to maintain a 3.95 GPA and has a very high ACT score. Because her family is not in a position to pay her tuition, Alice applied for an academic scholarship to State College. Two weeks later, Alice receives a letter from the scholarship committee. She nervously reads the letter and then runs to her bedroom to e-mail her best friend, letting her know that she received a full-ride scholarship to State College. Her friend reads the e-mail message two hours later and e-mails Alice her congratulations.

Identify the five components in this scenario. Working in pairs, prepare your own communication scenario and identify the five components of communication for it.

3. Synthesizing Information (▶1.1)

Approximately 1,500 words in this chapter were devoted to the discussion of the components of communication. Working in small groups, write a 200- to 250-word abstract (summary) of this discussion. Because this summary is an informational abstract, you may pick up the exact wording of the original discussion when appropriate. Ensure that all important points are covered, your narrative flows smoothly from one topic to another, and your writing is error-free.

4. Workplace Communication Issues (▶1.2)

For this exercise, your instructor will divide you into two-person teams.

a. Exchange e-mail addresses with your partner.
b. Send your partner an e-mail message in which you respond (in complete sentences) to the following two questions:
  1. Do you feel that it is right or wrong for an employer to maintain the right to read any e-mail message sent on company computers?
  2. Do you feel it is acceptable or unacceptable to use a company computer to send a short personal e-mail to a friend once or twice a day?
c. Send a copy of your e-mail message to yourself.
d. When you receive your partner's e-mail message, respond to it by agreeing or disagreeing with his or her position and giving the reason for your position. Again, send a copy of your response to yourself.
e. Print out and submit to your instructor a copy of (1) your original message, (2) your response to your partner's e-mail, and (3) your partner's response to your e-mail.

5. E-Mail (▶1.2)

Interview at least three full-time employees to learn about their experience with e-mail. Ask them questions such as the following:

a. How many e-mails do you send and receive each week?
b. Do you read all of the e-mails you receive? If not, why? How do you decide which ones to read and which to skip?
c. How important do you consider the subject line to be on an e-mail?
d. In your opinion, what makes an e-mail effective or ineffective? Present your findings in a 200- to 250-word report to your instructor.

6. Filter (▶ 1.2)

You are unique—as is every other person in class. List at least 10 ways in which you personally might filter information you receive, based on factors such as your individual experiences, culture, emotions at the moment, personality, knowledge, socioeconomic status, and demographic variables.

7. Euphemisms (▶ 1.3)

Working in two-person groups, see how many appropriate terms you can think of to substitute for the following concepts:

a. Dying
b. Elderly
c. Getting fired
d. Having no mobility in your legs
e. Going to the bathroom
f. Housewife
g. Jail

Additional exercises are available at the Online Study Center website: **college.hmco.com/pic/oberSASfund**.

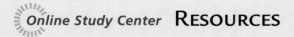

Online Study Center **RESOURCES**

Prepare for Class, Improve Your Grade, and ACE the Test. Student Achievement Series resources include:

ACE Practice Tests	Ask Ober	Audio Chapter Reviews and Quizzes
Chapter Outlines	Communication Objectives	Crossword Puzzles
Flashcards	Glossaries	Handouts
LAB Tests	Portfolio Project Stationery	Sample Reports

To access these learning and study tools, go to **college.hmco.com/pic/oberSASfund**.

Contemporary Issues in Business Communication

Working together in teams can result in higher productivity and creativity, if the proper communication exists. Just as these rowers use teamwork to achieve their goals, so do businesses and organizations.

3 *Communicate ethically.*

2 *Communicate effectively with diverse populations both internationally and within the United States.*

1 *Communicate effectively in small groups.*

Chapter Outline

Online Study Center
Prepare for Class
Chapter Outline

4 ▶ *Communicate effectively via e-mail.*

Teamwork:
The Core of Nucon

Entrepreneur Gilbert C. Morrell Jr. didn't need work-team communication for the first nine years of his company's existence because he *was* the company. Today Nucon, his temporary staffing and training company, has more than 500 employees, with revenues of $24 million last year.

If Morrell disagrees with an idea proposed in a work-team meeting, he can be convinced to change his mind "if the argument is sound or if it reflects information I don't have. I am willing to listen because there may be something I don't know that may persuade me." Not so with ideas that go against The Nucon Group's core values. In these situations, the CEO says, "I will respectfully listen to the other person's point and then explain why we won't follow that course of action." When turning down an idea, he often buffers his refusal with additional information to help the participants understand his position. "And always," he says, "I try to give constructive feedback—whether it is positive or negative." ■

Online Study Center college.hmco.com/pic/oberSASfund

KEY TERMS

ethics *p. 29*
ethnocentrism *p. 25*
groupthink *p. 21*
team *p. 20*

team A group of individuals who depend
on one another to accomplish a common
objective.

*At Samsung Electronics, Chairperson
Lee Kun Hee uses work groups, such as
this team of creative designers, to
launch a "design revolution."*

Gilbert Morrell of The Nucon Group is certainly aware of the role that work teams play in communicating in the contemporary organization. In fact, because communication is such a pervasive and strategic part of the organization, almost anything that affects the organization and its employees affects the communication function as well. However, four contemporary issues have special implications for business communication:

▎ *Work teams:* The dynamics of communicating within groups.

▎ *Diversity:* The effects of cultural differences in the workplace—both internationally and within the United States.

▎ *Ethics:* The moral implications of communicating in the contemporary business environment.

▎ *E-mail:* Communicating electronically.

COMMUNICATING IN WORK TEAMS

Communicate effectively in small groups.

A **team** is a group of individuals who depend on one another to accomplish a common objective. Teams are often superior to individuals because they can accomplish more work, are more creative, have more information available to them, and offer more interpersonal communication dynamics. A synergy can work to ensure that the group's total output exceeds the sum of the individuals' contributions.

Unfortunately, teams can also waste time, accomplish little work, and create an environment in which interpersonal conflict can rage. As anyone who has ever

worked in a group can attest, there is also the danger of *social loafing,* the psychological term for avoiding individual responsibility in a group setting.

Two to seven members seems to be the most appropriate size range for most effective work teams. Small-team research indicates that five is an ideal size for many teams.[1] Smaller teams often do not have enough diversity of skills and interests to function effectively as a team, whereas larger teams may lack healthy team interaction because just a few people may dominate the discussions.

The Variables of Group Communication

Three factors—conflict, conformity, and consensus—greatly affect the efficiency with which a team operates and the amount of enjoyment members derive from it.

Conflict

Conflict is a greatly misunderstood facet of group communication. Many group leaders work diligently to avoid conflict because they think it detracts from a group's goals. They take the attitude that a group experiencing conflict is not running smoothly and is destined to fail.

In fact, conflict is what group meetings are all about. One purpose of collaborating on a project is to ensure that various viewpoints are heard so that agreement about the most appropriate course of action can emerge. Groups can use conflict productively to generate and test ideas before they are implemented. Rather than indicating that a meeting is disorderly, the presence of conflict indicates that members are actively discussing the issues. If a group does not exhibit conflict by debating ideas or questioning others, there is little reason for it to exist. The members may as well be working individually.

Conflict, then, is the essence of group interaction. Competent communicators use conflict as a means to determine what is and what is not an acceptable idea or solution. Note, however, that the conflict discussed here involves debate about *issues,* not about *personalities.* Interpersonal conflict can, indeed, have serious negative consequences for work teams.

Conformity

Conformity is agreement with regard to ideas, rules, or principles. Members may be encouraged to disagree about the definition of a problem or possible solutions, but certain fundamental issues—such as how the group should operate—should be agreed on by everyone.

Although group conformity and group cohesiveness are necessary for successful small-group communication, too much cohesiveness can result in **groupthink**, a barrier to communication that results from an overemphasis on unity, which stifles opposing ideas and the free flow of information (Figure 2.1).[2]

The pressure to conform can become so great that negative information and contrary opinions are never even brought out into the open and discussed. As a consequence, the group loses the advantage of hearing and

CONCEPT CHECK 2.1

List two advantages and two disadvantages of working in teams.

CONCEPT CHECK 2.2

Give an example of a "good" conflict and an example of a "bad" conflict.

groupthink   The communication barrier that results from overemphasizing unity.

FIGURE 2.1

Effect of Excessive Conformity on a Group's Productivity

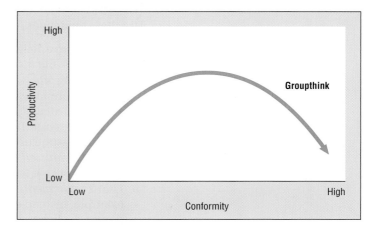

considering various perspectives. In effective work-team communication, conflicts, different opinions, and questions are considered an inevitable and essential part of the collaborative process.

Consensus

Consensus means reaching a decision that best reflects the thinking of all team members. It entails finding a solution that is acceptable enough that all members can support it (perhaps with reservations) and that no member actively opposes it. Consensus is not necessarily a unanimous vote, or even a majority vote, because in a majority vote only the majority are happy with the end result; people in the minority may have to accept something they don't like at all.

Not every decision, of course, needs to have the support of every member; to push for consensus on every matter would require a tremendous investment of time and energy. The group should decide ahead of time when to push for consensus—for example, when reaching decisions that have a major effect on the direction of the project or the conduct of the team.

Giving Constructive Feedback

The single most important skill applied when working through any problem is the ability to give constructive feedback. There are proven methods for giving and receiving criticism that work equally well for giving and receiving praise.[3]

Acknowledge the Need for Feedback

Feedback is vital; it is the only way to find out what needs to be improved and should thus be an overall part of the team's culture. Your team must agree that giving and receiving feedback is an acceptable part of how you will improve the way you work together. That way, no one will be surprised when he or she receives feedback.

Give Both Positive and Negative Feedback

Many people take good work for granted and give feedback only when problems arise. Unfortunately, this habit is counterproductive. People are far more likely to pay attention to your complaints if they have also received your compliments.

Learn How to Give Feedback

Use these guidelines for compliments as well as for complaints:

1. *Be descriptive.* Relate objectively what you saw or what you heard. Give specific examples—the more recent, the better.
2. *Avoid using labels.* Words such as *undependable, unprofessional, irresponsible,* and *lazy* are labels that we attach to behaviors, and these labels should be avoided. Instead, describe the behaviors and drop the labels.
3. *Don't exaggerate.* Be precise—and fair. To say, "You're always late for meetings" is probably untrue and therefore unfair.
4. *Speak for yourself.* Don't refer to absent, anonymous people ("A lot of people here don't like it when you . . .").
5. *Use "I" statements.* This point is perhaps the most important guideline. For example, instead of saying, "You are frequently late for meetings," say, "I feel annoyed when you are late for meetings." "I" statements create an adult/peer relationship.

Team Writing

The increasing complexity of the workplace makes it difficult for any one person to have either the time or the expertise to be able to identify and solve many of the problems that arise and then prepare written responses. Reflecting this trend, team writing is becoming quite prevalent in organizations. (In fact, collaborative communication has always been much more common in organizations than many people realize.)

In addition to the general team-building guidelines discussed in the previous section, writing teams should follow the strategies discussed in the following subsection.

Assign Tasks and Develop a Schedule

Start by determining the goals of the project and identifying the reader. Determine the components of the project, the research needed, and the date when each aspect needs to be completed. Then divide the tasks equitably, based on each member's needs, interests, expertise, and commitment to the project.

Meet Regularly

Schedule regular meetings throughout the project to pool ideas; keep track of new developments; assess progress; avoid overlap and omissions; and, if necessary, renegotiate the workload and redefine tasks. As soon as the initial data-gathering phase is complete, confer as a group to develop an outline for the finished project. This outline should show the sequence of major and subordinate topics in the document. Recognize that not all the information that you collect may need to be included in the report.

Draft the Document

The goal at this stage is not to prepare a finished product but rather to draft all the content. You have two options:

▌ Assign parts to different members. Having each member write a different part of the document provides an equitable distribution of the work and may produce a draft more quickly. You must ensure, however, that each member is writing in his or her area of expertise and that all have agreed on style issues such as the degree of formality, direct versus indirect organization, and use of preview and summary.

▌ Assign one person to draft the entire document. Assigning one member (presumably the most talented writer) to draft the entire document helps guarantee a more consistent writing style and lessens the risk of serious omissions or duplication. You must, however, provide sufficient guidance to the writer and allow ample time for one person to complete the entire writing task.

One common pitfall in team writing is the failure to achieve a single "voice" in the project. Regardless of who prepares each individual part of the report, the final report must look and sound as though it were prepared by one writer. Think of the report as a single document, rather than as a collection of parts. Organize and present the data so that the report comes across as coherent and unified.

Provide Helpful Feedback on Team Writing

Commenting on the writing of peers can be helpful both to you and to the colleague whose writing you're reviewing. As you respond to the writing of others, practice techniques that will help you react more effectively to your own writing. In addition, realizing that you are not alone with your writing problems and concerns is sometimes comforting. When reviewing a colleague's writing, follow the guidelines presented earlier in this chapter for providing feedback to team members.

As a writer, you benefit from the viewpoints of different audiences and from learning what does or doesn't work in your writing. Finally, in a team environment, peer comments create more active involvement and can help foster a sense of community within the team.

Revise the Draft

Be sure to allow enough time for editing the draft. This task is best accomplished by providing each member with a copy of the draft beforehand (to allow time for reading and annotating). You can then meet as a group to review each section for errors in content, gaps or repetition, and effective writing style.

Decide who will be responsible for making the changes to each section, how the document will be formatted, and who will be responsible for proofreading the final document. Typically, one person (preferably not the typist) is assigned the task of reviewing the final draft for consistency and correctness in content, style, and format.

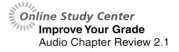

CONCEPT CHECK 2.3

What are five guidelines for effective team writing?

Online Study Center
Improve Your Grade
Audio Chapter Review 2.1

TEST PREPPER 2.1   ANSWERS CAN BE FOUND ON P. 410

True or False?

_____ 1. A group should strive to reach consensus on every decision.

_____ 2. All team members should be involved in revising the draft document.

_____ 3. Conflict is always a positive development in group interactions.

_____ 4. Effective methods for giving constructive positive feedback are the same as those for giving constructive negative feedback.

_____ 5. Giving feedback should be an accepted part of every group.

Vocabulary

Define the following terms in your own words.

6. Groupthink

7. Team

Critical Thinking

8. What do you think is the most important attribute of a team member for this course? Why?

Online Study Center
ACE the Test
ACE Practice Tests 2.1

Online Study Center
Improve Your Grade
Audio Chapter Quiz 2.1
PowerPoint Review 2.1

COMMUNICATING IN A DIVERSE ENVIRONMENT

 Communicate effectively with diverse populations both internationally and within the United States.

Paying attention to the needs of others indicates that we recognize and accept diversity. When we talk about diversity, we mean cultural differences not only within the American and Canadian work force but also in the worldwide marketplace.

Culture encompasses the customary traits, attitudes, and behaviors of a group of people. **Ethnocentrism** is the belief that one's own cultural group is superior to other such groups. Such an attitude hinders communication, understanding, and goodwill between trading partners. An attitude of arrogance is not only counterproductive but also unrealistic, considering that the U.S. population represents less than 5 percent of the world population.

Diversity will have profound effects on our lives and will pose a growing challenge for workers. (See, for example, Figure 2.2.)

The following discussion provides useful guidance for communicating with people from different cultures—both internationally as well as domestically. Although it is helpful to be aware of cultural differences, competent communicators recognize that each member of a culture is an individual, with individual needs, perceptions, and experiences, and should be treated as such.

ethnocentrism   The belief that one's own cultural group is superior to others.

Strategies for Communicating Across Cultures

When communicating with people from different cultures, use the strategies discussed in the following subsections.

Maintain Formality

Compared to the traditional American and Canadian cultures, most other cultures value and respect a much more formal approach to business dealings. Call others by their titles and family names unless specifically asked to do otherwise.

Show Respect

Withhold judgment, accepting the premise that attitudes held by an entire culture are probably based on sound reasoning. Listen carefully to what is being communicated and try to understand the other person's feelings.

Communicate Clearly

To ensure that your oral and written messages are understood, follow these guidelines:

▌ Avoid slang, jargon, and other figures of speech. Expressions such as "They'll eat that up" or "out in left field" are likely to confuse even a fluent English speaker.

▌ Be specific and illustrate your points with concrete examples.

▌ Provide and solicit feedback, summarize frequently, and encourage questions.

▌ Use a variety of media: handouts (distributed before the meeting to allow time for reading), audiovisual aids, models, and the like.

▌ Avoid attempts at humor; humor is likely to be lost on your counterpart.

▌ Speak plainly and slowly (but not so slowly as to appear condescending), choosing your words carefully.

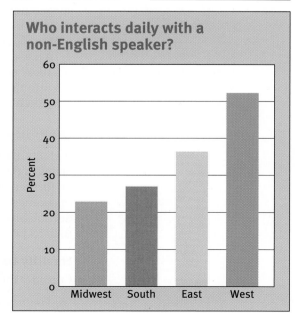

FIGURE 2.2

Who interacts daily with a non-English speaker?

When Exxon wanted to build a 660-mile pipeline through Chad and Cameroon, the company brought in anthropologist Ellen Brown to explain the process and its impact to the local residents. When she met with a local village chief, she politely left a gift of tea and sugar.

Value Diversity

CONCEPT CHECK 2.4

What are four strategies for communicating across cultures?

Those who view diversity among employees as a source of richness and strength for the organization can help bring a wide range of benefits to their organization. Whether you happen to belong to the majority culture or to one of the minority cultures where you work, you will share your work and leisure hours with people different from yourself—people who have values, mannerisms, and speech habits different from your own. This statement is true today, and it will be even more true in the future. The same strategies apply whether the cultural differences exist at home or abroad.

A person who is knowledgeable about, and comfortable with, different cultures is a more effective employee because he or she can avoid misunderstandings and tap into the greater variety of viewpoints that a diverse culture provides. In addition, such understanding provides personal satisfaction.

Diversity Within the United States

Perhaps, up to this point, you have been inferring that you must leave the United States and Canada to encounter cultures different from your own. Nothing could be further from the truth. In fact, the term *minority* is becoming something of a misnomer. For example, the white population in the United States is expected to decline from a total of 80 percent of the population in 1980 to a bare majority (less than 53 percent) in 2050.[4]

Ethnicity Issues in Communication

Consider these facts from the U.S. Census Bureau (Figure 2.3):[5]

▌ There is a 40 percent chance that two randomly selected North Americans will be of different racial or ethnic backgrounds.

▮ In 14 percent of U.S. homes, a language other than English is primarily spoken.

▮ Of all new entrants into the work force, 43 percent are people of color and immigrants.

▮ Women and people of color accounted for 70 percent of the work force in 2000.

When communicating about minorities, we should realize that ethnicity is not a characteristic limited to people of color; white Americans are ethnic, too. Each ethnic and racial group in the world—encompassing all 6 billion earth inhabitants—has its own physical and cultural characteristics. Of course, every person within an ethnic group has his or her own individual characteristics as well.

Is it any wonder, then, that communicating about ethnic and racial matters is so hazardous? Yet we have no choice. We must learn to communicate comfortably and honestly with one another. If we use the wrong terminology, make an unwarranted assumption, or present only one side of the story, our readers or listeners will let us know soon enough.

Gender Issues in Communication

Gender roles consist of the learned behavior associated with being male or female. Certain differences typically exist in male/female communication patterns, as shown in Table 2.1. Recognize that these differences often (but not always) do exist. Competent communicators seek to understand and adapt to these differences.

CONCEPT CHECK 2.5

What is the fastest growing group in the United States? The slowest growing group?

FIGURE 2.3

Percentage Distribution of U.S. Population, 1980–2050
The white American population is declining as a percentage of the total population, while Asian and Hispanic populations are increasing. As of the 2000 census, the sizes of the Hispanic and non-Hispanic black populations were about equal in the United States.[6] Even disregarding international implications, these findings will have major effects on the way Americans conduct business—and the way we communicate.

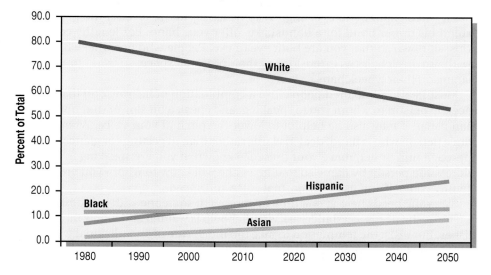

TABLE 2.1

Gender Differences in Communicating

Men	Women
Communicate primarily to preserve independence and status	Communicate primarily to build rapport
Prefer to work out their problems by themselves	Prefer to talk out solutions with another person
Are more likely to be critical of a coworker	Are more likely to compliment a coworker
Tend to interrupt to dominate a conversation or to change the subject	Tend to interrupt to agree with or support what another person is saying
Tend to be more directive	Tend to emphasize politeness
Tend to internalize successes ("That's one of my strengths") and to externalize failures ("We needed more time")	Tend to externalize successes ("I was lucky") and to internalize failures ("I'm just not good at that")
Speak differently to other men than they do to women	Speak differently to other women than they do to men

Sources: Jennifer Coates, *Women, Men, and Language,* Longman, New York, 1986; Deborah Tannen, *You Just Don't Understand,* Ballantine, New York, 1990; John Gray, *Men Are from Mars, Women Are from Venus,* HarperCollins, New York, 1992; Patti Hathaway, *Giving and Receiving Feedback,* rev. ed., Crisp Publications, Menlo Park, CA, 1998; Susan Herring, *Making the Net "Work,"* n.d., http://www.cs.nott.ac.uk/~azq97c/gender.htm (December 3, 2004); Deborah Tannen, *Talking from 9 to 5,* William Morrow, New York, 1994.

CONCEPT CHECK 2.6

When should you offer assistance to a disabled person?

Communicating with People with Disabilities

Since the Americans with Disabilities Act (ADA) was passed, more physically disabled individuals than ever before have been able to enter the workplace. The act guarantees that people with disabilities who are qualified to perform the essential functions of a job, with or without reasonable accommodation, will not be discriminated against in hiring and promotion in most public and private organizations.

Competent communicators go beyond these legal requirements. Depending on the individual situation, some reasonable changes in the way you communicate will be appreciated. For example, when being introduced to someone who uses a wheelchair, bend over slightly to be closer to eye level. If the person can extend his or her hand for a handshake, offer your hand. For lengthy conversations, sit down so that you are both eye to eye. People who use wheelchairs may see their wheelchairs as extensions of their personal space, so avoid touching or leaning on their wheelchairs.

Most hearing-impaired people use a combination of hearing and lip reading. Face the person to whom you're speaking, and speak a bit slower (but not louder) than usual. It may also be helpful to lower the pitch of your voice. When talking with a person who is blind, deal in words rather than in gestures or glances. As you approach him or her, make your presence known; if you are speaking in a group, address the person by name so that he or she will know to whom you are talking. Identify yourself and use your normal voice and speed.

Everyone needs help at one time or another. If someone with a disability looks as if he or she needs assistance, ask whether help is wanted and follow the person's wishes. But resist the temptation to take too much care of an individual with a disability. Don't be patronizing.

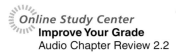

Online Study Center
Improve Your Grade
Audio Chapter Review 2.2

TEST PREPPER 2.2   ANSWERS CAN BE FOUND ON P. 410

True or False?

_____ 1. Cultures differ widely in the traits they value.

_____ 2. Humor is often an effective way to begin a presentation to an international audience.

_____ 3. In the year 2050, whites still are expected to be the largest ethnic group in the United States.

_____ 4. Males generally prefer to work out their problems by themselves, whereas females generally prefer to talk out solutions with another person.

_____ 5. You should always provide help for a disabled coworker.

Vocabulary

Define the following term in your own words and give an original example.

6. Ethnocentrism

Critical Thinking

7. In your opinion, are men or women generally more effective communicators in business? Why?

Online Study Center
ACE the Test
ACE Practice Tests 2.2

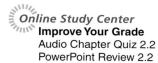
Online Study Center
Improve Your Grade
Audio Chapter Quiz 2.2
PowerPoint Review 2.2

ETHICS AND COMMUNICATION

3 ▷ *Communicate ethically.*

Each of us has a personal code of **ethics**, or system of moral principles, that might go beyond legal rules to tell us how to act when the law is silent. Our ethics represent our personal belief about whether something is right or wrong. We begin to form our ethical standards as children, as a result of our perceptions about the behavior of our parents, other adults, and our peer group.

There are three types of ethics:

ethics Rules of conduct that may go beyond legal rules.

▮ Professional ethics are defined by an organization (such as Texas Instruments or the American Bar Association). Employees and members are expected to follow these guidelines. They define what is right or wrong in the workplace. (See the Spotlight on page 38, "How Would You Respond?")

▮ Social ethics are defined by society. Thus, while accepting gifts from suppliers is strictly frowned upon in North American societies, such a practice may be commonplace and accepted in other societies.

▮ Individual ethics are defined by the person and are based on family values, heritage, personal experience, and the like.

What Affects Ethical Behavior?

According to Maxwell, when people make *unethical* decisions, they do so for one of three reasons:[7]

1. We do what's most convenient—in other words, we take the easy route.
2. We do what we must to win. Some people think that embracing ethics would limit their ability to succeed. They believe that "good guys finish last."
3. We rationalize our choices. We decide that the decision we make depends on the particular circumstances (this is called "situational ethics").

CONCEPT CHECK 2.7

Give an example of a professional, social, and personal ethical decision.

The corporate culture affects ethics. If everyone makes personal long-distance calls or sends personal e-mails on the job, you are likely to also (the "everybody-does-it" defense). If managers become aware of unethical practices and don't put a stop to them, they are condoning these actions.

The amount of freedom an organization gives an employee to behave unethically also affects behavior. At fast-food restaurants, for example, one employee takes your order and receives your payment and another employee fills the order. This means that the person filling your order doesn't handle the money and the person who handles the money doesn't fill your order. Thus, less opportunity for theft occurs.

If a strict code of ethics is in effect and enforced consistently and firmly, employees have less opportunity to be unethical. Employees know what is expected of them and what happens if they fail to live up to these expectations.

Framework for Ethical Decision Making

When faced with an ethical decision, follow these steps:

1. Get the facts. Determine who has an important stake in the outcome of your decision. Stakeholders might include employees, customers, suppliers, and the wider community. What is at stake for each group?
2. Evaluate the options. Which option produces the most good and does the least harm?

   ▌ Is it legal? This is the first question to ask. Does it abide by the law—laws relating to workplace safety, equal opportunity, performance appraisals, privacy, sexual harassment, and the like? If it is not legal, don't do it. If it is legal, does it abide by any contractual obligations of your firm?

   ▌ Does it comply with company values? If the company has a formal code of conduct or simply a culture of acting in a certain manner, does the action conform to those rules?

   ▌ Would you want the result of this decision to happen to you (the Golden Rule)? How would you like to be treated in this situation?

   ▌ How will you feel after the decision is known? Once people find out about it (workers in your company, members of the local community, and others), how will they perceive your actions? Can you face yourself? Even if it was a difficult decision, are you satisfied that you've acted in the best interests of everyone concerned? Often, we may come to regret our decisions as a result of subsequent information, but we have to make our decisions based on the information available at that time.

3. Make the decision.
4. Act on the decision and explain your rationale.

For more than 45 years, Texas Instruments (TI) has published an ethics booklet for its employees. According to Tom Engibous, TI president, "There simply is no room for unethical shortcuts or compromises. Our values will not be compromised."

Communicating Ethically

When communicating, we constantly make conscious decisions regarding what information to include and what information to exclude from our messages. For the information that is included, we make conscious decisions about how to phrase the message, how much to emphasize each point, and how to organize the message. Such decisions have legal and ethical dimensions—both for you as the writer and for the organization. For example, BMW, the German

Dilbert: © Scott Adams/Dist. by United Feature Syndicate, Inc.

automobile maker, was recently required to pay a $2 million judgment against a U.S. car buyer because it had failed to inform him that the paint on his car had been damaged and then retouched.[8] Competent communicators ensure that their oral and written messages are ethical, both in terms of what is communicated and in terms of what is left uncommunicated.

CONCEPT CHECK 2.8

According to Maxwell, why do people make unethical decisions?

Online Study Center
Improve Your Grade
Audio Chapter Review 2.3

TEST PREPPER 2.3

ANSWERS CAN BE FOUND ON P. 410

True or False?

_____ 1. Social ethics are defined by an organization.

_____ 2. Making ethical choices depending on circumstances is called situational ethics.

_____ 3. The corporate culture has a major effect on ethics in the workplace.

_____ 4. Following the Golden Rule is an excellent step toward behaving ethically.

_____ 5. Making ethical choices when communicating is not a frequent dilemma for most businesspeople.

Vocabulary

Define the following term in your own words.

6. Ethics

Critical Thinking

7. Economist Milton Friedman has argued that corporate officers have no right to spend corporate funds on social welfare projects, that they should do nothing but maximize profits. Do you agree or disagree? Why?

Online Study Center
ACE the Test
ACE Practice Tests 2.3

Online Study Center
Improve Your Grade
Audio Chapter Quiz 2.3
PowerPoint Review 2.3

COMMUNICATING VIA E-MAIL

4 ▶ *Communicate effectively via e-mail.*

In e-mail (electronic mail), messages are composed, transmitted, and read on the computer. E-mail is the most common form of communication today, easily outpacing telephone calls and letters sent via the U.S. Postal Service.[9] In an American Management Survey, 36 percent of executives reported that they favor e-mail for most management communication, compared with 26 percent who prefer the phone. (Surprisingly, one of the less-popular alternatives was a face-to-face meeting, favored by only 15 percent of the executives.)[10]

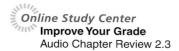

E-mail has, in fact, become so popular that it can be time-consuming to read and answer. Management consultant Christina Cavanagh, who has studied e-mail extensively, found that in 2002, business users received an average of 48 e-mails per day. Her research shows that an average of only 25 per day is realistic and manageable; this number of e-mails requires about two hours to process. She found that 64 percent of e-mail messages require a response, which takes five minutes on the average.[11]

You can never be sure who, other than your intended reader, will see your e-mail message. According to the Society for Human Resource Management, more than 36 percent of employers read employees' e-mail, and more than 70 percent believe it is the employer's right to read anything sent through the company's electronic communication system.[12]

In addition, as e-mail passes through various channels on its way from the sender to the receiver, the message can be intercepted or forwarded by unauthorized people in multiple ways. You should consider your e-mail messages like a postcard—available for anyone to read. And assume that they are permanent messages, available long after you and the recipient have deleted them from your files.

Because of its convenience and constant availability, it is easy to overuse e-mail. The guidelines contained in Table 2.2 show when four common forms of communication are used most effectively.

Format

To ensure maximum readability of your e-mail message, use short lines and short paragraphs (especially the first and last paragraphs). They are much easier to read. If the option exists on your e-mail program, set your left and right margins at 1 to 1.5 inches. Also avoid formatting a long message as one solid paragraph.

TABLE 2.2

Appropriate Uses of Communication Media

Medium	Use When the Message . . .
E-mail	▪ Consists of short, simple content. ▪ Involves mostly fact-based information where visual and nonverbal cues are not required. ▪ Requires prompt dissemination or response.
Face to face	▪ Benefits from visual, verbal, and nonverbal cues. ▪ Requires exploration of complex topics. ▪ Involves sensitive, personal, or bad-news information. ▪ Requires interactive or immediate feedback.
Telephone	▪ Benefits from a less formal environment. ▪ Requires an audience of one (usually). ▪ Requires discussion with immediate feedback of common ideas.
Written	▪ Requires a record for documentation or later reference. ▪ Contains complex, detailed, or lengthy content. ▪ Requires time to study and digest. ▪ Benefits from graphics or other visuals.

The use of all-capital letters for the entire body of your message is the text-based form of shouting at your reader and is considered rude (not to mention being more difficult to read). If words or phrases require emphasis, bold, italics, or quotation marks are more effective—and less obtrusive.

Always proofread your e-mail message before sending it. Don't let the speed and convenience of e-mail lull you into being careless. An occasional typo or other surface error will probably be overlooked by the reader. However, excessive errors or sloppy language creates an unprofessional image for your reader.

E-mail is typically written "on the fly"—composed and sent while keyboarding. Thus, writers sometimes ignore basic writing principles. According to one observer, e-mail may be

> desensitizing us to egregious grammatical gaffes. . . . Would you write a printed memo to your boss with typos in it? To what earthly purpose? How can someone on the other end of an e-mail message know that you're really an intelligent person?[13]

Model 1 on page 34 shows an appropriately formatted e-mail message.

Heading

Choose your recipients carefully. Don't send a message to an entire mailing list (for example, the whole department) if it applies to only one or two people. If needed, you can send a copy of your message by typing the address in the cc line (which stands for "carbon copy," the old-fashioned way of sending copies) or the bcc line (which stands for "blind carbon copy").

When using cc, the original recipient will be able to see who was copied on the message (to avoid hurt feelings, consider listing the names of the recipients in alphabetical order). When using bcc, the original recipient will not be aware that anyone else was copied on the message.

Send cc and bcc copies only when secondary readers need to be informed. Michael Eisner, former chairperson of Disney, once observed, "I have come to believe that if anything will bring about the downfall of a company, or maybe even a country, it is blind copies of e-mails that should never have been sent in the first place."[14]

Always use a descriptive subject line. In the course of a business day, your reader may receive dozens—perhaps, hundreds—of e-mail messages. Writing an effective subject line can help capture the reader's attention—and interest. The wording of the subject line may determine not only *when* but also *if* a message is read. Use a brief, descriptive subject line.

Most e-mail programs allow you to insert the original message into your reply. Use this feature judiciously. Occasionally, it may be helpful for the reader to see his or her entire message replayed. More often, however, you can save the reader time by establishing the content of the original message in your reply—for example, "Here is my opinion of the AlphaBat system that you asked about in your May 28 e-mail." If only part of the original message is relevant, delete the other parts. And always insert your reply above the original message.

Content

Downplay the seeming impersonality of electronic mail by starting your message with a friendly salutation, such as "Hi, Amos," or, more formally, "Dear Mr. Fisher."

MODEL 1

E-Mail Message

Is addressed only to the relevant readers.

Contains a descriptive subject line.

Starts with a friendly greeting.

Uses a direct style of writing—with the major news up front.

Ends with an appropriate closing.

Includes identifying information from a signature file.

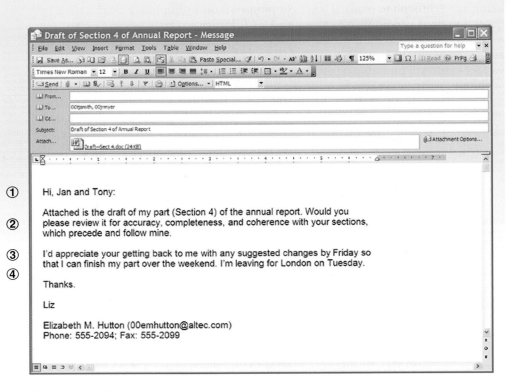

① Hi, Jan and Tony:

② Attached is the draft of my part (Section 4) of the annual report. Would you please review it for accuracy, completeness, and coherence with your sections, which precede and follow mine.

③ I'd appreciate your getting back to me with any suggested changes by Friday so that I can finish my part over the weekend. I'm leaving for London on Tuesday.

④ Thanks.

Liz

Elizabeth M. Hutton (00emhutton@altec.com)
Phone: 555-2094; Fax: 555-2099

Grammar and Mechanics Notes

1. Use a comma after "Hi" (before a noun of direct address).
2. For added readability, use short lines and paragraphs.
3. Use the possessive pronoun *your* before the gerund *getting*.
4. Leave a blank line between paragraphs (instead of indenting the first line).

While e-mail isn't as formal as a letter, neither is it as informal as a telephone call. The tone of your message depends, of course, on the situation—a message to your superior calls for a more formal tone than one to your friend.

Use a direct style of writing by putting your major idea in the first sentence or two. If the message is so sensitive or emotionally laden that a more indirect organization would be appropriate, you should reconsider whether e-mail is the most effective medium for the message. If a one-sentence e-mail message or reply serves your purpose, there is no need to pad the message to make it longer.

A variation of the carpenter's advice "Measure twice; cut once" applies to e-mail: "Think twice; write once." Because it is so easy to respond immediately to a message, you might be tempted to let your emotions take over. Such behavior is called "flaming" and should be avoided. Never say anything in an e-mail that you would not say to a person's face. Always assume the message you send will never be destroyed.

If you greet your reader at the beginning of your message, it is only logical to also tell him or her goodbye at the end. Use a friendly closing such as "Best regards," "Cheers," "Best wishes," or, more formally, "Sincerely."

Some e-mail programs provide only the e-mail address in the message header, for example, "kbio2@aol.com." Don't take a chance that your reader won't recognize you. Include your name, e-mail address, and any other appropriate identifying information at the end of your message. Most e-mail programs allow you to create a signature file containing this information; these lines are then automatically inserted at the end of every message. For example, you might create a signature file that reads as follows:

> Kristen Ahmed, Account Manager
> International Paper Company
> kahmed@ipc.com
> 317-555-7056, Ext. 339

CONCEPT CHECK 2.9

When is e-mail the preferred medium of communication in business?

The Office (Ad)dress Code

Different organizations have different cultures about the use of e-mail—just as they do about dressing, the use of first names, and the like. If you are new to an office, you would be wise to observe the corporate e-mail culture to learn the answers to questions such as these:[15]

- What is the general tone of e-mail messages sent in the organization—formal or informal?

- Does e-mail generally travel along a formal chain of command only, or is anyone free to e-mail comments or suggestions to top executives?

- How do employees generally contact colleagues down the hall—by e-mailing, phoning, or talking to them face-to-face?

- Do employees typically check (and respond to) e-mail messages immediately, daily, or over a period of days?

- What types of messages are typically sent by e-mail? Routine messages? Persuasive messages? Bad-news messages? Staff announcements? How long are these messages typically, and how long does a response usually take?

- What is the typical practice regarding the use of blind copies, forwarding, and e-mail attachments—both for intercompany and intracompany messages?

- What are the company's written policies regarding the use of personal e-mail on the job? Does the company tolerate a certain amount of personal e-mail? As noted in Figure 2.4, the average employee receives one to five personal e-mails at work each day.

- Does the company reserve the right to monitor all e-mail sent over the company's e-mail server?

Checklist 1 on page 37 summarizes the guidelines for writing and formatting e-mail messages.

Instant Messaging

In our fast-paced world, sometimes even traditional e-mail is not fast enough. You never know when the person to whom you sent the message will retrieve it

FIGURE 2.4

Number of Personal E-Mails

Personal e-mailing at work can seriously lower productivity rates, thus costing the company money. Know your company's policy on using company e-mail and IM for personal messages during business hours.

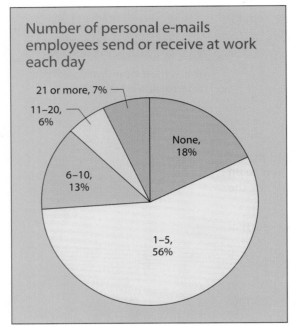

Number of personal e-mails employees send or receive at work each day

- 21 or more, 7%
- 11–20, 6%
- None, 18%
- 6–10, 13%
- 1–5, 56%

CONCEPT CHECK 2.10

Describe a business situation when the use of IM might be appropriate.

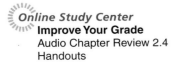

Online Study Center
Improve Your Grade
Audio Chapter Review 2.4
Handouts

and respond. Instant messaging (IM), however, uses Internet technology to allow people to send and receive text messages in real time. Today, anyone who owns a computer can go online and chat with family, friends, or colleagues throughout the world.

IM began in 1996 when a small Israeli company called Mirabilis launched ICQ ("I seek you"), which enabled people anywhere to type messages to each other in real time. Today, the largest IM provider by far is AOL, which purchased ICQ in 1998. MSN and Yahoo also provide the service, and Microsoft Windows XP comes with a free Windows Messenger IM service.

AOL Instant Messenger (AIM) carries 2 billion messages every day, and that figure is growing by 15 percent each month.[16] AIM is especially convenient because it can be accessed even if you do not have an AOL account.

How It Works

First, you have to download IM software and install it on your computer. You then register your screen name and compile a list of people with whom you might wish to interact; this list is called a buddy list. As soon as you log onto the Internet, most IM programs automatically detect your presence and alert others on your buddy list that you are online. Likewise, you see the names of those on your list who are online. You may then double-click the name of someone on your list who is also online and type a message. Your message appears instantly on that person's screen, and he or she may then type a response.

Other Forms of Electronic Communication

IM differs from e-mail because conversations occur instantly. Each party sees each line of text right after it is typed, thus making it more like a telephone conversation than exchanging letters or e-mail. A chat room allows a group of people to type messages that are seen by everyone in the "room." IM, on the other hand, typically involves one conversation between just two people. It is basically a private chat room for two people, both of whom have indicated their wish to communicate with each other.

Business Uses of IM

IM, of course, is not just for kids or families. Millions of corporate computer users have IM available on their work computers to enable them to connect with colleagues; to ask questions of team members; and, of course, to chat with friends and family. Assume, for example, you're on the phone with a client who asks you a question that you cannot answer. You can use IM to query a colleague down the hall (or across the country) to get an answer immediately. IM allows businesses to collaborate on projects easily and to hold virtual conferences.

Because of security concerns, most corporations have strict rules about individuals installing IM themselves. Corporate-installed IM systems contain more security features against unauthorized snooping. In addition, many corporations provide their own in-house server to keep private communications private. Many companies have also adopted policies against excessive use, nonbusiness use, and the like.

Competent communicators use e-mail and IM messages appropriately and format their messages for easy readability.

TEST PREPPER 2.4

ANSWERS CAN BE FOUND ON P. 410

True or False?

_____ 1. It takes five minutes to respond to the typical e-mail.

_____ 2. Using all-capital letters in the body of an e-mail message reinforces its importance.

_____ 3. The e-mail recipient does not know when another person has received a cc of the message.

_____ 4. You should put your major idea in the first sentence or two of an e-mail.

_____ 5. Salutations and friendly closings are not recommended for e-mail messages.

Critical Thinking

6. Assume that you typically receive 25 to 30 e-mails a day. How many of these e-mails would you reasonably consider to have a personal as opposed to a business purpose? Why?

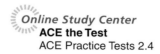

Online Study Center
ACE the Test
ACE Practice Tests 2.4

Online Study Center
Improve Your Grade
Audio Chapter Quiz 2.4
PowerPoint Review 2.4

CHECKLIST 1

Effective E-mail Practices

Format

✓ Use short lines and paragraphs.

✓ Avoid the use of all-capital letters.

✓ Proofread your message before sending it.

Heading

✓ Choose your recipients carefully.

✓ Use a descriptive subject line.

✓ Append the previous message only as needed when replying.

Content

✓ Start with a friendly salutation.

✓ Use a direct style of writing.

✓ Avoid flaming.

✓ Provide an appropriate closing.

Online Study Center *college.hmco.com/pic/oberSASfund*

SPOTLIGHT

How Would You Respond?

The following minicases on business ethics were developed by Kirk Hanson, a senior lecturer at the Stanford University Graduate School of Business and corporate ethics consultant. How would you respond to each? Formulate your responses before reading the suggested solutions.

Situations

1. You are about to take a job with Almost Perfect, Inc. You like everything you have learned about the company except the reputation the firm has for long working hours. You have a young family and are committed to spending time with them. What role should the number of working hours have in your decision?

2. You have been on the job for four days. Your boss hands you a report she hasn't had time to complete. "Just copy the numbers off last month's report," she says. "Nobody at headquarters ever really reads these." What do you do?

3. A new engineer who has just joined your group drops by your office and hands you a file stamped with the name of his former employer. "I thought you'd like to have a look at their list of key customers," he says. What do you do?

4. Despite a strongly worded company policy prohibiting gratuities from suppliers, you know your boss in the purchasing department is taking weeklong vacations paid for by a key vendor. What do you do?[17]

Suggested Solutions

1. Turn down the job or negotiate openly for more reasonable hours. You will never be satisfied if you take a job that sets up a constant value conflict. Be willing to pay the price for a family life that you value.

2. Offer to collect the real data for the report. Everyone is tested in the first weeks by coworkers who favor shortcuts or small ethical compromises. Establish your values; insist on getting the real data if push comes to shove.

3. Give him back the folder unread and tell him, "We don't do things like that around here." Be careful in your dealings with him. If he wasn't faithful to his obligations to his former employer, he won't be faithful to you.

4. Report him to a higher authority in the company, but be sure you have some proof before you do. He has violated such a clear standard that it is unlikely he can be persuaded to stop. Ask the higher authority to protect you from retaliation.

> ### THREE PS
> ### PROBLEM, PROCESS, PRODUCT

Reporting Research Results Ethically

Problem

Assume the role of Jason, a quality-control technician for an automobile manufacturer. You are responsible for testing a new airbag design. Your company is
eager to install the new airbags in next year's models because two competitors
have similar airbags on the market. However, your tests of the new design have
not been completely successful. All of the airbags tested inflated on impact, but
10 airbags out of every 100 tested inflated to only 60 percent of capacity. These
partially inflated airbags would still protect passengers from most of a collision
impact, but the passengers might receive more injuries than they would with
fully inflated airbags.

Before reporting the test results, you tell your supervisor that you would like
to run more tests to make sure that the airbags are reliable and safe. But your
supervisor explains that the company executives are eager to get the airbags on
the market and want the results in a few days. You now feel pressured to certify
that the airbags are safe (and indeed, they all inflated—at least partially).[18]

Process

1. What is the problem you are facing?

   I must decide exactly how I will phrase the certification sentence in
   my report.

2. What would be the ideal solution to this problem?

   I would be given additional time to conduct enough tests to assure
   myself that the airbags are reliable and safe.

3. Why can't the ideal solution be recommended?

   The company is pressuring me to certify the airbags now because
   two competitors have already introduced similar airbags.

4. Brainstorm possible certification statements that you might make.

   - All the airbags inflated.
   - None of the airbags failed to inflate.
   - Ninety percent of the airbags inflated fully; the rest inflated to
     only 60 percent of capacity.

5. Now evaluate each alternative in terms of these criteria.

   All the airbags inflated. This statement is true and is a positive
   statement that will probably satisfy management. However, it over-
   states the success of the tests and is somewhat misleading in what it
   omits—that 10 percent of the airbags inflated only partially. I may

THREE PS (CONTINUED)

be harming potential users by giving them a false sense of security; in addition, I may be leaving the company open to lawsuits resulting from failure of airbags to inflate fully.

None of the airbags failed to inflate. Again, this statement is true, but it omits important information the consumer needs. In addition, it is a negative statement, which will not please management.

Ninety percent of the airbags inflated fully; the rest inflated to only 60 percent of capacity. This statement provides the most accurate assessment of the test results. It emphasizes the positive and does state that some problems exist. The most serious risk with this alternative is that it could delay the release of the new design on the market. If this happens, my job might be at risk. In addition, it doesn't interpret the meaning of the partially inflated airbags.

6. Using what you've discovered about each alternative, construct the certification statement you will include in your report to management.

Product

Results of my testing of the new airbag design indicate that 90 percent of the airbags inflate fully on impact; the remaining 10 percent inflate to 60 percent of capacity, which is sufficient to protect passengers from most of a collision impact.

LEARNING OBJECTIVE REVIEW

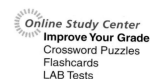

Online Study Center
Improve Your Grade
Crossword Puzzles
Flashcards
LAB Tests

1 ▶ *Communicate effectively in small groups.*

- Conflict, conformity, and consensus greatly affect the efficiency with which a team operates and the amount of enjoyment members derive from it.
- Use group conflict about ideas, not personalities, as a way of ensuring various viewpoints are heard to reach the best decision.
- Avoid groupthink or excessive conformity in group communication.
- Seek consensus when it is possible to do so.
- Learn how to give positive and negative feedback.
- Use team writing to benefit from the expertise of various individuals.
- Team writing works best when:
    - writing goals are established and the work is assigned to members based on ability
    - meetings to review work are regular
    - one member of the group writes the final draft to ensure "one voice" for the project
    - feedback is provided and drafts are revised before proofreading

2 ▶ *Communicate effectively with diverse populations both internationally and within the United States.*

- When communicating with people from other cultures:
    - maintain formality as some other cultures have a more formal approach to business dealings than Western cultures
    - show respect for the values of the other culture
    - communicate clearly by avoiding slang and other expressions that are unique to your culture
    - value diversity for the ways it benefits the organization
- When communicating with people within the United States, be sure to:
    - recognize ethnic differences in communication style
    - recognize differences in communication style due to gender
    - recognize and adapt to the communication needs of people with disabilities

3 ▶ *Communicate ethically.*

- Know your company's and your personal code of ethics.
- When faced with an ethical decision:
    - get the facts about the situation
    - evaluate all possible options for action
    - evaluate options by determining whether they are legal
    - evaluate options by comparing them to company values
    - evaluate options based on the outcome and how it will affect you and others
    - make the decision
    - act on the decision and explain your rationale

4 ▶ *Communicate effectively via e-mail.*

- When writing e-mail messages:
    - format for readability
    - identify the recipients who actually need to receive the message
    - use a descriptive subject line
    - use standard English
    - use an appropriate closing
    - provide identifying information about yourself at the end of the e-mail
    - follow the organizational culture's norms regarding e-mail
- When using instant messaging (IM):
    - follow the e-mail guidelines for readability and formatting
    - be aware of security concerns

EXERCISES

1. **Work-Team Communication (▶2.1)**

   Working in small groups, interview at least three international students or professors, each from a different country. For each country represented, determine the extent of team communications common in business, the extent of technological development, problems with the English language, and the like. Prepare a written report of your findings, proofread, revise as necessary, and submit it to your instructor.

2. **Domestic Intercultural Issues (▶2.2)**

   How would you respond to each of the following situations?

   a. Ryan gets angry when several of the people with whom he works talk among themselves in their native language. He suspects they are talking and laughing about him. As a result, Ryan tends to avoid his coworkers and to complain about them to others.

   b. Héctor, a slightly built office worker, feels intimidated when talking to his supervisor, a much larger man who is of a different racial background. As a result, Héctor often is unable to negotiate effectively.

   c. Darlene is embarrassed when she must talk to Galen, a subordinate who suffered major facial disfigurement from a grenade explosion during the Vietnam War. She doesn't know how to look at him. As a result, Darlene tends to avoid meeting with Galen face to face.

   d. Lillian, the only female manager on staff, gets incensed whenever her colleague Gilbert apologizes to her after using profanity during a meeting. First, she tells him that he shouldn't be using profanity at all. Second, if he does, he should not apologize just to her for using it.

   e. When Lance arrived as the only male real-estate agent in a small office, it was made clear to him that he would have to get his own coffee and clean up after himself—just like everyone else. Yet, whenever the FedEx truck delivers a heavy carton, the females always ask Lance to lift the package.

3. **Ethical Dilemmas (▶2.3)**

   Working in small groups and using the framework for ethical decision making discussed on page 30, make a decision regarding each of the following ethical dilemmas:

   a. *Confidentiality:* Your boss told you that one of your employees will have to be laid off because of budgetary cutbacks, but this information is confidential for the time being. You know that the employee is getting ready to buy a large, expensive house.

   b. *Copyright Issues:* You copied a computer program being used at work (and properly purchased) so that you can complete some work at home if you don't have time to finish it during normal working hours.

   c. *Employment:* You accepted a job but were then offered a much better job.

   d. *Hiring Minorities:* A Japanese candidate is the most qualified for a job, but the job requires quite a bit of face-to-face and telephone communication with customers, and you're concerned customers won't understand his accent.

   e. *Merit-Based Pay:* An employee has performed well all year and deserves a pay raise. However, she is at the top of her grade scale and can't be promoted.

4. **Sign of the Times (▶2.3)**

   You work part-time at a busy pawn shop in central San Antonio. A number of neighborhood stores have been burglarized in recent years, and the owner wants criminals to think twice before they break into his pawn shop. After thinking about the situation, he posts this sign in the window one night: "$10,000 reward offered to any officer of the law shooting and killing any person attempting to rob this property."

   When you come to work the next morning and see the sign, your first thought is that it will probably be an effective deterrent. As the day goes on, however, you begin to have doubts about the ethics of posting such a sign. Although you don't know of any law that would apply to this situation, you're not sure that your boss is doing the right thing. You decide to speak to him when he returns to lock up that evening. In preparation for this discussion, list the points you might make to convince the boss to take the sign down. Next, list the points in favor of leaving the sign up. If you were in charge, what would you do? Explain your answer in a brief report to the class.

5. E-Mail Format (▶2.4)

Evaluate the following e-mail message against the guidelines provided in Checklist 1 on page 37. Specifically, what would you change to make it more effective? Should this message have been sent as an e-mail message in the first place? Discuss.

6. Revising an E-Mail Message (▶2.4)

Revise the e-mail message shown below, following the e-mail guidelines in Checklist 1 on page 37. At the bottom of your message, list the specific practices of effective e-mails that you were able to follow in your communication.

7. Instant Messaging (▶2.4)

Set up a classmate as your buddy on your instant messaging system. Select a time to be online and, using IM, evaluate the following quotation from historian Daniel Boorstin: "Every advance in the history of communication has brought us in closer touch with people far away from us, but at the expense of insulating us from those nearest to us." What is meant by this statement? Do you agree or disagree? Why? While still in IM, write up a short report together summarizing the results of your discussion and your individual reactions to the IM session.

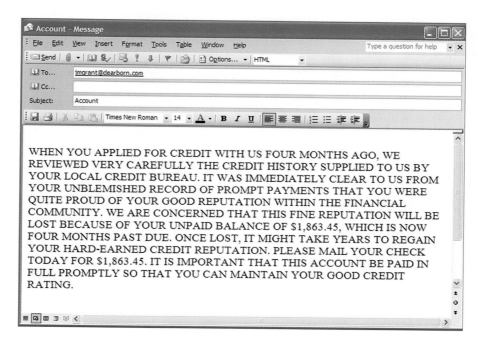

Additional exercises are available at the Online Study Center website: **college.hmco.com/pic/oberSASfund**.

Online Study Center **RESOURCES**

Prepare for Class, Improve Your Grade, and ACE the Test. Student Achievement Series resources include:

ACE Practice Tests	Ask Ober	Audio Chapter Reviews and Quizzes
Chapter Outlines	Communication Objectives	Crossword Puzzles
Flashcards	Glossaries	Handouts
LAB Tests	Portfolio Project Stationery	Sample Reports

To access these learning and study tools, go to **college.hmco.com/pic/oberSASfund**.

3 Interpersonal Communication Skills

Face-to-face meetings are one of the most effective ways to communicate and come to a decision as a group.

1 *Explain the meaning and importance of nonverbal communication.*

2 *Listen effectively in business situations.*

3 *Use the telephone effectively.*

Chapter Outline

Online Study Center
Prepare for Class
Chapter Outline

4 ▶ *Plan, conduct, and participate in business meetings.*

Meeting for Success

Need a decision? Call a meeting. That's the advice of Amy Hilliard, president and founder of The Hilliard Group, a firm that helps *Fortune* 500 businesses develop advertising, promotion, and public relations programs to reach out to African American, Hispanic, and Asian consumers across the country.

Although organizations hold meetings for a variety of reasons, one of the most important reasons is to come to a decision. "Face-to-face meetings expedite decisions," maintains Hilliard. "Many times, if you have the right people at the meeting, you can get a decision right away."

As a leader and a participant, Hilliard also understands the importance of listening. "Sometimes it's difficult to listen without having your response percolating in your mind, but you need to clear your mind and concentrate on what the other person is

on the job

AMY HILLIARD
President and Founder,
The Hilliard Group
(Chicago, Illinois)

KEY TERMS

agenda   *p. 56*
minutes   *p. 59*

saying." Nonverbal communication is a good way to convey that you are really listening. "For example, sitting with arms folded signals that you're closed," she explains, "but sitting with arms open and eyes focused on the speaker signals that you're listening and you welcome that person's input." ◼

In this chapter, we will explore four important interpersonal communication skills:

▮ Nonverbal communications
▮ Listening
▮ Using the telephone
▮ Participating in meetings

NONVERBAL COMMUNICATION

 Explain the meaning and importance of nonverbal communication.

Not all communication that occurs on the job is spoken, heard, written, or read—that is, verbal. According to management guru Peter Drucker, "The most important thing in communication is to hear what isn't being said."[1]

A nonverbal message is any message that is not written or spoken. It may accompany a verbal message (smiling as you greet a colleague), or it may occur alone (selecting the back seat when entering the conference room). Nonverbal messages are typically more spontaneous than verbal messages, but that doesn't mean that they are any less important. A classic study by Mehrabian found that only 7 percent of the meaning communicated by most messages comes from the verbal portion, with the remaining 93 percent being conveyed nonverbally.[2]

Many nonverbal messages have universal meanings (such as a nod of the head to indicate approval or agreement), while others (such as touching behavior) differ widely among cultures. The six most common types of nonverbal communication in business are discussed in the following sections.

Body Movement

By far, the most expressive part of the body is your face—especially your eyes. People tend to be quite consistent in their reading of facial expressions. In fact, many expressions have the same meaning across different cultures. Eye contact and eye movements tell you a lot about a person, although maintaining eye contact with the person to whom you're speaking is not perceived as important (or even polite) in some cultures.

Gestures are hand and upper-body movements that add important information to face-to-face interactions. More typically, gestures are used to help illustrate and reinforce your verbal message.

Body stance (posture, placement of arms and legs, distribution of weight, and the like) is another form of nonverbal communication. For example, leaning slightly toward the person with whom you're communicating would probably be taken as a sign of interest and involvement in the interaction. On the other hand, leaning back with arms folded across the chest might be taken (and intended) as a sign of boredom or defiance.

Physical Appearance

Our culture places great value on physical appearance. Attractive people tend to be seen as more intelligent, more likable, and more persuasive than unattractive people.

Your appearance is particularly important when you're trying to make a good first impression. Although you may not be able to change some of your physical features, understanding the importance of good grooming and physical appearance can help you to emphasize your strong points.

Voice Qualities

Voice qualities such as volume, speed, pitch, tone, and accent carry both intentional and unintentional messages. For example, when you are nervous, you tend to speak faster and at a higher pitch than normal. People who constantly speak too softly risk being interrupted or ignored, whereas people who constantly speak too loudly are often seen as being pushy or insecure.

Time

How do you feel when you're late for an appointment? When others are late? The meaning given to time varies greatly by culture, with Americans and Canadians being much more time conscious than people from South American or Middle Eastern cultures.

Time is related not only to culture but also to one's status within the organization. You would be much less likely to keep a superior waiting for an appointment than you would a subordinate. Time is also situation-specific. Although normally you might not worry about being five minutes late for a staff meeting, you would probably arrive early if you were the first presenter.

CONCEPT CHECK 3.1

What are the six most common types of nonverbal communication?

Touch

Touch is the first sense we develop, acquired even before birth. Some touches, such as those made by a physician during an examination, are purely physical; others, such as a handshake, are a friendly sign of willingness to communicate; and still others indicate intimacy. Although touching is a very important form of business communication, most people do not know how to use it appropriately and effectively. The person who never touches anyone in a business setting may be seen as cold and standoffish, whereas the person who touches others too frequently may cause the receiver to feel apprehensive and uncomfortable.

Space and Territory

When you are on a crowded elevator, you probably look at the floor indicator, at advertisements, at your feet, or just straight ahead—anywhere but at the person standing beside you. Most people in our culture are uncomfortable in such close proximity to strangers. Psychologists have identified four zones within which people in our culture interact:[3]

President George Bush congratulates miners who were rescued in Pennsylvania. He enters the "intimate" zone (from physical contact to about 18 inches) of one miner to clap him on the back.

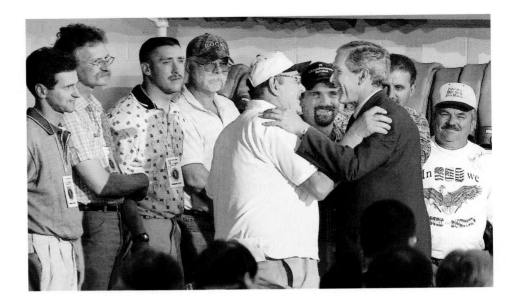

CONCEPT CHECK 3.2

Give an original example of a type of *business* communication that would typically occur in each of the following zones: Intimate Zone, Personal Zone, Social Zone, and Public Zone.

1. *Intimate Zone:* From physical contact to about 18 inches is where all your body movements occur; you move in this area throughout the day. This area is normally reserved for close, intimate interactions. Business associates typically enter this space infrequently and only briefly—perhaps to shake hands or pat someone on the back.

2. *Personal Zone:* This zone, extending from 18 inches to about 4 feet, is where conversation with close friends and colleagues takes place. Unlike interaction in the intimate zone, normal talking is frequent in the personal zone. Some, but not a great deal of, business interaction occurs here; for example, business lunches typically occur in this zone.

3. *Social Zone:* From 4 feet to 12 feet, the social zone is where most business exchanges occur. Informal business conferences and staff meetings occur within this space.

4. *Public Zone:* The public zone extends from 12 feet to as far as the eye can see and as far as the ear can hear. It is the most formal zone, and the least significant interactions typically occur here. Because of the great distance, communication in the public zone often goes one way, as from a speaker to a large audience.

Competent communicators recognize their own personal space needs and the needs of others. When communicating with people who prefer more or less space, the competent communicator makes the adjustments necessary to reach his or her objective.

Online Study Center
Improve Your Grade
Audio Chapter Review 3.1

TEST PREPPER 3.1

True or False?

_____ 1. A nonverbal message is any message that is not written.

_____ 2. Most of the meaning communicated by messages is communicated nonverbally.

_____ 3. Most business interaction occurs in the personal zone—from 18 inches to about 4 feet.

_____ 4. The meaning given to time varies greatly from one culture to the next.

_____ 5. People tend to be quite consistent in their interpretations of facial expressions.

Critical Thinking

6. If a nonverbal message contradicts a verbal message (for example, if a colleague claimed to like you but left you out of all his or her social interactions), which would you have more faith in—the verbal or nonverbal message? Why?

 Online Study Center
ACE the Test
ACE Practice Tests 3.1

Online Study Center
Improve Your Grade
Audio Chapter Quiz 3.1
PowerPoint Review 3.1

LISTENING

2 *Listen effectively in business situations.*

Effective communication—whether across continents or across a conference table—requires both sending and receiving messages—both transmission and reception. Whether you are making a formal presentation to 500 people or conversing with one person over lunch, your efforts will be in vain if your audience does not listen.

Listening involves much more than just hearing. You can hear and not listen (just as you can listen and not understand). Hearing is simply perceiving sound; sound waves strike the eardrum, sending impulses to the brain. Hearing is a passive process, whereas listening is an active process. When you *perceive* a sound, you're merely aware of it; you don't necessarily comprehend it. When you *listen*, you interpret and assign meaning to the sounds.

The Problem of Poor Listening Skills

Listening is the communication skill we use the most. White-collar workers typically devote at least 40 percent of their workday to listening. Yet immediately after hearing a ten-minute oral presentation, the average person retains only 50 percent of the information. Forty-eight hours later, only 25 percent of what was heard can be recalled.[4] Thus, listening is probably the least developed of the four verbal communication skills (writing, reading, speaking, and listening).

One of the major causes of poor listening is that most people simply have not been taught how to listen well. Think back to your early years in school. How much class time was devoted to teaching you to read and write? How many opportunities were you given to read aloud, participate in plays, or speak

THE LOCKHORNS

"LEROY'S HEARING IS GOOD. IT'S HIS LISTENING THAT'S BAD."

before a group? Chances are that reading, writing, and perhaps speaking were heavily stressed in your education. But how much formal training have you had in listening? If you're typical, the answer is "Not much."

Another factor that contributes to poor listening skills is the disparity between the speed at which we normally speak and the speed at which our brains can process data. We can think faster than we can speak—about four times faster, as a matter of fact. Thus, when listening to others, our minds begin to wander, and we lose our ability to concentrate on what is being said.

Here are some results of ineffective listening:

- Instructions not being followed
- Equipment broken from misuse
- Sales lost
- Feelings hurt
- Morale lowered
- Productivity decreased
- Rumors started
- Health risks increased

Still, poor listening skills are not as readily apparent as poor speaking or writing skills. It's easy to spot a poor speaker or writer but much more difficult to spot a poor listener because a poor listener can fake attention. In fact, the poor listener may not even be aware of this weakness. He or she may mistake hearing for listening.

Keys to Better Listening

The good news is that you can improve your listening skills. Tests at the University of Minnesota show that individuals who receive training in listening improve their listening skills by 25 percent to 42 percent.[5] To learn to listen more effectively, whether you're involved in a one-on-one dialogue or are part of a mass audience, give the speaker your undivided attention, stay open-minded, avoid interrupting, and involve yourself in the communication.

Give the Speaker Your Undivided Attention

During a business presentation, a member of the audience may hear certain familiar themes, think, "Oh, no, not that again," and proceed to tune the speaker out. Or during a conference with a subordinate, an executive may make or take phone calls, doodle, play around with a pen or pencil, or perform other distracting actions that give the speaker the impression that what he or she has to say is unimportant or uninteresting.

Physical distractions are the easiest to eliminate. Simply shutting the door or asking your assistant to hold all calls can eliminate many interruptions during personal conferences. If you're in a meeting where the environment is noisy, the temperature too cold or hot, or the chairs uncomfortable, try to tune out the distractions rather than the speaker. Learn to ignore those annoyances over which you have no control and to concentrate instead on the speaker and what he or she is saying.

Mental distractions are more difficult to eliminate. But with practice and effort, you can discipline yourself, for example, to temporarily forget about your fatigue or to put competing thoughts out of your mind so that you can give the speaker your attention.

We talk about giving the speaker your undivided attention. Actually, it would be more accurate to say that you give the speaker's *comments* your undivided attention; that is, you should focus on the content of the talk and not be overly concerned about how the talk is delivered. It is true, of course, that nonverbal clues do provide important information. However, do not be put off by the fact that the speaker may have dressed inappropriately, spoken too fast or in an unfamiliar accent, or appeared nervous. Almost always, *what* is said is more important than how it is said.

Likewise, avoid dismissing a topic simply because it is uninteresting or is presented in an uninteresting manner. Boring does not mean unimportant. Some information that may be boring or difficult to follow may in fact prove to be quite useful to you and thus be well worth your effort to give it your full attention.

Stay Open-Minded

Regardless of whom you're listening to or what the topic is, keep your emotions in check. Listen objectively and empathetically. Be willing to accept new information and new points of view, regardless of whether they mesh with your existing beliefs. Concentrate on the content of the message rather than on its source.

Don't look at the situation as a win/lose proposition; that is, don't consider that the speaker wins and you lose if you concede the merits of his or her position. Instead, think of it as a win/win situation: the speaker wins by convincing you of the merits of his or her position, and you win by gaining new information and insights that will help you perform your duties more effectively.

Maintain neutrality as long as possible, and don't jump to conclusions too quickly. Instead, try to understand *why* the speaker is arguing a particular point of view and what facts or experience convinced the speaker to adopt this position. When you assume this empathetic frame of reference, you will likely find that you neither completely agree with nor completely disagree with every point the speaker makes. This ability to evaluate the message objectively will help you gain the most from the exchange.

Don't Interrupt

Perhaps because of time pressures, we sometimes get impatient. As soon as we've figured out what a person is going to say, we tend to interrupt to finish the sentence for the speaker; this practice is especially a problem when listening to a slow speaker. Or as soon as we can think of a counterargument, we tend to rush right in—regardless of whether the speaker has finished or even paused for a breath.

Such interruptions have many negative consequences. First, they are rude. Second, instead of speeding up the exchange, such interruptions actually tend to drag it out because they often interfere with the speaker's train of thought, causing backtracking. The most serious negative consequence, however, is the nonverbal message such an interruption sends: "I have the right to interrupt you because what I have to say is more important than what you have to say!" Is it any wonder, then, that such a message hinders effective communication?

CONCEPT CHECK 3.3

What are four strategies for effective listening?

There is a difference between listening and simply waiting to speak. Even if you're too polite to interrupt, don't simply lie in wait for the first available opportunity to barge in with your version of the truth. If you're constantly planning what you'll say next, you can hardly listen attentively to what the other person is saying.

Americans tend to have low tolerance for silence. Yet waiting a moment or two after someone has finished before you respond has several positive effects—especially in an emotional exchange. It gives the person speaking a chance to elaborate on his or her remarks, thereby drawing out further insights. It also helps create a quieter, calmer, more respectful atmosphere, one that is more conducive to solving the problem at hand.

Involve Yourself

As we have said, hearing is passive whereas listening is active. You should be doing something while the other person is speaking (and we don't mean doodling, staring out the window, or planning your afternoon activities).

Much of what you should be doing is mental. Summarize to yourself what the speaker is saying; create what the experts call an *internal paraphrase* of the speaker's comments. We can process information much faster than the speaker can present it, so use that extra time for active listening—ensuring that you really are hearing not only what the person is saying but the motives and implications as well.

CONCEPT CHECK 3.4

What does the guideline "Be selfish in your listening" mean?

Some listeners find it helpful to jot down points, translating their mental notes into written notes. If you do so, keep your notes brief; don't become so busy writing down the facts that you miss the message. Concentrate on the main ideas; if you get them, you'll be more likely to remember the supporting details later. Recognize also that even if a detail or two of the speaker's message might be inaccurate or irrelevant, the major points may still be valid. Evaluate the validity of the overall argument; don't get bogged down in trivia.

Be selfish in your listening. Constantly ask yourself, How does this point affect *me*? How can I use this information to further my goals or to help me perform my job more effectively? Personalizing the information will help you to concentrate more easily and to weigh the evidence more objectively—even if the topic is difficult to follow or uninteresting and even if the speaker has some annoying mannerisms or an unpleasant personality.

Online Study Center
Improve Your Grade
Audio Chapter Review 3.2

TEST PREPPER 3.2   ANSWERS CAN BE FOUND ON P. 410

True or False?

_____ 1. Most people have been taught how to listen effectively.

_____ 2. Poor listening skills are not as readily apparent as poor speaking or writing skills.

_____ 3. You can hear but still not listen.

_____ 4. Research shows that formal training improves listening skills.

_____ 5. Physical distractions are more difficult to eliminate than mental distractions.

Critical Thinking

6. You're in a small group meeting when your superior begins to explain a new procedure by suggesting steps that you know might actually cause harm to an employee. What do you do?

Online Study Center
ACE the Test
ACE Practice Tests 3.2

Online Study Center
Improve Your Grade
Audio Chapter Quiz 3.2
PowerPoint Review 3.2

COMMUNICATING BY TELEPHONE

 3 *Use the telephone effectively.*

Consider the following statistics regarding telephone communication:[6]

▌ There is an average of more than one phone per person in the United States.

▌ AT&T processes more than 75 million calls every single day.

▌ The average length of phone calls is 6 minutes for local calls and 10 minutes for long-distance calls.

▌ Americans make more than 6.3 billion international calls every year (with an average cost of 34 cents per minute).

▌ More than 50 percent of Americans (143 million people) own a cell phone.

No wonder, then, that communicating effectively by telephone is a critical managerial skill, one that becomes increasingly important as the need for instantaneous information increases. Your telephone demeanor may be taken by the caller as the attitude of the entire organization. Every time the phone rings, your organization's future is on the line.

Your Telephone Voice

Because the person to whom you're speaking has no visual clues to augment the auditory clues, a voice that is raspy, hoarse, shrill, loud, or weak can make you sound angry, excited, depressed, or bored—even when you aren't. Therefore, try to control your voice and project a friendly, competent, enthusiastic image to the other party.

To make your voice as clear as possible, sit or stand tall and avoid chewing gum or eating while talking. If your head is tilted sideways to cradle the phone between your head and shoulder, your throat is strained and your words may sound unclear.

Your Telephone Technique

Always answer the phone by the second or third ring. Regardless of how busy you are, you do not want to give the impression that your company doesn't care about its callers. Answer clearly and slowly, giving the company's name. Remember that even if you give the same greeting 50 times a day, your callers probably hear it only once. Make sure they can understand it.

Be a good listener. Just as you would never continue writing or reading while someone speaks to you in person, do not engage in such distracting activities during phone calls. Pay attention especially to getting names correct and use the person's name during the conversation to personalize the message.

It is estimated that 70 percent of all business calls are placed on hold at some time during the conversation and that the average American business executive spends over 60 hours on hold every year.[7] If you must put a caller on hold, always ask, "May I put you on hold?" and then give the caller an opportunity to respond. Long-distance callers may prefer to call back rather than to be put on hold. When you get back on the line, do not appear rushed or exasperated. Give the patient caller your complete attention.

Voice Mail

Whether you love it or hate it, voice mail is here to stay. Although some callers find voice mail impersonal and irritating, most are grateful for the opportunity to leave a message when they're unable to reach their party.

Before you even make a call, recognize that you might have to leave a message, so plan your message beforehand. Be polite and get to the point quickly. Clearly define the purpose of the call and the desired action and always give your phone number—even if the caller has it on file. The calls that get returned the fastest are those that are easiest to make.

If you have voice mail on your own phone, follow these guidelines:

▌ Never use voice mail as a substitute for answering your phone when you are available. Your customers, suppliers, and fellow workers deserve more consideration than that.

▌ Record your outgoing message in your own voice and keep it short. Here is an example: "Hello, this is John Smith. Please leave me a message and I'll get back to you as quickly as I can. Thank you." Change your message when you will be away from the office for an extended period of time.

▌ Check your messages at least daily and return calls promptly. Callers assume that you've received their messages and may interpret a lack of response as rudeness.

Telephone Tag

The telephone would be a much more efficient instrument if we could be assured of reaching our party each time we called. Instead, we're often forced to play an unproductive game of telephone tag, in which Party A calls Party B, is unable to reach her, and leaves a message. Party B then returns Party A's call, is unable to reach him, and leaves a message. And the process continues until the connection is finally made or until one party gives up in frustration.

Only 17 percent of business callers reach their intended party on the first try, 26 percent by the second try, and 47 percent by the third try. Thus, it takes the majority of business callers at least three tries to reach their intended party.[8]

To avoid telephone tag, plan the timing of your calls. Try to schedule them at times when you're most likely to reach the person. Also, announce when you're returning a call. If you're returning someone's call and get a secretary on the line, begin by saying you're returning the boss's call. This will clue the secretary that the boss wants to speak to you. If necessary, find out what time would be best to call back or whether someone else in the organization can help.

Cell Phones

Nothing is more disconcerting than to have your business presentation interrupted by the ringing of someone's cell phone or the beeping of someone's pager. In public locations where conversation is expected (such as in airline terminals), using a cell phone or answering a page is appropriate. However, at formal meetings, restaurants, movies, and social occasions, you should either turn off your device or switch to the "silent-alert" mode (typically either a light or a vibrating device).

When calling someone on a cell phone, get down to business quickly; both you and the recipient are paying by-the-minute charges for using the phone.

And when driving, remember that safety comes first. Do not make (or answer) a call while maneuvering in difficult traffic.

Believing that such tiny devices have inadequate amplification, some cell phone users engage in what is known as "cell yell." Use your normal volume of voice when speaking on a cell phone.

TEST PREPPER 3.3   ANSWERS CAN BE FOUND ON P. 410

True or False?

_____ 1. The majority of all business calls are placed on hold at some time during the conversation.

_____ 2. The need for effective telephone communication skills is decreasing in the contemporary office.

_____ 3. It is acceptable to use voice mail as a substitute for answering your phone when you are available.

_____ 4. Fewer than one-fifth of business calls reach their intended party on the first try.

_____ 5. Using a cell phone in public places where conversation is expected is an accepted business practice.

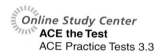
Online Study Center
ACE the Test
ACE Practice Tests 3.3

Online Study Center
Improve Your Grade
Audio Chapter Quiz 3.3
PowerPoint Review 3.3

BUSINESS MEETINGS

 Plan, conduct, and participate in business meetings.

Much of the listening you'll do in the workplace will be in the context of business meetings. Meetings serve a wide variety of purposes in the organization. They keep members informed of events related to carrying out their duties; they provide a forum for soliciting input, solving problems, and making decisions; and they promote unity and cohesiveness among the members through social interaction.

The ability to conduct and participate in meetings is a crucial managerial skill. One survey of more than 2,000 business leaders showed that executives who run a meeting well are perceived to be better managers by both their superiors and their peers.[9]

To use meetings as an effective managerial tool, you need to know not only how to run them but also when to call them and how to follow up afterward. Like so many decisions you will have to make about communication, your choices will be guided by what you hope to accomplish.

Planning the Meeting

When you add up the hourly salaries and fringe benefits of those planning and attending a meeting, the cost can be considerable. Managers must make sure they're getting their money's worth from a meeting, which requires careful planning: identifying the purpose and determining whether a meeting is really necessary, preparing an agenda, deciding who should attend, and planning the logistics.

Identifying Your Purpose

The first step is always to determine your purpose. The more specific you can be, the better results you will get. A purpose such as "to discuss how to make our marketing representatives more effective" is vague and therefore not as helpful as "to decide whether to purchase cellular phones for our marketing representatives." The more focused your purpose, the easier it will be to select a means of accomplishing that purpose.

Determining Whether a Meeting Is Necessary

Sometimes meetings are not the most efficient means of communication. For example, a short memo or e-mail message is more efficient than a face-to-face meeting to communicate routine information. Similarly, it doesn't make sense to use the weekly staff meeting of ten people to hold a long discussion involving only one or two of the members. A phone call or smaller meeting would accomplish that task more quickly and at less cost.

However, alternative means of conveying or securing information often present their own problems. Some people don't read written messages carefully, or they interpret them differently. Time is lost in transmitting and responding to written messages. And information may be garbled as it moves from person to person and from level to level.

Preparing an Agenda

agenda a list of topics to be considered at a meeting.

Once you've established your specific purpose, you need to consider in more detail what topics the meeting will cover and in what order. This list of topics, or the **agenda**, can accomplish two goals: (1) it helps you prepare for the meeting by showing what background information you'll need, and (2) it helps you run the meeting by keeping you focused on your plan.

Knowing what topics will be discussed also helps those attending the meeting to plan for the meeting effectively—reviewing needed documents, bringing pertinent records, deciding what questions need to be raised, and the like. The survey of 2,000 business leaders mentioned earlier revealed that three-fourths of the managers consider agendas to be essential for efficient meetings, yet nearly half the meetings they attend are *not* accompanied by written agendas.[10]

Formal, recurring business meetings might follow an agenda like the one below; of course, not every meeting will contain all these elements:

CONCEPT CHECK 3.6

What two purposes does an agenda serve for the meeting leader?

1. Call to order
2. Roll call (if necessary)
3. Reading and approval of minutes of previous meeting (if necessary)
4. Reports of officers and standing committees
5. Reports of special committees
6. Old business
7. New business
8. Announcements
9. Program
10. Adjournment

Each item to be covered under these headings should be identified, including the speaker (if other than the chairperson); for example:

7. NEW BUSINESS
   a. Review of December 3 press conference
   b. Recommendation for annual charitable contribution
   c. Status of remodeling—Jan Fischer

Deciding Who Should Attend

A great number of ad hoc meetings take place each business day for the purpose of solving a specific problem. If you must decide who will attend a particular meeting, your first concern is how the participants relate to your purpose. Who will make the decision? Who will implement the decision? Who can provide needed background information? On one hand, you want to include all who can contribute to solving the problem; on the other hand, you want to keep the meeting to a manageable number of people.

Consider also how the potential group members differ in status within the organization, in knowledge about the issue, in communication skills, and in personal relationships. The greater the differences, the more difficult it will be to involve everyone in a genuine discussion aimed at solving the problem.

Determining Logistics

It would be unwise to schedule a meeting that requires extensive discussion and creative problem solving at the end of the work day, when members may be exhausted emotionally and physically. Likewise, it would be counterproductive to schedule a three-hour meeting in a room equipped with uncushioned fold-up chairs, poor lighting, and extreme temperatures.

Instead, facilitate group problem solving by making intelligent choices about the timing and location of the meeting, room arrangements, types of audiovisual equipment, and the like. Doing so will increase the likelihood of achieving the goals of the meeting. With regard to seating arrangements, the most important tip is to make the decision *consciously*; that is, if you have a choice, use the arrangement that best fits your purpose (see Figure 3.1).

▌ The rectangular arrangement is most commonly used for formal meetings, with the chairperson sitting at the head of the table, farthest from the door.

▌ The circular arrangement is more informal and encourages an equal sharing of information and leadership functions.

▌ For larger meetings, a U-shaped setup is desirable because it allows each attendee to see all other meeting participants.

▌ A satellite arrangement is often useful for training sessions or when participants are to be divided into groups. This

FIGURE 3.1

Meeting Room Setups

Different meeting room arrangements lend themselves to different types of meetings.

Rectangular
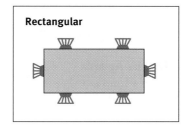

Circular
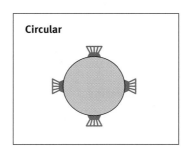

U-shaped
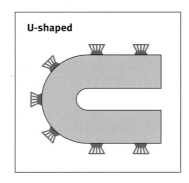

Satellite
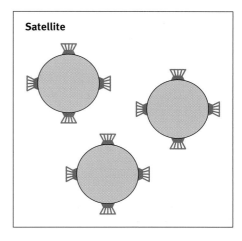

Classroom
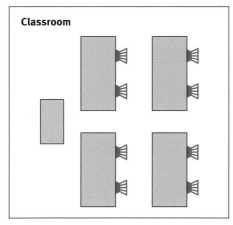

arrangement allows the chairperson to move freely around the room, addressing each group separately.

▌ A classroom arrangement is appropriate when most of the information is one way—from the leader to the audience; but even in this setup, the leader should encourage interaction among group members.

Conducting the Meeting

Planning for a meeting goes a long way toward ensuring its success, but the manager's job is by no means over when the meeting begins. A manager must be a leader during the meeting, keeping the group focused on the point and encouraging participation.

Punctuality

Unless a high-level member or one whose input is vital to the business at hand is tardy, make it a habit to begin every meeting on time. Doing so sends a powerful nonverbal message to chronic late arrivers that business will be conducted and decisions made whether or not they're present.

If you wait for latecomers, you send the message to those who *were* punctual that they wasted their time by being prompt. As a result, they will probably arrive late for subsequent meetings. And the habitual late arrivers will then begin arriving even later! Avoid this vicious cycle by beginning (and ending) at the appointed times.

Following the Agenda

One key to a focused meeting is to follow the agenda. At formal meetings, you will be expected to discuss all items on the published agenda and to omit all items not on the agenda. The less formal the meeting, the more flexibility you have in allowing new topics to be introduced. It's always possible that new information that has a bearing on your problem may arise. To prevent discussion simply because you didn't include the item on your agenda will make it more difficult for you to achieve your purpose. But as leader of the meeting, you must make certain that new topics are directly relevant.

Leading the Meeting

Begin the meeting with a statement of your purpose and an overview of the agenda. As the meeting progresses, keep track of time. Don't let the discussion get bogged down in details. If special meeting rules have not been adopted, most leaders follow standard parliamentary procedure.

Preventing people from talking too much or digressing from the topic requires tact. Comments like "I see your point, and that relates to what we were just discussing" can keep you on track without offending the speaker. You'll also need to encourage the participation of the quieter members of the group with comments like "Juan, how does this look from the perspective of your department?"

At the end of the meeting, summarize for everyone what the meeting has accomplished. What was decided? What are the next steps? Review any assignments and make sure that everyone understands his or her responsibilities.

During the meeting, someone—either an assistant, the leader, or someone the leader designates—should record what happens. That person must report objectively and not impose his or her own biases.

Following Up the Meeting

Routine meetings may require only a short memorandum or e-mail as a follow-up to what was decided. Formal meetings or meetings where controversial ideas were discussed may require a more formal summary.

Minutes are an official record of the proceedings; they summarize what was discussed and what decisions were made. Generally, they should emphasize what was done at the meeting, not what was *said* by the members. Minutes may, however, present an intelligent summary of the points of view expressed on a particular issue, without names attached, followed by the decision made. Avoid presenting minutes that are either so short they lack the "flavor" of what transpired or so long they tend to be ignored.

The first paragraph of minutes should identify the type of meeting (regular or special); the meeting date, time, and place; the presiding officer; the names of those present (or absent) if customary; and the fact that the minutes of the previous meeting were read and approved.

The body of the minutes should contain a separate paragraph for each topic. According to parliamentary procedure, the name of the maker of a motion, but not the seconder, should be entered in the minutes. The precise wording of motions, exactly as voted on, should also appear in minutes. It is often helpful to use the same subheadings as in the agenda.

The last paragraph of the minutes should state the time of adjournment and, if appropriate, the time set for the next meeting. The minutes should be signed by the person preparing them. If someone other than the chairperson prepares the minutes, the minutes should be read and approved by the chairperson before being distributed.

The minutes of a meeting are shown in Model 2, "Minutes of a Meeting" (see pages 60–61). Guidelines for conducting business meetings are summarized in Checklist 2, "Business Meetings" (see page 62).

minutes   An official record of the proceedings of a meeting.

Online Study Center
Improve Your Grade
Audio Chapter Review 3.4

TEST PREPPER 3.4   ANSWERS CAN BE FOUND ON P. 410

True or False?

_____ 1. The ability to conduct and participate in meetings is a crucial managerial skill.

_____ 2. A meeting is more efficient than an e-mail for communicating routine information.

_____ 3. Minutes of a meeting should be distributed before the meeting to identify the list of topics to be covered.

_____ 4. A circular arrangement of chairs at a meeting encourages equal sharing of information and leadership functions.

Vocabulary

Define the following terms in your own words.

5. Agenda
6. Minutes

Online Study Center
ACE the Test
ACE Practice Tests 3.4

Online Study Center
Improve Your Grade
Audio Chapter Quiz 3.4
PowerPoint Review 3.4

MODEL 2

Minutes of a Meeting

Report the events in the order in which they occurred.

Provide headings to aid readability.

Provide only enough detail to give an indication of what took place.

Provide exact wording of the motions made and indicate the action taken. Unless policy dictates, it is not necessary to identify the seconder of a motion or to provide a tally of the vote taken.

① **COMPUTER USE COMMITTEE**
Minutes of the Regular Meeting
May 18, 20—

② Members Present: S. Lindsey (Chair), L. Anderson-White, F. Griffin, T. King (Secretary), Z. Petropoulou, G. Ullom, J. West, K. Wolff

Shannon Lindsey called the meeting to order at 8:35 a.m. The minutes of the April 14 meeting were approved with the correction that Frank Griffin be recorded as present.

REPORT OF THE BUDGET SUBCOMMITTEE

Zoe Petropoulou reported that the Corporate Executive Council had approved an additional $58,000 for subcommittee allocation for hardware purchases through September 30, 20—. The subcommittee plans to send out RFPs by the end of the month and to make allocation recommendations to CUC at the June meeting. He also distributed a handout (Appendix A) showing the current-year hardware and software allocations through May 1.

OLD BUSINESS

None.

NEW BUSINESS

Standardization of Webpage-Development Software. Jenny West moved that "beginning September 1, 20—, CUC approve expenditures for webpage-development software only for Microsoft FrontPage 2003." She summarized the coordination, training, and site-maintenance problems that are now being encountered as a result of individual webmasters using different programs and answered questions from the floor. Gina Ullom moved to amend the motion by inserting the words "or later version" after "FrontPage 2003." The amendment passed, and the amended motion was adopted after debate.

Grammar and Mechanics Notes

1. Unless a different format is traditional, use regular report format for meeting minutes.
2. Identify the meeting attendees, listing the chair first, followed by others in either alphabetic or position order.

2

Speech-Recognition Software. Shannon Lindsey reported that she had received numerous requests for information or recommendations for purchasing speech-recognition software and asked for committee input. Extensive discussion followed concerning the cost, the amount of training required, accuracy, resulting noise level for carrel workers, and the overall implications of such software for touch-typing skills. The motion by Lisa Anderson-White that "the chair appoint a task force to study the issue and report back at the next meeting" passed. The chair appointed Lisa Anderson-White and Frank Griffin to the task force.

ANNOUNCEMENTS

Shannon Lindsey made the following announcements:

- She has received three positive comments and no negative feedback from her March 15 memo to department heads announcing the new repair and maintenance policy.
③ - She has been asked to represent CUC at the June 18 long-range planning meeting of the Corporate Executive Council to answer questions about planned hardware and software expenditures for the next three years.
- Anthem Computer Services has asked permission to make a 30-minute presentation to CUC. In accordance with committee policy, she rejected the request.

ADJOURNMENT

The meeting was adjourned at 10:40 a.m. The next regular meeting is scheduled for 8:30 a.m. on June 20.

④ Respectfully submitted,

Terry King

Terry King, Secretary

Enc: Appendix A: Hardware and Software Allocations
cc: Department Heads
Director of Purchasing
Corporate Executive Council

Announce the date and time of the next meeting. (Provide the location only if it differs from the regular meeting site.)

Grammar and Mechanics Notes

3. Use parallel language for enumerated or bulleted items.
4. Format the closing parts in a manner similar to that found in a business letter.

CHECKLIST 2

Business Meetings

Planning the Meeting

✓ Identify the purpose of the meeting.

✓ Prepare an agenda for distribution to the participants.

✓ Decide who should attend the meeting.

✓ Determine the logistics of the meeting—timing, location, room and seating arrangements, and types of audiovisual equipment needed.

✓ Assign someone (even if it is yourself) the task of taking notes during the meeting. These notes should be objective, accurate, and complete.

Conducting the Meeting

✓ Encourage punctuality by beginning and ending the meeting on time.

✓ Begin each meeting by stating the purpose of the meeting and reviewing the agenda.

✓ Establish ground rules that permit the orderly transaction of business. Many organizations follow parliamentary procedure.

✓ Control the discussion to ensure that it is relevant, that a few members do not monopolize the discussion, and that all members have an opportunity to be heard.

✓ At the end of the meeting, summarize what was decided, identify the next steps, and explain each member's responsibilities.

Following Up the Meeting

✓ If the meeting was routine and informal, follow up with a memorandum or e-mail summarizing the major points of the meeting. For more formal meetings, prepare and distribute minutes.

THREE Ps
PROBLEM, PROCESS, PRODUCT

A Plan for a Business Meeting

Problem

You are Dieter Ullsperger, director of employee relations for the city of Eau Claire, Wisconsin. The city manager has asked your department to develop a policy statement regarding the solicitation of funds from employees during work hours for employee weddings, retirements, anniversaries, and the like. Despite the good intentions of such efforts, the city manager questions whether they put undue pressure on some employees and take unreasonable time from official duties. You have already gathered secondary data regarding this matter and have spoken with your counterparts in Jacksonville, Florida; Milwaukee, Wisconsin; and Memphis, Tennessee. You are now ready to begin planning a first draft of the policy statement.

Process

1. What is the purpose of your task?

   To prepare a policy statement on soliciting funds from employees during office hours.

2. Is a meeting needed?

   Because this policy will affect every employee in city government, it should be developed on the basis of input from representatives of the work force. Therefore, a planning meeting is desirable.

3. What will be the agenda?

   My first reaction is that the meeting agenda is to write the new policy. I recognize that it is not reasonable, however, for a policy statement to be written during a meeting. Thus, the real agenda is to develop the broad outlines for the policy. The policy will be planned collaboratively, drafted individually, reviewed collaboratively, and revised individually.

4. Who should attend the meeting?

   Because I want to ensure broad consensus on this policy, I'll ask the union stewards of our two unions to attend. (I'll represent management.) I'll also ask the city attorney to attend to ensure that our policy is legal. Finally, I'll ask Lyn Paterson in Transportation to attend; she is a veteran city employee who is well respected among her peers and has served as the unofficial social chairperson for numerous fund-raising events over the past several years. I'll telephone each of those people to ask for his or her voluntary participation in this project.

THREE PS (CONTINUED)

5. What about logistics?

> Because I want the meeting to be informal, I'll hold it in the small conference room downstairs, which has an oval table. The only audiovisual equipment I'll need is a chalkboard to display any ideas we might have. I'll ask my assistant to take minutes. I was not given a specific deadline, so I'll delay the meeting for three weeks: two retirement parties are already scheduled in the meantime.

Product

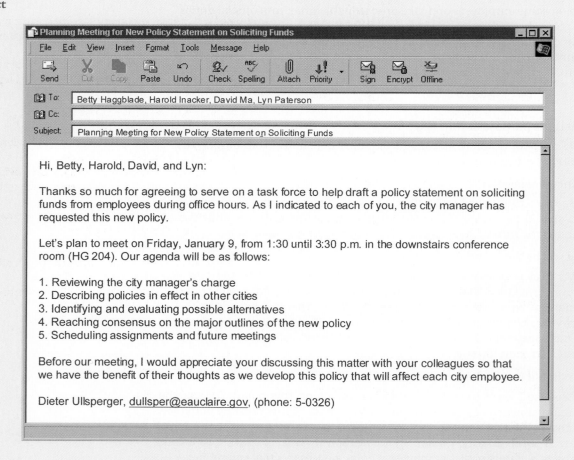

Planning Meeting for New Policy Statement on Soliciting Funds

File   Edit   View   Insert   Format   Tools   Message   Help

Send   Cut   Copy   Paste   Undo   Check   Spelling   Attach   Priority   Sign   Encrypt   Offline

To: Betty Haggblade, Harold Inacker, David Ma, Lyn Paterson

Cc:

Subject: Planning Meeting for New Policy Statement on Soliciting Funds

Hi, Betty, Harold, David, and Lyn:

Thanks so much for agreeing to serve on a task force to help draft a policy statement on soliciting funds from employees during office hours. As I indicated to each of you, the city manager has requested this new policy.

Let's plan to meet on Friday, January 9, from 1:30 until 3:30 p.m. in the downstairs conference room (HG 204). Our agenda will be as follows:

1. Reviewing the city manager's charge
2. Describing policies in effect in other cities
3. Identifying and evaluating possible alternatives
4. Reaching consensus on the major outlines of the new policy
5. Scheduling assignments and future meetings

Before our meeting, I would appreciate your discussing this matter with your colleagues so that we have the benefit of their thoughts as we develop this policy that will affect each city employee.

Dieter Ullsperger, dullsper@eauclaire.gov, (phone: 5-0326)

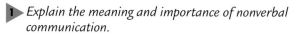
Online Study Center
Improve Your Grade
Crossword Puzzles
Flashcards
LAB Tests

LEARNING OBJECTIVE REVIEW

1 ▸ *Explain the meaning and importance of nonverbal communication.*

- Nonverbal messages are unwritten and unspoken.
- The most common types of nonverbal communication are:
  - body movement
  - physical appearance
  - voice qualities
  - time
  - touch
  - space and territory

2 ▸ *Listen effectively in business situations.*

- Implement the keys to better listening:
  - Give the speaker your undivided attention and pay attention to what is being said.
  - Stay open-minded and don't react emotionally to what the speaker says.
  - Don't interrupt.
  - Involve yourself in what the speaker is saying and consider how it applies to you.

3 ▸ *Use the telephone effectively.*

- Control your voice to project a professional image to the other party.
- Practice good telephone technique.
- Use voice mail effectively when leaving messages and answering messages.
- Avoid telephone tag by calling when the party is likely to be in the office.
- Use cell phones appropriately.

4 ▸ *Plan, conduct, and participate in business meetings.*

- When planning a meeting:
  - Identify the purpose and objective of the meeting.
  - Hold meetings only when another form of communication would not be effective.
  - Prepare an agenda that includes all important topics for discussion.
  - Invite only those who can make a significant contribution or who will be affected by the meeting's proceedings.
  - Make intelligent choices about the timing and location of the meeting, room arrangements, types of audiovisual equipment, and the like.

- When conducting a meeting:
  - Encourage members to be punctual.
  - Follow the agenda in formal meetings; allow some flexibility in informal meetings.
  - Be a leader by keeping the discussion moving forward according to the agenda and encouraging all to participate.
  - Conclude the meeting by summarizing what the meeting has accomplished.

- After the meeting:
  - Follow-up on short meetings with an e-mail or short memo.
  - Follow-up on formal meetings by distributing minutes.

EXERCISES

1. Communicating Without Talking (▶3.1)

Use nonverbal language only to communicate the following messages:

    a. Surprise
    b. Anger
    c. Sorrow
    d. Puzzlement
    e. Boredom
    f. Disinterest

2. Voice Qualities (▶3.1)

Read a journal article (either in print or online) on the effective use of your voice in a business setting. Next, write a one-page typed summary of the article. Proofread your summary for content and language errors and revise as needed. Staple a photocopy of the article to your summary, and submit both to your instructor.

3. Listening on TV (▶3.2)

Your instructor will assign you a television show to watch this week—a news program, talk show, or documentary. Using the listening techniques you learned in this chapter, take notes on the important points covered in the presentation. Listen for the major themes, not the details. Write a one-page memo to your instructor summarizing the important information you heard. Should every student's paper contain basically the same information? Explain your answer.

4. Serial Communication (▶3.2)

Divide into groups of four students each: A, B, C, and D. Within each group, have A and B leave the room. Then have C read aloud the one-page report that he or she prepared for Exercise 3 at a normal reading rate and without repeating any of the data, while D takes notes. Have A rejoin the group and take notes while D reads the notes taken of C's oral report. Then have B rejoin the group and take notes while A reads the notes taken of D's oral notes. Finally, have D reread aloud his or her original report and B reread aloud his or her notes. How much of the original story was lost in the respective transmissions?

How much was added to the original story? Think of some ways the accuracy could have been improved during each transmission. Write up your results in a typed e-mail to your instructor.

5. Communicating by Telephone (▶3.3)

Role-play the situation described below. Record the conversations for later evaluation. While two students are role-playing, the others in the class should be taking notes of what went well and what might have been improved. To help simulate a telephone environment, have the two student actors sit back to back so that they cannot see each other or the other class members.

Situation: You are Chris Renshaw, administrative assistant for Ronald Krugel, the marketing manager at Kraft Enterprises. Terry Plachta, an important customer whom you've never met, calls your boss with a complaint that an item ordered two weeks ago does not work as advertised. Your boss won't be back in the office until tomorrow afternoon.

6. Evaluating Telephone Communications (▶3.3)

Telephone two organizations in your area. Your purpose is to speak to the director of human relations to learn how much time he or she spends in meetings each week and to get an evaluation of the effectiveness of these meetings. Call at least three times if you're not successful the first time. Leave a message if necessary. Keep a log of each person with whom you speak at each organization, and evaluate the effectiveness of that person's telephone communication skills. Finally, write a summary of what you learned about meetings in that organization. Submit both your log and your summary to your instructor.

7. Leaving Effective Telephone Messages (▶3.3)

Assume that on your third try (see Exercise 6) you were still unsuccessful in reaching the director of human relations by telephone. Instead you got a recording, asking you to leave a message of no more than 30 seconds. Compose the message you would leave.

8. Planning a Business Meeting (▶ 3.4)

Assume that you are a dean at your institution, which does not celebrate Martin Luther King, Jr.'s birthday with a paid holiday. You are seeking the support of the college's four other deans for making the third Monday in January a holiday for all college employees and students. Will a meeting best serve your purpose? Why or why not? What alternatives exist for resolving the issue? Assuming you decide to call a meeting, prepare a memorandum, including the agenda, to send to the other deans. Submit both your memo and your responses to the above questions to your instructor.

9. Conducting a Meeting (▶ 3.4)

Divide into groups of five, with each person assuming the role of a dean at your institution (see Exercise 8). Draw straws to determine who will be the dean calling the meeting, and use this person's agenda. Conduct a 15- to 20-minute meeting. Following the meeting, evaluate its effectiveness. Did you achieve your objective? Explain your answer.

Additional exercises are available at the Online Study Center website: **college.hmco.com/pic/oberSASfund**.

 **RESOURCES**

Prepare for Class, Improve Your Grade, and ACE the Test. Student Achievement Series resources include:

ACE Practice Tests	Ask Ober	Audio Chapter Reviews and Quizzes
Chapter Outlines	Communication Objectives	Crossword Puzzles
Flashcards	Glossaries	Handouts
LAB Tests	Portfolio Project Stationery	Sample Reports

To access these learning and study tools, go to **college.hmco.com/pic/oberSASfund**.

The ability to display and present information online is exciting and invigorating but also requires the same core writing principles as printed material: clear organization, concise sentences, and correct grammar.

4 *Revise for content, style, and correctness.*

3 *Compose a first draft of your message.*

2 *Plan the purpose, content, and organization of your message.*

1 *Analyze the audience for your communication.*

Chapter Outline

Online Study Center
Prepare for Class
Chapter Outline

6 ► *Proofread your document.*

5 ► *Format your document.*

Perspectives on Writing

Editing for a global audience that moves on with each mouse click, Noel McCarthy knows that all the articles he posts must be clear, concise, and compelling. McCarthy is editor-in-chief of *Executive Perspectives,* the monthly online business magazine of the international accounting and consulting firm Pricewaterhouse-Coopers (PwC).

Every month, McCarthy and his editors read 150 business and economics publications to select six articles for the "Digest"

NOEL MCCARTHY
Editor-in-Chief,
Pricewaterhouse-
Coopers,
Executive Perspectives
(New York, New York)

KEY TERMS

audience analysis   *p. 71*
brainstorming   *p. 75*
drafting   *p. 76*
editing   *p. 79*
free writing   *p. 77*
organization   *p. 75*
revising   *p. 78*
writer's block   *p. 76*

section of the magazine. Then, he says, "[W]e whittle them down to their core arguments and add introductory paragraphs. Brevity and clarity are top priorities."

For the monthly "Re: Business" section of *Executive Perspectives,* McCarthy polishes four original articles submitted by PwC partners, managers, and directors. "We edit for grammar and style, yet we work hard to preserve the writer's individual voice," notes the editor-in-chief.

No matter how many times he reads an article on the screen, McCarthy finds he misses something if he doesn't proofread on the printed page. Then a professional proofreader reads every article and flags any errors for correction before the editors finalize that month's issue. ■

When faced with a writing task, some people just start writing. They try to do everything at once, figuring out what to say and how to say it, visualizing an audience and a goal, keeping watch on spelling and grammar, and choosing their words and building sentences—all at the same time. It's not easy to keep switching back and forth from one of these distinct writing tasks to another and still make headway. In fact, unless you're an expert writer, it's harder and slower than breaking the job into steps and completing each step in turn.

The idea of writing step by step may sound at first as if it will prolong the job, but it won't. The step of planning, for example, gives you a sense of where you want to go, which in turn makes getting there faster and easier. The clearer you are about your goals, the more likely your writing will accomplish those goals. And if you save a separate step for proofreading, that job will also go more smoothly and efficiently. After all, it's difficult to spot a typo while you're still trying to think up a big ending for your report.

There is no single "best" writing process. In fact, all good writers develop their own process that suits their own ways of tackling a problem. But one way or another, competent communicators typically perform the following steps when faced with a business situation that calls for a written response (see Figure 4.1).

The amount of time you devote to each step depends on the complexity, length, and importance of the document. Not all steps may be needed for all writing tasks. For example, you may go through all the steps if you are writing a business plan to get funding for a small business but not if you are answering an e-mail message inviting you to a meeting. Nevertheless, these steps are a good starting point for completing a writing assignment—either in class or on the job.

AUDIENCE ANALYSIS

> **1** *Analyze the audience for your communication.*

The audience for a message—the reader or readers—is typically homogeneous. Most of the time, of course, the audience comprises just one person, but even when it does not, the audience usually consists of people with similar levels of expertise, background knowledge, and the like. Thus, you can, and should, develop your message to take into account the needs of your reader. The success or failure of a message often depends on little things—the extra touches that say to the reader, "You're important, and I've taken the time to learn some things about you."

What can you learn about the personal interests or demographic characteristics of your audience that you can build into your message? Is the reader a take-charge kind of person who would prefer to have important information up front—regardless of whether the news is good or bad? What level of formality is expected? Would the reader be flattered or put off by the use of his or her first name in the salutation? Have good things or bad things happened recently at work or at home that may affect the reader's receptivity to your message?

To maximize the effectiveness of your message, you should perform an **audience analysis**; that is, you should identify the interests, needs, and personality of your receiver. Recall our discussion of mental filters in Chapter 1. Each person perceives a message differently because of his or her unique mental filter. Thus, we need to determine the level of detail, the language to be used, and the overall tone by answering the pertinent questions about audience discussed in the following sections (see Figure 4.2).

audience analysis   Identifying the interests, needs, and personality of the receiver.

Who Is the Primary Audience?

For most correspondence, the audience is one person, which simplifies the writing task immensely. It is much easier to personalize a message addressed to one individual than a message addressed to many individuals. Sometimes, however, you will have more than one audience. In this case, you need to identify your *primary* audience (the person whose cooperation is crucial if your message is to achieve its objectives) and then your *secondary* audience (others who will also read and be affected by your message). If you can satisfy no one else, try to satisfy the needs of the primary decision maker. If possible, also satisfy the needs of any secondary audience.

For example, if you are presenting a proposal that must be approved by the general manager but that will also require the cooperation of your colleagues in other departments, the general manager is the primary audience and your colleagues are the secondary audience. Gear your message—its content, organization, and tone—mainly to the needs of the general manager. Most often (but not always), the primary audience will be the highest-level person to whom you're addressing your communication.

What Does the Audience Already Know?

Understanding the audience's present grasp of the topic is crucial to making decisions about content and writing style. You must decide how much background information is necessary, whether the use of jargon is acceptable, and what readability level is appropriate. If you are writing to multiple audiences, gear the amount of detail to the level of understanding of the key decision maker (the primary audience). In general, it is better to provide too much rather than too little information.

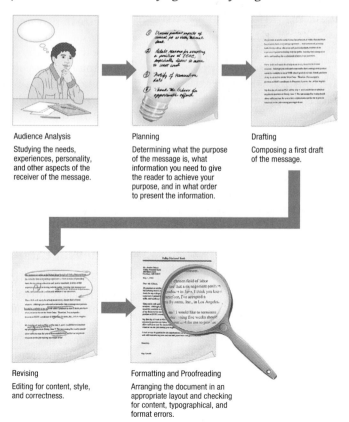

FIGURE 4.1

The Steps of the Writing Process
By following this process, the writer saves time by focusing on one particular task rather than trying to do everything at once.

Audience Analysis
Studying the needs, experiences, personality, and other aspects of the receiver of the message.

Planning
Determining what the purpose of the message is, what information you need to give the reader to achieve your purpose, and in what order to present the information.

Drafting
Composing a first draft of the message.

Revising
Editing for content, style, and correctness.

Formatting and Proofreading
Arranging the document in an appropriate layout and checking for content, typographical, and format errors.

Questions for Audience Analysis

Before you begin to write, consider the reader or readers to whom you are writing.

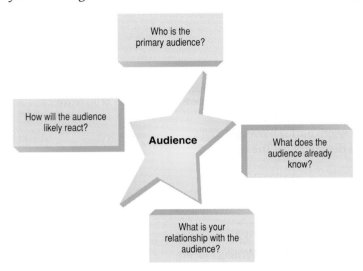

What Is Your Relationship With the Audience?

Does your audience know you? If not, you will first have to establish your credibility by assuming a reasonable tone and giving enough evidence to support your claims. Are you writing to someone inside or outside the organization? If outside, your message will often be a little more formal and will contain more background information and less jargon than if you are writing to someone inside the organization.

Communications to your superiors are obviously vital to your success in the organization. Such communications are typically a little more formal, less authoritarian in tone, and more information-filled than communications to peers or subordinates. In addition, such messages are typically "front-loaded"—that is, they use a direct organizational style and present the major idea in the first paragraph. Study your superior's own messages to get a sense of his or her preferred style and diction, and adapt your own message accordingly.

When you communicate with subordinates, be polite but not patronizing. Try to instill a sense of collaboration and of corporate ownership of your proposal. When praising or criticizing, be specific; and criticize the action—not the person. As always, praise in public but criticize in private.

What is your credibility with the reader? The more trustworthy you are, the more trustworthy your message will appear. Credibility comes from many sources. You may be perceived as being credible by virtue of the position you hold or by virtue of being a well-known authority. Or you may achieve credibility for your proposal by supplying convincing evidence, such as facts and statistics that can be verified.

Suppose, for example, you have worked in an advertising production department and have extensive experience with color reproduction. If you are writing a memo to a colleague suggesting that certain photos do not reproduce clearly and should therefore be replaced, you probably don't need to explain your expertise. Your colleague is likely to believe you. On the other hand, if you are writing a letter to the photographer, who does not know you, you would probably want to discuss past incidents that lead you to conclude that the photos should be replaced.

How Will the Audience Likely React?

If the reader's initial reaction to both you and your topic is likely to be *positive,* your job is relatively easy. You can use a direct approach—beginning with the most important information and then supplying the needed details. If the reader's initial reaction is likely to be *neutral,* you may want to use the first few lines of the message to get the reader's attention and convince him or her that what you have to say is important and that your reasoning is sound. Make sure your message is short and easy to read and that any requested action is easy to take.

Suppose, however, that you expect your reader's reaction—either to your topic or to you personally—to be *negative.* Here you have a real sales job to do.

CONCEPT CHECK 4.1

What is meant by a "front-loaded" message?

CONCEPT CHECK 4.2

What are two sources of writer credibility?

Your best strategy is to call on external evidence and expert opinion to bolster your position. Show that others, people whom the reader is likely to know and respect, share your opinions. Instead of one example, give two or three. Instead of quoting one external source, quote several.

Begin with the areas of agreement, stress reader benefits, and try to anticipate and answer any objections the reader might have. Use courteous, conservative language, and suggest ways the reader can cooperate without appearing to "give in"—perhaps by reminding the reader that new circumstances and new information call for new strategies. Through logic, evidence, and tone, build your case for the reasonableness of your position.

The reader wants to know "What's in it for me?" *You* are already convinced of the wisdom of your proposal. Your job is to let the reader know the benefits of doing as you ask. Put yourself in the reader's place. Discuss how the reader will benefit from your proposal. Emphasize the *reader* rather than the product or idea you're promoting.

> **NOT:** The San Diego Accounting Society would like you to speak to us on the topic of expensing versus capitalizing 401-C assets.

> **BUT:** Speaking to the San Diego Accounting Society would enable you to present your firm's views on the controversial topic of expensing versus capitalizing 401-C assets.

The type and amount of information you include in your message and the organization of that information reflect what you know (or can learn) about your audience. Competent communicators analyze their audience and then use this information to structure the content, organization, and tone of their messages.

Online Study Center
Improve Your Grade
Audio Chapter Review 4.1

TEST PREPPER 4.1

ANSWERS CAN BE FOUND ON P. 410

True or False?

_____ 1. Everyone should follow the same specific process when creating a written message.

_____ 2. A message to your superior is typically more formal than one to your peers or subordinates.

_____ 3. The secondary audience comprises your peers and subordinates.

_____ 4. If you're writing to a diverse audience, you should gear your message to the needs of the primary audience.

Vocabulary

Define the following term in your own words.

5. Audience analysis

Online Study Center
ACE the Test
ACE Practice Tests 4.1

Online Study Center
Improve Your Grade
Audio Chapter Quiz 4.1
PowerPoint Review 4.1

PLANNING

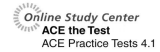 **2** *Plan the purpose, content, and organization of your message.*

Having identified your audience, the next step is to make conscious decisions about the purpose, content, and organization of the message.

Purpose

The first decision relates to the purpose of the message. If you don't know why you're writing the message (that is, if you don't know what you hope to accomplish), then later you'll have no way of knowing whether you've achieved your goal. In the end, what matters is not how well crafted your message was or how attractive it looked on the page; what matters is whether you achieved your communication objective. If you did, your communication was successful; if you did not, the communication was not successful.

Most writers find it easier to start with a general purpose and then refine the general purpose into a specific one. The specific purpose should indicate the response desired from the reader.

Assume, for example, that you are a marketing manager at Seaside Resorts, a chain of small hotels along the California, Oregon, and Washington coasts. You have noted that many of the larger hotel chains have instituted "frequent-stay" plans, which reward repeat customers with free lodging, travel, or merchandise. You want to write a message recommending a similar plan for your small hotel. Your general purpose might be this:

> *General Purpose:* To describe the benefits of a frequent-stay plan at Seaside Resorts.

Such a goal is a good starting point, but it is not specific enough. To begin with, it doesn't identify the intended audience. Are you writing a memo to the vice president of marketing recommending this plan, or are you writing a letter to frequent business travelers recommending that they enroll in this plan? Assume, for the moment, that you're writing to the marketing vice president. What is she supposed to *do* as a result of reading your memo? Do you want her simply to understand what you've written? Agree with you? Commit resources for further research? Agree to implement the plan immediately? How will you know if your message achieves its objective? Perhaps you decide that your specific purpose is the following:

> *Specific Purpose:* To persuade Cynthia to approve the development and implementation of a frequent-stay plan for a 12-month test period in Seaside's three Oregon resorts.

Now you have a purpose that's specific enough to guide you as you write the memo and to permit you to judge, in time, whether your message achieved its goal.

In another situation, your general purpose might be to resolve a problem regarding a shipment of damaged merchandise, and your specific purpose might be to persuade the manufacturer to replace the damaged shipment at no cost to you within 10 days. Or your general purpose might be to refuse a customer's claim, and your specific purpose might be to convince the customer that your refusal is reasonable and to maintain the customer's goodwill. Having a clear-cut statement of purpose lets you focus on the content and organization, eliminating any distracting information and incorporating all relevant information.

Content

Once you have identified the needs and interests of your audience and determined the purpose of your message, the next step is to decide what information to include. For simple messages, such as routine e-mail, this step presents few problems. However, many communication tasks require numerous decisions about what to include. How much background information is needed? What statistical data best supports the conclusions? Is expert opinion needed? Would examples, anecdotes, or graphics aid comprehension? Will research be necessary, or do you have what you need at hand?

The trick is to include enough information so that you don't lose or confuse the reader, yet avoid including irrelevant material that wastes the reader's time and obscures the important data. Different writers use different methods for identifying what information is needed. Some simply jot down notes on the points they plan to cover. For all but the simplest communications, the one thing you should *not* do is to start drafting immediately, deciding as you write what information to include. Instead, start with at least a rudimentary outline of your message—whether it's in your head, in a well-developed typed outline, or in the form of notes on a piece of scratch paper.

One useful strategy is **brainstorming**—jotting down ideas, facts, possible leads, and anything else you think might be helpful in constructing your message. Aim for quantity, not quality. Don't evaluate your output until you've run out of ideas. Then begin to refine, delete, combine, and otherwise revise your ideas to form the basis for your message.

Organization

The final step in the planning process is to establish the **organization** of the message—that is, to determine in what order to discuss each topic. After you have brainstormed or mapped out your ideas around a main idea, you need to organize them into an outline that you can use to draft your message into its most effective form.

Classification (grouping related ideas) is the first step in organizing your message. Once you've grouped related ideas, you then need to differentiate between the major and minor points so that you can line up minor ideas and evidence to support the major ideas.

The most effective sequence for the major ideas often depends on the reaction you expect from your audience. If you expect a positive response, you may want to use a direct approach, in which the conclusion or major idea is presented first, followed by the reasons. If you expect a negative response, you may decide to use an indirect approach, in which the reasons are presented first and the conclusion follows.

Because of the importance of the sequence in which topics are discussed, the recommended organization of each specific type of communication is discussed in detail in the chapters that follow.

brainstorming   Writing down ideas to help in solving a problem.

organization   The sequence in which each topic is discussed.

CONCEPT CHECK 4.4

Assume that you have jotted down the following points you want to include in your letter to FedEx. Number the points in the order that you think will help you achieve your purpose.

____ Provide needed details about the problem
____ Tell what remedy you want
____ Identify the problem
____ Close on a positive note
____ Describe the inconvenience that you experienced

Online Study Center
Improve Your Grade
Audio Chapter Review 4.2

TEST PREPPER 4.2

ANSWERS CAN BE FOUND ON P. 410

True or False?

____ 1. You should compose a general objective before composing a specific objective for your message.
____ 2. Even the simplest message requires considering what information to include before beginning to write the message.
____ 3. Brainstorming involves generating ideas and evaluating their worth.

Vocabulary

Define the following terms in your own words.
4. Brainstorming
5. Organization

Online Study Center
ACE the Test
ACE Practice Tests 4.2

Online Study Center
Improve Your Grade
Audio Chapter Quiz 4.2
PowerPoint Review 4.2

Online Study Center   college.hmco.com/pic/oberSASfund

DRAFTING

> **3** ▸ *Compose a first draft of your message.*

drafting   Composing a preliminary version of a message.

Having now finished planning, you are finally ready to begin **drafting**—that is, composing a preliminary version of a message.

Probably the most important thing to remember about drafting is to just let go—let your ideas flow as quickly as possible onto paper or the computer screen, without worrying about style, correctness, or format. Separate the drafting stage from the revising stage. Although some people revise as they create, most find it easier to first get their ideas down on paper in rough-draft form and then revise. It's much easier to polish a page full of writing than a page full of *nothing*.

So avoid moving from author to editor too quickly. Your first draft is just that—a *draft*. Don't expect perfection, and don't strive for it. Concentrate instead on recording in narrative form all the points you identified in the planning stage. When you have finished and then begin to revise, you will likely discover that a surprising amount of your first draft is usable and will be included in your final draft.

If a report is due in five weeks, some managers (and students) spend four weeks worrying about the task and one week (or even one long weekend) actually writing the report. Similarly, when given 45 minutes to write a letter or memo, some people spend 35 minutes anxiously staring at a blank page or blank screen and 10 minutes actually writing. These people are experiencing **writer's block**—the inability to focus on the writing process and to draft a message. The causes of writer's block are typically one or more of the following:

writer's block   The inability to focus on the writing process and draft a message.

▊ *Procrastination:* Putting off what we dislike doing.

▊ *Impatience:* Growing tired of the naturally slow pace of the writing process.

▊ *Perfectionism:* Believing that our draft must be perfect the first time.

CONCEPT CHECK 4.5

What are three causes of writer's block?

These factors naturally interfere with creativity and concentration. In addition, they undermine the writer's self-image and make him or her even more reluctant to tackle the next writing task. The treatment for writer's block lies in the strategies discussed in the following paragraphs.

For Portland, Oregon, ad agency Wieden+Kennedy, promoting a creative environment in which to create advertising copy is a necessity. They even provide a rooftop hammock to help copy writers generate ideas and even draft their copy.

1. Choose the right environment. The ability to concentrate on the task at hand is one of the most important components of effective writing. The best environment may *not* be the same desk where you normally do your other work. Even if you can turn off the phones and shut the door to visitors, silent distractions can bother you—a notation on your calendar reminding you of an important upcoming event, notes about a current project, even a photograph of a loved one. Many people write best in a library-type environment, with a low noise level, relative anonymity, and the space to spread out notes and other resources on a large table. Others find a computer room conducive to thinking and writing, with its low level of constant background noise and the presence of other people similarly engaged.

2. Schedule a reasonable block of time. If the writing task is short, you can block out enough time to plan, draft, and revise the entire message at one sitting. If the task is long or complex, however, schedule blocks of no more than two hours or so. After all, writing is hard work. When your time is up or your work completed, give yourself a reward—take a break or get a snack.

"I wish you would make up your mind, Mr. Dickens. Was it the best of times or was it the worst of times? It could scarcely have been both."

3. State your purpose in writing. Having identified your specific purpose during the planning phase, write it at the top of your blank page or tack it on the bulletin board in front of you. Keep it visible so that it will be uppermost in your consciousness as you compose.

4. Engage in free writing. Review your purpose and your audience. Then, as a means of releasing your pent-up ideas and getting past the block, begin **free writing**; that is, write continuously for five to ten minutes, literally without stopping. Although free writing is typically considered a predrafting technique, it can also be quite useful for helping writers "unblock" their ideas.

   While free writing, don't look back and don't stop writing. If you cannot think of anything to say, simply keep repeating the last word or keep writing some sentence such as, "I'll think of something soon." Resist the temptation to evaluate what you've written. At the end of five or ten minutes, take a breather, stretch and relax, read what you've written, and then start again, if necessary.

free writing Writing continuously for a short period of time without stopping.

5. Avoid the perfectionism syndrome. Remember that the product you're producing now is a *draft*—not a final document. Don't worry about style, coherence, spelling or punctuation errors, and the like. The artist in you must create something before the editor can refine it.

6. Think out loud. Some people are more skilled at *speaking* their thoughts than at writing them. Picture yourself telling a colleague what you're writing about, and explain aloud the ideas you're trying to get across. Hearing your ideas will help sharpen and focus them.

7. Write the easiest parts first. The opening paragraph of a letter or memo is often the most difficult one to compose. If that is the case, skip it and begin in the middle. In a report, the procedures section may be easier to write than

CONCEPT CHECK 4.6

What are seven strategies for avoiding writer's block?

the recommendations. Getting *something* down on paper will give you a sense of accomplishment, and your writing may generate ideas for other sections.

Try each of these strategies for avoiding writer's block at least once; then build into your writing routine those strategies that work best for you. Just as different athletes and artists use different strategies for accomplishing their goals, so do different writers. There is no one best way, so choose what is effective for you.

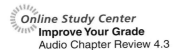
Online Study Center
Improve Your Grade
Audio Chapter Review 4.3

TEST PREPPER 4.3   ANSWERS CAN BE FOUND ON P. 410

True or False?

_____ 1. Composing a finished version of a message is known as drafting.

_____ 2. You should draft the parts of your message in the order in which they will appear in the final document.

_____ 3. You should use all of the strategies for avoiding writer's block each time you draft a complex message.

Vocabulary

Define the following terms in your own words.

4. Drafting
5. Free writing
6. Writer's block

Online Study Center
ACE the Test
ACE Practice Tests 4.3

Online Study Center
Improve Your Grade
Audio Chapter Quiz 4.3
PowerPoint Review 4.3

REVISING

 4 ▶ *Revise for content, style, and correctness.*

revising   Modifying a document to increase its effectiveness.

Revising is the process of modifying a document to increase its effectiveness. Having the raw material—your first draft—in front of you, you can now refine it into the most effective document possible, considering its importance and the time constraints under which you are working. If possible, put your draft away for a period of time—the longer the better. Leaving time between creation and revision helps you distance yourself from your writing. If you revise immediately, the memory of what you "meant to say" rather than what you actually wrote may be so strong that it keeps you from spotting weaknesses in logic or diction.

If you're a typical writer, you will have made numerous minor revisions even as you were composing; as noted earlier, however, you should save the major revisions until later. For important writing projects, you will probably want to solicit comments about your draft from colleagues as part of the revision process.

Although we have discussed revising as the fourth step of the writing process, in fact it involves several steps. Most writers revise first for content, then for style, and finally for correctness. All types of revision are most efficiently done from a typed copy of the draft rather than from a handwritten copy.

Revising for Content

After an appropriate time interval, first reread your purpose statement and then the entire draft to get an overview of your message. Ask yourself questions such as the following:

- Is the content appropriate for the purpose I've identified?
- Will the purpose of the message be clear to the reader?
- Have I been sensitive to the needs of the reader?
- Is all the information necessary?
- Is any needed information missing?
- Is the order of presentation of the points effective?

Although it is natural to have a certain pride of authorship in your draft document, don't be afraid to make whatever changes you think will strengthen your document—even if it means striking out whole sections and starting again from scratch. The aim is to produce a revised document in which you can have even more pride.

Revising for Style

Next, read each paragraph again. Reading aloud gives you a feel for the rhythm and flow of your writing. Long sentences that made sense as you wrote them may leave you out of breath when you read them aloud.

If time permits and the importance of the document merits it, try reading your message aloud to friends or colleagues, or have them read your revised draft. Ask them what is clear or unclear. Can they identify the purpose of your message? What kind of image do they get of the writer just from reading the message?

Revising for Correctness

The final phase of revising is **editing**, the process of ensuring that writing conforms to standard English.

Editing involves checking for correctness—that is, identifying problems with grammar, spelling, punctuation, and word usage. You may want to use your word processor's grammar checker as a starting point for editing. Editing should follow revision because there is no need to correct errors in passages that may later be revised or deleted. Writers who fail to check for grammar, mechanical, and usage errors risk losing credibility with their reader. Such errors may distract the reader, delay comprehension, cause misunderstandings, and reflect negatively on the writer's abilities. All three types of revision—for content, style, and correctness—can be accomplished most efficiently on a computer.

> **CONCEPT CHECK 4.7**
>
> What are the three steps of revision?

editing Making the writing conform to standard English.

Online Study Center
Improve Your Grade
Audio Chapter Review 4.4

TEST PREPPER 4.4   ANSWERS CAN BE FOUND ON P. 411

True or False?

_____ 1. Immediately after drafting a document, you should revise it to make it more effective.

_____ 2. Most writers make minor revisions even as they are drafting a document.

_____ 3. Revision is accomplished most efficiently on a computer.

Vocabulary

Define the following terms in your own words.

4. Editing
5. Revising

Critical Thinking

6. Most word processing programs provide a grammar and spelling checker that flags many types of grammatical and mechanical errors. To what extent do you believe you can trust such tools? Why?

Online Study Center
ACE the Test
ACE Practice Tests 4.4

Online Study Center
Improve Your Grade
Audio Chapter Quiz 4.4
PowerPoint Review 4.4

Online Study Center college.hmco.com/pic/oberSASfund

FORMATTING

 5 ▶ *Format your document.*

Letters are external documents sent to people outside the organization; *memos* are internal documents sent to people inside the same organization as the writer. Today, most traditional memos have been replaced by e-mail; and, in fact, many letters are now sent as e-mail attachments rather than through the mail. E-mail and reports may be either internal or external. No one format for any type of business document is universally accepted as standard; a fair amount of variation is common in industry. Detailed guidelines for the most common formatting standards are presented in the Style Manual at the back of this text.

To some extent, technology is changing formatting standards. For example, although formatting is traditionally the next-to-last step in the writing process, you may in fact make some formatting decisions at the planning or drafting stages. For example, your word processing program has probably been set with default side margins of 1 to 1¼ inches, which are appropriate for most documents.

In addition, e-mail messages all look like memorandums—whether they are sent to someone inside or outside the organization. They typically contain *To:*, *From:*, *Date:*, and *Subject:* lines just as memos do, and they do not contain an inside address, as is typical in letters. The important point is to use the format that is appropriate for each specific message.

Regardless of who actually types your documents, *you* are the one who signs and submits them, so *you* must accept responsibility for not only the content but also the mechanics, format, and appearance of your documents. In addition, the increasing use of word processing means that executives now keyboard many of their own documents—without the help of an assistant.

Another advantage of standard formatting is simply that it is more efficient. Formatting documents the same way each time means that you do not need to make individual layout decisions for every document. Thus, a standard format not only saves time but also gives a consistent appearance to the organization's documents.

Finally, readers *expect* to find certain information in certain positions in a document. If the information is not there, the reader is unnecessarily distracted. For all these reasons, you should become familiar with the standard conventions for formatting documents.

CONCEPT CHECK 4.8

What are three advantages of using a standard format?

PROOFREADING

6 ▶ *Proofread your document.*

Proofreading is the final quality control check for your document. Remember that a reader may not know whether an incorrect word resulted from a simple typo or from the writer's ignorance of correct usage. And even one such error can have adverse effects (see Figure 4.3).

Being *almost* perfect is not good enough; for example, if your telephone directory were only 99 percent perfect, each page would contain about four wrong numbers! And imagine the embarrassment of the tax preparer who submitted supporting statements for a client's tax return that contained this direction: "Please reference *Lie 12* on Schedule C." Or how about the newspaper ad that Continental

Airlines ran in the *Boston Herald,* in which the company advertised one-way fares from Boston to Los Angeles for $48? The actual one-way fare was *$148*. That typographical error cost Continental $4 million, because it sold 20,000 round-trip tickets at a loss of $200 each.[1]

Take responsibility for ensuring the accuracy of your communications, just as you take responsibility for your other managerial tasks. Proofread for content, typographical, and format errors.

■ *Content Errors:* First, read through your document quickly, checking for content errors. Was any material omitted unintentionally? Unfortunately, writers who use word processing to move, delete, and insert material sometimes omit passages unintentionally or duplicate the same passage in two different places in the document. In short, check to be sure that your document *makes sense.*

■ *Typographical Errors:* Next, read through your document slowly, checking for typographical errors. Watch especially for errors that form a new word—for example, "I took the figures *form* last month's reports." Such errors are difficult to spot. Also be on the lookout for repeated or omitted words. Double-check all proper names and all figures, using the original source if possible. Professional proof-readers find that writers often overlook errors in the titles and headings of reports, in the opening and closing parts of letters and memos, and in the last paragraph of all types of documents.

■ *Format Errors:* Visually inspect the document for appropriate format. Are all the parts included and in the correct position? What will be the receiver's first impression before reading the document? Does the document look attractive on the page? Do not consider the proofreading stage complete until you are able to read through the entire document without making any changes. There is always the possibility that in correcting one error you inadvertently introduced another.

Finally, after planning, drafting, revising, formatting, and proofreading your document, transmit it—confident and satisfied that you've taken all reasonable steps to ensure that it achieves its objectives. The steps in the writing process are summarized in Checklist 3 on page 82.

FIGURE 4.3

The Need for Competent Proofreading Skills

If 99.9% accuracy is acceptable to you, then

Every hour:
- 18,300 pieces of mail will be mishandled.
- 22,000 checks will be credited to the wrong bank accounts.
- 72,000 phone calls will be misplaced by telecommunication services.

Every day:
- 12 newborn babies will be given to the wrong parents.
- 107 incorrect medical procedures will be performed.

Every year:
- 2.5 million books will be shipped with the wrong cover.
- 20,000 incorrect drug prescriptions will be written.

Not to mention that:
- 315 entries in *Webster's Third New International Dictionary of the English Language* will be misspelled.

CONCEPT CHECK 4.9

What three types of errors should you look for when proofreading?

Online Study Center
Improve Your Grade
Audio Chapter Review 4.5, 4.6
Handouts

TEST PREPPER 4.5, 4.6   ANSWERS CAN BE FOUND ON P. 411

True or False?

_____ 1. Most traditional memos have been replaced by e-mail.

_____ 2. Technology is changing formatting standards.

_____ 3. The proofreading stage should not be considered finished until you can read through the entire document without making any changes.

Critical Thinking

4. Some companies have developed their own unique formatting standards for their written communications. Why do you think they chose to develop their own formats rather than using commonly accepted formatting standards?

Online Study Center
ACE the Test
ACE Practice Tests 4.5, 4.6

Online Study Center
Improve Your Grade
Audio Chapter Quiz 4.5, 4.6
PowerPoint Review 4.5, 4.6

Online Study Center   college.hmco.com/pic/oberSASfund

CHECKLIST 3

The Writing Process

Audience Analysis

✓ Who is the primary audience?

✓ What does the audience already know?

✓ What is your relationship with the audience?

✓ How will the audience likely react?

Planning

✓ Determine the purpose of the message.

    a. Make it as specific as possible.

    b. Identify the type of response desired from the reader.

✓ Determine what information to include in the message, given its purpose and your analysis of the audience.

✓ Organize the information.

    a. Prefer a direct approach for routine and good-news messages and for most messages to superiors: present the major idea first, followed by supporting details.

    b. Prefer an indirect approach for persuasive and bad-news messages written to someone other than your superior: present the reasons first, followed by the major idea.

Drafting

✓ Choose a productive work environment and schedule a reasonable block of time to devote to the drafting phase.

✓ Let your ideas flow as quickly as possible, without worrying about style, correctness, or format.

✓ Do not expect a perfect first draft; avoid the urge to revise at this stage.

✓ If possible, leave a time gap between writing and revising the draft.

Revising

✓ Revise for content: determine whether all information is necessary, whether any needed information has been omitted, and whether the content has been presented in an appropriate sequence.

✓ Revise for style.

✓ Revise for correctness: use correct grammar, mechanics, punctuation, and word choice.

Formatting and Proofreading

✓ Format the document according to commonly used standards (see the Style Manual at the end of this text).

✓ Proofread for content errors, typographical errors, and format errors.

THREE PS
PROBLEM, PROCESS, PRODUCT

A Simple Memo

Problem

Today is December 3, 20—, and you are Alice R. Stengren, president of the Entrepreneurial Association of Baker College. EABC is the newest of the six student organizations in the school of business and has 38 members. It was formed two years ago when the department of management instituted a major in entrepreneurship.

The association recently voted to institute an annual $1,000 EABC scholarship. The scholarship will be awarded on the basis of merit to a junior or senior business student majoring in entrepreneurship at Baker College. Funds for the scholarship will be raised by selling coffee and doughnuts each day from 7:30 to 10:30 a.m. in the main lobby of the building. Write a memo to Dean Richard Wilhite, asking permission to start this fund-raising project in January.

Process

1. What is the purpose of your memo?

   To convince the dean to let EABC sell coffee and doughnuts in the main lobby from 7:30 to 10:30 a.m. daily, beginning in January.

2. Describe your primary audience

   Dean Richard Wilhite:
   - Former president of Wilhite Energy Systems (started the company—an entrepreneur himself)
   - 46 years old; has been business dean at Baker for six years (very familiar with the school and college)
   - Nationally known labor expert
   - Holds tenure in the department of management (which offers an entrepreneurship major)
   - Has spoken about the need to increase scholarships
   - Devotes a great deal of time to lobbying the legislature and raising funds (recognizes the need for fund-raising)
   - Doesn't know me personally but is familiar with EABC

3. Is there a secondary audience for your memo? If so, describe.

   No secondary audience.

4. Considering your purpose, what information should you include in the memo?

   Either brainstorm and jot down the topics you might cover, or construct a mind map.

5. Jot down the major topics in the order in which you'll discuss them.

   a. Dean's interest in increasing scholarships
   b. Introduce scholarship and our fund-raising proposal
   c. Practical work experience that members will get

THREE Ps (CONTINUED)

> d. Possible drawbacks (where to store supplies; special treatment for EABC)
> e. Other needed details
> f. Closing—convenient for faculty, staff, students

6. Using the rough outline developed in Step 5, write your first draft. Concentrate on getting the needed information down. Do not worry about grammar, spelling, punctuation, transitions, unity, and the like at this stage.

7. Print your draft and revise it for content, style, and correctness. (As needed, refer to the Modules in Language Arts Basics at the back of the book for guidance on grammar, mechanics, punctuation, and usage and to Checklist 3 on page 82 for style pointers.)

8. How will you transmit this message; that is, what format will you use?

> I could, of course, send the dean an e-mail message. Given the importance of this request, however, I'll format it as a memo on the college letterhead. That way, the request will look more professional, and the dean will have a printed copy for review.

9. Format your revised draft, using a standard memo style. Then proofread.

Product

Baker College
Since 1911

Baker College
1020 South Washington
Owosso, Michigan 48867-4400
Telephone (989) 729-3300
Fax (989) 729-3411

MEMO TO: Dean Richard Wilhite

FROM: Alice R. Stengren, President *ARS*
Entrepreneurial Association of Baker College

DATE: December 3, 20—

SUBJECT: Establishment of EABC Scholarship

The Entrepreneurial Association of Baker College (EABC) shares your interest in increasing the number of scholarships available to business majors. Toward that end, we recently voted to establish an annual $1,000 scholarship for a junior or senior student majoring in entrepreneurship. To fund this scholarship, we propose selling doughnuts and coffee in the main lobby from 7:30 to 10:30 a.m. daily. All profits will be earmarked for the scholarship fund.

A secondary benefit of this project is that it will provide practical work experience for our club members. We will purchase our own supplies and equipment and keep careful records. When not in use, the supplies and equipment will be stored in the office of Professor Grant Edwards, our sponsor. The Data Processing Management Association follows similar procedures with its fund-raising project of selling computer disks in the main lobby.

We look forward to receiving your approval of this fund-raising project in time for us to begin in January. In addition to raising new scholarship money and providing work experience for our members, we will also be providing a convenient service for faculty, staff, and students.

Baker College / Auburn Hills • Cadillac • Cass City • Flint • Fremont • Jackson • Mount Clemens • Muskegon • Owosso • Port Huron
Regionally Accredited by North Central Association of Colleges and Schools Commission on Institutions of Higher Education / Member, Association of Independent Colleges and Universities of Michigan

Online Study Center
Improve Your Grade
Crossword Puzzles
Flashcards
LAB Tests

LEARNING OBJECTIVE REVIEW

 Analyze the audience for your communication.

- To provide your reader with a message that is readable and useful, determine the reader's interests, needs, and personality.
- Determine the primary audience as the reader who must approve your request or whose cooperation you will need on the project.
- Identify what the reader already knows so you can present the information the reader will need to understand and act on your message.
- Determine the status of your reader and your relationship to the reader in order to determine the appropriate tone of your message.
- Consider audience reaction:
  - A positive or neutral reaction allows a direct communication style.
  - A negative reaction will require a persuasive approach.
- Focus on how your request or idea will benefit the reader.

2 *Plan the purpose, content, and organization of your message.*

- Identify a specific purpose for your message to focus the content.
- Develop content that is relevant to your audience by brainstorming.
- Organize your message by grouping related ideas.
- Organize your ideas in a sequence that depends on the reaction you expect from your audience.

3 *Compose a first draft of your message.*

- Overcome writer's block by:
  - choosing the right environment to facilitate concentration
  - scheduling a reasonable block of time to get the job done
  - stating your purpose in writing
  - engaging in free writing
  - avoiding the perfectionism syndrome
  - thinking out loud
  - writing the easiest parts first

4 *Revise for content, style, and correctness.*

- Reread your draft and determine if the content meets the reader's needs and the purpose of the message.
- Check for readability.
- Edit the draft to ensure the writing conforms to standard English.

5 *Format your document.*

- Use standard formatting whenever possible to save time.

6 *Proofread your document.*

- Proofread for content, typographical, and format errors.

EXERCISES

1. Audience Analysis (4.1)

Assume that you must write an e-mail message to your current business communication professor, asking him or her to let you take your final examination one week early so that you can attend your friend's wedding.

a. Perform an audience analysis of your professor. List everything you know about this professor that might help you compose a more effective message.

b. Write two good opening sentences for this message, the first one assuming that you are an A student who has missed class only once this term and the second assuming that you are a C student who has missed class six times this term.

2. Audience Analysis Revisited (▶4.1)

Now assume the role of the professor (see Exercise 1) who must reply to the request of the student with the C grade who has missed class six times. You'll tell the student that you are not willing to schedule an early exam.

a. Perform an audience analysis of yourself (as the student). What do you know about yourself that would help the professor write an effective message?
b. Should the professor use a direct or an indirect organization? Why?
c. Write the first sentence of the professor's message.

3. Brainstorming and Organizing (▶4.2)

Assume that you are going to write a letter to your state senator about a proposed state surcharge on college tuition fees. Determine a specific purpose, and then brainstorm at least six facts, ideas, and questions you might want to raise in your letter. Next, decide which items are major points and which are minor points. Once you've selected either a direct or an indirect organization, arrange the items on your list in a logical order.

4. Brainstorming (▶4.2)

Working in groups of three or four, come up with as many uses for a brick as you can. Make a list of all the suggestions, and then share your list with the other groups in the class. How does your list compare to those of the other groups? How many new ideas did the other groups come up with that your group hadn't thought of? How big was the combined list?

5. Drafting (▶4.3)

Building on the process of brainstorming and organizing in Exercise 3, draft the letter to your legislator.

a. Write the specific purpose at the top of your blank page.
b. Write the easiest part of the letter first. With which part did you start? Why?
c. Continue to draft the remaining sections of the letter. In what order did you complete your letter? Why?
d. Did you use every fact, question, or idea on your list? Explain your choices.

6. Revising a Composition (▶4.4)

Bring in a one-page composition you have written in the past—an essay exam response, a business letter, or the like. Make sure your name is *not* on the paper. Exchange papers among several colleagues (so that you are not revising the paper of the person who is revising yours) and complete the following revision tasks.

a. Read the paper once, revising for content. Make sure that all needed information is included, all unneeded information is excluded, and the information is presented in a logical sequence.
b. Read the paper a second time, revising for style. Make sure that the words, sentences, paragraphs, and overall tone are appropriate.
c. Read the paper a third time, revising for correctness. Make sure that grammar, mechanics, punctuation, and word choice are error-free.
d. Return the paper to the writer. Using the revisions on your paper as a guide only (after all, *you* are the author), prepare a final version of the paper. Submit both the marked-up version and the final version of your paper to your instructor.

7. Revising Your Legislator Letter (▶4.4)

Now revise your letter to the legislator (see Exercise 5), taking into consideration content, style, and correctness.

8. Work-Team Communication (▶4.5)

You will work in groups of four for this assignment. Assume that a large shopping center is next to your campus and that many day students park there for free while attending classes. The shopping center management is considering closing this lot to student use, citing the need for additional space for customer parking. The four members of your group represent four student organizations that have decided to write a joint letter trying to convince Martin Uthe, the manager of the shopping center, to maintain the status quo.

Following the writing process outlined in this chapter, compose a one-page letter to the manager. Brainstorm to generate ideas for the content of the letter; have each member of the group call out possible points to include while one person writes down all the ideas. Don't evaluate any of the ideas until you have worked for ten to fifteen minutes. Then discuss each point listed and decide which ones to include and in what order.

Format your letter in block style. Address it to Mr. Martin Uthe, Executive Manager, Fairview Shopping Center, P.O. Box 1083, DeKalb, IL 60115. Type an envelope, sign and fold the letter, and insert it into the envelope before submitting it to your instructor.

9. Proofreading (▶ 4.6)

Assume that you are Michael Land and that you wrote and typed the letter shown below. Proofread the letter for content, typographical errors, and format, using the line numbers to indicate the position of each error. Indicate with a yes or no whether the error would have been identified by using a computer's spelling checker. (*Hint:* Can you find 31 content, typographical, or format errors?)

```
 1   April 31 2007

 2   Mr. Thomas Johnson, Manger

 3   JoAnn @ Friends, Inc.
 4   1323 Charleston Avenue
 5   Minneapolis, MI 55402

 6   Dear Mr. Thomas:

 7   As a writing consultant, I have often aksed aud-
 8   iences to locate all teh errors in this letter.

 9   I am allways surprized if the find all the errors.
10   The result being that we all need more practical
11   advise in how to proof read.

12   To aviod these types of error, you must ensure that
13   that you review your documents carefully. I have
14   preparred the enclosed exercises for each of you
15   to in your efforts at JoAnne & Freinds, Inc.

16   Would you be willing to try this out on you own
17   workers and let me know the results.

18   Sincerly Yours

19   Mr. Michael Land,
20   Writing Consultant
```

Additional exercises are available at the Online Study Center website: **college.hmco.com/pic/oberSASfund**.

Online Study Center RESOURCES

Prepare for Class, Improve Your Grade, and ACE the Test. Student Achievement Series resources include:

ACE Practice Tests	Ask Ober	Audio Chapter Reviews and Quizzes
Chapter Outlines	Communication Objectives	Crossword Puzzles
Flashcards	Glossaries	Handouts
LAB Tests	Portfolio Project Stationery	Sample Reports

To access these learning and study tools, go to **college.hmco.com/pic/oberSASfund**.

5 Revising Your Writing

Gary Davis is in charge of corporate communications for World Wrestling Entertainment (WWE). He emphasizes the importance of capturing the attention of the audience at wrestling events and in company communications. WWE communications must be as positive, engaging, and to the point as the moves each wrestler performs on stage.

3 Develop logical paragraphs.

2 Write effective sentences.

1 Choose the right words for your message.

> *"From a business communication standpoint, less is more."*
> —Gary Davis, Vice President of Corporate Communications,
> World Wrestling Entertainment

Chapter Outline

Online Study Center
Prepare for Class
Chapter Outline

4 ▶ *Convey an appropriate tone.*

Wrestling With Writing

No matter who manages to stay in the ring—or who lands outside, Gary Davis uses positive language to describe the situation. He is vice president of corporate communications for World Wrestling Entertainment (WWE), which arranges more than 300 professional wrestling events around the world every year.

Whether drafting a routine announcement or explaining the company's response to an unexpected problem, the WWE executive emphasizes that "the key is to write as if the glass is half full. If you do that, your message will come out positive." Another way Davis helps audiences grasp his meaning is by writing simply and concisely. "Although it is very easy to overwrite, to say too much, to be too flowery, this obscures what you're trying to say," he notes. "From a business communication standpoint, less is more."

Demonstrating the power of concrete, positive language in the service of an important ideal, Davis recently wrote a letter

on the job

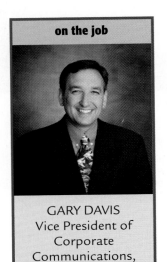

GARY DAVIS
Vice President of
Corporate
Communications,
World Wrestling
Entertainment
(Stamford,
Connecticut)

mechanics Those elements in communication that show up only in written form.

showcasing the SmackDown Your Vote! initiative. The letter quoted WWE stars talking about registering young voters. The result: hundreds of thousands of young voters are becoming involved in the election process—and the WWE is enhancing its credibility with key audiences. ■

A technically and grammatically correct message may still not achieve its objective because it may lack style. By *style*, we mean the manner in which an idea is expressed (not its *substance*). Style consists of the particular words that the writer uses and the manner in which those words are combined into sentences, paragraphs, and complete messages.

While writing the first draft of a message, you should be more concerned with content than with style. Your major objective should be to get your ideas down in *some* form, without worrying about style and mechanics. (**Mechanics** are elements in communication that show up only in written form—including spelling, punctuation, abbreviations, capitalization, number expression, and word division.) Apply the principles of style shown in Figure 5.1 as you revise drafts of the letters, memos, e-mails, and reports that are assigned in later chapters and on the job.

CHOOSING THE RIGHT WORDS

 Choose the right words for your message.

Individual words are the basic units of writing, the bricks with which we build meaningful messages. All writers have access to the same words. The care with which we select and combine words can make the difference between a message that achieves its objective and one that does not. Discussed below and in the following sections are five principles of word choice to help you write more effectively.

Write Clearly

The basic guideline for writing, and the one that must be present for the other principles to have meaning, is to write clearly—to write messages the reader can understand, depend on, and act on. You can achieve clarity by making your message accurate and complete, by using familiar words, and by avoiding dangling expressions and unnecessary jargon.

Be Accurate

A writer's credibility is perhaps his or her most important asset, and credibility depends greatly on the accuracy of the message. If by carelessness, lack of preparation, or a desire to manipulate, a writer misleads the reader, the damage is immediate and long-lasting. A reader who has been fooled once may not trust the writer again.

Accuracy can take many forms. The most basic is the truthful presentation of facts and figures. But accuracy involves much more. For example, consider the following sentence from a memo to a firm's financial backers:

> The executive committee of Mitchell Financial Services met on Thursday, May 28, to determine how to resolve the distribution fiasco.

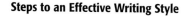

FIGURE 5.1

Steps to an Effective Writing Style

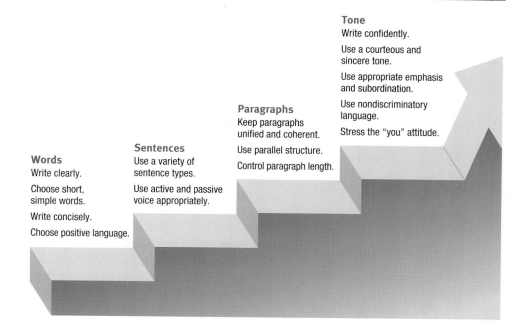

Tone
Write confidently.

Use a courteous and sincere tone.

Use appropriate emphasis and subordination.

Use nondiscriminatory language.

Stress the "you" attitude.

Paragraphs
Keep paragraphs unified and coherent.

Use parallel structure.

Control paragraph length.

Sentences
Use a variety of sentence types.

Use active and passive voice appropriately.

Words
Write clearly.

Choose short, simple words.

Write concisely.

Choose positive language.

Suppose, on checking, the reader learns that May 28 fell on a Wednesday this year—not on a Thursday. Immediately, the reader may suspect everything else in the message. The reader's thinking might be, "If the writer made this error that I *did* catch, how many errors that I *didn't* catch are lurking there?"

Now consider more subtle shades of truth. The sentence implies that the committee met, perhaps in an emergency session, for the *sole* purpose of resolving the distribution fiasco. But suppose this matter was only one of five agenda items being discussed at a regularly scheduled meeting. Is the statement still accurate? Suppose the actual agenda listed the topic as "Recent Distribution Problems." Is *fiasco* the same as *problems*?

The accuracy of a message, then, depends on what is said, how it is said, and what is left unsaid (see, for example, the next section on the importance of completeness). Competent writers assess the ethical dimensions of their writing and use integrity, fairness, and sound judgment to make sure their communication is ethical.

Be Complete

Closely related to accuracy is completeness. A message that lacks important information may create inaccurate impressions. A message is complete when it contains all the information the reader needs to react appropriately—no more and no less.

As a start, answer the five Ws: Tell the reader *who, what, when, where,* and *why.* Omitting any of this information may either result in decisions based on incomplete information or require extra follow-up correspondence to gather the needed information.

Use Familiar Words

Your message must be understood before someone can act on it. For this reason, you should use words that are familiar both to you (so that you will not misuse the word) and to your readers.

NOT: When promulgating your esoteric cogitations or articulating your superficial sentimentalities and amicable philosophical and psychological observations, beware of platitudinous ponderosity. Let your verbal evaporations have lucidity, intelligibility, and veracious vivacity without rodomontade or thespian bombast. Sedulously avoid all polysyllabic profundity, pompous propensity, and sophomoric vacuity.[1]

BUT: Don't use big words.

Long words are sometimes useful in business communication, of course, and should be used when appropriate. The larger your vocabulary and the more you know about your reader, the better equipped you will be to choose and use correctly those words that are familiar to your reader.

Avoid Dangling Expressions

dangling expression Any part of a sentence that does not logically connect to the rest of the sentence.

A **dangling expression** is any part of a sentence that doesn't logically fit in with the rest of the sentence. Its relationship with the other parts of the sentence is unclear; it *dangles*. The two most common types of dangling expressions are misplaced modifiers and unclear antecedents. To correct dangling expressions, use one of the following techniques:

❚ Make the subject of the sentence the doer of the action expressed in the introductory clause.

❚ Move the expression closer to the word that it modifies.

❚ Make sure that the specific word to which a pronoun refers (its *antecedent*) is clear.

❚ Revise the sentence for coherence.

NOT: After reading the proposal, a few problems occurred to me. *(As written, the sentence implies that "a few problems" read the proposal.)*

BUT: After reading the proposal, I noted a few problems.

NOT: Dr. López gave a presentation on the use of drugs in our auditorium. *(Are drugs being used in the auditorium?)*

BUT: Dr. López gave a presentation in our auditorium on the use of drugs.

NOT: Ming explained the proposal to Lupe, but she was not happy with it. *(Who was not happy—Ming or Lupe?)*

BUT: Ming explained the proposal to Lupe, but Lupe was not happy with it.

Use Short, Simple Words

CONCEPT CHECK 5.1

Substitute a shorter, more familiar word for each of the following words: aggregate, analogous, inexhaustible, perpetuate.

Short and simple words are more likely to be understood, less likely to be misused, and less likely to distract the reader.

NOT: To recapitulate, our utilization of adulterated water precipitated the interminable delays.

BUT: In short, our use of impure water caused the endless delays.

Dilbert: © Scott Adams/Dist. by United Feature Syndicate, Inc.

It is true, of course, that often no short, simple word is available to convey the precise shade of meaning you want. Our guideline is not to use *only* short and simple words but to *prefer* short and simple words.

Here are some examples of needlessly long words, gleaned from various business documents, with their preferred shorter substitutes shown in parentheses:

ascertain (learn)	modification (change)
endeavor (try)	recapitulate (review)
enumerate (list)	substantial (large)
fluctuate (vary)	termination (end)
indispensable (vital)	utilization (use)

You need not strike these long words totally from your vocabulary; any one of them, used in a clear sentence, is acceptable. The problem is that a writer may tend to fill his or her writing with very long words when simpler ones could be used. Use long words in moderation.

Avoid Clichés and Slang

A cliché is an expression that has become monotonous through overuse. It lacks freshness and originality and may also send the unintended message that the writer couldn't be bothered to choose language geared specifically to the reader.

NOT: Enclosed please find an application form that you should return at your earliest convenience.

BUT: Please return the enclosed application form before May 15.

Here are some examples of other expressions that have become overused and that therefore sound trite and boring. Avoid them in your writing.

According to our records	It goes without saying that
Company policy requires	Needless to say
Do not hesitate to	Our records indicate that
For your information	Please be advised that
If I can be of further help	If you have any other questions

Online Study Center college.hmco.com/pic/oberSASfund

Slang is an expression, often short-lived, that is identified with a specific group of people. If you understand each word in an expression but still don't understand what it means in context, chances are you're having trouble with a slang expression. For example, read the following sentence:

> It turns my stomach the way you can break your neck and beat your brains out around here, and they still stab you in the back.

To anyone unfamiliar with American slang (a nonnative speaker, perhaps), this sentence might seem to be about the body because it refers to the stomach, neck, brains, and back. The real meaning, of course, is something like this:

> I am really upset that this company ignores hard work and loyalty when making personnel decisions.

Avoid slang in most business writing for several reasons:

▌ Slang is informal, and much business writing, although not formal, is still *businesslike* and calls for standard word usage.

▌ Slang is short-lived. An expression used today may not be in use—and thus may not be familiar—in three years, when your letter is retrieved from the files for reference.

▌ Slang is identified with a specific group of people, and others in the general population may not understand the intended meaning.

For these reasons, avoid terms such as the following in most business writing:

can of worms	pay through the nose
chew out	play up to
go for broke	security blanket
use your noodle	knock it off
wiped out	once-over

Write Concisely

Business people are *busy* people. The information revolution has created more paperwork, giving people access to more data. Having more data to analyze (but not necessarily having the ability to read faster or more time in which to read), managers want information presented in the fewest possible words. To achieve conciseness, make every word count. Avoid redundancy, wordy expressions, hidden verbs and nouns, and other space-eaters.

Avoid Redundancy

redundancy The unnecessary repetition of an idea that has already been expressed or intimated.

A **redundancy** is the unnecessary repetition of an idea that has already been expressed or intimated. Eliminating the repetition contributes to conciseness.

> NOT: Signing both copies of the lease is a necessary requirement.
> BUT: Signing both copies of the lease is necessary.

> NOT: Combine the ingredients together.
> BUT: Combine the ingredients.

A *requirement* is by definition *necessary,* so only one of the words is needed. Similarly, to *combine* means to bring *together,* so using both words is redundant.

Don't confuse redundancy and repetition. Repetition—using the same word more than once—is occasionally effective for emphasis (as we will discuss later in this chapter). Redundancy, however, serves no purpose and should always be avoided.

Most redundancies are simply *verbiage—excess* words that consume time and space. Avoid them. In addition, avoid the following common redundancies (use the words in parentheses instead):

advance planning (planning)

any and all (any *or* all)

basic fundamentals
(basics *or* fundamentals)

plan ahead (plan)

but nevertheless (but *or* nevertheless)

over again (over)

true facts (facts)

free gift (gift)

repeat again (repeat)

each and every (each *or* every)

Avoid Wordy Expressions

Although wordy expressions are not necessarily writing errors (as redundancies are), they do slow the pace of the communication and should be avoided. To solve this problem, try substituting one word for a phrase whenever possible.

NOT: In view of the fact that the model failed twice during the time that we tested it, we are at this point in time searching for other options.

BUT: Because the model failed twice when we tested it, we are now searching for other options.

The original sentence contains 28 words; the revised sentence, 16. Thus, you've "saved" 12 words. Here are examples of other wordy phrases and their preferred one-word substitutes in parentheses:

are of the opinion that (believe)

due to the fact that (because)

for the purpose of (for *or* to)

in the event that (if)

pertaining to (about)

with regard to (about)

Avoid Hidden Verbs

A hidden verb is a verb that has been changed into a noun form, thereby weakening the action. Verbs are *action* words and should convey the main action in the sentence. They provide interest and forward movement. Consider this example:

NOT: Scott made an announcement that he will give consideration to our request.

BUT: Scott announced that he will consider our request.

What is the real action? It is not that Scott *made* something or that he will *give* something. The real action is hiding in the nouns: Scott *announced* and will *consider*. These two words, then, should be the main verbs in the sentence. Notice that the revised sentence is more direct—and four words shorter. Here are some other actions that should be conveyed by verbs instead of being hidden in nouns:

arrived at the conclusion (concluded)

came to an agreement (agreed)

gave a demonstration of (demonstrated)

performed an analysis of (analyzed)

has a requirement for (requires)

held a meeting (met)

made a payment (paid)

gave an explanation (explained)

expletive   An expression such as *there is* or *it has been* that begins a clause and for which the pronoun has no antecedent.

CONCEPT CHECK 5.2

Give an original example of each of the following terms: cliché, hidden subject, hidden verb, redundancy, slang.

Avoid Hidden Subjects

Like verbs, subjects play a prominent role in a sentence and should stand out. An **expletive** is an expression such as *there is* or *it is* that begins a clause or sentence and for which the pronoun has no antecedent. The subject always follows the expletive. Because the topic of a sentence that begins with an expletive is not immediately clear, you should use such sentences sparingly in business writing. Avoiding expletives also contributes to conciseness.

NOT: There was no indication that it is necessary to invite Zhao. *(11 words)*

BUT: No one indicated that Zhao should be invited. *(8 words)*

Imply or Condense

Sometimes you do not need to state certain information explicitly; you can imply it instead. In other situations, you can use adjectives and adverbs to convey the needed information in a more concise format.

NOT: We have received your recent letter and are happy to provide the data you requested. *(15 words)*

BUT: We are happy to provide the data you recently requested. *(10 words)*

NOT: This brochure, which is available free of charge, will answer your questions. *(12 words)*

BUT: This free brochure will answer your questions. *(7 words)*

Use Positive Language

Words that create a positive image are more likely to help you achieve your objective than are negative words. For example, you are more likely to persuade someone to do as you ask if you stress the advantages of doing so rather than the disadvantages of *not* doing so. Positive language also builds goodwill for you and your organization and often gives more information than negative language does. Note the differences in tone and amount of information given in the following pairs of sentences:

NOT: The briefcase is not made of cheap imitation leather.

BUT: The briefcase is made of 100% belt leather for years of durable service.

NOT: We cannot ship your merchandise until we receive your check.

BUT: As soon as we receive your check, we will ship your merchandise.

Expressions such as *cannot* and *will not* are not the only ones that convey negative messages. Other words, such as *mistake, damage, failure, refuse,* and *deny,* carry negative connotations and should be avoided when possible.

NOT: Failure to follow the directions may cause the blender to malfunction.

BUT: Following the directions will ensure many years of service from your blender.

In short, stress what *is* true and what *can* be done rather than what is not true and what cannot be done. This is not to say that negative language has no place in business writing. Negative language is strong and emphatic, and sometimes you will want to use it. Unless the situation clearly calls for negative language, however, you are more likely to achieve your objective and to build goodwill for yourself and your organization by stressing the positive.

Because words are the building blocks for your message, choose them with care. Using short, simple words, writing with clarity and conciseness, and using positive language will help you construct effective sentences and paragraphs.

Online Study Center
Improve Your Grade
Audio Chapter Review 5.1

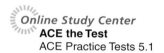

ANSWERS CAN BE FOUND ON P. 411

True or False?

____ 1. Any word that you use in your writing should be familiar both to you and to all of your readers.

____ 2. Long words should not be used in business writing.

____ 3. Both redundancies and repetition weaken your writing.

Online Study Center
ACE the Test
ACE Practice Tests 5.1

Online Study Center
Improve Your Grade
Audio Chapter Quiz 5.1
PowerPoint Review 5.1

Vocabulary

Define the following terms in your own words and give an original example of each.

4. Dangling expression
5. Expletive
6. Redundancy

Critical Thinking

7. Describe a business communication situation in which it might be preferable to use *negative* language rather than positive language.

Writing Effective Sentences

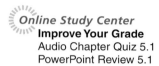

2 ▶ *Write effective sentences.*

A sentence has a subject and predicate and expresses at least one complete thought. Beyond these attributes, however, sentences vary widely in style, length, and effect. They are also very flexible; writers can move sentence parts around, add and delete information, and substitute words to express different ideas and emphasize different points. To build effective sentences, use a variety of sentence types, and use active and passive voice appropriately.

Use a Variety of Sentence Types

There are four basic sentence types—simple, compound, complex, and compound-complex—all of which are appropriate for business writing.

Simple Sentence

A **simple sentence** contains one independent clause (that is, a clause that can stand alone as a complete thought). Because it presents a single idea and is usually short, a simple sentence is often used for emphasis. Although a simple sentence contains only one independent clause, it may have a compound subject or compound verb (or both). All of the following sentences are simple.

> I quit.

> Individual Retirement Accounts are a safe option.

> Both Individual Retirement Accounts and Simplified Employee Pension Plans are safe and convenient options as retirement investments for the entrepreneur.

simple sentence A sentence that contains one independent clause.

Compound Sentence

A **compound sentence** contains two or more independent clauses and no dependent clauses. Because each clause presents a complete idea, each idea receives *equal*

compound sentence A sentence that contains two or more independent clauses.

When you're given only 15 minutes to convince venture capitalists to invest $8 million in your small start-up high-tech company, you must make sure every word of your presentation counts. Krishna Subramanian, CEO of Kovair, was successful in her presentation to 300 investors at a Silicon Valley forum.

complex sentence   A sentence that contains one independent clause and one or more dependent clauses.

compound-complex sentence   A sentence that contains two or more independent clauses and one or more dependent clauses.

CONCEPT CHECK 5.3

Write simple, compound, and complex sentences to express the following ideas: Mr. Esquibel was given a promotion. Mr. Esquibel was assigned additional responsibilities. For the complex sentence, emphasize the first idea.

emphasis. (If the two ideas are not closely related, they should be presented in two separate sentences.) Here are three compound sentences:

Stacey listened, but I nodded.

Morris Technologies made a major acquisition last year, and it turned out to be a disaster.

Westmoreland Mines moved its headquarters to Prescott in 1984; however, it stayed there only five years and then moved back to Globe.

Complex Sentence

A **complex sentence** contains one independent clause and one or more dependent clauses. For example, in the first sentence below, "The scanner will save valuable input time" is an independent clause because it makes sense by itself. "Although it cost $235" is a dependent clause because it does not make sense by itself.

Although it cost $235, the scanner will save valuable input time.

George Bosley, who is the new CEO at Hubbell, made the decision.

I will be moving to Austin when I assume my new position.

The dependent clause provides additional, but *subordinate*, information related to the independent clause.

Compound-Complex Sentence

A **compound-complex sentence** contains *two or more* independent clauses and *one or more* dependent clauses.

I wanted to write the report myself, but I soon realized that I needed the advice of our legal department. (*Two independent clauses and one dependent clause*)

If I can, I'll do it; if I cannot, I'll ask Sheila to do it. (*Two independent clauses and two dependent clauses*)

Sentence Variety

Using a variety of sentence patterns and sentence lengths helps keep your writing interesting. Note how simplistic and choppy too many short sentences can be and how boring and difficult too many long sentences can be.

Too Choppy:

Golden Nugget will not purchase the Claridge Hotel. The hotel is 60 years old. The asking price was $110 million. It was not considered too high. Golden Nugget had wanted some commitments from New Jersey regulators. The regulators were unwilling to provide such commitments. Some observers believe the refusal was not the real reason for the decision. They blame the weak Atlantic City economy for the cancellation. Golden Nugget purchased the Stake House in Las Vegas in 1990. It lost money on that purchase. It does not want to repeat its mistake in Atlantic City. (*Average sentence length = 8 words*)

Too Difficult:

Golden Nugget will not purchase the Claridge Hotel, which is 60 years old, for an asking price of $110 million, which was not considered too high, because the company had wanted some commitments from New Jersey regulators, and the regulators were unwilling to provide such commitments. Some observers believe the refusal was not the real reason for the decision but rather that the weak Atlantic City economy was responsible for the cancellation; and since Golden Nugget purchased the Stake House in Las Vegas in 1990 and lost money on that purchase, it does not want to repeat its mistake in Atlantic City. *(Average sentence length = 50 words)*

The sentences in these paragraphs should be revised to show relationships between ideas more clearly, to keep readers interested, and to improve readability. Use simple sentences for emphasis and variety, compound sentences for coordinate (equal) relationships, and complex sentences for subordinate relationships.

> *Appropriate Variety:*
>
> Golden Nugget will not purchase the 60-year-old Claridge Hotel, even though the $110 million asking price was not considered too high. The company had wanted some commitments from New Jersey regulators, which the regulators were unwilling to provide. However, some observers blame the cancellation on the weak Atlantic City economy. Golden Nugget lost money on its 1990 purchase of the Stake House in Las Vegas, and it does not want to repeat its mistake in Atlantic City. *(Average sentence length = 20 words)*

The first two sentences in the revision are complex, the third sentence is simple, and the last sentence is compound. The lengths of the four sentences range from 12 to 27 words. To write effective sentences, use different sentence patterns and lengths. Most sentences in good business writing range from 16 to 22 words.

Use Active and Passive Voice Appropriately

Voice is the characteristic of a verb that shows whether the subject of the sentence acts or is acted on. In the **active voice**, the subject *performs* the action expressed by the verb. In the **passive voice**, the subject *receives* the action expressed by the verb.

active voice   The sentence form in which the subject performs the action expressed by the verb.

passive voice   The sentence form in which the subject receives the action expressed by the verb.

ACTIVE:	Inmac offers a full refund on all orders.
PASSIVE:	A full refund on all orders is offered by Inmac.
ACTIVE:	Shoemacher & Doerr audited the books in 2006.
PASSIVE:	The books were audited in 2006 by Shoemacher & Doerr.

Passive sentences add some form of the verb *to be* to the main verb, so a passive sentence is always longer than the equivalent active sentence. In the first set of sentences just given, for example, compare *offers* in the active sentence with *is offered by* in the passive sentence.

Use active sentences most of the time in business writing, just as you unconsciously use active sentences in most of your conversations. Note that verb *voice* (active or passive) has nothing to do with verb *tense*, which shows the time of the action. As the following sentences show, the action in both active and passive sentences can occur in the past, present, or future.

NOT:	A very logical argument was presented by Troy. *(Passive voice, past tense)*
BUT:	Troy presented a very logical argument. *(Active voice, past tense)*
NOT:	An 18 percent increase will be reported by the eastern region. *(Passive voice, future tense)*
BUT:	The eastern region will report an 18 percent increase. *(Active voice, future tense)*

Online Study Center   college.hmco.com/pic/oberSASfund

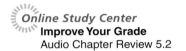

CONCEPT CHECK 5.4

Compose an effective compound sentence in which both clauses are in the active voice.

Passive sentences are most appropriate in three circumstances: (1) when you want to emphasize the receiver of the action, (2) when the person doing the action is either unknown or unimportant, or (3) when you want to be tactful in conveying negative information. All of the following sentences are appropriately stated in the passive voice:

> Protective legislation was blamed for the drop in imports. *(Emphasizes the receiver of the action)*

> Transportation to the construction site will be provided. *(The doer of the action is not important.)*

> Several *complaints* have been received regarding the new policy. *(Tactfully conveys negative news)*

Words, sentences, and paragraphs are all building blocks of communication. You have seen how using a variety of sentence types and using active and passive voice appropriately can help make your sentences more effective. Now you are ready to combine these sentences to form logical paragraphs.

Online Study Center
Improve Your Grade
Audio Chapter Review 5.2

TEST PREPPER 5.2

ANSWERS CAN BE FOUND ON P. 411

True or False?

_____ 1. Most active sentences are in the present tense, and most passive sentences are in the past tense.

_____ 2. A compound-complex sentence contains two or more independent clauses and two or more dependent clauses.

_____ 3. All passive sentences add some form of the verb *to be* to the main verb.

_____ 4. Passive sentences should be avoided in business writing.

Vocabulary

Define the following terms in your own words and give an original example of each.

5. Active voice
6. Simple sentence
7. Compound sentence
8. Compound-complex sentence
9. Passive voice
10. Complex sentence

Online Study Center
ACE the Test
ACE Practice Tests 5.2

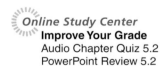

Online Study Center
Improve Your Grade
Audio Chapter Quiz 5.2
PowerPoint Review 5.2

DEVELOPING LOGICAL PARAGRAPHS

3 *Develop logical paragraphs.*

A paragraph is a group of related sentences that focus on one main idea. The main idea is often identified in the first sentence of the paragraph, which is then known as a *topic sentence*. The body of the paragraph supports this main idea by giving more information, analysis, or examples. A paragraph is typically part of a longer message, although one paragraph can contain the entire message, especially in informal communications such as e-mail.

Paragraphs organize the topic into manageable units of information for the reader. Readers need a cue to tell them when they have finished a topic so that they can pause and refocus their attention on the next topic. To serve this purpose, paragraphs must be unified and coherent, be stated in parallel structure, and be of an appropriate length.

Keep Paragraphs Unified and Coherent

Although closely related, unity and coherence are not the same. A paragraph has *unity* when all its parts work together to develop a single idea consistently and logically. A paragraph has *coherence* when each sentence links smoothly to the sentences before and after it.

Unity

A unified paragraph gives information that is directly related to the topic, presents this information in a logical order, and omits irrelevant details. The following excerpt is a middle paragraph in a memorandum arguing against the proposal that Collins, a baby-food manufacturer, should expand into producing food for adults:

> **NOT:**   [1] We cannot focus our attention on both ends of the age spectrum. [2] In a recent survey, two-thirds of the under-35 age group named Collins as the first company that came to mind for the category "baby-food products." [3] For more than 50 years we have spent millions of dollars annually to identify our company as the baby-food company, and market research shows that we have been successful. [4] Last year, we introduced Peas 'N Pears, our most successful baby-food introduction ever. [5] To now seek to position ourselves as a producer of food for adults would simply be incongruous. [6] Our well-defined image in the marketplace would make producing food for adults risky.

The paragraph obviously lacks unity. You may decide that the overall topic of the paragraph is Collins's well-defined image as a baby-food producer. So sentence 6 would be the best topic sentence. You might also decide that sentence 4 brings in extra information that weakens paragraph unity and should be left out. The most unified paragraph, then, would be sentences 6, 3, 2, 5, and 1, as shown here:

> **BUT:**   Our well-defined image in the marketplace would make producing food for adults risky. For more than 50 years we have spent millions of dollars annually to identify our company as the baby-food company, and market research shows that we have been successful. In a recent survey, two-thirds of the under-35 age group named Collins as the first company that came to mind for the category "baby-food products." To now seek to position ourselves as a producer of food for adults would simply be incongruous. We cannot focus our attention on both ends of the age spectrum.

A topic sentence is especially helpful in a long paragraph. It usually appears at the beginning of a paragraph. This position helps the writer focus on the topic, so the paragraph will have unity. It also lets the reader know immediately what the topic is.

Coherence

A coherent paragraph weaves sentences together so that the discussion is integrated. The reader never needs to pause to puzzle out the relationships or reread to get the intended meaning. To achieve coherence:

▌ Use transitional words.

▌ Use pronouns.

▌ Repeat key words and ideas.

▌ Use parallel structure.

Transitional words help the reader see relationships between sentences. Such words may be as simple as *first* and other indicators of sequence.

> Ten years ago, Collins tried to overcome market resistance to its new line of baby clothes. <u>First</u>, it mounted a multimillion-dollar ad campaign featuring the Mason quintuplets. <u>Next</u>, it sponsored a Collins Baby look-alike contest. <u>Then</u>, it sponsored two network specials featuring Dr. Benjamin Spock. <u>Finally</u>, it brought in the Madison Avenue firm of Morgan & Modine to broaden its image.

CONCEPT CHECK 5.5

What are four methods for achieving coherence?

The words *first, next, then,* and *finally* clearly signal step-by-step movement. Transitional words act as road signs, indicating where the message is headed and letting the reader know what to expect. Here are some commonly used transitional expressions grouped by the relationships they express:

Relationship	*Transitional Expressions*
addition	*also, besides, in addition, too*
cause and effect	*as a result, because, consequently, so, therefore*
comparison	*in the same way, likewise, similarly*
contrast	*although, but, however, on the other hand, yet*
illustration	*for example, in other words, to illustrate*
sequence	*first, second, third, then, next, finally*
summary/ conclusion	*at last, finally, in conclusion, to summarize, therefore*

A second way to achieve coherence is to use pronouns. Because a pronoun stands for a word already named, using pronouns ties sentences and ideas together. The pronouns are underlined in the sentences below:

> If Collins branches out with additional food products, one possibility would be a fruit snack for youngsters. Funny Fruits were tested in Columbus last summer, and <u>they</u> were a big hit. Roger Johnson, national marketing manager, says <u>he</u> hopes to build new food categories into a $200 million business. <u>He</u> is also exploring the possibility of acquiring other established name brands. <u>These</u> acquired brands would let Collins expand faster than if it had to develop a new product of <u>its</u> own.

A third way to achieve coherence is to repeat key words. In a misguided attempt to appear interesting, writers sometimes use different terms for the same idea. For example, a writer may use the words *administrator, manager, supervisor,* and *executive* all to refer to the same person. Such "elegant variation" merely confuses the reader, who has no way of knowing whether the writer is referring to the same concept or to slightly different variations of that concept. Avoid needless repetition, but use purposeful repetition to link ideas and thus promote paragraph coherence. Here is a good example:

> Collins has taken several <u>steps</u> recently to enhance profits and project a stronger leadership position. One of these <u>steps</u> is streamlining operations. Collins's

line of children's clothes was <u>unprofitable</u>, so it discontinued the <u>line</u>. Its four produce farms were likewise <u>unprofitable</u>, so it hired an outside professional team to manage them.

Ensure paragraph unity by developing only one topic per paragraph and by presenting the information in logical order. Ensure paragraph coherence by using transitional words and pronouns and by repeating key words.

Use Parallel Structure

The term **parallelism** means using similar grammatical structure for similar ideas—that is, matching adjectives with adjectives, nouns with nouns, infinitives with infinitives, and so on. Much widely quoted writing uses parallelism—for example, Julius Caesar's "I came, I saw, I conquered" and Abraham Lincoln's "government of the people, by the people, and for the people." Parallel structure smoothly links ideas and adds a pleasing rhythm to sentences and paragraphs, thereby enhancing coherence.

parallelism   Using similar grammatical structure to express similar ideas.

> NOT: The new dispatcher is competent and a fast worker.
> BUT: The new dispatcher is competent and fast.

> NOT: The new grade of paper is lightweight, nonporous, and it is inexpensive.
> BUT: The new grade of paper is lightweight, nonporous, and inexpensive.

> NOT: The training program will cover
>   1. Vacation and sick leaves
>   2. How to resolve grievances
>   3. Managing your workstation
> BUT: The training program will cover
>   1. Vacation and sick leaves
>   2. Grievance resolution
>   3. Workstation management

> NOT: One management consultant recommended either selling the children's furniture division or its conversion into a children's toy division.
> BUT: One management consultant recommended either selling the children's furniture division or converting it into a children's toy division.

In the last set of sentences above, note that correlative conjunctions (such as *both/and, either/or,* and *not only/but also*) must be followed by words in parallel form. Be especially careful to use parallel structure in report headings that have equal weight and in numbered or bulleted lists.

CONCEPT CHECK 5.6

Compose a sentence using *either/or* phrases that illustrate parallel structure.

Control Paragraph Length

How long should a paragraph of business writing be? As with other considerations, the needs of the reader, rather than the convenience of the writer, should determine the answer to this question. Paragraphs should help the reader by signaling a new idea as well as by providing a physical break.

Long blocks of unbroken text look boring and needlessly complex. Also, they may unintentionally obscure an important idea buried in the middle. On the other hand, a series of extremely short paragraphs can weaken coherence by obscuring underlying relationships.

Essentially, there are no fixed rules for paragraph length, and occasionally one- or ten-sentence paragraphs might be effective. However, most paragraphs of good business writers fall into the 60- to 80-word range—long enough for a topic sentence and three or four supporting sentences. Although a single paragraph should never discuss more than one major topic, complex topics may need to be divided into several paragraphs. Your purpose and the needs of your reader should ultimately determine paragraph length.

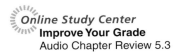

Online Study Center
Improve Your Grade
Audio Chapter Review 5.3

TEST PREPPER 5.3   ANSWERS CAN BE FOUND ON P. 411

True or False?

_____ 1. A topic sentence usually appears at the beginning of a paragraph.

_____ 2. To avoid monotony, business writers should use different terms to refer to the same idea.

_____ 3. It is acceptable to divide a long paragraph into separate paragraphs even if they both discuss the same topic.

_____ 4. Parallel structure is required in report headings that have equal weight as well as in numbered and bulleted lists.

Vocabulary

Define the following term in your own words and give an original example.

5. Parallelism

Critical Thinking

6. Assume that today you wrote one e-mail to your boss and another to your best friend. How do you think they might differ in terms of (a) sentence type, (b) coherence and logic, (c) parallel structure, and (d) paragraph length?

Online Study Center
ACE the Test
ACE Practice Tests 5.3

Online Study Center
Improve Your Grade
Audio Chapter Quiz 5.3
PowerPoint Review 5.3

WHAT DO WE MEAN BY *TONE*?

 ▶ *Convey an appropriate tone.*

Having chosen the right words to construct effective sentences and then having combined these sentences into logical paragraphs, we now examine the tone of the complete message—the complete letter, memorandum, report, or the like. *Tone* in writing refers to the writer's attitude toward both the reader and the subject of the message. The overall tone of your written message affects your reader just as your tone of voice affects your listener in everyday exchanges.

The business writer should strive for an overall tone that is confident, courteous, and sincere; that uses emphasis and subordination appropriately; that contains nondiscriminatory language; and that stresses the "you" attitude.

Write Confidently

Your message should convey the confident attitude that you have done a competent job of communicating and that your reader will do as you ask or will accept your decision. If you believe that your explanation is complete, that your request is reasonable, or that your decision is based on sound logic, you are likely to write with confidence. Such confidence has a persuasive effect on your audience. Avoid using language that makes you sound unsure of yourself. Be especially wary of beginning sentences with "I hope," "If you agree," and similar self-conscious terms.

> **NOT:** If you'd like to take advantage of this offer, call our toll-free number.
> **BUT:** To take advantage of this offer, call our toll-free number.

> **NOT:** I hope that you will agree that my qualifications match your job needs.
> **BUT:** My qualifications match your job needs in the following respects.

A word of caution: Do not appear overconfident; that is, avoid sounding presumptuous or arrogant. Be especially wary of using strong phrases such as "I know that" and "I am sure you will agree that."

> **NOT:** I'm sure you'll agree our offer is reasonable.
> **BUT:** This solution should enable you to collect the data you need while still protecting the privacy of our clients.

Competent communicators are confident communicators. They write with conviction, yet avoid appearing to be pushy or presumptuous.

Use a Courteous and Sincere Tone

A tone of courtesy and sincerity builds goodwill for you and your organization and increases the likelihood that your message will achieve its objective. For example, lecturing the reader or filling a letter with platitudes (trite, obvious statements) implies a condescending attitude. Likewise, readers are likely to find offensive expressions such as "you failed to," "we find it difficult to believe that," "you surely don't expect," or "your complaint."

> **NOT:** Companies like ours cannot survive unless our customers pay their bills on time.
> **BUT:** By paying your bill before May 30, you will maintain your excellent credit history with our firm.

> **NOT:** You sent your complaint to the wrong department. We don't handle shipping problems.
> **BUT:** We have forwarded your letter to the shipping department. You should be hearing from them within the week.

Your reader is sophisticated enough to know when you're being sincere. To achieve a sincere tone, avoid exaggeration (especially using too many modifiers or too strong modifiers), obvious flattery, and expressions of surprise or disbelief.

> **NOT:** Your satisfaction means more to us than making a profit, and we shall work night and day to see that we earn it.
> **BUT:** We value your goodwill and have taken these specific steps to ensure your satisfaction.

Competent communicators use both verbal and nonverbal signals to convey courtesy and sincerity. However, it is difficult to fake these attitudes. The best way to achieve the desired tone is to assume a courteous and sincere outlook toward your reader.

Use Appropriate Emphasis and Subordination

Not all ideas are created equal. Some are more important and more persuasive than others. If you want your writing to be credible, you must make sure that your reader views the relative importance of each idea in the same way you do. To achieve this objective, use appropriate emphasis and subordination techniques.

Techniques of Emphasis

To emphasize an idea, use any of the following strategies (to subordinate an idea, simply use the opposite strategy):

1. Put the idea in a short, simple sentence. However, if you need a complex sentence to convey the needed information, put the more important idea in the independent clause. (The ideas communicated in each independent clause of a *compound* sentence receive *equal* emphasis.)

   SIMPLE: The Repro 100 is the better photocopier for our purposes.

   COMPLEX: Although the Copy Cat is faster, 98 percent of our copying requires fewer than five copies per original. *(Emphasizes the fact that speed is not a crucial consideration for us)*

2. Place the major idea first or last. The first paragraph of a message receives the most emphasis, the last paragraph receives less emphasis, and the middle paragraphs receive the least emphasis. Similarly, the middle sentences within a paragraph receive less emphasis than the first sentence in a paragraph.

   The first criterion examined was cost. The Copy Cat sells for $2,750, and the Repro 100 sells for $2,100, or 24 percent less than the cost of the Copy Cat.

3. Make the noun you want to emphasize the subject of the sentence. In other words, use active voice to emphasize the doer of the action and passive voice to emphasize the receiver.

   ACTIVE: The Repro 100 costs 24 percent less than the Copy Cat. *(Emphasizes the Repro 100 rather than the Copy Cat)*

   PASSIVE: The relative costs of the two models were compared first. *(Emphasizes the relative costs rather than the two models)*

4. Devote more space to the idea.

   The two models were judged according to three criteria: cost, speed, and enlargement/reduction capabilities. Total cost is an important consideration for our firm because of the large number of copiers we use and our large volume of copying. Last year our firm used 358 photocopiers and duplicated more than 6.5 million pages. Thus, regardless of the speed or features of a particular model, if it is too expensive to operate, it will not serve our purposes.

5. Use language that directly implies importance, such as "most important," "major," or "primary."

   The most important factor for us is cost. *(In contrast, use terms such as* least important *or* a minor point *to subordinate an idea.)*

6. Use repetition (within reason).

   However, the Copy Cat is expensive—expensive to purchase and expensive to operate.

7. Use mechanical means (within reason)—enumeration, italics, solid capitals, second color, indenting from left and right margins, or other elements of design—to emphasize key ideas.

> But the most important criterion is cost, and the Repro 100 costs 24 percent *less* than the Copy Cat.

The Ethical Dimension

In using emphasis and subordination, your goal is to ensure a common frame of reference between you and your reader; you want your reader to see how important you consider each idea to be. Your goal is *not* to mislead the reader. For example, if you believe that the Repro 100 is a *slightly* better choice, you would not want to intentionally mislead your reader into concluding that it is *clearly* a better choice. Such a tactic would be not only unethical but also unwise. Use sound business judgment and a sense of fair play to help you achieve your communication objectives.

Use Nondiscriminatory Language

Nondiscriminatory language treats everyone equally, making no unwarranted assumptions about any group of people. Using nondiscriminatory language is smart business because it is ethical and because we risk offending others if we do otherwise. Consider the types of bias in this report:

> The finishing plant was the scene of a confrontation today when two ladies from the morning shift accused a foreman of sexual harassment. Marta Maria Valdez, a Hispanic inspector, and Margaret Sawyer, an assembly-line worker, accused Mr. Engerrand of making suggestive comments. Mr. Engerrand, who is 62 years old and an epileptic, denied the charges and said he thought the girls were trying to cheat the company with their demand for a cash award.

Were you able to identify the following instances of bias or discriminatory language?

▮ The women were referred to as *ladies* and *girls*, although it is unlikely that the men in the company are referred to as *gentlemen* and *boys*.

▮ The term *foreman* (and all other *-man* occupational titles) has a sexist connotation.

▮ The two women were identified by their first and last names, without personal titles, whereas the man was identified by a personal title and last name only.

▮ Valdez's ethnicity, Engerrand's age, and Engerrand's disability were identified, although they were irrelevant to the situation.

Competent communicators make sure that their writing is free of sexist language and free of bias based on factors such as race, ethnicity, religion, age, sexual orientation, and disability.

Instead of	*Use*
chairman	chair, chairperson
best man for the job	best person for the job
using foul language around the ladies	using foul language

No one understands the importance of a courteous and sincere tone better than Ali Kasikci, general manager of the Peninsula Beverly Hills hotel, the only hotel in southern California to win both the Mobil Travel Guide Five-Star Award and the AAA Five-Diamond Award.

Instead of	Use
Lloyd, a broker, and his wife, a beautiful brunette	Lloyd, a broker, and his wife, a lawyer (*or* homemaker)
each manager and his assistant	managers and their assistants
Dick McKenna, noted black legislator,	Dick McKenna, noted legislator,
Geraldine, an epileptic,	Geraldine, who has epilepsy,

Most of us like to think of ourselves as sensitive, caring people who do not wish to offend others. Our writing and speaking should reflect this attitude.

Stress the "You" Attitude

Are you more interested in how well *you* perform in your courses or in how well your classmates perform? When you hear a television commercial, are you more interested in how the product will benefit *you* or in how your purchase of the product will benefit the sponsor?

If you're like most people reading or hearing a message, your conscious or unconscious reaction is likely to be "What's in it for *me*?" Recognizing this tendency provides you with a powerful strategy for structuring your messages to maximize their impact: Stress the "you" attitude, not the "me" attitude.

The **"you" attitude** emphasizes what the receiver (the listener or the reader) wants to know and how he or she will be affected by the message. It requires developing empathy—the ability to project yourself into another person's position and to understand that person's situation, feelings, motives, and needs. To avoid sounding selfish and uninterested, focus on the reader—adopt the "you" attitude.

> **NOT:** I am shipping your order this afternoon.
> **BUT:** Your order should arrive by Friday.

> **NOT:** We will be open on Sundays from 1 to 5 p.m., beginning May 15.
> **BUT:** You will be able to shop on Sundays from 1 to 5 p.m., beginning May 15.

"you" attitude A viewpoint that emphasizes what the reader wants to know and how the reader will be affected by the message.

Reader Benefits

reader benefits The advantages a reader would derive from granting the writer's request or from accepting the writer's decision.

An important component of the "you" attitude is the concept of **reader benefits**—emphasizing how the reader (or the listener) will benefit from doing as you ask. Sometimes, especially when asking a favor or refusing a request, the best we can do is to show how someone (not necessarily the reader) will benefit. Whenever possible, however, we should show how someone *other than ourselves* benefits from our request or from our decision.

> **NOT:** Our decorative fireplace has an oak mantel and is portable.
> **BUT:** Whether entertaining in your living room or den, you can still enjoy the ambience of a blazing fire because our decorative fireplace is portable. Simply take it with you from room to room.

Note that the revised sentence, which stresses reader benefits, is longer than the original sentence—because it contains *more information*. Yet it is not verbose; that is, it does not contain unnecessary words. You can add information and still write concisely.

Exceptions

Stressing the "you" attitude focuses the attention on the reader, which is right where the attention should be—most of the time. In some situations, however, you may want to avoid focusing on the reader; these situations all involve conveying negative information. When you refuse someone's request, disagree with someone, or talk about someone's mistakes or shortcomings, avoid connecting the reader too closely with the negative information. In such situations, avoid second-person pronouns (*you* and *your*), and use passive sentences or other subordinating techniques to stress the receiver of the action rather than the doer.

NOT: You should have included more supporting evidence in your presentation.

BUT: Including more supporting evidence would have made the presentation more convincing.

NOT: You failed to return the merchandise within the 10-day period.

BUT: We are happy to give a full refund on all merchandise that is returned within 10 days.

Note that neither of the revised sentences contains the word *you*. Thus, they help to separate the reader from the negative information, making the message more tactful and palatable.

Effective Business Writing

Writing style goes beyond *correctness*. Although a document that contains numerous grammatical, mechanical, or usage errors could hardly be considered effective, a document that contains no such errors might still be ineffective because it lacks style. Style involves choosing the right words, writing effective sentences, developing logical paragraphs, and setting an appropriate overall tone. Checklist 4 on page 110 summarizes the principles discussed in this chapter.

CONCEPT CHECK 5.7

Revise the following sentences to make them more effective:

a. I think we should proceed with the expansion for three reasons.
b. Why not take advantage of this offer?
c. We didn't have the manpower to handle the job.
d. My girl will set up the appointment.

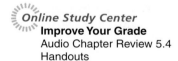
Online Study Center
Improve Your Grade
Audio Chapter Review 5.4
Handouts

TEST PREPPER 5.4

ANSWERS CAN BE FOUND ON P. 411

True or False?

_____ 1. The last paragraph of a message receives the most emphasis.

_____ 2. Your objective in using emphasis and subordination should be to ensure that your reader understands the importance you placed on each aspect of the situation.

_____ 3. "Every nurse supplies her own uniform" would be an example of sexist language.

_____ 4. You should never mention a physical or mental disability in business writing.

_____ 5. Sometimes you should *not* stress the "you" attitude in business writing.

Vocabulary

Define the following terms in your own words and give an original example of each.

6. Reader benefits
7. "You" attitude

Critical Thinking

8. Assume you are giving a speech rather than writing a message. What are some ways you might emphasize an important idea orally?

Online Study Center
ACE the Test
ACE Practice Tests 5.4

Online Study Center
Improve Your Grade
Audio Chapter Quiz 5.4
PowerPoint Review 5.4

CHECKLIST 4

Writing With Style

Words

✓ Write clearly.

✓ Choose short, simple words.

✓ Write concisely.

✓ Choose positive language.

Sentences

✓ Use a variety of sentence types.

✓ Use active and passive voice appropriately.

Paragraphs

✓ Keep paragraphs unified and coherent.

✓ Use parallel structure.

✓ Control paragraph length.

Overall Tone

✓ Write confidently.

✓ Use a courteous and sincere tone.

✓ Use appropriate emphasis and subordination.

✓ Use nondiscriminatory language.

✓ Stress the "you" attitude.

THREE Ps
PROBLEM, PROCESS, PRODUCT

Writing an Unbiased Message

Problem

As chair of your company's employee grievance committee, you must approve the minutes of each meeting before they are distributed. Following is the draft of a paragraph from the minutes that the secretary has forwarded for your approval:

> Mr. Timmerman argued that the 62-year-old Kathy Bevier should be replaced because she doesn't dress appropriately for her seamstress position in the alteration department. However, the human resources director, who is female, countered that we don't pay any of the girls in the alteration department well enough for them to buy appropriate attire. Mr. Timmerman did acknowledge that the seamstress performs her job well, considering her age and the fact that she suffers from arthritis. He added that he just wished she would dress more businesslike instead of wearing the colorful clothes and makeup that reflect her immigrant background.

Process

1. List any examples of gender bias contained in this paragraph.
   - "Mr. Timmerman" versus "Kathy Bevier"
   - "seamstress"
   - "who is female"
   - "any of the girls"

2. Are there examples of age bias?
   - "62-year-old"
   - "considering her age"

3. Are there instances of other discriminatory biases that you would want to correct?
   - Disability bias: "suffers from arthritis"
   - Nationality bias: "colorful clothes and makeup that reflect her immigrant background"

Product

Ralph Timmerman argued that Kathy Bevier should be replaced because she doesn't dress appropriately for her sewing position in the alteration department. However, the human resources director countered that we don't pay these employees well enough for them to buy appropriate attire. Timmerman acknowledged that Bevier performs her job well. He added that he just wished she would dress more businesslike.

PORTFOLIO PROJECT 1

Writing an Informational Message

Online Study Center
Prepare for Class
Portfolio Stationery

This exercise is the first of eight portfolio projects that will provide you with actual evidence to demonstrate your communication competence to potential employers. The forms for these projects and blank letterheads are available on the Internet at http://college.hmco.com/pic/oberSASfund. See the sample portfolio project shown on page 112. The problem is shown at the left, and the student's finished document is shown at the right.

Problem

You are the head of the catalog sales department of Branford's, a large department store located in Albuquerque, New Mexico. Most of your 17 full-time employees are high school graduates, and many of them are female. For beginning workers, you pay $2.50 per hour over the minimum wage, plus fringe benefits. Send a message to your employees informing them that management has decided that no one can take vacation or personal days during the months of November and December. The reason, of course, is that the holiday season is your busiest sales period.

PORTFOLIO PROJECT 1 (CONTINUED)

Process

Compose a few paragraphs describing how you solved this problem. In narrative form, provide information such as the following:

1. What is the purpose of your message?
2. Describe your audience.
3. Will you use a direct or an indirect organizational plan? (What is your audience's likely reaction to this memo?)
4. What reasons can you give for your decision?
5. How can you stress the "you" attitude and use positive language to explain the reasons for this decision?
6. Will you format this document as a letter or memo? Why?

Product

Compose your document and follow the steps of the writing process (audience analysis, planning, drafting, revising, formatting, and proofreading). Format the final version on letterhead stationery (refer to the Style Manual at the back of the book for formatting guidelines).

Sample Portfolio Project

OBER

PORTFOLIOPROJECT

ROUTINE RESPONSE TO A REQUEST FOR PRODUCT INFORMATION

PROBLEM

As the assistant business manager for Maison Richard, a 200-seat restaurant in Seattle, you received an inquiry from Chris Shearing, 1926 Second Avenue, Seattle, WA 98101. She had several questions about the meat and fish served in your restaurant. Here are her questions and your answers.

a. *Are the cattle from which your beef comes allowed to roam freely on an open range instead of being fattened in cramped feedlots?* No, allowing free-roaming would increase the muscle tissue in the beef, making it less tender.
b. *Are the cattle fed antibiotics and hormones?* Yes, to ensure a healthy animal and to promote faster growth.
c. *Do your trout come from lakes and streams?* No, they're farm-grown, which is more economical and results in less disease.

Ms. Shearing is a well-known animal-rights activist, and you want to present your case as positively as possible to avoid the loss of her goodwill and any negative publicity that might result. Respond to her letter, supplying whatever other appropriate information you feel is reasonable.

PROCESS

I decided to use a direct organizational plan for this letter because it was a routine reply to a routine request for product information. I used a descriptive subject line and direct opening paragraph to set the stage for my comments.

Most of the answers to Ms. Shearing's questions are probably not what she wanted to hear. Thus, I took pains to explain the reasons for our decisions and to avoid using negative language. The reasons show how people other than Maison Richard (for example, our customers and employees) benefit from our decision. The "you" approach is stressed throughout.

Finally, I closed on a positive, confident note, assuming that I had answered all of her questions in a satisfactory manner.

I formatted the letter in standard block style and did not include reference initials, because I typed my own letter.

PRODUCT

The document follows on the next page.

CERTIFICATION

I certify that this document was composed and formatted by this student.

Jorge Corey   *April 10, 20--*
Student   Date

Virginia Perkins   *April 15, 20--*
Instructor   Date

OBER, *FUNDAMENTALS OF CONTEMPORARY BUSINESS COMMUNICATION.* COPYRIGHT © HOUGHTON MIFFLIN COMPANY. ALL RIGHTS RESERVED. HANDOUT **5.0**

Maison Richard   WORLD TRADE CENTER, SEATTLE, WA 98100
PHONE: 317-555-1083 WEB: *HTTP://MAISONRICHARD*

October 8, 20--

Ms. Chris Shearing
1926 Second Avenue
Seattle, WA 98101

Dear Ms. Shearing:

Subject: Your Inquiry of October 1, 20--

I am happy to provide you with the information you requested about our restaurant. You will be pleased to know that we purchase only top-quality government-inspected meat, fish, and fowl.

The U.S. Department of Agriculture provides strict guidelines for meat products. Most cattle today are raised in specially designed lots that are cleaned daily to ensure animal and human health. Also, to ensure healthy animals and promote faster growth, antibiotics and hormones that have been approved safe for both animals and humans are fed to the animals. The highest-quality beef, in demand by beef consumers in stores as well as by top restaurants such as ours, is produced this way.

The trout we serve in our restaurant is grown on a farm, where careful monitoring of water and other conditions results in less disease. This process provides a safer, higher-quality product for our customers.

I am pleased to answer your questions about the food we serve and look forward to seeing you soon at Maison Richard.

Sincerely,

Ima Student
Assistant Business Manager

OBER, *FUNDAMENTALS OF CONTEMPORARY BUSINESS COMMUNICATION.* COPYRIGHT © HOUGHTON MIFFLIN COMPANY. ALL RIGHTS RESERVED. HANDOUT **5.0**

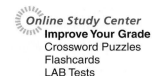

LEARNING OBJECTIVE REVIEW

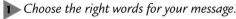 *Choose the right words for your message.*

- Write clearly.
    - Be accurate.
        - Write truthfully.
        - Avoid misleading implications.
        - Be aware of what is said, how it is said, and what is left unsaid.
    - Be complete.
        - Give the reader all the information the reader needs to act appropriately.
        - Answer the five Ws: *who, what, when, where,* and *why.*
    - Use words that are familiar to you and your reader.
    - Avoid dangling expressions.
        - Make the doer of the action the subject of the sentence.
        - Place modifiers close to the word they are modifying.
        - Use antecedents for all pronouns.
        - Revise for coherence.
    - Use short, simple words.
    - Avoid clichés and slang.

- Write concisely.
    - Avoid redundancy.
    - Avoid wordy expressions.
    - Avoid hidden verbs.
    - Eliminate expletives.
    - Imply or condense.

- Use positive language.

2 *Write effective sentences.*

- Vary the types of sentence to avoid monotony.
- Use active voice in most situations.
- Use passive voice when conveying negative information.

3 *Develop logical paragraphs.*

- Keep paragraphs unified and coherent.
- Use parallel structure to express similar ideas.
- Control paragraph length.

4 *Convey an appropriate tone.*

- Write confidently.
- Use a courteous and sincere tone.
- Use appropriate emphasis and subordination.
- Use nondiscriminatory language.
- Stress the "you" attitude.

EXERCISES

1. Short and Simple Words (▶ 5.1)

Revise the following paragraph to incorporate more short and simple words:

> The consultant demonstrated how our aggregate remuneration might be ameliorated by modifications in our propensities to utilize credit for compensating for services. She also endeavored to ascertain which of our characteristics were analogous to those of other entities for which she had fabricated solutions. She recommended we commence to initiate innumerable modifications in our procedures to increase cash flow, which she considers indispensable for facilitating increased corporate health.

2. Positive Language (▶ 5.1)

Revise the following paragraph to incorporate more positive language:

> We cannot issue a full refund at this time because you did not enclose a receipt or an authorized estimate. I'm sorry that we will have to delay your reimbursement. We are not like those insurance companies that promise you anything but then disappear when you have a claim. When we receive your receipt or estimate, we will not hold up your check. Our refusal to issue reimbursement without proper supporting evidence means that we do not have to charge you outlandish premiums for your automobile insurance.

3. Sentence Variety (▶ 5.2)

Revise the following paragraph by varying sentence types and sentence lengths to keep the writing interesting.

> Health Foods was founded by Floyd Morales in 1994. The product was the first snack food to combine cheddar cheese and popcorn. Morales perfected the Health Foods recipe in his home kitchen after much trial and error. Health Foods sales were reportedly only $65,000 in 1995. During that time, the product was available only in the Midwest. By 1998, sales had soared to $12 million. This attracted the attention of Norton. The snack-food giant bought Health Foods in 1999 for $15 million. Since the purchase, Norton has not revised the popular Health Foods formula. It has used its marketing prowess to keep sales growing, despite the growing number of challengers crowding the market.

4. Active and Passive Voice (▶ 5.2)

For each of the following sentences, first identify whether the sentence is active or passive. Then, if necessary, revise the sentence to use the more effective verb voice.

   a. We will begin using the new plant in 2003, and the old plant will be converted into a warehouse.
   b. A very effective sales letter was written by Paul Mendleson. The letter will be mailed next week.
   c. You failed to verify the figures on the quarterly report. As a result, $5,500 was lost by the company.

5. Paragraph Unity (▶ 5.3)

From the following sentences, select the best topic sentence; then list the other sentences in an appropriate order.

   a. Businesses will spend $150 billion a year on goods and services marketed by telephone.
   b. The telephone is becoming one of the nation's chief timesavers.
   c. Telephones save time, save money, and establish goodwill.
   d. Telephones can sell an idea, service, or product.
   e. Telephones can be used to answer questions, clear up confusion, and produce immediate responses.
   f. More and more business is being conducted by telephone.
   g. The telephone is on its way to becoming the number 1 marketing tool.

6. **Writing Confidently (▶ 5.4)**

   Revise the following sentences to convey an appropriately confident attitude.

   a. Can you think of any reason not to buy a watch for dressy occasions?
   b. I hope you agree that my offer provides good value for the money.
   c. Of course, I am confident that my offer provides good value for the money.
   d. You might try to find a few minutes to visit our gallery on your next visit to galleries in this area.

7. **Using Appropriate Emphasis and Subordination (▶ 5.4)**

   Assume that you have evaluated two candidates for the position of sales assistant. The following is what you have learned:

   a. Herbert Garcia has more sales experience.
   b. Marcia Ford has more appropriate formal training (a college degree in marketing, attendance at several three-week sales seminars, and the like).
   c. Marcia Ford's personality appears to mesh more closely with the prevailing corporate attitudes at your firm.

   You must write a memo to Jordan Gardner, the company's vice president, recommending one of these candidates. First, assume that personality is the most important criterion and write a memo recommending Marcia Ford. Second, assume that experience is the most important criterion and write a memo recommending Herbert Garcia. Use appropriate emphasis and subordination in each message. You may make up any reasonable information needed to complete the assignment.

8. **Using Nondiscriminatory Language (▶ 5.4)**

   Revise the following sentences to eliminate discriminatory language.

   a. The mayor opened contract talks with the union representing local policemen.
   b. While the salesmen are at the convention, their wives will be treated to a tour of the city's landmarks.
   c. Our company gives each foreman the day off on his birthday.
   d. Our public relations director, Aurelia Gordon, will ask her young secretary, Teresa Moretti, to take notes during the president's speech.
   e. Both Dr. Marcos and his assistant, Terry Derek, attended the new-product seminar.

Additional exercises are available at the Online Study Center website: **college.hmco.com/pic/oberSASfund**.

Online Study Center **RESOURCES**

Prepare for Class, Improve Your Grade, and ACE the Test. Student Achievement Series resources include:

ACE Practice Tests	Ask Ober	Audio Chapter Reviews and Quizzes
Chapter Outlines	Communication Objectives	Crossword Puzzles
Flashcards	Glossaries	Handouts
LAB Tests	Portfolio Project Stationery	Sample Reports

To access these learning and study tools, go to **college.hmco.com/pic/oberSASfund**.

6 Routine Letters, Memos, and E-Mail Messages

Annie's Homegrown is a business that promotes all-natural products that are good for your health and the environment, but the business doesn't just stop there. Annie's Homegrown interacts and communicates with its customers in the same genuine, caring way that it produces its food. The result is a brand that speaks not only to the product, but also to the person.

3 *Compose a routine claim letter.*

2 *Compose a routine reply.*

1 *Compose a routine request.*

Before I write, I try to envision [the reader]. This helps me plan a genuine, unique letter that addresses each person's concerns."

—Ann Withey, Cofounder, Annie's Homegrown

Chapter Outline

▶ ROUTINE REQUESTS
Major Idea First
Explanation and Details
Friendly Closing

▶ ROUTINE REPLIES

▶ ROUTINE CLAIM LETTERS

▶ ROUTINE ADJUSTMENT LETTERS
Overall Tone
Good News First
Explanation
Positive, Forward-Looking Closing

Online Study Center
Prepare for Class
Chapter Outline

4 ▶ *Compose a routine adjustment letter.*

Routine Communication Is Best When Homegrown

Ann Withey, the cofounder of Annie's Homegrown, a $10 million business that makes packaged, all-natural macaroni and cheese products, responds to roughly 1,500 letters every month. Most are requests for free information about one of the causes promoted on product packages, such as a listing of scholarships or a "Be Green" bumper sticker. In response, Withey sends a form letter that is headed "Dear Friend" and opens with an expression of sincere appreciation for the reader's support and loyalty. The letter refers to the enclosed information and again thanks the reader. Making the most of every customer contact, this routine reply also includes an order form, a coupon, and information about related products.

About 20 letters every week require a customized response. Withey tailors the content of these letters for each reader. "Before I write, I try to envision that person. This helps me plan a genuine,

Online Study Center college.hmco.com/pic/oberSASfund

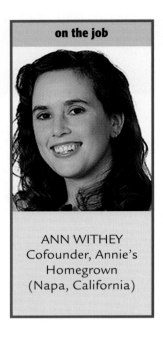

on the job

ANN WITHEY
Cofounder, Annie's
Homegrown
(Napa, California)

KEY TERMS

adjustment letter   *p. 127*
claim letter   *p. 125*
direct organizational plan   *p. 118*
indirect organizational plan
   p. 118
resale   *p. 129*

direct organizational plan   A plan in which the major purpose of the message is communicated first, followed by any needed details.

indirect organizational plan   A plan in which the reasons or rationale are presented first, followed by the major idea.

unique letter that addresses each person's concerns." She first thanks the reader for his or her support, then picks out a specific detail from the original letter that she can discuss in her response. Finally, she closes on a friendly note by thanking the reader for "bringing a smile to my face." ∎

Most of the typical manager's correspondence involves communicating about routine matters. For example, a small-business owner asks for a catalog and credit application from a potential supplier, a manager at a large corporation sends an e-mail informing employees of a change in policy, a consumer notifies a company that an ordered product arrived in damaged condition, or a government agency responds to a request for a brochure.

Although routine, such messages are of interest to the reader because the information contained in the message is necessary for day-to-day operations. Although no company is pleased when a customer is dissatisfied with one of its products, firms *are* interested in learning about such situations so that they can correct the problems and prevent their recurrence.

When the purpose of a message is to convey routine information, and our analysis of the audience indicates that the reader will probably be interested in its contents, we use a **direct organizational plan**. The main idea is stated first, followed by any needed explanation, and then a friendly closing. The advantage of using a direct organizational plan for routine correspondence is that it puts the major news first—where it stands out and gets the most attention. This strategy saves the reader time because he or she can quickly see what the message is about by scanning the first one or two sentences.

The **indirect organizational plan**, in which the reasons are presented before the major idea, is often used for bad-news and persuasive messages and is covered in a later chapter.

ROUTINE REQUESTS

 Compose a routine request.

A request is routine if you anticipate that the reader will readily do as you ask without having to be persuaded. For example, a request for specific information about an organization's product is routine because all organizations appreciate the opportunity to promote their products. However, a request for free samples of a company's product to distribute at your store's anniversary sale might not be routine because the company might have concluded that such promotion efforts are not cost-effective; thus, you would have to *persuade* the reader to grant the request.

Major Idea First

When making a routine request, present the major idea—your request—clearly and directly in the first sentence or two (see, however, the Spotlight "When in Rome . . . ," on page 133). You may use a direct question, a statement, or a polite request to present the main idea. Always pose your request clearly and politely, and give any background information needed to set the stage. All of the following are effective routine requests:

Direct Question: Does Black & Decker offer educational discounts for public institutions making quantity purchases of tools? Blair Junior High School will soon be replacing approximately 50 portable electric drills used by our industrial technology students.

Statement: Please let me know how I might invest in your deferred money-market fund. As an American currently working in Bangkok, Thailand, I cannot easily take advantage of your automatic monthly deposit plan.

Polite Request: Would you please answer several questions about the work performance of Casandra Naser. She has applied for the position of industrial safety officer at Inland Steel and has given your name as a reference.

Decide in advance how much detail you are seeking. If you need only a one-sentence reply, it would be unfair to word your request in such a way as to prompt the writer to provide a three-page answer. Define clearly the type of response you want and phrase your request to elicit that response.

NOT: Please explain the features of your Interact word processing program.

BUT: Does your Interact word processing program automatically number lines and paragraphs?

Remember that you are imposing on the goodwill of the reader. Ask as few questions as possible—and never ask for any information that you can easily obtain on your own. If many questions *are* necessary, number them; most readers will answer questions in the order in which you pose them and will thus be less likely to skip one unintentionally. Yes-or-no questions or short-answer questions are easy for the reader to answer, but when you need more information, use open-ended questions.

Arrange your questions in logical order (for example, order of importance, chronological order, or simple-to-complex order), word each question clearly and objectively (to avoid bias), and limit the content to one topic per question. If appropriate, assure the reader that the information provided will be treated confidentially.

Explanation and Details

Most of the time you will need to give additional explanation or details about your initial request. Include any needed background information (such as the reason for asking) either immediately before or after making the request. Suppose you received the polite request given earlier asking about Casandra Naser's job performance. Unless you were also told that the request came from a potential employer and that Casandra Naser had given your name as a reference, you might be reluctant to provide such confidential information.

Or assume that you're writing to a former employer or professor asking for a letter of recommendation. You might need to give some background about yourself to jog the reader's memory. Also, you might need to justify or expand on your request. Put yourself in the reader's position. What information would you need to answer the request accurately and completely?

A reader is more likely to cooperate if you can show how he or she will benefit from agreeing to your request. In fact, it is often the communication of such benefits that makes the message routine rather than persuasive.

Will you please help us serve you better by answering several questions about your banking needs. We're building a branch bank in your neighborhood and would like to make it as convenient for you as possible.

FIGURE 6.1

Example of an Ineffective Routine Request

Uses a subject line that is too general to be helpful. (It is not even clear to the reader whether you're providing or requesting product information.)

Begins in an indirect, roundabout manner and introduces irrelevant background information.

Embeds the requests for information in the middle of a long paragraph.

Closes with a cliché, without providing any incentive for responding.

Provides incomplete sender identification.

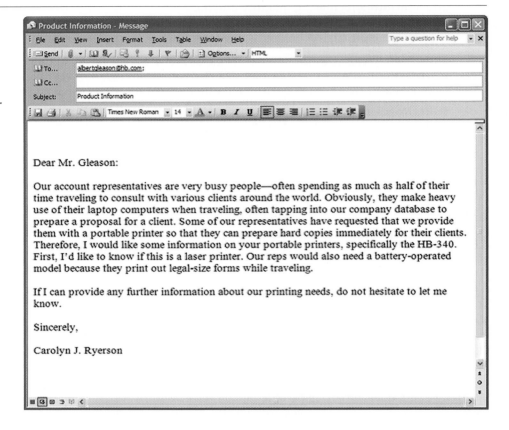

Dear Mr. Gleason:

Our account representatives are very busy people—often spending as much as half of their time traveling to consult with various clients around the world. Obviously, they make heavy use of their laptop computers when traveling, often tapping into our company database to prepare a proposal for a client. Some of our representatives have requested that we provide them with a portable printer so that they can prepare hard copies immediately for their clients. Therefore, I would like some information on your portable printers, specifically the HB-340. First, I'd like to know if this is a laser printer. Our reps would also need a battery-operated model because they print out legal-size forms while traveling.

If I can provide any further information about our printing needs, do not hesitate to let me know.

Sincerely,

Carolyn J. Ryerson

In general, you should identify reader benefits when they may not be obvious to the reader, but you need not belabor the point if such benefits are obvious. For example, a memo asking employees to recycle their paper and plastic trash would probably not need to discuss the value of recycling because most readers would already be familiar with the advantages of doing so.

Friendly Closing

In your final paragraph, assume a friendly tone. Close by expressing appreciation for the assistance to be provided (but without seeming to take the recipient's cooperation for granted), by stating and justifying any deadlines, or by offering to reciprocate. Make your ending friendly, positive, and original, as illustrated by the following examples:

> Please let me know if I can return the favor.

> We appreciate your providing this information, which will help us make a more fair evaluation of Casandra Naser's qualifications for this position.

> May I please have the product information by October 1, when I place my Christmas wholesale orders. That way, I will be able to include Kodak products in my holiday sales.

Figure 6.1 illustrates how *not* to write an effective routine request. Model 3 is a revised version of the ineffective example, illustrating the guidelines discussed previously for writing an effective routine request.

CONCEPT CHECK 6.1

You're beginning your last year at school and are interested in securing a full-time paid internship in computer networking for the spring term. You decide to send an e-mail inquiry to the human services resource department at Dell Inc.

a. Compose an appropriate subject line for your e-mail.

b. Compose the first paragraph of your message.

c. Compose the last sentence of your message.

MODEL 3

Routine Request

This message is from a potential customer to a manufacturer.

① Dear Mr. Gleason:

Presents the request in the first sentence, followed by the reason for asking.

② Would you provide me with information regarding your HB-340 portable printer. I'm interested in purchasing 74 lightweight printers that our account representatives can use with their Toshiba 1200XE notebook computers when they travel.

Specifically, I would like answers to the following three questions:

Enumerates questions for emphasis and clarity; makes questions easy to answer.

1. Is the HB-340 a laser printer?

2. Is it battery operated? Because we wish to use the printer for traveling, such a feature is important.

3. Will the printer accept legal-size paper?

Expresses appreciation; hints at a reader benefit.

③ I would appreciate your faxing me the information I need to make a purchase decision. I would also appreciate receiving ordering information.

Sincerely,

Carolyn J. Ryerson (cryerson@pricewinston.com)
Assistant Purchasing Director, Price Winston
1855 Avenue of the Americas
New York, NY 10019
Phone: 212-555-6109
Fax: 212-555-0327

E-mail header fields:

To...: albertgleason@hb.com;
Subject: Request for HB-340 Product Information

Grammar and Mechanics Notes

1. Format e-mail messages for easy readability—and always proofread before sending.
2. *your HB-340 portable printer.:* Use a period after a polite request.
3. *appreciate your faxing:* Use the possessive form of a pronoun (*your*) before a gerund (*faxing*).

CATHY   **by Cathy Guisewite**

ROUTINE REPLIES

2 ▶ *Compose a routine reply.*

Routine replies provide the information requested in the original message or otherwise comply with the writer's request. Like the original request letters, they are organized in a direct organizational style, putting the "good news"—the fact that you're responding favorably—up front.

Probably one of the most important guidelines to follow is to answer promptly. If a potential customer asks for product information, ensure that the information arrives before the customer must make a purchase decision. Otherwise, the time it took you to respond will have been wasted. Also, delaying a response might send the unintentional nonverbal message that you do not want to comply with the writer's request.

Your response should be courteous. If you appear to be acting grudgingly, you will probably lose any goodwill that a gracious response might have earned for you or your organization.

> NOT: Although we do not generally provide the type of information you requested, we have decided to do so in this case.
>
> BUT: We are happy to provide the information you requested.

Grant the request or give the requested information early in the message. Doing so not only saves the reader's time but also puts him or her in a positive state of mind immediately. Although the reader may be pleased to hear that "We have received your letter of June 26," such news is not nearly so eagerly received as telling the reader that "I would be pleased to speak at your Engineering Society meeting on August 8; thanks for thinking of me." Put the good news up front—where it will receive the most emphasis.

Be sure to answer all the questions asked or implied, using objective and clearly understood language. Although it is often helpful to provide additional information or suggestions, you should never fail to at least address all the questions asked. Questions are usually answered in the order in which they were asked, but consider rearranging them if a different order makes more sense.

Determining what your reader already knows about the topic should help you decide what information to include and how to phrase it.

In the body of your message, refer to any enclosure and then add an enclosure notation at the bottom of the letter. Refer to a specific page of an enclosed brochure or to a particular paragraph of an enclosed document to help ensure that such enclosures will be read.

Close your letter on a positive, friendly note. Avoid such clichés as "If you have additional questions, please don't hesitate to let me know." Instead, use original wording, personalized especially for the reader. After all, the reader might receive many letters like yours, and if he or she has already encountered "Thank you for your interest in our products" five times that day, the expression will sound trite and insincere.

Model 4 on page 124 is a routine reply to the request shown in Model 3 on page 121. The original request asked three questions about the printer, and the answers are as follows:

1. No, the HB-340 is not a laser printer.
2. No, it is not battery-operated.
3. Yes, it does accept legal-size paper.

As you can see, only one of the three questions can be answered with an unqualified "yes," and that is the question the respondent chose to answer first. Positive language helps soften the impact of the negative responses to the other two questions. Also, reader benefits are stressed throughout the letter. Instead of just describing the features, the writer shows how the features can benefit the reader.

Checklist 5 on page 132 summarizes the points you should consider when writing and responding to routine requests. Use this checklist as a guide in structuring your message and in evaluating the effectiveness of your first draft.

Online Study Center
Improve Your Grade
Audio Chapter Review 6.1, 6.2

TEST PREPPER 6.1, 6.2

ANSWERS CAN BE FOUND ON P. 411

True or False?

_____ 1. Most routine requests should be written using the direct organizational pattern.

_____ 2. One of the most important guidelines in responding to a request is to grant the request.

_____ 3. In responding to a request for information, you should always answer the questions in the order in which they were asked.

_____ 4. If you enclose an item with your letter, you should refer to the enclosure in the body of your letter.

_____ 5. Even for routine requests, you should generally tell the reader why you're making the request.

Vocabulary

Define the following terms in your own words.

6. Direct organizational plan
7. Indirect organizational plan

Critical Thinking

8. You're beginning your last year at school and are interested in securing a full-time paid internship in computer networking for the spring term. Do you think e-mail or a telephone call would be the best medium for this inquiry? Why?

Online Study Center
ACE the Test
ACE Practice Tests 6.1, 6.2

Online Study Center
Improve Your Grade
Audio Chapter Quiz 6.1, 6.2
PowerPoint Review 6.1, 6.2

Online Study Center college.hmco.com/pic/oberSASfund

MODEL 4

Routine Reply

This letter responds to the request in Model 3 on page 122.

Begins by answering the "yes" question first.

Answers all questions by using positive language and pointing out the benefits of each feature.

Uses paragraphs instead of enumeration to answer each question because each answer requires elaboration.

Gives important purchase information; closes on a forward-looking note.

September 12, 20—

Ms. Carolyn J. Ryerson
Assistant Purchasing Director
Price Winston
1855 Avenue of the Americas
New York, NY 10019

Di–Mark
320 Industrial Avenue
Palo Alto, CA 94300
TEL 650.555.1200

Dear Ms. Ryerson:

Subject: Information You Requested About the HB-340

Yes, our popular HB-340 printer does accept legal-size paper. Its 15-inch carriage will enable your representatives to print out complex spreadsheets while on the road. Of course, it also adjusts easily to fit standard 8½-by-11-inch paper.

① For quiet operation and easy portability, the HB uses ink-jet printing on plain paper. This technology provides nearly the same quality output as a laser printer at less than half the cost.

② Although many travelers use their computers on a plane or in their automobiles, they typically wait until reaching their destination to print out their documents. Thus, the HB uses AC power only, thereby reducing its weight by nearly a pound. The extra-long 12-foot power cable will let you power-up your printer easily no matter where the electrical outlet is hidden.

③ To take the HB-340 for a test drive, call your local Best Buy at 800-555-2189. They will show you how to increase your productivity while increasing your luggage weight by only 4 pounds.

Sincerely yours,

Albert Gleason

Albert Gleason, Sales Manager

juc
④ By Fax

Grammar and Mechanics Notes

1. *ink-jet printing:* Hyphenate a compound adjective before a noun.
2. *its:* Do not confuse *its* (the possessive pronoun) with *it's* (the contraction for "it is").
3. *a test drive,:* Place a comma after an introductory expression.
4. *By Fax:* For reference purposes, include a delivery notation if appropriate.

ROUTINE CLAIM LETTERS

 3 ▶ *Compose a routine claim letter.*

A **claim letter** is written by a buyer to a seller, seeking some type of action to correct a problem with the seller's product or service. The purchaser may be an individual or an organization. The desired adjustment might be nothing more than an explanation or apology, but the mere fact that you request some direct action will increase your chances of getting a satisfactory response.

A claim letter can be considered routine if you can reasonably anticipate that the reader will comply with your request. If, for example, you ordered a shipment of shoes for your store that were advertised at $23.50 each and the wholesaler charged you $32.50 instead, you would write a routine claim letter, asking the seller to correct the error. But suppose the wholesaler marked the price down to $19.50 two days after you placed your order. Then, instead of writing a routine claim letter, you might want to write a persuasive letter, trying to convince the wholesaler to give you the lower price. (Persuasive letters are discussed in Chapter 7.)

Although you may be frustrated or angry as a result of the situation, remember that the person to whom you're writing was not *personally* responsible for your problem. Be courteous and avoid emotional language. Assume that the company is reasonable and will do as you reasonably ask. Avoid any hint of anger, sarcasm, threat, or exaggeration. A reader who becomes angry as a result of the strong language in your claim letter will be less likely to do as you ask. Instead, using factual and unemotional language, begin your routine claim letter directly, telling exactly what the problem is.

> **NOT:** You should be ashamed at your dishonest advertising for the videotape *Safety Is Job One.*
>
> **BUT:** The videotape *Safety Is Job One* that I rented for $125 from your company last week lived up to our expectations in every way but one.

> **NOT:** I am disgusted at the way United Express cheated me out of $17.50 last week. What a rip-off!
>
> **BUT:** An overnight letter that I mailed on December 3 did not arrive the next day, as promised by United Express.

After you have identified the problem, begin your explanation. Provide as much background information as necessary—dates, model numbers, amounts, photocopies of canceled checks or correspondence, and the like. Use a confident tone and logic (rather than emotion) to present your case. Write in an impersonal style, avoiding the use of "you" pronouns to avoid linking your reader too closely to the negative news.

> **NOT:** I delivered this letter to you sometime in the early afternoon on December 3. Although you promised to deliver it by 3 p.m. the next day, you failed to do so.
>
> **BUT:** As shown on the enclosed copy of my receipt, I delivered this letter to United Express at 3:30 p.m. on December 3. According to the sign prominently displayed in the office, any package received by 4 p.m. is guaranteed to arrive by 3 p.m. the following business day.

claim letter A letter from a buyer to a seller, seeking some type of action to correct a problem with the seller's product or service.

MODEL 5

Routine Claim

This claim letter is about a defective product.

OTIS CANDY COMPANY   BOX 382, EDEN, NC 27932, 919-555-4822, FAX: 919-555-4831, WWW.OTISCANDY.COM

April 14, 20—

① Customer Relations Representative
Sir Speedy, Inc.
26722 Plaza Drive
Mission Viejo, CA 92690-9077

Dear Customer Relations Representative:

Subject: Poor Quality of Photocopying

Identifies the problem immediately and tells how the writer was inconvenienced.

The poor quality of the 13-page full-color handout you duplicated for me on April 8 made the handouts unsuitable for use in my recent presentation. As a result, I had to use black-and-white copies duplicated in-house instead.

Provides the needed details in a nonemotional, businesslike manner.

② As you can see from the enclosed handout, the colors often run together and the type is fuzzy. The photocopying is not equivalent in quality to that illustrated in
③ Sir Speedy's advertisement on page 154 of the April issue of *Business Management.*

Identifies and justifies the specific remedy requested.

I have already given the presentation for which these handouts were made, so re-duplicating them would not solve the problem. Because I have not yet paid your Invoice 4073 for $438.75, would you please cancel this charge.

Closes on a confident note.

④ I know that despite one's best efforts, mistakes will occasionally happen, and I am confident that you will correct this problem promptly.

Sincerely,

Claire D. Scriven

Claire D. Scriven
Marketing Manager

ric
Enclosure

Grammar and Mechanics Notes

1. If an addressee's name is unknown, you may use a title in both the inside address and the salutation.
2. *run together and:* Do not insert any punctuation before the *and* separating the two independent clauses because the second clause, "the type is fuzzy," is so short.
3. *Business Management:* Italicize magazine titles.
4. *occasionally:* Note that this word has two *c*'s and one *s.*

Tell exactly what went wrong and how you were inconvenienced. If it is true and relevant, mention something positive about the company or its products to make your letter appear reasonable.

> According to the enclosed arrival receipt, my letter was not delivered until 8:30 a.m. on December 5. Because the letter contained material needed for a dinner meeting on December 4, it arrived too late to be of any use. This is not the type of on-time service I've routinely received from United Express during the eight years I've been using your delivery system.

Finally, tell what type of adjustment you expect. Do you want the company to replace the product, repair it, issue a refund, simply apologize, or what? End the letter on a confident note.

> I would appreciate your refunding my $17.50, thereby reestablishing my confidence in United Express.

In some situations, you may not know what type of adjustment is reasonable; in that case, you would leave it up to the reader to suggest an appropriate course of action. This might be the situation when you suffered no monetary loss but simply wish to avoid an unpleasant situation in the future (such as discourteous service, long lines, or ordering the wrong model because of having received incomplete or misleading information).

> Please let me know how I might avoid this problem in the future.

Model 5 illustrates a routine claim letter about a defective product, asking for a specific remedy.

When Wayne Inouye took over as CEO of faltering consumer-PC maker eMachines, Inc., he decided that to understand how to fix the company, he would respond to calls from irate customers personally. His customer focus began when he sold guitars.

ROUTINE ADJUSTMENT LETTERS

 4 ▶ *Compose a routine adjustment letter.*

An **adjustment letter** is written to inform a customer of the action taken in response to the customer's claim letter. Few people bother to write a claim letter unless they have a real problem, so most claims that companies receive are legitimate and are adjusted according to the individual situation. If the action taken is what the customer requested or expected, you should write a routine adjustment letter using the direct organizational plan.

Note that *anyone* in an organization may be called upon to write claim and adjustment letters—not just those working in purchasing or sales or customer service. For example, an accounting manager may send (and receive) a letter complaining of poor service from an employee.

Overall Tone

A claim represents a possible loss of goodwill and confidence in your organization or its products. Because the customer is upset, the overall tone of your adjustment letter is crucial. Because you have already decided to honor the claim, your best

---

CONCEPT CHECK 6.2

The *Accounting Principles* textbook (ISBN: 0618191496) that you purchased online at textbooks.com arrived on time as advertised but in damaged condition. The front cover and several of the pages were torn—certainly not what you'd expect when you paid $45.99 for the used book. You complain via e-mail.

a. Compose an appropriate subject line for your e-mail.

b. Compose the first paragraph of your message.

c. Compose the last sentence of your message.

---

adjustment letter   A letter written to inform a customer of the action taken in response to the customer's claim letter.

strategy is to adopt a gracious, trusting tone. Give your customer the benefit of the doubt. It does not make sense to adopt a grudging or resentful tone and risk losing whatever goodwill you might have gained from granting the adjustment.

NOT: Although our engineers do not understand how this problem could have occurred if the directions had been followed, we are nevertheless willing to repair your generator free of charge.

BUT: We are happy to repair your generator free of charge. Within ten days, a factory representative will call you to schedule a convenient time to make the repair.

Your overall tone should show confidence both in the reader's honesty and in the essential worth of your own organization and its products. To the extent possible, use neutral or positive language in referring to the claim (for example, write "the situation" instead of "your complaint"). Also, avoid appearing to doubt the reader. Instead of saying "you claim that," use more neutral wording, such as "you state that."

Finally, respond promptly. Your customer is already upset; the longer this anger remains, the more difficult it will be to overcome.

Good News First

Nothing that you are likely to tell the reader will be more welcomed than the fact that you are granting the claim, so put this news up front—in the very first sentence if possible. The details and background information will come later, as illustrated by the following examples:

A new copy of the *American World Dictionary* is on its way to your office, and I assure you that no pages are missing from this copy. I checked it myself!

The enclosed check for $17.50 reimburses you for your company's delayed overnight letter. Thank you for bringing this matter to my attention.

It is often appropriate to thank the reader for giving you an opportunity to resolve the situation, but what about apologizing? An apology, which tends to emphasize the negative aspects of the situation, is generally not advised for small, routine claims that are promptly resolved to the customer's satisfaction. Instead, emphasize the positive aspects and look forward to future transactions. If the customer has been severely inconvenienced or embarrassed and the company is clearly at fault, however, a sincere apology would be in order. In such a situation, first give the good news and then apologize in a businesslike manner; avoid repeating the apology in the closing lines.

I have contracted with a local mason to rebuild your home's brick walkway, which our driver damaged on February 23. I am truly sorry for the inconvenience this situation has caused you and am grateful for your understanding.

Explanation

After presenting the "good news," you must educate your reader about why the problem occurred and, if appropriate, what steps you've taken to make sure it doesn't recur. Explain the situation in sufficient detail to be believable, but don't belabor the reason for the problem. Emphasize the fact that you stand behind your products. Use positive language, don't pass the buck, and don't hide behind a "mistakes-will-happen" attitude.

> Let me explain what happened. On December 4, the plane that had your letter in its cargo bay could not land at O'Hare Airport because of a snowstorm and was diverted to Detroit. Although our Detroit personnel worked overtime to reload the mail onto a delivery truck, which was then driven to Chicago, the shipment did not arrive until early on December 5.

Because the reader's faith in your products has been shaken, you also have a sales job to do. You must build into your letter subtle **resale**—that is, information that reestablishes the customer's confidence in the product purchased or in the company that sells the product. To be believable, do not promise that the problem will never happen again; that's unrealistic. Do use specific language, however, including facts and figures when possible.

resale Information that reestablishes a customer's confidence in the product or company.

> NOT: We can assure you that this situation will not happen again.
>
> BUT: Fortunately, such incidents are rare. For example, even considering bad weather, airline strikes, and the like, United Express has maintained an on-time delivery record of 97.6 percent during the past 12 months. No other delivery service comes even close to this record.

Positive, Forward-Looking Closing

End your letter on a positive note. Do not refer to the problem again, do not apologize again, do not suggest the possibility of future problems, and do not imply that the reader might still be upset. Instead, use strategies that imply a continuing relationship with the customer, such as including additional resale, a comment about the satisfaction the reader will receive from the repaired product or improved service, or appreciation for the reader's interest in your products.

> NOT: Again, I apologize for the delay in delivering your letter. If you experience such problems again, please don't hesitate to write.
>
> BUT: We have enjoyed serving your delivery needs for the past eight years, Ms. Clarke, and look forward to many more years of service.

Include sales promotion only if you are confident that your adjustment has restored the customer's confidence in your product or service; otherwise, it might backfire. If used, sales promotion should be subtle and should involve a new product or accessory rather than promoting a new or improved model of what the reader has already bought.

Model 6 on page 131 illustrates an adjustment letter, and Checklist 6 on page 132 summarizes the guidelines for writing routine claim and adjustment letters.

Online Study Center
Improve Your Grade
Audio Chapter Review 6.3, 6.4
Handouts

TEST PREPPER 6.3, 6.4   ANSWERS CAN BE FOUND ON P. 411

True or False?

_____ 1. If your computer broke down during the 90-day warranty period, you would probably write a routine adjustment letter.

_____ 2. You should avoid using "you" pronouns when describing the problem with the company's product.

_____ 3. "Thank you for letting us know about your problem with our product" would be an effective way to begin a routine adjustment letter.

_____ 4. In an adjustment letter, you should not promise that the problem will not recur.

_____ 5. It is not advisable to apologize for small, routine claims.

Vocabulary

Define the following terms in your own words.

6. Adjustment letter
7. Claim letter
8. Resale

Critical Thinking

9. Some consumer advocates recommend addressing your claim letter directly to the company president instead of to the customer service manager. Do you agree or disagree? Why?

Online Study Center
ACE the Test
ACE Practice Tests 6.3, 6.4

Online Study Center
Improve Your Grade
Audio Chapter Quiz 6.3, 6.4
PowerPoint Review 6.3, 6.4

MODEL 6

Routine Adjustment Letter

This adjustment letter responds to the claim letter in Model 5 on page 126.

Tells immediately that the adjustment is being made; thanks the reader.

Explains briefly, but specifically, what happened.

Looks forward to a continuing relationship with the customer; does not mention the problem again.

Sir Speedy, Inc.

April 22, 20—

① Ms. Claire D. Scriven
Marketing Manager
Otis Candy Company
Box 302
Eden, NC 27932

Dear Ms. Scriven:

② Subject: Cancellation of Invoice 4073

Sir Speedy is, of course, happy to cancel the $438.75 charge for Invoice 4073. I appreciate your taking the time to write and send us a sample hand-out.

③ Upon receiving your letter, I immediately sent your handout to our quality-control personnel for closer examination. They agreed that the handouts should have been redone before they left our facilities. We have now revised our procedures to ensure that before each order is shipped, it is inspected by someone other than the person preparing it.

To better serve the media needs of our corporate customers, we are installing the Xerox DocuCenter 480 copier, the most sophisticated industrial color copier system available. Thus, when you send us your next order, you'll see that your handouts are of even higher quality than those in the *Business Management* advertisement that impressed you.

Sincerely yours,

David Foster

David Foster
Customer Relations

CORPORATE OFFICES
26772 Plaza Drive
P.O. Box 9077
Mission Viejo, CA 92690-9077
Tel: (949) 348-5000
Fax: (949) 348-5010
www.sirspeedy.com

Grammar and Mechanics Notes

1. Type the position title either on the same line as the person's name or, as here, on a line by itself.
2. *Invoice 4073:* Capitalize a noun that precedes a number.
3. *personnel:* Do not confuse *personnel* (employees) with *personal* (private).

CHECKLIST 5

Routine Requests and Replies

Routine Requests

✓ Present the major request in the first sentence or two, preceded or followed by reasons for making the request.

✓ Provide any needed explanation or details.

✓ Phrase each question so that it is clear, is easy to answer, and covers only one topic. Ask as few questions as possible, but if several questions are necessary, number them and arrange them in logical order.

✓ If appropriate, incorporate reader benefits and promise confidentiality.

✓ Close on a friendly note by expressing appreciation, justifying any necessary deadlines, offering to reciprocate, or otherwise making your ending personal and original.

Routine Replies

✓ Answer promptly and graciously.

✓ Grant the request or begin giving the requested information in the first sentence or two.

✓ Address all questions asked or implied; include additional information or suggestions if either or both would be helpful.

✓ Include subtle sales promotion if appropriate.

✓ Refer to any items you enclose with the letter, and insert an enclosure notation at the bottom.

✓ Close on a positive and friendly note, and use original wording.

CHECKLIST 6

Routine Claim and Adjustment Letters

Routine Claim Letters

✓ Write your claim letter promptly—as soon as you've identified a problem. Try to determine the name of the appropriate individual to whom to write; if that determination is not possible, address your letter to the customer relations department.

✓ Strive for an overall tone of courtesy and confidence; avoid anger, sarcasm, threats, and exaggeration. If true and relevant, mention something positive about the company or its products somewhere in the letter.

✓ Begin the letter directly, identifying the problem immediately.

✓ Provide as much detail as necessary. Using impersonal language, tell specifically what went wrong and how you were inconvenienced.

✓ If appropriate, tell what type of adjustment you expect—replacement, repair, refund, or apology. End on a confident note.

Routine Adjustment Letters

✓ Respond promptly; your customer is already upset.

✓ Begin the letter directly, telling the reader immediately what adjustment is being made.

✓ Adopt a courteous tone. Use neutral or positive language throughout.

- ✓ If appropriate, somewhere in the letter thank the reader for writing, and apologize if the customer has been severely inconvenienced or embarrassed because of your company's actions.

- ✓ In a forthright manner, explain the reason for the problem in sufficient detail to be believable, but don't belabor the point. If appropriate, briefly tell what steps you've taken to prevent a recurrence of the problem.

- ✓ Provide information that reestablishes your customer's confidence in the product or your company. Be specific enough to be believable.

- ✓ If the customer was at fault, explain in impersonal and tactful language the facts surrounding the case.

- ✓ Close on a positive note. Include additional resale, subtle sales promotion, appreciation for the reader's interest in your products, or some other strategy that implies customer satisfaction and the expectation of a continuing relationship.

SPOTLIGHT

When in Rome . . .

The direct organizational style is suggested for routine messages. This style can be summarized in five words: *Present the major idea immediately.* American business executives have little time and patience for needless formalities and "beating around the bush."

Such is not always the case, however, when writing to someone whose culture and experiences are quite different from your own. Businesspeople in some countries may find letters written in the direct style too harsh and abrupt, lacking in courtesy. You should therefore adapt your writing style to the expectations of the reader.

For example, an American manufacturer sent a form sales letter to many domestic and foreign retail stores inviting inquiries about stocking its line of fishing tackle. Note the differences in two of the responses the manufacturer received, shown below.

The moral is simple. Write as your receiver expects you to write. Take a cue from his or her writing. If the letters you receive from an international associate are written in a direct style, you may safely respond in a similar style. However, if the letters you receive are similar to the Chinese response below, you might try a more formal, less direct style when responding. Although you would not want to *adopt* the reader's style, you might need to *adapt* your own style on the basis of your analysis of the audience.

American Response

Would you please send me a sample of the fishing tackle you advertised in your October 3 letter, along with price and shipping information. As a long-time retailer of fishing tackle, I would be especially interested in any items you might have for fly fishing.

Since the trout season starts in six weeks, I would appreciate having this information as soon as possible.

Chinese Response

It was with great pleasure that we received your letter dated 3 October. We send our deepest respects and wish to inform you that Yoon Sung Fishing Tackle Company, Ltd., has been selling fishing items for 38 years.

We would be pleased to consider your merchandise. May we ask you to please send us samples, price, and shipping information. It will be a great pleasure to conduct business with your company.

THREE Ps
PROBLEM, PROCESS, PRODUCT

A Routine Message

Problem

As the owner of Parker Central, a small plumbing business, you try to instill in all your employees a *customer-first* attitude. Therefore, you were quite put off by your own treatment yesterday (July 13) at the hands of the receptionist at Englehard Investment Service (231 East 50th Street, Indianapolis, IN 46205). You showed up 20 minutes early for your 2:30 p.m. appointment with Jack Nutley, an investment counselor with the firm. You were meeting with him for the first time to discuss setting up a simplified employee pension (SEP) plan for your 20 employees.

To begin with, the receptionist ignored you for at least five minutes until she finished the last paragraph of a document she was typing. Then, after finding out whom you wanted to see, she did not even call Jack's office to announce your arrival until 2:30 p.m. Finally, you learned that Jack had just become ill and had to go to the doctor. So you wasted half an afternoon and were also insulted by the receptionist's rude treatment.

You decide to write to Jack Nutley about the receptionist's office behavior. Your *claim* is for better service in the future. You want him to know that if his organization continues to treat you in such a manner, you will have no interest in doing business with his firm. Write the claim letter.

Process

1. What is the purpose of your letter?

    To ensure that you will not receive rude treatment on future visits to this office.

2. Describe your audience.

    - A potential supplier
    - Well qualified (or you wouldn't have selected him)
    - A professional used to dealing with the public and maintaining good public relations

3. List in the appropriate order the topics you will discuss.

    - Gently introduce the problem.
    - In nonemotional language, provide specific details of what happened.
    - Tell what you expect the company to do.

4. Write the opening sentence of your letter.

    In your work as an investment counselor, you work with people daily and want your employees to treat clients courteously.

5. Using confident and polite language, write your closing paragraph in which you tell what you want to happen.

> I was offended by your receptionist's rudeness. My time is important, and I shall expect better treatment in the future if I am going to use your investment service to establish my company's pension plan.

Product

July 14, 20—

Mr. Jack Nutley
Investment Counselor
Englehard Investment Service
231 East 50th Street
Indianapolis, IN 46205

Dear Mr. Nutley:

As an investment counselor, you work with people daily, and I know that you want your employees to treat clients well. Therefore, I believe you will be interested in my encounter with a receptionist in your office yesterday.

As you will recall, I had an appointment scheduled with you at 2:30 p.m. on July 13 to discuss setting up a pension plan for my employees. I arrived 20 minutes early, but the receptionist did not acknowledge my presence for at least 5 minutes while she finished typing a document. In fact, she did not call your office until 2:30 p.m. to announce my arrival. At that time, she informed me that you had taken ill and had left for an appointment with your doctor. I ended up wasting half the afternoon.

The name on the receptionist's nameplate was Linda Evans. I was offended by her rudeness. My time is very important, and I shall expect better treatment in the future if I am going to use your investment service to establish my company's pension plan.

Sincerely,

Robert Maston

Robert Maston, Owner

PORTFOLIO PROJECT 2

Writing a Routine Adjustment Letter

Problem

You are Kathryn Smith, a correspondent in the customer service department of Branford's Department Store. This morning (May 25, 20—), you received the following letter from Mrs. Henrietta Daniels, an angry customer:

> Dear Customer Service Manager:
>
> I am really upset at the poor-quality shades that you sell. Two months ago I purchased two pairs of your pleated fabric shades in Wedgwood Blue at $35.99 each for my two bathroom windows. A copy of my $74.32 bill is enclosed.
>
> The color has already begun to fade from these shades. I couldn't believe it when I checked and found that they now look tie-dyed! That is not the look I wish for my home.
>
> Since these shades did not provide the type of wear that I paid for, please refund my $74.32.
>
> Sincerely,
>
> Mrs. Henrietta Daniels

You take Mrs. Daniels' itemized bill down to the sales floor and find the model of shades she purchased. You conclude that Mrs. Daniels' home must have large bathroom windows because the only size this particular shade comes in is 64 inches long by 32 inches wide. Printed right on the tag attached to the shade is this caution: "Warning: The imported fabric in this shade makes it unsuitable for use in areas of high humidity." Clearly, these shades were not made for bathroom use. You call up Mrs. Daniels' account on your computer and find that she has been a loyal customer for many years. You decide, therefore, to refund her $74.32, even though she misused the product. Write the adjustment letter (Mrs. Henrietta Daniels, 117 Pine Forest Drive, Atlanta, GA 30345).

Process

Compose a few paragraphs describing how you solved this problem. In narrative form, provide information such as the following:

1. What is the purpose of your letter?
2. Describe your audience.
3. Will you use a direct or an indirect organizational plan?
4. How will you convey the information that Mrs. Daniels misused the product?

5. How can you promote your cotton and polyester bathroom curtains (which are appropriate for high-moisture environments)?
6. What is the purpose of your closing sentence?

Product

Compose your document and follow the steps of the writing process (audience analysis, planning, drafting, revising, formatting, and proofreading). Format the final version on letterhead stationery (refer to the Style Manual at the back of the book for formatting guidelines).

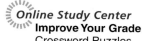

Online Study Center
Improve Your Grade
Crossword Puzzles
Flashcards
LAB Tests

LEARNING OBJECTIVE REVIEW

1 *Compose a routine request.*

- A request is routine if you anticipate that the reader will readily do as you ask without having to be persuaded.
- When making a routine request:
  - Present the major idea first.
  - Provide the necessary explanation and details.
  - End with a friendly closing statement.

2 *Compose a routine reply.*

- Routine replies provide the information requested in the original message or otherwise comply with the writer's request.
- When writing routine replies:
  - Answer promptly.
  - Use a courteous tone.
  - Grant the request early in the message.
  - Answer all the questions asked or implied.
  - Refer to any enclosure and then add an enclosure notation at the bottom of the letter.
  - End with a positive closing statement.

3 *Compose a routine claim letter.*

- A claim letter is routine if you can reasonably anticipate that the reader will comply with your request.
- When writing a routine claim letter:
  - Be courteous and avoid emotional language.
  - Begin by stating the problem.
  - Provide the necessary background and explanation.
  - Explain what went wrong and how you were inconvenienced.
  - State the adjustment you expect.

4 *Compose a routine adjustment letter.*

- A routine adjustment letter is written to inform a customer of the action taken in response to the customer's claim letter.
- When writing a routine adjustment letter:
  - Maintain a respectful, trusting tone.
  - Tell the reader you are granting the claim up front.
  - Provide details that will help the reader understand why the problem occurred.
  - Close with a positive statement that emphasizes a continuing relationship.

EXERCISES

1. Routine Request—Product Information (▶6.1)

Luis St. Jean (LSJ) is a famous design house in France with annual sales of $1.2 billion in clothing, perfume, scarves, and other designer items. Each year it prepares more than 150 original designs for its seasonal collections. As head buyer for Cindy's, an upscale women's clothing store at Mall of America in Minneapolis, you think you might like to begin offering LSJ's line of perfume. You need to know more about pricing, types of perfume offered, minimum ordering quantities, marketing assistance provided by LSJ, and the like. You'd also like to know if you can have exclusive marketing rights to LSJ perfumes in the Minneapolis area and whether you would have to carry LSJ's complete line (you don't think the most expensive perfumes would be big sellers). Write to Mr. Henri Vixier, License Supervisor, Luis St. Jean, 90513 Cergy, Pointoise Cedex, France, seeking answers to your questions.

2. Routine Response—Comedian on Board (▶6.2)

You are the director of entertainment for a cruise ship, the *Sea Princess*. You are always looking for new acts to book on your cruises. Yesterday, you received a letter from Barbara Greensburg, manager of Houston Entertainment, Inc., who requested that you book one of her clients, Herman Thayer.

Herman is a young comedian from Houston, Texas, who has appeared in local comedy clubs in Houston and the surrounding area. He has received great reviews for these shows. Herman also recently finished a college campus tour that, according to Barbara, was very successful.

Barbara is now trying to get Herman a "gig" for a few weeks in May. You have made a few calls to promoters in Houston and found that Herman is very good. You would like to meet with him and Barbara to discuss the possibility of having him perform on some of your cruises.

Write a letter to Barbara inviting her and Herman to come to Mobile, Alabama, on March 15 for a visit. If things work out, you have two cruises that you could book him on during the month of May. Barbara's address is P.O. Box 4790, Houston, TX 77590.

3. Work-Team Communication—Routine Response (▶6.2)

You are a member of the Presidents' Council, an organization made up of the presidents of each stu-

dent organization on campus. You just received a memorandum from Dr. Robin H. Hill, dean of students, wanting to know the types of social projects in which the student organizations on campus have been engaged during the past year. The dean must report to the board of trustees on the important role played by student organizations—both in the life of the university and community and in the development of student leadership and social skills. She wants to include information on topics such as student-run programs on drug and alcohol abuse, community service, and fund-raising.

Working in groups of four, identify and summarize the types of social projects that student organizations at your institution have completed this year. Then organize and synthesize your findings in a one-page memo to Dr. Hill. After writing your first draft, have each member review and comment on the draft. Then revise as needed and submit it to your instructor. Use only factual data for this assignment.

4. Claim Letter—Inaccurate Reporting (▶6.3)

As the assistant marketing manager for ReSolve, a basic computer spreadsheet program for Windows, you were pleased that your product was reviewed in the current issue of *Computing Trends*. The review praised your product for its "lightning-fast speed and convenient user interface." You were not pleased, however, that your product was downgraded because it lacked high-level graphics capability. The reviewer compared ReSolve with full-featured spreadsheet programs costing, on average, $200 more than your program. No wonder, then, that your program rated a 6.6 out of 10, coming in third out of the five programs reviewed. If it had been compared with similar low-level programs, you feel certain that ReSolve would have easily come out on top.

Although you do not want to get the magazine upset with your company (Software Entrepreneurs, Inc.), you do feel that it should compare apples with apples and should conduct another review of your program. Write to Roberta J. Horton, the magazine's review editor, at 200 Public Square in Cleveland, OH 44114, and tell her so.

5. Routine Claim—Defective Product (▶6.3)

You are J. R. McCord, purchasing agent for People's Energy Company. On February 3, you ordered a box of four laser cartridges for your Sampson Model 25 printers at $69.35 each, plus $6.85 shipping and handling—for a total price of $284.25. The catalog description for this cartridge (Part No. 02-8R01656) stated, "Fits Epson and Xerox printers and most compatibles." Because the Sampson is advertised as a Xerox clone printer, you assumed the cartridges would work with it. When the order arrived, you discovered that the cartridges didn't fit your Sampson printer. Although the cartridges are the same shape, the new cartridges are about ¼ inch thicker and won't sit properly on the spindles.

You believe that your supplier's misleading advertising caused you to order the wrong model cartridge. You'd like the company to either refund the $284.25 you paid on its Invoice 95-076 or replace the cartridges with ones that do work with your printers. You'll be happy to return all four cartridges if the company will give you instructions for doing so. Write your letter to the Customer Service Department of Nationwide Office Supply, located at 2610 Kerper Boulevard in Dubuque, IA 52001.

6. Adjustment Letter—Company at Fault (▶ 6.4)

Assume the role of customer service representative at Nationwide Office Supply (see Exercise 5). You've received J. R. McCord's letter (People's Energy Company, Wheatley Road, Old Westbury, NY 11568). You've done some background investigation and have learned that what the customer said is true— the Sampson Model 25 *is* a Xerox clone and your catalog does state that this cartridge fits Xerox printers and most compatibles. The problem arose because the Model 25, Sampson's newest printer, was intro-

duced shortly after your catalog went to press. This model's spindle is slightly shorter than those of previous Sampson models.

You do not carry in your inventory a cartridge that fits the Sampson Model 25. The customer should return the cartridges cash on delivery (COD), marking on the address label "Return Authorization 95-076R." In the meantime, you've authorized a refund of $284.25; J. R. McCord should receive the check within ten days. Convey this information to J. R. McCord.

7. Adjustment Letter—Customer at Fault (▶ 6.4)

Assume the role of customer service representative at Nationwide Office Supply (see Exercise 5). You've done some background investigation and have learned that J. R. McCord was somewhat mistaken in stating that the Sampson Model 25 is a Xerox clone. Sampson advertises that the Model 25 uses the same character set as Xerox printers, which means that all fonts available from Xerox can also be downloaded to the Model 25. The company neither states nor implies that Xerox-compatible cartridges or other supplies fit its machines.

Because the customer made an innocent mistake and you will be able to resell the unused cartridges, you decide to honor the claim anyway. The customer should return the cartridges prepaid, marking on the address label "Return Authorization 95-076R." In the meantime, you're shipping the customer four cartridges (Part No. 02-9R32732) that *will* work on the Model 25; the customer can expect to receive them within ten days. You're also enclosing your summer catalog.

Additional exercises are available at the Online Study Center website: **college.hmco.com/pic/oberSASfund**.

Online Study Center RESOURCES

Prepare for Class, Improve Your Grade, and ACE the Test. Student Achievement Series resources include:

ACE Practice Tests	Ask Ober	Audio Chapter Reviews and Quizzes
Chapter Outlines	Communication Objectives	Crossword Puzzles
Flashcards	Glossaries	Handouts
LAB Tests	Portfolio Project Stationery	Sample Reports

To access these learning and study tools, go to **college.hmco.com/pic/oberSASfund**.

7 Persuasive Letters, Memos, and E-Mail Messages

As any sales representative knows, making the sale is about not only promoting the benefits of a product or service, but also anticipating a client's needs, questions, and objections, and turning them around in a positive way. Wurzburg, Inc., an industrial packaging distributor, emphasizes its 100 years of experience to demonstrate to clients that the company is knowledgeable and honorable.

1 ▶ *Compose a persuasive message promoting an idea.*

2 ▶ *Compose a persuasive message requesting a favor.*

3 ▶ *Compose a persuasive claim.*

Online Study Center
Prepare for Class
Chapter Outline

4 ▶ *Compose a sales letter.*

Persuasive Messages in an Industrial-Strength Package

As a sales representative for industrial packaging distributor Wurzburg, Inc., Patrick Vijiarungam can provide everything that a manufacturer needs to pack items so shipments arrive at their destinations safely. "When I write a persuasive letter," he says, "I use both emotional and logical appeals." The audience for his persuasive messages includes purchasing agents, project engineers, and plant managers.

After an initial telephone call to discuss the client's general needs, Vijiarungam uses the opening of his follow-up sales letter to show appreciation for the reader's time and interest. Next, he addresses the reader's problem and suggests how the company can solve it.

Using a logical appeal, Vijiarungam touches on specific product benefits. "Wurzburg has been in business for almost a

Online Study Center college.hmco.com/pic/oberSASfund

PATRICK VIJIARUNGAM
Sales Representative,
Wurzburg, Inc.
(Memphis, Tennessee)

KEY TERMS

central selling theme   *p. 155*
rhetorical question   *p. 145*

hundred years," he says. "Our reputation as a knowledgeable and honorable company is a key selling point." He sees objections—to pricing, for example—as opportunities "to turn the situation around and come out a hero to the customer." To motivate action, he closes by mentioning a possible schedule or offering his company's technical expertise for other problems. ■

PLANNING THE PERSUASIVE MESSAGE

 Compose a persuasive message promoting an idea.

Persuasion is the process of motivating someone to take a specific action or to support a particular idea. Persuasion motivates someone to believe something or to do something that he or she would not otherwise have done. Every day many people try to persuade you to do certain things or to believe certain ideas. Likewise, you have many opportunities to persuade others each day.

As a businessperson, you will also need to persuade others to do as you want. You may need to persuade a superior to adopt a certain proposal, a supplier to refund the purchase price of a defective product, or a potential customer to buy your product or service. In a sense, *all* business communication involves persuasion. Even if your primary purpose is to inform, you still want your reader to accept your perspective and to believe the information you present.

The essence of persuasion is overcoming initial resistance. The reader may resist your efforts for any number of reasons. Your proposal may require the reader to spend time or money—at the very least, you're asking the reader to make the effort to *read* your message. Or perhaps the reader has had bad experiences in the past with similar requests or holds opinions that predispose him or her against your request.

Your job in writing a persuasive message, then, is to talk your readers into something, to convince them that your point of view is appropriate. You'll have the best chance of succeeding if you tailor your message to your audience, provide your readers with reasons they will find convincing, and anticipate and deflect or disarm their objections. Such tailor-made writing requires careful planning; you need to define your purpose clearly and analyze your audience thoroughly.

Purpose

The purpose of a persuasive message is to motivate the reader to agree with you or to do as you ask. Unless you are clear about the specific results you wish to achieve, you won't be able to plan an effective strategy that will achieve your goals.

Suppose, for example, you want to convince your boss to adopt a complex proposal. The purpose of your memo might be to persuade your superior to either:

▮ Adopt your proposal,

▮ Approve a pilot test of your proposal, or

▮ Schedule a meeting where you can present your proposal in person and answer any questions.

Achieving any one of these three goals may require a different strategy. Knowing your purpose lets you know what kind of information to include in your persuasive message. "Knowledge is power," and never is this saying truer than when you write persuasive messages. To write effectively about an idea or product, you must know the idea or product intimately. If you're promoting an idea, consider all of the ramifications of your proposal.

▌ Are there competing proposals that should be considered?

▌ What are the implications for the organization (and for you) if your proposal is adopted and it *fails*?

▌ How does your proposal fit in with the organization's existing plans and direction?

Audience Analysis

The more you can promote the features of your idea or product as satisfying a *specific* need of your audience, the more persuasive your message will be. Suppose, for example, you're promoting a line of men's shoes; you should stress different features, depending on your audience.

Young executive:	stylish . . . comes in various shades of black and brown . . . a perfect accessory to your business wardrobe
Mid-career executive:	perfect detailing . . . 12-hour comfort . . . stays sharp-looking through days of travel
Retired executive:	economical . . . comfortable . . . a no-nonsense type of shoe

The point to remember is to know your audience and to personalize your message to best meet its needs and interests. Stress the "you" attitude to achieve the results you want.

Knowledge and Attitude of the Reader

What does the reader already know about the topic? Determining this level of understanding will tell you how much background information you should include. What is the reader's predisposition toward the topic? If it is negative, then where one or two reasons might ordinarily suffice, you will need to give more justifications. Initial resistance also calls for more objective, verifiable evidence than if the reader were initially neutral. You also need to learn *why* the reader is resistant so that you can tailor your arguments to overcome those specific objections.

Effect on the Reader

How will your proposal affect the reader? If the reader is being asked to commit resources (time or money), discuss the rewards for doing as you ask. If the reader is being asked to endorse some proposal, provide enough specific information to enable the reader to make an informed decision. The reader wants to know "What's in it for me?" *You* are already convinced of the wisdom of your proposal. Your job is to let the reader know the benefits of doing as you ask.

To be persuasive, you must present *specific, believable* evidence. One of the worst mistakes you can make, however, would be simply to describe the

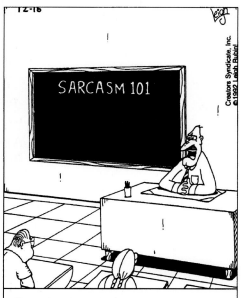

"I can't tell you what a pleasure and a privilege it is to teach such a bright-looking group of individuals."

By permission of Leigh Rubin and Creators Syndicate, Inc.

features of the product or list the advantages of doing as you ask. Instead, put yourself in the reader's place. Discuss how the reader will benefit from your proposal. Emphasize the *reader* rather than the product or idea you're promoting.

> NOT: The San Diego Accounting Society would like you to speak to us on the topic of expensing versus capitalizing 401-C assets.

> BUT: Speaking to the San Diego Accounting Society would enable you to present your firm's views on the controversial topic of expensing versus capitalizing 401-C assets.

Sometimes your readers won't benefit *directly* from doing as you ask. If you are trying to entice your employees to contribute to the United Way, for example, it would be difficult to discuss direct reader benefits. In such situations, discuss the *indirect* benefits of reader participation; for example, show how someone other than you, the solicitor of the funds, will benefit.

> Your contribution will enable inner-city youngsters, many of whom have never even been outside the city of Columbus, to see pandas living and thriving in their natural habitat.

Writer Credibility

What is your credibility with the reader? The more trustworthy you are, the more trustworthy your message will appear. Credibility comes from many sources. You may be perceived as being credible by virtue of the position you hold or by virtue of being a well-known authority. Or you may achieve credibility for your proposal by supplying convincing evidence, such as facts and statistics that can be verified.

Suppose, for example, you have worked in an advertising production department and have extensive experience with color reproduction. If you are writing a memo to a colleague suggesting that certain photos will not reproduce clearly and should therefore be replaced, you probably don't need to explain your expertise. Your colleague is likely to believe you. On the other hand, if you are writing a letter to the photographer, who does not know you, you would probably want to discuss past incidents that lead you to conclude the photos should be replaced.

ORGANIZING A PERSUASIVE REQUEST

A persuasive request seeks to motivate the reader to accept your idea (rather than to buy your product). The purpose of your message and your knowledge of the reader help to determine the content of your message and the sequence in which you discuss each topic.

Determining How to Start the Message

In the past, it was common practice to organize *all* persuasive messages by using an indirect organizational plan—presenting the rationale first, followed by the major idea (the request for action). Many persuasive messages continue to follow this format. Nevertheless, writers today should determine which organizational plan (direct or indirect) will help them better achieve their objectives.

Direct Plan—Present the Major Idea First

Most superiors prefer to have messages from their subordinates organized in the direct style, which was introduced in Chapter 6. Thus, when writing persuasive memos that travel up the organization, you should generally present the main idea (your recommendation) first, followed by the supporting evidence. The direct organizational plan saves time and immediately satisfies the reader's curiosity about your purpose. To get readers to accept your proposal when using the direct plan, present your recommendation along with the criteria or brief rationale in the first paragraph.

> NOT: I recommend we hold our Pittsburgh sales meeting at the Mark-Congress Hotel.

> BUT: I have evaluated three hotels as possible meeting sites for our Pittsburgh sales conference and recommend we meet at the Mark-Congress Hotel. As discussed below, the Mark-Congress is centrally located, has the best meeting facilities, and is moderately priced.

In general, choose the direct organizational plan for persuasive messages when any of the following conditions apply:

▍ You are writing to superiors within the organization.

▍ Your audience is predisposed to listen objectively to your request.

▍ The proposal does not require strong persuasion (that is, no major obstacles to it exist).

▍ The proposal is long or complex. (Your reader may become impatient if you bury your main point in a long report.)

▍ You know that your reader prefers the direct approach.

Indirect Plan—Gain the Reader's Attention First

Your job is to explain the merits of your proposal and show how the reader will benefit from doing as you ask. Because a reluctant reader is more likely to agree to an idea *after* he or she understands its merits, your plan of organization is to convince the reader before asking for action.

You should use the indirect organizational plan when:

▍ Writing to subordinates.

▍ Strong persuasion is needed.

▍ You know that your reader prefers the indirect plan.

When using the indirect plan, delay asking for action until after you've presented your reasons. A subject line that does not disclose your recommendation should be used in persuasive letters. Don't announce your purpose immediately, but rather lead up to it gradually.

> NOT: SUBJECT: Proposal to Purchase Color Copier *(Too direct)*
> NOT: SUBJECT: Proposal *(Too general)*
> BUT: SUBJECT: Analysis of Color-Copy Needs

The first test of a good opening sentence in a persuasive request is whether it is interesting enough to catch and keep the reader's attention. It won't matter how much evidence you have marshaled to support your case if the recipient does not bother to continue reading carefully after the first sentence.

A **rhetorical question** often proves effective as an opening sentence. A rhetorical question is asked strictly to get the reader thinking about the topic of your message; a literal answer is not expected. Of course, questions with obvious answers

rhetorical question   A question asked to encourage the reader to think about the topic; a literal answer is not expected.

are not effective motivators for further reading and, in fact, may insult the reader's intelligence. Similarly, yes-or-no questions rarely make good lead-ins because forming an answer doesn't require much thought.

> What is black and white and red (read) all over? Very few things, as a matter of fact!

Sometimes an unusual fact or unexpected statement will draw the reader into the message. At other times, you might want to select a statement about which the reader and writer will agree—to immediately establish some common ground.

> A study conducted by IBM showed that participants remembered almost twice as much of the information presented on color slides as on black-and-white slides.

> Almost 95 percent of the participants at our four seminars last month gave us an overall rating of "Outstanding."

Your opening statement must also relate to the purpose of your message. If it is too far off the topic or misleads the reader, you risk losing goodwill, and the reader may simply stop reading. At the very least, the reader will feel confused or deceived, making persuasion more difficult.

Keep your opening statement short. Often an opening paragraph of just one sentence makes the message inviting to read. Few readers have the patience to wade through a long introduction to figure out the purpose of the message. In summary, make the opening for a persuasive message written in the indirect organizational plan interesting, relevant, and short. The purpose is to make sure your reader is drawn into the body of your message.

Creating Interest and Justifying Your Request

Regardless of whether you write your opening in a direct or indirect style, you must now begin the process of convincing the reader that your request is reasonable. This effort may require several paragraphs of discussion, depending on how much evidence you think is needed to convince the reader. Because it takes more space to state *why* something should be done than simply to state *that* it should be done, persuasive requests are typically longer than other types of messages.

To convince your reader, you must be objective, specific, logical, and reasonable. Avoid emotionalism, obvious flattery, insincerity, and exaggeration. Let your evidence carry the weight of your argument.

> NOT: Locating our plant in Suffolk instead of in Norfolk would result in considerable savings.

> BUT: Locating our plant in Suffolk instead of in Norfolk would result in annual savings of nearly $175,000, as shown in Table 3.

The type of evidence you present depends, of course, on the circumstances. The usual types of evidence are the following:

▮ *Facts and statistics:* Facts are objective statements whose truth can be verified; statistics are facts consisting of numbers. Both must be relevant and accurate. For example, statistics that were accurate five years ago may no longer hold true today. But avoid overwhelming the reader with statistical data. Instead, highlight a few key statistics—for emphasis.

> The Lexcraft prints a one-page, four-color handout in 30 seconds at a cost of 28 cents.

▌ *Expert opinion:* Testimony from authorities on the topic might be presented if their input is relevant and, if necessary, you can supply the experts' credentials. Expert opinion is especially persuasive to readers who don't recognize you as an authority on the subject.

> The Lexcraft rated a "Best-Buy" award in the February issue of *Personal Computing.*

▌ *Examples:* Specific cases or incidents used to illustrate the point under discussion should be relevant, representative, and complete.

> We spent $147.50 to have Imagemaster print the 250 handouts we used in last month's purchasing managers' seminar. We could have printed them on the Lexcraft for less than $80—with same-day service.

Present the benefits (either direct or indirect) that accompany the adoption of your proposal, and provide enough background and objective evidence to enable the reader to make an informed decision.

Dealing With Obstacles

Ignoring any obvious obstacles to granting your request provides the reader with a ready excuse to refuse your request. Instead, your strategy should be to show that even considering such an obstacle, your request is still reasonable. Such a strategy is used in the following example:

> Although the vice president has asked for a moratorium on equipment expenditures until June, if we purchase the $750 Lexcraft printer before December 31, we'll actually save that amount in printing costs by April—before our quarterly budget is due.

If you're asking someone to speak to a professional organization but cannot provide an honorarium, emphasize the free publicity the speaker will receive and the impact that the speaker's remarks will have on the audience. If you're asking for confidential information, discuss how you will treat it as such. If you're asking for a large donation, explain how payment can be made on the installment plan or by payroll deduction and point out the tax-deductible feature of the donation.

Even though you must address the major obstacles, do *not* emphasize them. Subordinate this discussion by devoting relatively little space to it, by dealing with obstacles in the same sentence that you highlight a reader benefit, or by putting the discussion in the middle of a paragraph. Regardless of how you do it, show the reader that you're aware of the obvious obstacles and that despite them, your proposal still has merit.

Motivating Action

Although your request has been stated (direct organizational plan) or implied (indirect organizational plan) earlier, give a direct statement of the request late in the message—after most of the background information and reader benefits have been covered thoroughly. Make the specific action that you want clear and easy to take. For example, if the reader agrees to do as you ask, how should he or she let you know? Will a phone call suffice, or is a written reply necessary? If a phone call is adequate, have you provided a phone number? If you're asking for a favor that requires a written response, have you included a stamped, self-addressed envelope?

Ask for the desired action in a confident tone. If your request or proposal is reasonable, there is no need to apologize. And, of course, you do not want to

CONCEPT CHECK 7.1

Assume that you want to convince your fellow employees to volunteer one weekend (all day Saturday and Sunday) to help on a Habitat for Humanity construction project.

a. Would you use a direct or indirect plan of organization?

b. Construct an appropriate subject line for your e-mail message.

c. Construct an effective opening attention-getter.

d. Construct an effective closing sentence.

supply the reader with excuses for refusing. Take whatever steps you can to ensure a prompt reply.

> So that we can have this copier installed in time for us to use it at our January sales meeting, may I order this copier for $750 by December 1? The ability to update our handouts right up to an hour before our presentation will mean that our figures are always the latest available.

Checklist 7 on page 160 summarizes guidelines to use in writing persuasive requests. Although you will not be able to employ all of these suggestions in every persuasive request, you should consider them as an overall framework for structuring your persuasive message.

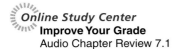
Online Study Center
Improve Your Grade
Audio Chapter Review 7.1

TEST PREPPER 7.1   ANSWERS CAN BE FOUND ON P. 411

True or False?

_____ 1. Most persuasive messages to your superior should be written in the direct organizational style.

_____ 2. Even when making your recommendation directly, you should also include your criteria or a brief rationale in the first paragraph.

_____ 3. To help you achieve your objective, it is often desirable to ignore major obstacles in your persuasive letter.

_____ 4. In a persuasive letter written in the indirect style, the actual request should come early in the letter.

Vocabulary

Define the following term in your own words and give an original example.

5. Rhetorical question

Critical Thinking

6. See Concept Check 7.1 on page 147. In the body of your message, how much space should you devote to explaining what Habitat for Humanity is and how it helps others? What should you stress in your message?

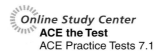
Online Study Center
ACE the Test
ACE Practice Tests 7.1

Online Study Center
Improve Your Grade
Audio Chapter Quiz 7.1
PowerPoint Review 7.1

COMMON TYPES OF PERSUASIVE REQUESTS

In many ways, writing a persuasive request is more difficult than writing a sales letter because reader benefits are not always so obvious in persuasive requests. This section provides specific strategies and examples for selling an idea, requesting a favor, and writing a persuasive claim letter.

Selling an Idea

You will have many opportunities to use your education and experience to help solve problems faced by your organization. On the job, you will frequently write messages proposing one alternative over another, suggesting a new procedure, or in some other way recommending a course of action. Organize such messages logically, showing what the problem is, how you intend to solve the problem, and why your solution is sound. Write in an objective style and provide evidence to support your claims. The memo in Model 7 on page 149 illustrates the selling of an idea.

MODEL 7

Persuasive Request— Selling an Idea

This persuasive memo uses the direct plan because the memo travels up the organization.

NEWTON
Electrical
Systems

1034 York Road
Baltimore, MD 21204
Phone: 301.555.1086
Fax: 301.555.3926
www.nes.com

Serving the automotive industry for more than 50 years

① **MEMO TO:**   Elliott Lamborn, Vice President

   FROM: Jenson J. Peterson, Marketing Supervisor *JJP*

   DATE: April 3, 20—

   SUBJECT: Proposal to Reassign Employee Parking Lots

Begins by introducing the recommendation, along with a brief rationale.

As one way of showing our support for the Ford Motor Company, which accounts for nearly half of our annual sales, I propose that the close-in employee parking lots around our headquarters be restricted to use by owners of Ford vehicles.

Provides a smooth transition to the necessary background information. Cites statistics and external testimony for credibility.

② During their frequent visits to our headquarters, Ford personnel must pass the employee parking lot. When they do, they will see that approximately 70 percent of our employees drive vehicles manufactured by competitors of Ford. In fact, a Ford purchasing agent asked me last week, "How can you expect us to support you if you don't support us?"

Repeats the recommendation after presenting most of the rationale.

The purpose of this memo, then, is to seek approval to have our close-in employee parking lot restricted to use by Ford vehicles. The maintenance department estimates that it will need four weeks and about $500 to make the needed signs.

Neutralizes an obvious obstacle.

Our labor contract requires union approval of any changes in working conditions. However, Sally Marsh, our shop steward, has told me that she would be willing to consider this matter—especially if similar restrictions are imposed on the executive parking lot.

Closes on a positive note; motivates prompt action.

③ Since our next managers' meeting is on May 8–10, I look forward to being able to announce the new plan to them. By approving this change, Newton will be sending a powerful positive message to our visitors: Our employees believe in the products we sell.

Grammar and Mechanics Notes

1. Because of its more readable format, writers often prefer a standard memo format for persuasive messages—even when e-mail is available. Often, the memo is sent as an attachment to an e-mail message.
2. *70 percent:* Use figures and the word *percent* in business correspondence.
3. *managers' meeting:* Place the apostrophe *after* the *s* to form the possessive of a plural noun *(managers)*.

Requesting a Favor

 Compose a persuasive message requesting a favor.

A request for a favor differs from a routine request because routine requests are granted almost automatically, whereas favors require persuasion. For example, asking a colleague to trade places with you on the program for the monthly managers' meeting might be considered a routine request. Asking the same colleague to prepare and give your presentation for you would more likely be a favor and require some persuasion.

Although friends and close colleagues often do each other favors as a matter of course, many times in business the granting of a favor might not be so automatic—especially if you don't know the person to whom you're writing. In such situations, you will want to begin your request with an attention-getter and stress the reader benefits from granting the favor.

Discuss at least one reader benefit before making your request. Explain why the favor is being asked and continue to show how the reader (or at least someone other than you) will benefit from the favor. Keep a positive, confident tone throughout, and make the action clear and easy to take.

Often the favor is requested because the reader is an expert on some topic. If that is the case, you may legitimately make a complimentary remark about the reader. Make sure, however, that your compliment sounds sincere. Readers are rightfully suspicious, for example, when they read in a form letter that they have been specifically chosen to participate in some project. ("Me and how many thousands of others?" they might wonder.) On the other hand, such a compliment in a letter that is personally typed and signed has much more credibility.

The most important factor to remember in asking for a favor has to do with the favor itself rather than with the writing process: keep your request reasonable. Don't ask someone else to do something that you can or should do for yourself.

Figure 7.1 on page 152 illustrates how *not* to write an effective persuasive request. Model 8 on page 153, a revised version of the ineffective request, illustrates how to write an effective persuasive request. The reader and writer do not know each other, which makes persuasion a little more challenging and which calls for an indirect organizational plan. Reader benefits (the opportunity to promote the reader's organization and the flattering prospect of being the center of attention) are included.

Writing a Persuasive Claim

 Compose a persuasive claim.

As discussed in Chapter 6, most claim letters are routine letters and should be written using a direct plan of organization—stating the problem early in the letter. Because it is to the company's benefit to keep its clientele happy, most reasonable claims are settled to the customer's satisfaction. Therefore, persuasion is not ordinarily necessary.

Suppose, however, that you wrote a routine claim letter and the company, for some reason, denied your claim. If you still feel that your original claim is legitimate, you might then write a *persuasive* claim letter—using all the techniques discussed earlier in this chapter for writing persuasive requests. Or assume that

When the beanbag chair that you purchased split after only four months' use, you immediately called the discount store where you purchased it to ask for either a replacement or a refund of your $49.95 purchase price. The store declined, stating that it had no way of knowing if the person using the chair was heavy and reminding you that the chair was guaranteed to support only a maximum of 200 pounds. Now you're really mad and decide to write a persuasive claim letter.

a. What is the purpose of your letter?

b. Should you hint at how angry you are at the store's refusal to honor the guarantee?

c. Construct an effective opening attention-getter.

d. Construct an effective closing sentence.

your new photocopier broke three days after the warranty period expired. The company is not legally obligated to honor your claim, but you may decide to try to persuade it to do so anyway.

Showing anger in your persuasive claim letter is counterproductive, even if the company turned down your original claim. The goal of your letter is not to vent your anger but rather to solve a problem. A solution is more likely to happen when a calm atmosphere prevails.

As in a routine claim letter, you will need to explain in sufficient detail precisely what the problem is, how it came about, and how you want the reader to solve the problem. Use a calm, objective, courteous tone, avoiding anger and exaggeration. Although similar in some respects to a routine claim letter, the persuasive claim differs in two important ways: it has an attention-getting opening and it presents more evidence.

Attention-Getting Opening

Recall that you begin a routine claim letter by stating the problem. This type of opening would not be wise for a persuasive claim because the reader may conclude that the claim is unreasonable until he or she reads your rationale.

> **NOT:** Would you please repair my Minolta 203 copier without charge, even though the 12-month warranty expired last week.

> **BUT:** We took a chance and lost! We bet that the Minolta 203 we purchased from you 12 months ago would prove to be as reliable as the other ten Minoltas our firm uses.

The original opening is counterproductive, providing a ready excuse for denying the claim. The revised version holds off making the request until enough background information has been provided. Note also the personal relationship the writer is beginning to establish with the reader in the revised version—disclosing not only that the company owns ten other Minolta copiers but also that the other copiers have all been very reliable. Such an understanding tone will make the reader more likely to grant the request.

More Evidence

Because your claim either is not routine or has been rejected once, you need to present as much convincing evidence as possible. Explain fully the basis for your claim; then request a specific adjustment. Model 9 on page 154 illustrates the guidelines for writing a persuasive claim letter.

Online Study Center
Improve Your Grade
Audio Chapter Review 7.2, 7.3

TEST PREPPER 7.2, 7.3   ANSWERS CAN BE FOUND ON P. 411

True or False?

_____ 1. Regardless of whether you're using a direct or an indirect organizational plan, you should discuss at least one reader benefit before actually requesting the favor.

_____ 2. A persuasive claim letter needs an attention-getting opening, whereas a routine claim letter does not.

Critical Thinking

3. Do you think that persuasive messages that attempt to sell an idea are more frequently written to one's superiors or to one's subordinates?

Online Study Center
ACE the Test
ACE Practice Tests 7.2, 7.3

Online Study Center
Improve Your Grade
Audio Chapter Quiz 7.2, 7.3
PowerPoint Review 7.2, 7.3

Online Study Center college.hmco.com/pic/oberSASfund

FIGURE 7.1

An Ineffective Persuasive Request

Uses a subject line that is too specific.

Begins by directly asking for the favor, using "me"-attitude language.

Omits important information. (Who will be attending the conference? How many will attend? How long will the presentation be?)

Identifies the obstacle in a selfish manner— without including any reasons that minimize the obstacle.

Gives a deadline for answering—without providing any rationale.

Closes with a cliché.

January 15, 20—

Ms. Tanya Porrat, Editor
Autoimmune Diseases Monthly
1800 Ten Hills Road, Suite B
Boston, MA 02145

Dear Ms. Porrat

Subject: Request for You to Speak at the Multiple Sclerosis Congress

I have a favor to ask—a rather large one, I'm afraid. Having served as editor of a professional journal myself, I know how busy editors are, but I was wondering if you would be willing to fly to Washington, D.C. on April 25 and speak at the closing banquet of our seventh annual congress.

The problem, of course, is that as a nonprofit association, we cannot afford to pay you an honorarium. I trust that this won't be a problem for you. We would, however, be willing to reimburse you for air travel and hotel accommodations.

Our conference attendants would benefit tremendously from your vast knowledge of multiple sclerosis, so we're really hoping you'll say yes. Just let me know your decision by March 3 in case we have to make other arrangements.

Please call me if you have any questions.

Cordially

May Lyon

May Lyon, Banquet Chair

MODEL 8

Persuasive Request— Asking a Favor

This persuasive request uses the indirect plan because the writer does not know the reader personally and because strong persuasion is needed.

Opens by quoting the reader, thus complimenting her.

Intimates the request; provides the necessary background information.

Subordinates a potential obstacle by putting it in the dependent clause of a sentence.

Closes with a restatement of a reader benefit.

NATIONAL MULTIPLE SCLEROSIS SOCIETY

National Multiple Sclerosis Society
733 Third Avenue
New York, NY 10017-3288

Tel 212 986 3240
1 800 FIGHT MS
Fax 212 986 7981
E-Mail: nat@nmss.org
www.nmss.org

January 21, 20—

① Ms. Tanya Porrat, Editor
Autoimmune Diseases Monthly
1800 Ten Hills Road, Suite B
Boston, MA 02145

Dear Ms. Porrat

Subject: Program Planning for the Multiple Sclerosis Congress

② "The average person has about 1 chance in 1,000 of developing MS." That comment of yours in a recent interview in the *Boston Globe* made me sit up and think.

Your knack for exploring little-known facts like that would certainly be of keen interest to those attending our annual congress in Washington, D.C. on April 23–25. As the keynote speaker at the banquet at the Mayflower Hotel on April 25, you would be able to present your ideas on current initiatives to the 200 people present. You would, of course, be our guest for the banquet, which begins at 7 p.m. Your 45-minute presentation would begin at about 8:30 p.m.

We will reimburse you for air travel and hotel accommodations. Although our nonprofit association is unable to offer an honorarium, we do offer you an opportunity to introduce your journal and to present your ideas to representatives of major autoimmune groups in the country.

③ We'd like to announce your presentation in our next newsletter, which goes to press on March 3. Won't you please call to let me know that you can come. We'll have a large, enthusiastic audience of medical researchers waiting to hear you.

Cordially

May Lyon

④ May Lyon, Banquet Chair

The National MS Society...One thing people with MS can count on.

Grammar and Mechanics Notes

1. To increase readability, do not italicize publication titles in addresses.
2. *Boston Globe:* Italicize the titles of separately published works, such as newspapers, magazines, and books.
3. *that you can come:* Use a period after a courteous request.
4. The writer's title may go on the same line as the writer's name, separated by a comma, or on a line by itself.

MODEL 9

Persuasive Claim

This persuasive claim letter uses the indirect plan.

Begins on a warm and relevant note.

Provides a smooth transition from the opening sentence.

Provides the necessary background information.

Tells exactly what the problem is in a neutral, courteous tone.

Provides a rationale for granting the claim; asks confidently for specific action; mentions the reader benefit of keeping a satisfied customer.

June 18, 20—

Customer Service Supervisor
Northern Airlines
P.O. Box 619616
Dallas/Fort Worth Airport, TX 75261-9616

Dear Customer Services Supervisor:

① I think you will agree that a relaxing 90-minute flight on Northern Airlines is more enjoyable than a grueling six-hour automobile trip. Yet on June 2, my wife and I found ourselves doing just that—driving from Saginaw, Michigan, to Indianapolis—in the middle of the night and in the company of three tired children.

We had made reservations on Northern Flight 126 a month earlier. When we arrived at the airport, we were told that Flight 126 had been canceled. Your gate agent (Ms. Nixon) had graciously rebooked us on a flight leaving at 9:45 the next morning.

Since the purpose of our trip was to attend a family wedding on June 3, we had no choice but to cancel our rebooked flight and to drive to Indianapolis instead. When we tried to turn in our tickets for a refund, Ms. Nixon informed us that because the flight had been canceled due to inclement weather, she would be unable to credit my American Express charge card.

② As a frequent flier on Northern, I've often experienced the "Welcome Aboard!" feeling that is the basis for your current advertising, and I believe you will want to extend that same feeling to your ticket operations as well. Please credit my American Express charge card (No. 4102 817 171) for the $680 cost of the five tickets, thus putting out the welcome mat again for my family.

Sincerely,

Oliver J. Arbin

Oliver J. Arbin
③ 518 Thompson Street
Saginaw, MI 48607

Grammar and Mechanics Notes

1. *just that—driving:* To insert a dash, type two hyphens (--) with no space before or after. The word processing program automatically converts two hyphens into a printed dash.
2. *"Welcome Aboard!":* Position the exclamation point inside the closing quotation marks where it applies to the term itself.
3. For personal business letters printed on plain paper, type your address below your name.

WRITING A SALES LETTER

 4 ► *Compose a sales letter.*

The heart of most business is sales—selling a product or service. Much of a company's sales effort is accomplished through the writing of effective sales letters—either individual letters for individual sales or form letters for large-scale sales.

In large companies, the writing of sales letters is centered in the advertising department and is a highly specialized task performed by advertising copywriters and marketing consultants. Within a few years after graduation, however, a growing number of college students aim to own their own businesses. These start-up companies are typically quite small, having only a few employees.

In such a situation, the company must mount an aggressive sales effort to develop business but is typically too small to hire a copywriter or marketing consultant. Thus, the owner often ends up writing these sales letters, which are vital to the firm's ongoing health. So no matter where you intend to work, chances are that at some point you will need to write sales letters.

Selecting a Central Selling Theme

Your first step is to become thoroughly familiar with your product, its competition, and your intended audience. Then, you must select a **central selling theme** for your letter. Most products have numerous features that you will want to introduce and discuss. For your letter to make a real impact, however, a single theme should run through it—a major reader benefit that you introduce early and emphasize throughout the letter.

central selling theme   The major reader benefit that is introduced early and emphasized throughout a sales letter.

It would be unrealistic to expect your reader to remember five different product features that you mention. In any case, you have only a short time to make a lasting impression on your reader. Use that time wisely to emphasize what you think is the most compelling benefit of owning your product. Two means of achieving this emphasis are *position* and *repetition*. Introduce your central selling theme early (in the opening sentence, if possible), and keep developing it throughout the letter.

Gaining the Reader's Attention

A reply to a request for product information from a potential customer is called a *solicited sales letter*. An *unsolicited sales letter*, on the other hand, is a letter promoting a firm's products that is mailed to potential customers who have not expressed any interest in the product. (Unsolicited sales letters are also called *prospecting letters*. Some recipients, of course, call them *junk mail*.)

Because most sales letters are unsolicited, you have only a line or two in which to grab the reader's attention. Unless a sales letter is addressed to the reader personally and is obviously not a form letter, the reader is likely just to skim it—either out of curiosity or because the opening sentence was especially intriguing.

Most readers will scan the opening of even a form letter, perhaps just to learn what product is being promoted. If you can capture their attention in these first few lines, they may continue reading. Otherwise, all your efforts will have been wasted. The following examples of opening sentences have proven effective for sales letters.

Technique	*Example*
Rhetorical question	What is the difference between extravagance and luxury? *(Promoting a high-priced car)*
Thought-provoking statement	Most of what we had to say about business this morning was unprintable! *(Promoting an early morning television news program)*
Unusual fact	If your family is typical, you will wash one ton of laundry this year. *(Promoting a laundry detergent)*
Current event	The new Arrow assembly plant will bring 1,700 new families to White Rock within three years. *(Promoting a real estate company)*
Anecdote	During six years of college, the one experience that helped me the most did not even occur in the classroom. *(Promoting a weekly business magazine)*
Direct challenge	Drop the enclosed Pointer pen on the floor, writing tip first, and then sign your name with it. *(Promoting a no-blot ballpoint pen)*

Creating Interest and Building Desire

If your opening sentence is directly related to your product, the transition to the discussion of features and reader benefits will be smooth and logical. Make sure that the first sentence of the paragraph that follows relates directly to the idea introduced in your opening sentence. Unrelated ideas will make the reader pause and feel puzzled.

Interpreting Features

The major part of your letter (typically several paragraphs) will probably be devoted to creating interest and building desire for your product. You should not only describe the product and its features but, more important, *interpret* these features by showing specifically how each will benefit the reader. Make the reader—not the product—the subject of most of your sentences.

> NOT: The JT Laser II prints at the speed of 15 pages per minute.
>
> BUT: After pressing the print key, you'll barely have time to reach over and retrieve the page from the bin. The JT Laser II's print speed of 15 pages per minute is twice that of the typical printer.
>
> NOT: Masco binoculars zoom from 3 to 12 power.
>
> BUT: With Masco binoculars, you can look a ruby-throated hummingbird squarely in the eye at 300 feet and see it blink.

Using Objective, Ethical Language

To be convincing, you must present specific, objective evidence. Simply saying that a product is great is not enough. You must provide evidence to show *why* or *how* the product is great. Here is where you'll use all the data you gathered before you started to write. Avoid generalities, unsupported superlatives and claims, and too many or too strong adjectives and adverbs.

> NOT: At $595, the Sherwood moped is the best buy on the market.
>
> BUT: The May *Independent Consumer* rated the $595 Sherwood moped the year's best buy.
>
> NOT: We know you will enjoy the convenience of our Bread Baker.
>
> BUT: Our Bread Baker comes with one feature we don't think you'll ever use: a 30-day, no-questions-asked return policy.

Although the law allows you to promote your product aggressively, you will want to operate under certain legal and ethical constraints. The guidelines provided in the Spotlight ("What May You Say in a Sales Letter?") on page 161 apply to American laws and customs. When operating in the international environment, you should follow local laws and customs.

Focusing on the Central Selling Theme

The recurring theme of your letter should be the one feature that sets your product apart from the competition. If your reader remembers nothing else about your product, this one feature is what you want him or her to remember. Whenever possible, unify the features under a single umbrella theme—whether that theme is convenience, ease of use, flexibility, price, or some other distinguishing characteristic around which you can build your case.

Discussing and fully interpreting these features may take a considerable amount of space, and some readers may be unwilling to read through a long sales letter. Those who do, however, will be more motivated to respond favorably. The test of an effective sales letter is the number of sales it generates—*not* the number of people who read the letter.

Mentioning Price

If price is your central selling theme, introduce it early and emphasize it. In most cases, however, price is not the central selling theme and should therefore be subordinated. Introduce the price late in the message, after you have discussed most of the advantages of owning the product. To subordinate price, state it in a long complex or compound sentence, perhaps in a sentence that also mentions a reader benefit.

> You'll consider the $250 cost of this spreadsheet seminar repaid in full the very next time your boss asks you to revise the quarterly sales budget—on a Friday afternoon!

Sometimes it is helpful to present the price in terms of small units—for example, showing how subscribing to a weekly magazine costs less than $1 per week, rather than $50 per year. Or compare the price to that of a familiar object—"about what you'd pay for your morning newspaper or cup of coffee."

Motivating Action

Although the purpose of your letter should be apparent right from the start, delay making your specific request until late in the letter—after you have created interest and built desire for the product. Then state the specific action you want.

If the desired action is an actual sale, make the action easy to take by including a toll-free number, enclosing an order blank, accepting credit cards, and the like.

CONCEPT CHECK 7.3

While studying for your bar exams, you decide to start a part-time business delivering singing telegrams throughout the Atlanta metropolitan area. For a flat fee of $150, you'll personally deliver a greeting card and sing any song (in good taste) of the customer's choice—using either the actual wording of the song or special lyrics composed by the customer. You promote your company (Musical Messages) as appropriate for birthdays, graduations, promotions, and other special occasions.

a. What will be your central selling theme?
b. Construct an appropriate attention-getter for your opening paragraph.
c. Construct an effective sentence that mentions the price.
d. Construct an effective closing sentence.

Online Study Center
Improve Your Grade
Audio Chapter Review 7.4
Handouts

For high-priced items, it would be unreasonable to expect to make an actual sale by mail. Probably no one has read a sales letter promoting a new automobile and then phoned in an order for the automobile. For such items, your goal is to get the reader to take just a small step toward purchasing—sending for more information, stopping by the dealer for a demonstration, or asking a sales representative to call. Again, make the step easy for the reader to take.

Provide an incentive for prompt action: for example, offer a gift to the first 100 people who respond or stress the need to buy early while a good selection remains, before the holiday rush begins, or while the three-day sale is in full swing. Make your push for action *gently*, however. Any tactic that smacks of high-pressure selling at this point is likely to increase reader resistance.

Use confident language when asking for action, and avoid hesitant phrases such as "If you want to save money" or "I hope you agree that this product will save you time." When asking the reader to part with money, it is always a good idea to mention a reader benefit in the same sentence.

NOT: Hurry! Hurry! Hurry! These sale prices won't be in effect long. *(Too strong)*

NOT: If you agree that this ice cream maker will make your summers more enjoyable, you can place your order by telephone. *(Too self-conscious)*

BUT: To have your Jiffy Ice Cream Maker available for use during the upcoming July 4 weekend, simply call our toll-free number today.

These guidelines for writing an effective sales letter are illustrated in Model 10 on page 159 and are summarized in Checklist 8 on pages 160–161. As always, the test of the effectiveness of a message is whether it achieves its goal. Use whatever information you have available (especially in terms of audience analysis) to help your letter achieve its goal.

TEST PREPPER 7.4

ANSWERS CAN BE FOUND ON P. 411

True or False?

_____ 1. Owners of small businesses often write their sales letters themselves.
_____ 2. If your product or service has three major advantages over the competition, you should stress all of them in your letter.
_____ 3. Unsolicited sales letters require more persuasion than solicited sales letters do.
_____ 4. If price is your biggest advantage over the competition, you should stress price throughout your letter.
_____ 5. You should devote most of the space in a sales letter to describing the features of your product or service.

Vocabulary

Define the following term in your own words and give an original example.
6. Central selling theme

Critical Thinking

7. Your boss has asked you to write a form sales letter advertising a new diet supplement for men that is "guaranteed to add at least 2 inches to your chest size or double your money back." Although the product is legal (and very popular), you personally feel that it is a sham and are hesitant to promote it. What do you tell your boss?

Online Study Center
ACE the Test
ACE Practice Tests 7.4

Online Study Center
Improve Your Grade
Audio Chapter Quiz 7.4
PowerPoint Review 7.4

MODEL 10

Sales Letter

Starts with a rhetorical question.

Introduces need for safety and security as the central selling theme.

Presents specific evidence and discusses it in terms of reader benefits.

Emphasizes "you" instead of the product in most sentences.

Subordinates price in a long paragraph that also discusses benefits.

Makes the desired action clear and easy to take; ends with a reader benefit.

①

2455 Paces Ferry Road, N.W. • Atlanta, GA 30339-4024
(770) 433-8211

② Dear Homeowner:

Do you view your home as an investment or as your castle? Is it primarily a tax write-off or a place of refuge?

Most of us view our homes as places where we can feel safe from outside intrusions. Thus, we feel threatened by government statistics showing that 5.3 percent of all U.S. households were burglarized last year. How can we protect ourselves?

Today, there's a simple and dependable alarm that protects up to 2,500 square feet. Just plug in the Safescan Home Alarm System and turn the key. You then have 30 seconds to leave and 15 seconds to switch off the alarm once you return.

③ Worried that your dog might trigger the alarm? Safescan screens out normal sounds like crying babies, outside traffic, and rain. But hostile noises like breaking glass and splintering wood trigger the alarm. The 105-decibel siren is loud enough to alert neighbors and to drive away even the most determined burglar.

What if a smart burglar disconnects the electricity to your home or pulls the plug? Built-in batteries ensure that Safescan operates through power failures, and batteries recharge automatically. Best of all, installation is easy. Simply mount the 4-pound unit on a wall, and plug it in. Nothing could be faster. Finally, there is a $259 home alarm that you can trust. And the one-year warranty and ten-day return policy ensure your complete satisfaction.

Last year, 3.2 million burglaries occurred in the United States, but you can now tip the odds back in your favor. To order the Safescan Home Alarm System, stop by your nearest Home Depot. Within minutes, Safescan can be guarding your home, giving you peace of mind.

Sincerely yours,

Jeffrey Parret

Jeffrey Parret
National Sales Manager

Grammar and Mechanics Notes

1. In general, omit the date and inside address in form sales letters. Subject lines are also frequently omitted.
2. *Dear Homeowner:* Note the generic salutation.
3. *crying babies, outside traffic, and:* Separate items in a series by commas.

CHECKLIST 7

Persuasive Requests

Determine How to Start the Message

✓ Direct Plan—Use a direct organizational plan when you write to superiors, your audience is predisposed to listen objectively to your request, the proposal does not require strong persuasion, the proposal is long or complex, or you know your reader prefers the direct approach. Present the recommendation, along with the criteria or brief rationale, in the first paragraph.

✓ Indirect Plan—Use an indirect organizational plan when you write to subordinates, strong persuasion is needed, or you know your reader prefers the indirect approach. Start by gaining the reader's attention.

- Make the first sentence motivate the reader to continue reading. For example, use a rhetorical question, unusual fact, unexpected statement, or common-ground statement.

- Keep the opening paragraph short (often just one sentence); relevant to the message; and, when appropriate, related to a reader benefit.

Create Interest and Justify Your Request

✓ Devote the major part of your message to justifying your request. Give enough background and evidence to enable the reader to make an informed decision.

✓ Use facts and statistics, expert opinion, and examples to support your proposal. Ensure that the evidence is accurate, relevant, representative, and complete.

✓ Use an objective, logical, reasonable, and sincere tone. Avoid obvious flattery, emotionalism, and exaggeration.

✓ Present the evidence in terms of either direct or indirect reader benefits.

Minimize Obstacles

✓ Do not ignore obstacles or any negative aspects of your request. Instead, show that even considering them, your request is still reasonable.

✓ Subordinate the discussion of obstacles by the position of and the amount of space devoted to the topic.

Ask Confidently for Action

✓ State (or restate) the specific request late in the message—after most of the benefits have been discussed.

✓ Make the desired action clear and easy for the reader to take, use a confident tone, do not apologize, and do not supply excuses.

✓ End on a forward-looking note, continuing to stress reader benefits.

CHECKLIST 8

Sales Letters

Prepare

✓ Learn as much as possible about the product, the competition, and the audience.

✓ Select a central selling theme—your product's most distinguishing feature.

Gain the Reader's Attention

✓ Make your opening brief, interesting, and original. Avoid obvious, misleading, and irrelevant statements.

✓ Use any of these openings: rhetorical question, thought-provoking statement, unusual fact, current event, anecdote, direct challenge, or some similar attention-getting device.

✓ Introduce (or at least lead up to) the central selling theme in the opening.

✓ If the letter is in response to a customer inquiry, begin by expressing appreciation for the inquiry and then introduce the central selling theme.

Create Interest and Build Desire

✓ Make the introduction of the product follow naturally from the attention-getter.

✓ *Interpret* the features of the product; instead of just describing the features, show how the reader will benefit from each feature. Let the reader picture owning, using, and enjoying the product.

✓ Use action-packed, positive, and objective language. Provide convincing evidence to support your claims—specific facts and figures, independent product reviews, endorsements, and so on.

✓ Continue to stress the central selling theme throughout.

✓ Subordinate price (unless price is the central selling theme). State the price in small terms, in a long sentence, or in a sentence that also talks about benefits.

Motivate Action

✓ Make the desired action clear and easy to take.

✓ Ask confidently, avoiding the hesitant "if you'd like to" or "I hope you agree that."

✓ Encourage prompt action (but avoid a hard-sell approach).

✓ End your letter with a reminder of a reader benefit.

SPOTLIGHT

What May You Say in a Sales Letter?

May I say that our product is the best on the market?

Yes. You may legally express an opinion about your product; this is called *puffery*. You may not, however, make a claim that can be proven false, such as saying that your product is cheaper than a competing product when, in fact, your product is not cheaper.

The typist mistakenly typed the price of our product as $19.95, instead of the correct price of $29.95. Do I have to sell it for $19.95?

No. You are not legally responsible for an honest mistake, as long as your intent was not to deceive the buyer.

May I include a sample of my product with my letter and require the reader to either send payment or return the product at my expense?

No. Readers do not have to pay for or return any unordered goods. They may legally treat them as a gift from you.

I want to send a sales letter promoting our rock music to high school students. May I legally accept orders from minors?

Yes. You may accept their orders, and if you do, you are legally bound to honor the contract. Until they reach the age of adulthood (18 years in some states and 21 years in others), however, minors may legally cancel a contract and return the merchandise to you.

In my showroom, I want to sell the furniture that has small nicks and scratches on it. If I state in my sales letter that all sales are final and sale items are marked "as is," do I have to issue refunds to anyone who complains?

No. By using the term "as is," you are telling the consumer that you are not promising new merchandise.

Without my knowledge, my assistant wrote a letter in which she promised a customer a 10 percent price break; such a price reduction is clearly against store policy. Do we have to honor my assistant's price?

Yes. Your assistant was acting as your agent, and her promise is legally binding on your firm.

> ## THREE PS
> ## PROBLEM, PROCESS, PRODUCT

A Sales Letter

Problem

You are the marketing manager at Motorola for the C2K chip. This chip was designed for the Voice Note, a digital recorder that allows you to record messages to yourself rather than scribbling them on scraps of paper.

The recorder is $2\frac{1}{2} \times 1 \times \frac{1}{2}$ inches, weighs 3 ounces, and is made in Japan from sturdy plastic. It records messages that are a maximum of 3 minutes long and holds $4\frac{1}{2}$ hours of dictation. A lock button prevents recording over a message. After the message has been played back, the chip automatically resets for use the next time. The Voice Note is operated by pressing the Record button and speaking. It runs on two AAA batteries that are included and comes with a 90-day warranty and a 30-day full-refund policy.

To field-test this product, you decide to try a local direct-mail campaign directed at the business community. You purchase a mailing list containing the names and addresses of the 800 members of the Phoenix Athletic Club, a downtown facility used by businesspeople for lunch, after-work drinks, exercise, and social affairs. The club has racquetball and tennis courts, an indoor pool, and exercise rooms. Its yearly membership fee is $3,000. You decide to send these 800 members a form letter promoting the Voice Note for $29.95. You'll include your local phone number (555-2394) for placing credit-card orders by phone, or the readers may stop by the store to purchase the recorder in person.

Process

1. Describe your audience.

   - Businesspeople
   - Active (sports and exercise facilities)
   - Upscale (can afford $3,000 annual membership)
   - Probably very busy professionally and socially

2. What will be your central selling theme?

   Convenience/portability is the unique benefit of Voice Note.

3. Write an attention-getter that is original, interesting, and short; that is reader-oriented; that relates to the product; and that, if possible, introduces the central selling theme.

   You're driving home on the freeway in bumper-to-bumper traffic when the solution to a nagging problem facing you at work suddenly pops into your head. But by the time you get home 30 minutes later, your good idea has vanished.

4. Jot down the features you might discuss and the reader benefits associated with each feature.

- Size is 2½ × 1 × ½ inches, weighs 3 ounces: *smaller and lighter than a microcassette recorder; fits in shirt pocket or purse; easy to use on the go.*
- Records 3-minute messages—a maximum of 4½ hours: *room enough for most "to-do" messages—90 different reminders.*
- Press Record button and then speak; lock function prevents overrecording: *easy to use, even in car; not a lot of buttons to fiddle with.*
- Powered by two AAA batteries (included): *real portability.*

5. Write the sentence that mentions price. (Because price is not the central selling theme, it should be subordinated.)

The Voice Note's price of $29.95 is less than you'd pay for a bulky microcassette recorder that is much less convenient for on-the-go use.

6. What action are you seeking from the reader?

To purchase the Voice Note.

7. How can you motivate prompt action?

Make the action easy to take; offer warranty and guarantee satisfaction; stress that the sooner you buy, the sooner you'll enjoy using it.

Product

Lee's Consumer Products
Fiesta Mall ▪ 1200 Dobson Road ▪ Mesa, Arizona 85201
TEL: 480-555-2394 ▪ www.leesconsumerproducts.com

Dear Club Member:

You leave the Phoenix Athletic Club and are heading home on the freeway in bumper-to-bumper traffic when the solution to a nagging problem at work pops into your head. But by the time you get home, your good idea has vanished.

Next time, carry Voice Note, the 3-ounce digital recorder with the new Motorola C2K chip that allows you to record reminders to yourself on the go. Now you can "jot" down your ideas as soon as they occur. As you know, inspiration often strikes far from a pad and pencil!

Much smaller than a microcassette (2½ × 1 × ½ inches), Voice Note slips into your shirt pocket or purse. And there aren't a lot of buttons to fiddle with. Just press Record and speak. A lock prevents overrecording your earlier messages.

You can record up to 90 different messages of 3 minutes each—"to-do" messages like "Call Richard about the Apple computer contract" or "Place order for 200 shares of SRP stock" or even "Pick up Jenny from soccer practice at 5:30." After playback, the tape automatically resets for immediate use.

For true portability, the Voice Note is powered by two AAA batteries (included). Your satisfaction is guaranteed by our 90-day warranty and 30-day refund policy.

The Voice Note's price of $29.95 is less than you'd pay for a bulky microcassette recorder that is much less convenient for on-the-go use. For credit-card orders, simply call us at 555-2394. Or stop by our retail store at Fiesta Mall for a personal demonstration.

The next time you need to pick up a quart of milk on the way home, make a Voice Note. You won't come home empty-handed.

Sincerely,

Richard E. Lee

Richard E. Lee

PORTFOLIO PROJECT 3

Writing a Persuasive Message

Online Study Center
Prepare for Class
Portfolio Stationery

Problem

You are Cesar Gutiérrez, a claims adjuster for Statewide Insurance. Your job requires you to investigate automobile accident claims, negotiate settlements, and authorize payments. Customers are already distressed, of course, over their accidents and possible physical injury. The last thing they need is a delay in settling their insurance claims and getting their vehicles repaired.

Because you travel the entire eastern half of your state to physically examine the damaged vehicles and talk with those involved, you constantly have to search maps and the Internet for directions to out-of-the-way places.

It occurs to you that you could be more productive and provide better customer service if you had an onboard automotive navigation system that relies on the federally operated Global Positioning System (GPS). The device in which you're interested is the Street Pilot III, which boasts a large color display as well as voice prompts (such as "turn right at the next intersection") and automatic routing capability. It's portable, so you can use it on any vehicle—which is particularly useful given that you sometimes have to fly to your destination and then rent an automobile. The cost is $699.99, but there is no monthly access charge.

Send a memo to your boss, Lisette Washington, vice president of operations, trying to sell her on the idea. She will be concerned, of course, about whether the other two adjusters will request the same device.

Process

Compose a few paragraphs describing how you solved this problem. In narrative form, provide information such as the following:

1. What is the purpose of your letter?
2. Describe your audience.
3. Will you use a direct or an indirect organizational pattern?
4. List the reasons you might discuss for approving your proposal—including any reader benefits associated with each reason.
5. What is an obstacle that might prevent you from achieving your objective?

Product

Compose your document, following the steps of the writing process (audience analysis, planning, drafting, revising, formatting, and proofreading). Format the final version on letterhead stationery (refer to the Style Manual at the back of this text for formatting guidelines).

LEARNING OBJECTIVE REVIEW

1 *Compose a persuasive message promoting an idea.*

- Consider your message's purpose.
- Familiarize yourself with the idea or product.
- Determine the audience's specific needs and interests as they relate to the central idea of the message.
- Analyze the audience's knowledge and attitude toward the product.
- Consider how the message will affect the reader.
- Determine your credibility with the reader.
- Write the message.
    - Use a direct plan when you are writing to superiors or your audience is likely to grant the request.
    - Use an indirect plan when writing to a subordinate or when strong persuasion is needed.
- Begin your request with an attention-getter and stress reader benefits from granting the request.
- Subordinate obstacles.
- State (or restate) the specific request late in the message—after most of the benefits have been discussed.

2 *Compose a persuasive message requesting a favor.*

- Discuss at least one reader benefit before you ask for the favor.
- If the reader is an expert, make a complimentary remark about the reader.

3 *Compose a persuasive claim.*

- Begin with a neutral opening that gets the reader's attention.
- Explain the problem specifically.
- Request a specific adjustment.

4 *Compose a sales letter.*

- Start with a rhetorical question or other attention-getter.
- Introduce the central selling theme in terms of a major reader benefit.
- Provide specific evidence to support the selling theme.
- Subordinate price.
- Provide an incentive for prompt action.
- End with a reader benefit.

1. Helping a Friend (▶ 7.1)

You are the plant manager of the Monterey Manufacturing Company in Pearl River, Louisiana. You manufacture automotive ball bearings. Currently you have
125 employees. One of your employees, Francis
Benoit, has been diagnosed with throat cancer.

Francis is well known and well liked at the plant,
but his illness has kept him out of work for over two
months, and he has exhausted all of his sick leave.
His doctor believes he will probably be out of work
for at least three more months. You want to encourage your employees to donate sick-leave time to
Francis. Employees can donate up to five days of sick
leave each. No one is required to participate, but
anyone who can should give at least a few hours of
sick leave.

To donate sick-leave time to Francis, employees
must fill out a form in the Human Resource Management department. Forms must be submitted before
the end of the month for accounting purposes. Any
unused hours and days will return to those who have
donated on a proportional basis.

Write a memo to be posted in the break room
encouraging the employees to donate time to
Francis.

2. Field Trip (▶ 7.2)

You are David Pearson, owner and manager of Jack
'n' Jill Preschool. During the next few weeks, you will
be discussing food and nutrition with the youngsters;
and you want to end the unit by having the children
walk to the nearby Salad Haven, take a tour of the
kitchens, and then make their own salads for lunch
from the restaurant's popular salad bar. Of course,
each family would pay for its child's meal. In fact, to
help make the visit easier, you'll collect the money
beforehand and pay the cashier for everyone at once.
You will ask several parents to come with you to help
supervise the 23 children, ages three through five,
although they will probably need some extra help
from the salad-bar attendants. You can come any day
during the week of October 10 to 14. State regulations require that the children eat lunch between
11 a.m. and 12:30 p.m. Write to Donna Jo Luse (Manager, Salad Haven, 28 Grenvale Road, Westminster,
MD 21157) asking for permission to make the field
trip.

3. Celebrity Donation (▶ 7.2)

Coming out of the movie theater after watching the
Academy Award–winning movie *Rocky Mountain
Adventure,* starring Robert Forte, you suddenly have
an idea. As executive director of the Wilderness Fund,
you've been searching for an unusual raffle prize for
your upcoming fundraiser. You wonder whether you
could persuade Robert Forte to donate some item
used in this popular movie (perhaps a stage prop or
costume item) for the raffle. The Wilderness Fund is
an 8,000-member nonprofit agency dedicated to pre-
serving forest lands—the very type of lands photo-
graphed so beautifully in Forte's latest movie. Write
to the actor at Century Studios, 590 North Vermont
Avenue, Los Angeles, CA 90004.

4. Azaleas (▶ 7.3)

You are Vera Malcolm, the facilities manager for
Public Service Company of Arkansas. In preparation
for the recent dedication of your new hydroelectric
plant, you spruced up the grounds near the viewing
stand. As part of the stage decorations, you ordered
ten potted azaleas at $27.50 each (plus $10.50 shipping) from Jackson-Parsons Nurseries (410 Wick
Avenue, Youngstown, OH 44555) on February 3. The
bushes were guaranteed to arrive in show condition—ready to burst into bloom within three days—
or your money would be cheerfully refunded.

The plants arrived in healthy condition but were
in their final days (perhaps hours) of flowering—
certainly in no shape to display at the dedication.
You decided, instead, to plant the azaleas as part of
your permanent landscaping. Because the plants
arrived only three days before the dedication, you
had to purchase substitute azaleas from the local
florist—at a much higher price. In fact, you ended
up paying $436 for the florist plants—$140.50 more
than the Jackson-Parsons price. You feel that the
nursery was responsible for your having to incur the
additional expenditure. Write a letter asking Jackson-
Parsons to reimburse your company for the $140.50.

5. Inaccurate Reporting (▶ 7.3)

As the CEO of Software Entrepreneurs, Inc., you just
received a memo from the marketing manager for
your ReSolve spreadsheet program. The manager

had written to the review editor at *Computing Trends* protesting inaccurate reporting; the reply (from Roberta J. Horton) was a form letter describing the magazine's policy on product reviews. Although you are glad to know that your product will be included in the yearly software review, you agree with your marketing manager that the editor made an error in downgrading your program. Apparently the reviewer worked with the original version of ReSolve and not with the improved version that was released one month before the review appeared. The new version is so powerful that it outperforms the competition on nearly every test used by the reviewer to determine product rankings.

Because magazine deadlines require that articles be completed well in advance of the printing date, you realize that the magazine could not possibly have included the improved version in its tests. However, you would like the review editor to print a small item noting the availability of the improved ReSolve in an upcoming issue. Write to Horton (*Computing Trends*, 200 Public Square, Cleveland, OH 44114) with this request.

6. Work-Team Communication (▶ 7.4)

Select an ad from a newspaper or journal published within the past month. Working in groups of three or four, write an unsolicited form sales letter for the advertised product, to be signed by the sales manager. (You may need to gather additional information about the product, perhaps from the Internet.) The audience for your letter will be either the students or the faculty at your institution (you decide which). Include only actual data about the product and about the audience. Submit a copy of both the advertisement and your letter.

7. Selling for Charity (▶ 7.4)

As the director of fund-raising for the Buckeye Bread Basket, a Cleveland, Ohio, charity that buys food for people in need, you are starting a new program. You plan to sell holiday greeting cards to raise money for your annual Thanksgiving Day dinner. This year, more than 400 needy people (including both single people and families) are expected to attend the dinner. An Ohio artist created the original watercolor scene on the cards, which come in boxes of ten, with green envelopes. People who buy the cards can take a tax deduction for their donations; the money from the sale of a single box can feed a hungry family of four on Thanksgiving. Write a form letter that will persuade people to order your cards. The price is $22 per box, plus $2.50 postage and handling, and orders can be placed using the enclosed form and return envelope.

Additional exercises are available at the Online Study Center website: **college.hmco.com/pic/oberSASfund**.

Online Study Center   RESOURCES

Prepare for Class, Improve Your Grade, and ACE the Test. Student Achievement Series resources include:

ACE Practice Tests	Ask Ober	Audio Chapter Reviews and Quizzes
Chapter Outlines	Communication Objectives	Crossword Puzzles
Flashcards	Glossaries	Handouts
LAB Tests	Portfolio Project Stationery	Sample Reports

To access these learning and study tools, go to **college.hmco.com/pic/oberSASfund**.

8 Bad-News Letters, Memos, and E-Mail Messages

To retain a competitive edge, a large company must be able to communicate openly and honestly with its customers—even if the news it has to share is unfavorable.

1 *Communicate your message politely, clearly, and firmly.*

2 *Compose a message that rejects an idea.*

3 *Compose a message that refuses a favor.*

"We would rather err on the side of being open and truthful so people don't ask, 'Why didn't you tell us about this problem?'"
—Howard High, Strategic Communications Manager, Intel Corporation

Chapter Outline

Online Study Center
Prepare for Class
Chapter Outline

Compose a message that refuses a claim.

Intel's Strategic Communication

Open disclosure is the way Howard High deals with messages about potential problems. High is strategic communications manager for Intel, the global leader in the production of microprocessors. As a company spokesperson, he shares information about the $21 billion company and its products with reporters from U.S. and foreign business publications. Intel products have a high profile, thanks to the "Intel Inside" brand-building campaign that has established the company's worldwide reputation for quality.

As Intel adds innovative features and more processing power to its new chips, the company faces the challenge of managing public perceptions and expectations of product performance. This endeavor is where insightful audience analysis and open disclosure pay off. "We would rather err on the side of being open

HOWARD HIGH
Strategic Communications
Manager,
Intel Corporation
(Santa Clara, California)

and truthful so people don't ask, 'Why didn't you tell us about this problem?'" comments High.

When High has to communicate a bad-news message about a problem that may affect a large number of customers, he takes additional steps to publicize the issue. "We would probably involve a senior-level manager as the spokesperson or the quoted source in the news," he says. ■

PLANNING THE BAD-NEWS MESSAGE

 Communicate your message politely, clearly, and firmly.

At some point in our lives, we all probably have been both the senders and the recipients of bad news. And just as most people find it difficult to accept bad news, they also find it difficult to convey bad news. How you write your messages won't change the news you have to deliver, but it may determine whether your reader accepts your decision as reasonable—or goes away mad.

As noted in Chapter 6, every letter can be considered a persuasive letter. This idea is especially true for bad-news letters, where you must persuade the reader of the reasonableness of your decision.

Your purpose in writing a bad-news message is twofold: first, to say "no" or to convey bad news and, second, to retain the reader's goodwill. To accomplish these goals, you must communicate your message politely, clearly, and firmly. In addition, you must show the reader that you've seriously considered the request but that as a matter of fairness and good business practice, you must deny it.

Organizing to Suit Your Audience

The reader's needs, expectations, and personality—as well as the writer's relationship with the reader—largely determine the content and organization of a bad-news message. Thus you need to put yourself in the place of the reader.

To decide whether to use the direct or the indirect plan for refusing a request, check the sender's original message. If the original message was written in the direct style, the sender may have considered it a routine request, and you would be safe in answering in the direct style. If the original message was written in the indirect style, the sender probably considered it a persuasive request, and you should consider answering in the indirect style. (Messages written to one's superior are typically written in the direct style, however, regardless of whether the reader considers the original request routine or persuasive.)

For example, an e-mail message telling employees that the company cafeteria will be closed for one day to permit installation of new equipment can be written directly and in a paragraph or two. A message telling employees that the company cafeteria will be closed permanently and that employees will now have to go outside for lunch (and pay higher prices) would require more explanation and should probably be written in the indirect style.

Direct Plan—Present the Bad News Immediately

As discussed earlier, many requests are routine; the writer simply wants a yes-or-no decision and wants to hear it in a direct manner. Similarly, if an announcement of bad news is not likely to generate an emotional response from the reader, you should use a direct approach. The direct plan for bad-news messages is basically the same plan used for routine messages discussed in Chapter 6: present the major idea (the bad news) up-front. To help readers accept your decision when using the direct plan, however, give a brief rationale along with the bad news in the first paragraph.

NOT: The annual company picnic originally scheduled for August 3 at Riverside Park has been canceled.

BUT: Because ongoing construction at Riverside Park might present safety hazards to our employees and their families, the annual company picnic originally scheduled for August 3 has been canceled.

As usual, state the message in language as positive as possible, while still maintaining honesty.

NOT: Our departmental compliance report will be late next month.

BUT: The extra time required to resolve the New Orleans refinery problem means that our departmental compliance report will be submitted on March 15 rather than on March 1.

Follow this information with any needed explanation and a friendly closing. Use the direct organizational plan in the following circumstances:

▪ The bad news involves a small, insignificant matter and can be considered routine. If the reader is not likely to be emotionally involved and thus not seriously disappointed by the decision, use the direct approach.

▪ The reader prefers directness. Superiors typically prefer that *all* messages from subordinates be written in the direct style.

▪ The writer wants to emphasize the negative news. Suppose that you have already refused a request once and the reader writes a second time; under these circumstances, a forceful "no" might be in order. Or consider the situation where negative information will be included in a form letter—perhaps as an insert in a monthly statement. Because the reader might otherwise discard or merely skim an "unimportant-looking" message, you should consider placing the bad news up front—where it will be noticed.

Indirect Plan—Buffer the Bad News

You will often want to use an indirect plan—especially when giving bad news to

▪ Subordinates
▪ Customers
▪ Readers who prefer the indirect approach
▪ Readers you don't know

With the indirect approach, present the reasons first, then the negative news. This approach emphasizes the *reasons* for the bad news, rather than the bad news itself.

Suppose, for example, a subordinate expects a "yes" answer upon receiving your e-mail message. Putting the negative news in the first sentence might be too harsh and emphatic, and your decision might sound unreasonable until the reader has heard the rationale for it. In such

Being forthright and up-front about bad news is generally the best tactic. Many observers feel that if Martha Stewart had simply admitted the details of her phone call with stockbroker Peter Bacanovic, the entire incident would not have made the headlines or have had the serious repercussions it had on her company, Martha Stewart Living Omnimedia.

a situation, you should begin with a neutral and relevant statement—one that helps establish or strengthen the reader–writer relationship. Such a statement serves as a *buffer* between the reader and the bad news that follows.

An effective opening buffer for bad-news messages has these characteristics:

1. It is *neutral.* To serve as a true buffer, the opening must not convey the negative news immediately. At the same time, guard against implying that the request will be *granted*, thereby building up the reader for a big letdown.
2. It is *relevant.* The danger with starting *too* far from the topic is that the reader might not recognize that the letter is intended as a response to his or her request. In addition, an irrelevant opening seems to avoid the issue, thus sounding insincere or self-serving. To show relevance and to personalize the opening, you might include some reference to the reader's letter in your first sentence. A relevant opening provides a smooth transition to the reasons that follow.
3. It is *supportive.* The purpose of the opening is to help establish compatibility between the reader and the writer. If the opening is controversial or seems to lecture the reader, it will not achieve its purpose.
4. It is *interesting.* Buffer openings should motivate the recipient to continue reading. Therefore, avoid giving obvious information.
5. It is *short.* Readers become impatient if they have to wait too long to reach the major point of the message.

Assume that the owner of an appliance store has written you, one of his suppliers, asking you to provide an in-store demonstrator of your firm's products during his anniversary sale. For sound business reasons, you must refuse the request. Because you're writing to a good customer, you decide to use an indirect plan. You might effectively start your message by using any of the following types of buffers:

Buffer Type	*Example*
Agreement	We both recognize the promotional possibilities that often accompany big anniversary sales such as yours.
Appreciation	Thanks for letting us know of your success in selling Golden Microwaves. *(Avoid, however, thanking the reader for asking you to do something that you're going to refuse to do; such expressions of appreciation sound insincere.)*
Compliment	Congratulations on having served the community of Greenville for ten years.
Facts	Three-fourths of the Golden Microwaves distributors who held anniversary sales last year reported at least a 6 percent increase in annual sales of our home products.
General principle	We believe in furnishing Golden Microwaves distributors a wide range of support in promoting our products.
Good news	Golden Microwaves' upcoming 20 percent-off sale will be heavily advertised and will certainly provide increased traffic for your February anniversary sale.
Understanding	I wish to assure you of Golden Microwaves' desire to help make your anniversary sale successful.

Ethical communicators use a buffer *not* to manipulate or confuse the reader but rather to help the reader accept the disappointing information in an objective manner.

Justifying Your Decision

Presumably, you reached your negative decision by analyzing all the relevant information. Whether you began in a direct or an indirect manner, now explain your analysis to help convince the reader that your decision is reasonable. The major part of your message should, therefore, focus on the *reasons* rather than on the bad news itself.

Provide a smooth transition from the opening buffer and present the reasons honestly and convincingly. If possible, explain how the reasons benefit the reader or, at least, benefit someone other than your organization. For example, refusing to exchange a worn garment might enable you to offer better-quality merchandise to your customers, raising the price of your product might enable you to switch to nonpolluting energy in its manufacture, or refusing to provide copies of company documents might protect the confidentiality of customer transactions. Presenting reader benefits keeps your decision from sounding selfish.

Sometimes, of course, granting the request is simply not in the company's best interests. In such situations, don't "manufacture" reader benefits; instead, just provide whatever short explanation you can and let it go at that.

DILBERT

Dilbert: © Scott Adams/Dist. by United Feature Syndicate, Inc.

> Because this data would be of strategic importance to our competitors, we treat the information as confidential. Similar information about our entire industry (SIC Code 1473), however, is collected in the annual *U.S. Census of Manufacturing*. These census reports are available in most public and university libraries and online.

Show the reader that your decision was a *business* decision, not a personal one. Indicate that the request was taken seriously, and don't hide behind company policy. If the policy is a sound one, it was established for good reasons; therefore, explain the rationale for the policy.

NOT: Company policy prohibits our providing an in-store demonstrator for your tenth-anniversary sale.

BUT: A survey of our dealers three years ago indicated that they felt the space taken up by in-store demonstrators and the resulting traffic problems were not worth the effort; they were also concerned about the legal liability of having someone cooking in their stores.

The reasons justifying your decision should take up the major part of the message, but be concise or your reader may become impatient. Do not belabor a point and do not provide more background than is necessary. If you have several reasons for refusing a request, present the strongest one first—where it will receive the most emphasis. Avoid mentioning any weak reasons. If the reader feels he or she can effectively rebut even one of your arguments, you're simply raising false hopes and inviting needless correspondence.

Giving the Bad News

The bad news is communicated up-front in directly written messages. Even in an indirectly written message, if you have done a convincing job of explaining the reasons, the bad news itself will come as no surprise; instead, the decision will appear logical and reasonable—indeed, the *only* logical and reasonable decision that could have been made under the circumstances.

To retain the reader's goodwill, state the bad news in positive or neutral language, stressing what you *are* able to do rather than what you are *not* able to do. Avoid, for example, words and phrases such as *cannot, are not able to, impossible, unfortunately, sorry,* and *must refuse.* To subordinate the bad news, put it in the middle of a paragraph, and include in the same sentence (or immediately afterward) additional discussion of reasons.

> In response to these dealer concerns, we eliminated in-store demonstrations and now advertise exclusively in print. Doing so has enabled us to begin featuring a two-page spread in each major Sunday newspaper, including your local paper, the *Greenville Courier.*

When using the indirect plan, phrase the bad news in impersonal language, avoiding the use of *you* and *your.* The objective is to distance the reader from the bad news so that it will not be perceived as a personal rejection. To avoid pointing out the bad news that lies ahead, avoid using *but* and *however* to introduce it. Most readers won't remember what was written before the *but*—only what was written after it.

Resist any temptation to apologize for your decision. You may reasonably assume that if the reader were faced with the same options and had the same information available, he or she would act in a similar way. There is no reason to apologize for any reasonable business decision.

In some situations, the refusal can be implied, making a direct statement of refusal unnecessary. But don't be evasive. If you think a positive, subordinated refusal might be misunderstood, go ahead and state it directly. Of course, even under these circumstances, you should use impersonal language and include reader benefits.

Closing on a Pleasant Note

Any refusal, even when handled skillfully, carries negative overtones. Therefore, you need to end your message on a more pleasant note. Avoid statements such as the following:

Problem to Avoid	Example of Problem
Apologizing	Again, I am sorry that we were unable to grant this request.
Anticipating problems	If you run into any problems, please write me directly.
Inviting needless communication	If you have any further questions, please let me know.

Problem to Avoid	Example of Problem
Referring again to bad news	Although we are unable to supply an in-store demonstrator, we do wish you much success in your tenth-anniversary sale.
Repeating a cliché	If we can be of any further help, please don't hesitate to call on us.
Revealing doubt	I trust that you now understand why we made this decision.
Sounding selfish	Don't forget to feature Golden Microwave prominently in your anniversary display.

Instead, make your closing original, friendly, and positive by using any of the following techniques (avoid referring again to the bad news):

Technique	Example
Best wishes	Best wishes for success with your tenth-anniversary sale. We have certainly enjoyed our ten-year relationship with Parker Brothers and look forward to continuing to serve your needs in the future.
Counterproposal	To provide increased publicity for your tenth-anniversary sale, we would be happy to include a special 2-by-6-inch boxed notice of your sale in the *Greenville Courier* edition of our ad on Sunday, February 8. Just send us your camera-ready copy by January 26.
Other sources of help	A dealer in South Carolina switched from using in-store demonstrators to showing a video continuously during his microwave sale. He used the ten-minute film *Twenty-Minute Dinners with Pizzazz* (available for $45 from the Microwave Research Institute, P.O. Box 800, Chicago, IL 60625) and reported a favorable reaction from customers.
Resale or subtle sales	You can be sure that the new Golden promotion Mini-Micro we're introducing in January will draw many customers to your store during your anniversary sale.

To sound sincere and helpful, make your ending original. If you provide a counterproposal or offer other sources of help, provide all the information the reader needs to follow through. If you include sales promotion, make it subtle and reader-oriented.

In short, the last idea the reader hears from you should be positive, friendly, and helpful. Checklist 9 on page 183 summarizes guidelines for writing bad-news letters. The rest of this chapter discusses strategies for writing bad-news replies and bad-news announcements.

REJECTING AN IDEA

 Compose a message that rejects an idea.

One of the more challenging bad-news messages to write is one that rejects someone's idea or proposal. Put yourself in the role of the person making the suggestion. He or she has probably spent a considerable amount of time in developing the idea; studying its feasibility; perhaps doing some research; and, of course, writing the original persuasive message.

Consider, for example, the situation faced by Elliott Lamborn of Newton Electrical Systems. He has just received a memo from Jenson Peterson, his marketing supervisor, proposing that the company restrict its close-in employee parking lots to use by drivers of Ford vehicles because Ford Motor Company accounts for nearly half of the company's annual sales. Peterson obviously thought his idea had merit and likely expects Lamborn to approve it. If—or in this case *when*—his proposal is rejected, Peterson will be surprised and disappointed.

Because Lamborn is Peterson's superior, he could send Peterson a directly written memo saying, in effect, "I have considered your proposal and must reject it." But Peterson is obviously intelligent and enterprising, and Lamborn does not want to discourage future initiatives on his part. As with all such bad-news replies, then, Lamborn's twin objectives are to refuse the proposal and to retain Peterson's goodwill.

To be successful, Lamborn has an educating job to do. He must give Peterson the reasons for the rejection, reasons of which Peterson is probably unaware. He must also show that he recognizes Peterson's proposal as carefully considered and that the rejection is based on business—not personal—considerations.

Given the amount of effort Peterson has devoted to this project, Lamborn's response will be most effective if written in the indirect pattern. This pattern will let Lamborn move his subordinate gradually into agreeing that the proposal is not in the firm's best interests.

Model 11 on page 177 shows Lamborn's memo rejecting Peterson's proposal. Although we label this memo a bad-news message, it is also a *persuasive* message. Like all bad-news messages, the memo seeks to persuade the reader that the writer's position is reasonable.

REFUSING A FAVOR

 Compose a message that refuses a favor.

Many favors are asked and granted almost automatically. Doing routine favors for others in the organization shows a cooperative spirit, and a spirit of reciprocity often prevails—we recognize that the person asking us for a favor today may be the person from whom we'll need a favor next week. Sometimes, however, for business or personal reasons, we are not able to accommodate the other person and must decline an invitation or a request for a favor.

The type of message written to refuse a favor depends on the particular circumstances. Occasionally, someone asks a "big" favor—perhaps one involving a major investment of time or resources. In that case, the person has probably written a thoughtful, reasoned message trying to persuade you to do as he or she

MODEL 11

Bad-News Reply— Rejecting an Idea

This memo responds to the persuasive request in Model 7 (see page 149).

**NEWTON
Electrical
Systems**

1034 York Road
Baltimore, MD 21204
Phone: 301.555.1086
Fax: 301.555.3926
www.nes.com

+ — + — + — + — + — + — + — + — + — + — + — + — + — + — + — + — + — + —
Serving the automotive industry for more than 50 years

MEMO TO: Jenson J. Peterson, Marketing Supervisor

FROM: Elliott Lamborn, Vice President *EL*

DATE: October 15, 20—

SUBJECT: Employee Parking Lot Proposal

Your October 3 memo certainly enlightened me regarding the automobile habits of our employees. I had no idea that our workers drive such a variety of models.

Uses a neutrally worded subject line.

Starts with a supportive buffer; the second sentence provides a smooth transition to the reason.

The increasing popularity of foreign-made vehicles recently led management to conclude that we should consider taking advantage of this expanding market. President Wrede has appointed a task force to determine how we might also promote our electrical systems to Asian automakers, as well as to Ford.

Begins discussing the reason.

Our successful push into the international market will mean that many of the foreign-made vehicles our employees drive will, in fact, be supplied with Newton Electrical Systems components. Thus, our firm will benefit from the continuing presence of these cars in all our lots.

Presents the refusal in the last sentence of the paragraph, using positive and impersonal language.

① Your memo got me to thinking, Jenson, that we might be missing an opportunity to promote our products to headquarters visitors. Would you please develop some type of awareness campaign (such as a bumper sticker for employee cars that contain a Newton electrical system) that shows our employees support the products we sell. I would appreciate having a memo from you with your ideas by November 3 so that ② I might include this project in next year's marketing campaign.

Closes on a forward-looking, off-the-topic note.

amp

Grammar and Mechanics Notes

1. *thinking, Jenson, that:* Set off nouns of direct address *(Jenson)* with commas.
2. *year's:* Use apostrophe plus *s* to form the possessive of a singular noun *(year)*.

MODEL 12

Bad-News Reply— Refusing a Favor

① From... Peter Gates <pgates@kempman>
To... Wanda K. Berenson <wberenson@kempman>
Cc...
Subject: Your Memo of May 9, 20--

Gives a quick reason, immediately followed by the refusal.

Provides additional details.

Closes on a helpful note.   ②

Hi, Wanda:

You did such a good job of explaining the merits of our new Executive-in-Residence program that I've tentatively decided to apply for the program myself. To keep my options open, then, I must ask you to select someone else to serve on the evaluation committee.

Since I may be an applicant myself, I believe it would be inappropriate for me to suggest an alternative committee member.

I will know by July 1 whether my workload for the fall semester will allow me to apply. If I decide not to apply, I'll be back in touch with you then to see if there is some way I can assist you in getting this important program off to a successful start.

Peter

Peter Gates (pgates@kempman)
Western Regional Manager
818-555-3854

Grammar and Mechanics Notes

1. Most e-mail programs will automatically insert the "From:" line in the header.
2. *July 1 whether:* Do not use a comma after an incomplete date.

asks. If you must refuse such a significant request, you should probably present your refusal indirectly, following the guidelines given earlier.

Most requests for favors are routine, however, and a routine request should receive a routine response—that is, a response written in the direct organizational plan. A colleague asking you to attend a meeting in her place, a superior asking you to serve on a committee, or a business associate inviting you to lunch is not going to be deeply disappointed if you decline. The writer probably has not spent a great deal of energy composing the request; the main thing he or she wants to know from you is "yes" or "no."

In such situations, give your refusal in the first paragraph, but avoid curtness and coldness. Courtesy demands that you buffer the bad news somewhat and that you at least give a quick, reasonable rationale for declining. Although the refusal itself might not lose the reader's goodwill, a poorly written refusal message might! The e-mail message in Model 12 on page 178 declines a request to serve on a corporate committee and is written using a direct plan.

Assume for a moment, however, that Peter Gates had decided, instead, that his best strategy would be to write the message (Model 12) in the indirect pattern, explaining his rationale before refusing. His opening buffer might then have been as follows:

> Like you, I believe our new Executive-in-Residence program will prove to be effective for both Utah State and the executives who participate.

REFUSING A CLAIM

 4 ▸ *Compose a message that refuses a claim.*

The indirect plan is almost always used when refusing an adjustment request because the reader (a dissatisfied customer) is emotionally involved in the situation. The customer is already upset by the failure of the product to live up to expectations. If you refuse the claim immediately, you risk losing the customer's goodwill.

The tone of your refusal must convey respect and consideration for the customer—even when the customer is at fault. To separate the reader from the refusal, begin with a buffer, using one of the techniques presented earlier (for example, showing understanding).

> Frequent travelers like you depend on luggage that "can take it"—luggage that will hold up for many years under normal use.

When explaining the reasons for denying the claim, do not accuse or lecture the reader. At the same time, don't appear to accept responsibility for the problem if the customer is at fault. In impersonal, neutral language, explain why the claim is being denied.

> **NOT:** The reason the handles ripped off your Sebastian luggage is that you overloaded it. The tag on the luggage clearly states that you should use the luggage only for clothing, with a maximum of 40 pounds. However, our engineers concluded that you had put at least 65 pounds of items in the luggage.

> **BUT:** On receiving your piece of Sebastian luggage, we sent it to our testing department. The engineers there found stretch marks on the leather

FIGURE 8.1

An Ineffective Bad-News Message

Uses a direct, negative subject line.

Begins by apologizing, giving the bad news first (where it is emphasized), and using personal language.

Uses an accusatory tone; hides behind company policy without explaining the reason for the policy.

Repeats the apology (thereby emphasizing the negative aspects), sounds insincere in its sales promotion, and ends with a cliché.

June 27, 20—

Mr. Oliver J. Arbin
518 Thompson Street
Saginaw, MI 48607

Dear Mr. Arbin

Subject: Denial of Your Claim of June 18, 20—

Although we were certainly sorry to learn of your troubles with Northern Airlines, I'm afraid that we won't be able to refund your money. Let me explain why.

Flight 126 was scheduled to depart at 8 P.M. and was canceled at 7:10 P.M. because of inclement weather. If you and your family had remained in the boarding area as requested, you would have been rebooked on Flight 3321, which arrived in Indianapolis just 75 minutes later than your scheduled flight. Company policy forbids our refunding money when a flight is canceled because of inclement weather.

Although I'm sorry we could not help you this time, Mr. Arbin, I hope you will call upon us in the future when your travel plans take you to one of the 200 cities Northern Airlines is proud to serve. Please let me know if you have any questions about this matter.

Sincerely

Madelyn Masarani

Madelyn Masarani
Service Representative

eta

MODEL 13

Bad-News Reply— Refusing a Claim

This message is a response to the persuasive claim presented in Model 9 on page 154.

NORTHERN
AIRLINES

June 27, 20—

Mr. Oliver J. Arbin
518 Thompson Street
Saginaw, MI 48607

Opens on an agreeable and relevant note.

① Dear Mr. Arbin

Subject: Further Information About Flight 126

We make no money when our customers are forced to take long trips by car rather than by flying Northern Airlines; and when that happens, we want to find out why.

Begins the explanation; presents the refusal in impersonal language.

② A review of the June 2 log of the aborted Flight 126 shows that it was scheduled to depart at 8 p.m. and was canceled at 7:10 p.m. because of inclement weather. Passengers were asked to remain in the boarding area; those who did were rebooked on Flight 3321, which departed at 9:15 p.m. Flight 3321 arrived in Indianapolis at 10:40 p.m., just 75 minutes later than the scheduled arrival of Flight 126. Given these circumstances, the ticket agent was correct in disallowing any refund on nonrefundable tickets.

Closes on a helpful note; assumes that the reader will continue to fly on Northern Airlines.

Because you indicated that you're a frequent traveler on Northern, I've asked our scheduling department to add you to the mailing list to receive a complimentary subscription to our quarterly Saginaw flight schedule. A copy of the current schedule is enclosed. From now on, you'll be sure to know exactly when every Northern flight arrives at and departs from Tri-Cities Airport.

Sincerely

Madelyn Masarani

Madelyn Masarani
Service Representative

eta
③ Enclosure

Grammar and Mechanics Notes

1. Insert no punctuation after the salutation and complimentary closing when using open punctuation.
2. *boarding area;:* Use a semicolon to separate two closely related independent clauses not connected by a conjunction.
3. Use an enclosure notation to alert the recipient to look for some inserted material.

and a frayed nylon stitching cord. They concluded that such wear could have been caused only by contents weighing substantially more than the 40-pound maximum weight that is stated on the luggage tag. Such use is beyond the "normal wear and tear" covered in our warranty.

Note that in the second example, the pronoun *you* is not used at all when discussing the bad news. By using third-person pronouns and the passive voice, the example avoids directly accusing the reader of misusing the product. The actual refusal, given in the last sentence, is conveyed in neutral language.

As with other bad-news messages, close on a friendly, forward-looking note. If you can offer a compromise, it will take the sting out of the rejection and show the customer that you are reasonable. It will also help the customer save face. Be careful, however, that your offer does not imply any assumption of responsibility on your part. The compromise can either come before or be a part of the closing.

> Although we replace luggage only when it is damaged in normal use, our repair shop tells me the damaged handle can easily be replaced. We would be happy to do so for $39.50, including return shipping. If you will simply initial this letter and return it to us in the enclosed, addressed envelope, we will return your repaired luggage within four weeks.

Somewhere in your letter you might also include a subtle pitch for resale. The customer has had a negative experience with your product. If you want your reader to continue to be a customer, you might restate some of the benefits that led him or her to buy the product in the first place. But use this technique carefully; a strong pitch may simply annoy an already unhappy customer.

Consider the situation in which a customer wrote to an airline company upset that his family's flight to Indianapolis was canceled and they were forced to make a six-hour drive instead (see Model 9 on page 154). The customer wanted a refund of the $680 cost of his five nonrefundable tickets. For good business reasons, the company decided not to accept the claim, showing that sometimes even well-written claims must be rejected.

Figure 8.1 on page 180 illustrates how *not* to write an effective bad-news message. Model 13 on page 181, a revised version of the ineffective example, illustrates how to write an effective claims refusal.

CONCEPT CHECK 8.1

Now assume the role of the customer service manager at textbooks.com (see Concept Check 6.2 on page 127). The front cover and two of the pages of the textbook were torn when you shipped it. That's why you sold it as a used book at a deep discount. Customers must check a box on the online order form acknowledging their understanding that used books may have been marked up or show signs of wear and tear. The only thing you guarantee is that no pages are missing from the used books you sell. Decline the claim.

a. Compose an appropriate subject line for your e-mail.
b. Compose the first sentence of your message.
c. Compose the sentence in which you actually refuse the claim.
d. Compose the final paragraph of your letter.

Online Study Center
Improve Your Grade
Audio Chapter Review 8.1–8.4
Handouts

TEST PREPPER 8.1–8.4

ANSWERS CAN BE FOUND ON P. 411

True or False?

_____ 1. Bad-news messages should be written in the direct organizational pattern.

_____ 2. The buffer opening of a bad-news letter should not indicate the topic of the letter.

_____ 3. Most of the focus of the bad-news message should be on the reasons for the refusal.

_____ 4. To establish good rapport with the reader, you should apologize for having to deliver bad news.

_____ 5. Bad-news messages are also persuasive messages.

Critical Thinking

6. What advice could you give to a friend who has to send a bad-news message to an Asian colleague?

Online Study Center
ACE the Test
ACE Practice Tests 8.1–8.4

Online Study Center
Improve Your Grade
Audio Chapter Quiz 8.1–8.4
PowerPoint Review 8.1–8.4

CHECKLIST 9

Bad-News Messages

Determine How to Start the Message

✓ **Direct Plan:** Use a direct organizational plan when the bad news is insignificant, the reader (such as your superior) prefers directness or expects a "no" response, the writer wants to emphasize the bad news, or the reader-writer relationship is either extremely close or extremely poor. Present the bad news (see "Give the Bad News" at right), along with a brief rationale, in the first paragraph.

✓ **Indirect Plan:** Use an indirect organizational plan when writing to subordinates, customers, readers who prefer the indirect plan, or readers you don't know. Start by buffering the bad news, following these guidelines:

a. Remember the purpose: to establish a common ground with the reader.

b. Select an opening statement that is neutral, relevant, supportive, interesting, and short.

c. Consider establishing a point of agreement, expressing appreciation, giving a sincere compliment, presenting a fact or general principle, giving good news, or showing understanding.

d. Provide a smooth transition from the buffer to the reasons that follow.

Justify Your Decision

✓ If possible, stress reasons that benefit someone other than yourself.

✓ State reasons in positive language.

✓ Avoid relying on "company policy"; instead, explain the reason behind the policy.

✓ State reasons concisely to avoid reader impatience. Do not overexplain.

✓ Present the strongest reasons first; avoid discussing weak reasons.

Give the Bad News

✓ If using the indirect plan, subordinate the bad news by putting it in the middle of a paragraph and including additional discussion of reasons.

✓ Present the bad news as a logical outcome of the reasons given.

✓ State the bad news in positive and impersonal language. Avoid terms such as *cannot* and *your*.

✓ Do not apologize.

✓ Make the refusal definite—by implication if appropriate; otherwise, by stating it directly.

Close on a Positive Note

✓ Make your closing original, friendly, off the topic of the bad news, and positive.

✓ Consider expressing best wishes, offering a counterproposal, suggesting other sources of help, or building in resale or subtle sales promotion.

✓ Avoid anticipating problems, apologizing, inviting needless communication, referring to the bad news, repeating a cliché, revealing doubt, or sounding selfish.

> ### THREE PS
> ### PROBLEM, PROCESS, PRODUCT

A Bad-News Message

Problem

You are a facilities manager at General Mills. Your firm recently constructed a new administrative building on a five-acre lot, and you've landscaped the unused four acres with lighted walkways, fountains, and ponds for employees to enjoy during their lunch hours and before and after work. Your lovely campuslike site is one of the few such locations within the city limits.

Joan Bradley, the mayor of your city, is running for reelection. She has written to you asking permission to hold a campaign fund-raiser on your grounds on July 7 from 8 p.m. until midnight. This event will be for "heavy" contributors; as many as 150 people, each paying $500, are expected. Her reelection committee will take care of all catering, security, and cleanup.

You do not want to become involved in this event for numerous reasons. Write to the mayor (The Honorable Joan Bradley, Mayor of Clarkfield, Clarkfield, MN 56223) and decline her request.

Process

1. Describe your primary audience.

   - Very important person (Don't want to offend her)
   - Holds political views different from my own
   - Possibility of her losing the election (Don't want to appear to be backing a loser)

2. Describe your secondary audience.

   - The 150 big contributors (What will be their reaction to my refusal?)
   - The other candidates (Do not wish to offend anyone who might become the next mayor)

3. Brainstorm: List as many reasons as you can think of why you might refuse the mayor's request. Then, after you've come up with several, determine which one will be most effective. Underline that reason.

   - Other sites in the city offer a more suitable environment for the event
   - Would have to provide the same favor for every other candidate
   - <u>Possible harm to lawn, plants, and animals</u>
   - Company policy prohibits outside use

4. Write your buffer opening—neutral, relevant, supportive, interesting, and short.

   > Thank you for your kind comments about our lovely grounds. Our staff has been able to create an environment in which plants and animals not normally found in the Midwest are able to thrive.

5. Now skip to the actual refusal itself. Write the statement in which you refuse the request—making it positive, subordinated, and unselfish.

   To protect this delicate environment, we restrict the use of these grounds to company employees.

6. Write the closing for your letter—original, friendly, off the topic of the refusal, and positive. *Suggestions:* best wishes, counterproposal, other sources of help, or subtle resale.

   As an alternative, may I suggest the beautiful grounds at the Minnesota Educational Consortium on Lapeer Street. They were designed with a Minnesota motif by Larry Miller, the designer for our grounds.

Product

General Mills
General Offices

Post Office Box 1113
Minneapolis, Minnesota 55440

May 20, 20—

The Honorable Joan Bradley
Mayor of Clarkfield
Clarkfield, MN 56223

Dear Mayor Bradley:

Thank you for your kind comments about our lovely grounds. Our staff has been able to create an environment here in which plants and animals not normally found in the Midwest are able to thrive.

For example, after much effort, we have finally been able to attract a family of Eastern Bluebirds to our site. At this very moment, the female is sitting on three eggs, and members of our staff unobtrusively check on her progress each day.

Similar efforts have resulted in the successful introduction of beautiful but sensitive flowers, shrubs, and marsh grasses. To protect this delicate environment, we restrict the use of these grounds to company employees, many of whom have contributed ideas, plants, and time in developing the grounds.

As an alternative, may I suggest the beautiful grounds at the Minnesota Educational Consortium on Lapeer Street. They were designed with a Minnesota motif by Larry Miller, who designed our grounds. Various public events have been held there without damage to the environment. Susan Siebold, their executive director (555-9832), is the person to contact about using MEC's facilities.

Sincerely,

J. W. Hudson

J. W. Hudson
Facilities Manager

tma

> ## PORTFOLIO PROJECT 4

Online Study Center
Prepare for Class
Portfolio Stationery

Writing a Bad-News Letter

Problem

You are Charles J. Redding, national sales manager for Midland Medical Supplies. You have received a memo from O. B. Presley, a sales representative, asking that the company purchase a new notebook computer with built-in printer (the Canon NoteJet) for all sales reps. You have, of course, considered all kinds of options to make the sales representatives more productive—notebook computers with built-in printers, cellular telephones for their cars, computerized answering and call-forwarding services, and the like. The fact is that your firm simply cannot afford these items for every sales representative. Also, some of the less energetic representatives clearly do not need them. Instead, your company's philosophy is to pay your representatives top salary and commission and then have them purchase out of their commission earnings whatever "extra" devices or services they deem worthwhile.

   You have checked with your purchasing department and found that your corporate price for the Canon NoteJet is $1,350, instead of the retail price of $1,999 quoted by Presley. You would be happy to have the company purchase this machine for Presley and deduct the cost from his commission check. Even though Presley will be disappointed in what you have to say, send him a memo conveying this information.

Process

Compose a few paragraphs describing how you solved this problem. In narrative form, provide information such as the following:

1. What is the purpose of your letter?
2. Describe your audience.
3. Will you use a direct or an indirect organizational plan?
4. What attributes should your opening sentence have?
5. What attributes should the refusal sentence have?
6. When and how will you discuss your counteroffer?
7. What attributes should your closing paragraph have?
8. How can you use the "you" attitude and positive language throughout your letter?

Product

Compose your document, following the steps of the writing process (audience analysis, planning, drafting, revising, formatting, and proofreading). Format the final version on letterhead stationery (refer to the Style Manual for formatting guidelines).

LEARNING OBJECTIVE REVIEW

1▶ *Communicate your message politely, clearly, and firmly.*

- Recognize your twofold purpose:
  - To convey bad news
  - To maintain the reader's goodwill
- Decide whether to use the direct or the indirect plan.
  - Use the direct plan when the bad news involves a small, insignificant matter and can be considered routine; the reader prefers directness; or you want to emphasize the bad news.
  - Use the indirect approach when giving bad news to subordinates, customers, readers who prefer the indirect approach, and readers you do not know.
- When using the indirect plan:
  - Use a buffer statement.
  - Justify your decision with an explanation that includes reader benefits.
  - Subordinate the bad news.
  - Close on a pleasant note.

2▶ *Compose a message that rejects an idea.*

- Strive to refuse the proposal while retaining the reader's goodwill.
- Try to persuade the reader that your position is reasonable.

3▶ *Compose a message that refuses a favor.*

- Refuse significant requests indirectly.
- Refuse routine requests directly.
- Provide a brief rationale for all refusals.

4▶ *Compose a message that refuses a claim.*

- Use the indirect plan.
- Begin with a buffer.
- Explain why the claim is being denied.
- Close on a friendly, forward-looking note.

EXERCISES

1. McDonald's Franchise (▶ 8.1)

As the director of franchise operations for McDonald's, Inc., you must evaluate the hundreds of applications for franchises you receive each month. Today you received an application from Maxine Denton, who is developing a large shopping-center complex in Austin, Texas. Her corporation wants to open a McDonald's restaurant in her shopping center. Of course, the company will have no trouble coming up with the initial investment. It will also select a qualified manager, who will then go through McDonald's extensive training and orientation course.

But McDonald's has a policy against granting franchises to corporations, real estate developers, and other absentee owners. The firm wants its owners to manage their stores personally. McDonald's prefers high-energy types who will devote their careers to their restaurants and not be involved in numerous other business ventures. Write to Ms. Denton (she's the president of Lone Star Development Corporation, P.O. Box 1086, Houston, TX 77001), turning down her application.

2. Getting Around a Long Wait (▶ 8.1)

You're new to the management staff of Cedar Point, a large amusement park in Sandusky, Ohio. Cedar Point is renowned for its 14 roller coasters and dozens of other exciting rides. Each ride can accommodate many people at once, so the lines don't stand still for very long. Even so, on summer holidays and weekends, the wait for Cedar Point's most popular rides, such as the Millennium Force roller coaster, can be lengthy. In fact, when *Wall Street Journal* reporters sampled the mid-day waiting time at parks around the United States, they wound up standing for an hour in the line for the two-minute Millennium Force ride. At the other end of the spectrum, the reporters waited only 11 minutes or less to jump on rides at Coney Island in Brooklyn, New York, an old-fashioned park where the lines lengthen after dark.

Imagine that your boss, Cedar Point's top operational officer, has asked all supervisors to submit ideas for a system that would make the wait less onerous for customers. One supervisor suggests that parents with strollers be allowed to go to the front of the line, on the theory that this policy reduces the likelihood of noisy scenes with fussy youngsters. You believe that other customers would resent this system; you also don't believe that it would dramatically affect either the wait or customers' perceptions of it. With your boss's approval, you decide to reject this idea.

3. Job Too Big (▶8.1)

You are the owner of AMX Construction in Loveland, Colorado. You are putting together a proposal for a construction loan to build the Eagle's Nest apartments, a 100-unit apartment complex, in Fort Collins, Colorado. You will be the general contractor on the project, and you have accepted bids from subcontractors for the plumbing work on the apartments.

You reviewed the bids very carefully and narrowed the field of 15 to 2 bidders. The second lowest bid was from a plumbing firm in Denver. This firm specializes in plumbing for large apartment complexes. You have worked with them before, and their work is good.

The lowest bidder was Alpine Plumbing from Golden, Colorado. You have worked with Alpine before, and although their work was also good, the company took longer than expected to complete jobs. Alpine Plumbing is a small firm with only three plumbers. They usually work on small complexes of between 20 and 30 units and have never tackled a job this big.

You are concerned that Alpine won't be able to meet the deadlines you have proposed. Therefore,

you elected to go with the company from Denver rather than Alpine. Write a letter to Mr. Alex Gephardt, General Manager, Alpine Plumbing, P.O. Box 245, Golden, Colorado, 75221, giving him the bad news.

4. No Hotel Reservation (▶8.1)

You are the manager of the Daytona 100, a 100-room hotel in Daytona, Florida, that caters to businesspeople. You've received a reservation from Alpha Kappa Psi fraternity at Ball State University to rent 24 double rooms during the college's spring break (April 6 to 13). The fraternity has offered to send a $1,000 deposit to guarantee the rooms if necessary.

As a former AKPsi yourself, you know that these fraternity members are responsible students who would cause no problems. You also recognize that when these students graduate and assume positions in industry, they are the very type of people you hope will stay at your hotel. Because of previous bad experiences, however, you now have a strict policy against accepting reservations from student groups. Write to the AKPsi treasurer (Scott Rovan, 40 Cypress Grove Court, No. 25, Muncie, IN 47304), conveying this information.

5. Work-Team Communication— Dealing with AIDS (▶8.1)

Working in teams of three or four, assume the role of the grievance committee of your union. Your small company has its first known case of an employee with AIDS. The employee, an assistant manager (non-union position), has indicated that she intends to continue working as long as she is physically able. The company has upheld her right to do so.

You've received a memo signed by six union members who work in her department, objecting to her continued presence at work. They are worried about the risks of contracting the disease from a coworker. Although they have compassion for the assistant manager, they want the union to step in and require that she either resign or be reassigned so that union members do not have to interact with her in the course of completing their own work.

Your committee does some Internet research on the topic and based on your findings decides not to intervene in this matter. Do the research and write a memo to Katherine Kellendorf, chair of the Committee of Concerned Workers, giving her your decision.

6. Declining a Field Trip (▶ 8.2)

You are Donna Jo Luse and you have received the letter written by David Pearson (see Exercise 2 of Chapter 7). Lunch is, of course, your busiest time, and no one has the time then (or the patience) to provide a tour of the kitchens and help 23 youngsters make their salads. Perhaps, instead, they could come for a tour and snack midmorning or midafternoon. Write to Mr. Pearson (Jack 'n' Jill Preschool, 113 Grenvale Road, Westminster, MD 21157), refusing his request.

7. No Magic (▶ 8.2)

Today you received in the mail a letter you have come to expect. The letter is from Olivia Frances, a close personal friend in Steubenville, Ohio. Olivia has been the chairperson of NHP, a nonprofit organization that helps raise money for a children's hospital near Steubenville.

Because of your national reputation as a magician and your friendship with Olivia, you have been invited for several years in a row to do a magic show at the organization's annual conference. The magic show has been a big moneymaker for the hospital, and you have enjoyed volunteering your time to help

such a worthy cause and to help a dear friend. However, this year you have a prior family commitment and must deny your friend's request to do the magic show. Write a personal letter to Olivia (965 West Cloverdale Avenue, Steubenville, OH 45810) letting her know the bad news.

8. Azaleas Do Not Grow (▶ 8.3)

You are a customer service representative for Jackson-Parsons Nurseries and have received the letter written by Vera Malcolm (see Exercise 4 of Chapter 7). Jackson-Parsons goes to great expense to use only the highest-quality patented stock and to pack each order in dampened sphagnum moss. However, there is no way that any nursery can control the care that plants receive on reaching their destination. Your obligation in this matter clearly ended when Ms. Malcolm did not notify you of the problem immediately. If she had, you would have refunded her money. But evidently the azaleas are now thriving where they were planted, and you feel you have no further obligation. Tell this to Ms. Malcolm in a letter (Public Service Company of Arkansas, 189 Blackwood Lane, Little Rock, AR 72207).

Additional exercises are available at the Online Study Center website: **college.hmco.com/pic/oberSASfund**.

Online Study Center RESOURCES

Prepare for Class, Improve Your Grade, and ACE the Test. Student Achievement Series resources include:

ACE Practice Tests	Ask Ober	Audio Chapter Reviews and Quizzes
Chapter Outlines	Communication Objectives	Crossword Puzzles
Flashcards	Glossaries	Handouts
LAB Tests	Portfolio Project Stationery	Sample Reports

To access these learning and study tools, go to **college.hmco.com/pic/oberSASfund**.

Marketing and advertising are only as effective as the research on which they are based, especially for a nonprofit organization like the Rock and Roll Hall of Fame and Museum. Working with limited resources, it must identify who its clients are and from where they come so it can communicate with them effectively and efficiently to meet its goals.

1 Learn the guidelines to achieving report accuracy.

2 Identify the different purposes for writing reports.

3 Evaluate the quality of data already available.

4 Collect and evaluate data on the Internet.

190

> *"I use bar graphs for age or basic demographic information. When I want to show a trend or data movement over time, I use a line graph."*
>
> —Todd Mesek, Director of Marketing and Communications, Rock and Roll Hall of Fame and Museum

Chapter Outline

▶ REPORT ACCURACY

▶ PURPOSES OF REPORTS
Informing
Analyzing
Recommending

▶ COMMON TYPES OF DATA
Evaluating Secondary Data

▶ COLLECTING DATA ON THE INTERNET
Browsing the Internet
Searching the Internet
Evaluating the Quality of Electronic Information

▶ COLLECTING DATA THROUGH QUESTIONNAIRES
Constructing the Questionnaire
Writing the Cover Letter

▶ CONSTRUCTING TABLES AND CHARTS
Preparing Tables
Preparing Charts
A Word of Caution

▶ INTERPRETING THE DATA
The Three-Step Process of Analysis
Making Sense of the Data

Online Study Center
Prepare for Class
Chapter Outline

7 ▶ *Interpret data for the report reader.*

6 ▶ *Construct effective tables and charts.*

5 ▶ *Develop an effective questionnaire and cover letter.*

Marketing Rock and Roll

How can a nonprofit museum with a modest research budget and an ambitious mission collect and analyze data about half a million visitors yearly? As director of marketing and communications for the Rock and Roll Hall of Fame and Museum, Todd Mesek is responsible for its marketing, advertising, public relations, and website. He needs research to understand the public's view of the museum so that management can determine how to allocate its resources most effectively.

Online Study Center college.hmco.com/pic/oberSASfund

TODD MESEK
Director of Marketing
and Communications,
Rock and Roll Hall of
Fame and Museum
(Cleveland, Ohio)

KEY TERMS

bar chart   *p. 207*
line chart   *p. 207*
pie chart   *p. 207*
primary data   *p. 196*
questionnaire   *p. 200*
secondary data   *p. 196*
survey   *p. 200*
table   *p. 202*

When preparing reports, Mesek uses charts to help readers grasp the significance of the data. "I use bar graphs for age or basic demographic information," he explains. "When I want to show a trend or data movement over time, I use a line graph. Often, I use pie charts to show the origin of our visitors."

From research, he has learned that more than 95 percent of the visitors are from out of town, and 10 percent are from out of the country. Because of these findings, the museum now invests more of its resources in reaching out to potential visitors beyond Cleveland who want to see Eric Clapton's guitar and other artifacts of rock and roll. ■

REPORT ACCURACY

 Learn the guidelines to achieving report accuracy.

Organizations like the Rock and Roll Hall of Fame and Museum need comprehensive, up-to-date, accurate, and understandable information to achieve their goals. Much of this information is communicated in the form of reports—such as progress reports, proposals, and policies and procedures. Also, in any organization, unique problems and opportunities appear that require one-time-only reports. Many of these situations call for information to be gathered and analyzed and for recommendations to be made. These so-called *situational reports* are perhaps the most challenging for the report writer. Because they involve a unique event, the writer has no previous reports to use as a guide; he or she must decide what types of information and how much information are needed and how best to organize and present the findings. Model 14 on page 194 shows a sample situational report.

No report weakness—including making major grammatical mistakes, misspelling the name of the report reader, or missing the deadline for submitting the report—is as serious as communicating inaccurate information. It's a basic tenet of management that bad information leads to bad decisions. In such situations, the bearer of the "bad" news will surely suffer the consequences. To achieve accuracy, follow these guidelines:

1. *Report all relevant facts.* Errors of *omission* are just as serious as errors of *commission.* Don't mislead the reader by reporting just those facts that tend to support your position.

   NOT: During the two-year period of 2002–2004, our return on investment averaged 13 percent.

   BUT: Our return on investment was 34 percent in 2002 but −8 percent in 2004, for an average of 13 percent.

2. *Use emphasis and subordination appropriately.* Your goal is to help the reader see the relative importance of the points you discuss. If you honestly think a certain idea is of minor importance, subordinate it—regardless of whether it reinforces or weakens your ultimate conclusion. Don't emphasize a point simply because it reinforces your position, and don't subordinate a point simply because it weakens your position.

3. *Give enough evidence to support your conclusions.* Make sure that your sources are accurate, reliable, and objective and that enough evidence exists to support your position. Sometimes your evidence (the data you gather) may be so sparse or of such questionable quality that you cannot draw a valid conclusion. If so, simply present the findings and don't draw a conclusion. To give the reader confidence in your statements, discuss your procedures thoroughly and cite all your sources.

4. *Avoid letting personal biases and unfounded opinions influence your interpretation and presentation of the data.* Sometimes you will be asked to draw conclusions and to make recommendations; such judgments inevitably involve a certain amount of subjectivity. You must make a special effort to look at the data objectively and to base your conclusions solely on the data. Avoid letting your personal feelings influence the outcomes. Sometimes the use of a single word can unintentionally convey bias.

> NOT: The accounting supervisor *claimed* the error was unintentional.
>
> BUT: The accounting supervisor *stated* the error was unintentional.

CONCEPT CHECK 9.1

What are four guidelines for ensuring report accuracy?

PURPOSES OF REPORTS

 2 *Identify the different purposes for writing reports.*

At the outset, you need to determine why you are writing the report. Business reports generally aim to inform, analyze, or recommend.

Informing

Informational reports relate objectively the facts and events about a particular situation. No attempt is made to analyze and interpret the data, draw conclusions, or recommend a course of action. Most progress reports, as well as policies and procedures, are examples of informational reports. In most cases, these types of reports are the easiest to complete. The report writer's major interest is in presenting all of the relevant information objectively, accurately, and clearly, while refraining from including unsolicited analysis and recommendations.

Analyzing

One step in complexity above the informational report is the analytical report, which not only presents information but also analyzes it. Data by itself may be meaningless; the information must be put into some context before readers can make use of it.

Consider, for example, this informational statement: "Sales for the quarter ending June 30 were $780,000." Was this performance good or bad? We cannot possibly know unless the writer *analyzes* the information for us. Here are two possible, very different interpretations of this statement:

> EITHER: Sales for the quarter ending June 30 were $780,000, up 7 percent from the previous quarter. This strong showing was achieved despite an industry-wide slump and may be attributed to the new "Tell One—Sell One" campaign we introduced in January.

MODEL 14

Situational Report

Begins by introducing the topic and discussing the procedures used. This report uses the indirect pattern, saving the recommendations until the end.

Is organized according to the criteria used to solve the problem.

Uses the author-date format for citing references (see the Style Manual).

Closes by making a recommendation based on the findings presented.

THE FEASIBILITY OF AN MXD IN MEMPHIS
David M. Beall

① Mixed-use development (MXD) integrates three or more land uses (for example, office, retail, hotel, residential, and recreation) in a high-density configuration with uninterrupted circulation from one component to another. Interviews with seven local real estate developers and bankers and secondary sources provided information on the feasibility of constructing a mixed-use development in Memphis.

Low Land Prices and Low-Density Population Weaken Potential

② Land prices are a key economic factor in real estate development. High prices force developers to develop land with intensive uses to justify land costs. The much more expensive cost of an MXD makes economic sense only when high land prices justify the investment. Land prices in Memphis, however, are relatively low compared to prices in other major U.S. cities. The Galleria in Houston and the Wolfchase Galleria in Memphis are similar-sized developments that offer an excellent comparison of how land prices dictate development intensity. The Galleria site cost $85,000 per acre; six years later, the Wolfchase Galleria site cost only $10,000 per acre (Rogers, 1998, p. 148)

Successful MXDs tend to be located in high-density urban cores. The Memphis market, however, is a low-density environment. Approximately 67% of the Memphis housing stock is single-family homes, and relatively few commercial buildings reach over six stories high ("Inside Memphis," 2006).

③ **Financing Would Be Difficult**

The area bankers interviewed are reluctant to become involved with a new type of large-scale commercial development. Instead, they prefer to sponsor projects with which they have had experience. According to one banker, "A bank is only as successful as its last loan" (Weiss, 2007). The bankers believe the economic risks associated with developing an MXD outweigh the rewards. They cite such adverse factors as high development costs, complexity, and lack of experience (Allen, 2006)

Davenport Should Delay MXD Project

Because of Memphis's relatively low land costs and low-density population and the difficulty of securing financing, Davenport Development Corp. should not pursue a mixed-use development in the Memphis area now. However, because the Southeast is growing so rapidly, we should reevaluate the Memphis market in three years.

Grammar and Mechanics Notes

1. *real estate developers:* Do not hyphenate a compound noun *(real estate)* that comes before another noun *(developers).*
2. *site:* location *(cite:* "to quote"; *sight:* "to view").
3. Be consistent in formatting report side headings; there is no one standard format (other than consistency). This report uses "talking" headings, which identify both the topic and the major conclusion of each section.

OR: Sales for the quarter ending June 30 were $780,000, a decline of
5.5 percent from the same quarter last year. All regions experienced
a 3 percent to 5 percent *increase* except for the western region,
which experienced an 18 percent decrease in sales. John Manilow,
western regional manager, attributes his area's sharp drop in sales to
the budgetary problems now being experienced by the state govern-
ments in California and Arizona.

The report writer must ensure that any conclusions drawn are reasonable,
valid, and fully supported by the data presented. Although the writer must attempt
to avoid inserting his or her own biases or preexisting opinions into the report,
analysis and interpretation can never be completely objective. The report writer
makes numerous decisions that call for subjective evaluations. Note the difference
in effect of the following two statements, which contain the same information but
in reversed order:

ORIGINAL: Although it is too early to determine the effectiveness of
Mundrake's efforts, he believes the steps he is taking will bring
Limerick's absentee rate down to the industry average of
3.6 percent by December.

REVERSED: Although Mundrake believes the steps he is taking will bring
Limerick's absentee rate down to the industry average of
3.6 percent by December, it is too early to determine the
effectiveness of his efforts.

The original order leaves a confident impression of the probable success of the
steps taken, whereas the reversed order leaves a much more skeptical impression.
Only the report writer can determine which version leaves the more accurate
impression.

CONCEPT CHECK 9.2

What are three major purposes of reports?

Recommending

Recommendation reports add the element of endorsing a specific course of action.
The writer presents the relevant information, interprets it, and then suggests a
plan of attack. The important point is that you must let the *data* form the basis for
any conclusions you draw and any recommendations you make. You want to analyze and present your data so that the truth, the whole truth, and nothing but the
truth emerges. In other words, avoid the temptation of beginning with a precon-
ceived idea and then marshaling evidence and manipulating data to support it.

In a sense, your final recommendation represents only the tip of the iceberg,
but it is a very visible tip. The logic, clarity, and strength of your recommendation can have major implications for your career and for your organization's
well-being.

COMMON TYPES OF DATA

3 *Evaluate the quality of data already available.*

Before collecting any data, you must define the report purpose and analyze
the intended audience. Then you must determine what data is needed to solve the
problem. Sometimes the data you need will be in your mind or in documents you
already have in hand, sometimes it will be in documents located elsewhere, and
sometimes the data is not available at all but must be generated by you.

Start the data-collection phase by breaking your problem into its component parts so that you will know what data you need to collect. The easiest way to do so is to think about what questions you need to answer before you can solve the problem. The answers to these questions will ultimately provide the solution to the overall problem under investigation, and the question topics may, in fact, ultimately serve as the major divisions of your report.

The two major types of data you will collect are secondary and primary data. **Secondary data** consists of data collected by someone else for some other purpose; it may be published or unpublished. Published data includes any material that is widely disseminated, including the following:

secondary data   Data collected by someone else for some other purpose.

- World Wide Web and other Internet resources
- Journal, magazine, and newspaper articles; these articles may be located in print format or retrieved from an electronic database.
- Books
- Brochures and pamphlets
- Technical reports

Unpublished secondary data includes any material that is not widely disseminated, including the following:

- Company records (such as financial records, personnel data, previous correspondence, and reports)
- Legal documents (such as court records and minutes of regulatory hearings)
- Personal records (such as diaries, receipts, and checkbook registers)
- Medical records

primary data   Data collected by the researcher to solve the specific problem at hand.

Primary data consists of data collected by the researcher to solve the specific problem at hand. Because you are collecting the data yourself, you have more control over its accuracy, completeness, objectivity, and relevance. Although secondary and primary data both serve as important sources for business reports, we usually start our data collection by reviewing the data that is already available. Not all report situations require collecting new (primary) data, but it would be unusual to write a report that did not use some type of secondary data.

Studying what is already known about a topic and what remains to be learned makes the reporting process more efficient because the report writer can then concentrate scarce resources on generating new information rather than rediscovering existing information. Also, studying secondary data can highlight sources for additional information, suggest methods of primary research, or give clues for questionnaire items—that is, provide guidance for primary research. For these reasons, our discussion of data collection focuses first on secondary sources.

Secondary data is neither better nor worse than primary data; it is simply *different*. The source of the data is not as important as its quality and its relevance for your particular purpose. The major advantages of using secondary data are economic: using secondary data is less costly and time-consuming than collecting primary data. Its disadvantages relate not only to the availability of sufficient secondary data but also to the quality of the data that is available. Never use any data before you have evaluated its appropriateness for the intended purpose.

Evaluating Secondary Data

By definition, secondary data was gathered for some purpose other than your particular report needs. Therefore, the categories used, the population sampled, and the analyses reported might not be appropriate for your use. Ask yourself the questions in the following subsections about any secondary sources you're considering incorporating into your report.

What Was the Purpose of the Study?

If the study was undertaken to find a legitimate answer to a question or problem, you can have more confidence about the accuracy and objectivity of the results than if, for example, the study was undertaken merely to prove a point. People seeking honest answers to honest questions are more likely to select their samples carefully, to ask clear and unbiased questions, and to analyze the data appropriately.

Be wary of secondary data if the researcher had a vested interest in the outcome of the study. For example, you would probably have more faith in a study extolling the merits of the Toyota Camry automobile if it had been conducted by *Consumer Reports* than if it had been conducted by Toyota, Inc.

How Was the Data Collected?

Were appropriate procedures used? Although you may not be an experienced researcher yourself, your reading of secondary data will likely alert you to certain standard research procedures that should be followed. For example, if you are interested in learning the reactions of all factory workers in your organization to a particular proposal, you would not gather data from just the newly hired workers. Likewise, if a questionnaire were sent to all the factory workers and only 10 percent responded, you probably would not conclude that the opinions of these few respondents represented the views of all workers.

How Was the Data Analyzed?

As we shall see later, different types of data lend themselves to different types of analyses. Sometimes the low number of responses to a particular question or ambiguity in the question itself prevents us from drawing any valid conclusions.

In some situations, even though the analysis was appropriate for the original study, it may not be appropriate for your particular purposes. For example, suppose you're interested in the reactions of teenagers and the only available secondary data used the category "younger than 21 years of age." You would not know whether the responses came mostly from those younger than 13 years old, those 13 to 19 years old (your target group), or those older than 19 years old.

How Consistent Is the Data Compared to That from Other Studies?

When you find the same general conclusions drawn in several independent sources, you can have greater confidence in the data. On the other hand, if four studies on a particular topic reached one conclusion and a fifth study reached the

Researching his comparable value guided the New York Jets in signing tackle Jason Fabini to a multiyear contract. Their salary-cap analysts constructed charts listing the contracts of 15 to 20 comparable players and compared the financial and performance statistics for each player.

opposite conclusion, you would need to scrutinize the fifth study carefully before accepting its findings.

Avoid accepting something as true simply because you read it in print or saw it on the Internet. Because the reader of your report will be making decisions based on the data you present, take care to include only accurate data in your report.

How Old Is the Data?

Data that was true at the time it was collected might or might not be true today. A job-satisfaction study completed at your organization last year may have yielded accurate data at the time. If your organization has since merged with another company, moved its headquarters, or been torn by a strike, however, the job-satisfaction data may have no relevance today. On the other hand, some data may remain accurate years after its collection. For example, a thorough study of the origins of the labor movement in the United States may have almost permanent validity.

Your data must pass these five tests, whether it comes from company records or printed sources on the Internet. Data that fails even one of the tests should probably be discarded and not used in your report. At the very least, such data requires extra scrutiny and perhaps extra explanation in the report itself if you do choose to use it.

CONCEPT CHECK 9.3

What five questions should you answer before relying on secondary data?

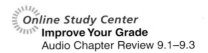

Online Study Center
Improve Your Grade
Audio Chapter Review 9.1–9.3

TEST PREPPER 9.1–9.3

ANSWERS CAN BE FOUND ON P. 412

True or False?

_____ 1. Reports written in response to a one-time-only, unique situation are called situational reports.

_____ 2. The most important trait of a report is that it be formatted in an easy-to-read manner.

_____ 3. Recommendations typically involve a certain degree of subjectivity on the part of the report writer.

_____ 4. Most reports require the use of secondary data.

_____ 5. Secondary data has been published; primary data has not been published.

Vocabulary

Define the following terms in your own words and give an original example.

6. Primary data

7. Secondary data

Online Study Center
ACE the Test
ACE Practice Tests 9.1–9.3

Online Study Center
Improve Your Grade
Audio Chapter Quiz 9.1–9.3
PowerPoint Review 9.1–9.3

COLLECTING DATA ON THE INTERNET

4 *Collect and evaluate data on the Internet.*

Nobody "owns" the Internet; that is, no one governing authority can make rules and impose order. Thus, it should not surprise you that the massive amount of information available on the Internet is not neatly and logically organized for easy search and retrieval. Fortunately, several search sites are available on the Internet to make accessing Internet resources, if not painless, at least more pleasant and productive. Basically, these sites fall into two categories—directories for browsing the Internet and indexes for searching for specific information.

Browsing the Internet

Web directories are hyperlinked lists of websites, hierarchically organized into topical categories and subcategories. Clicking your way through these lists will lead you to website links for the subject you're investigating.

Use these directories when you need to find common information quickly and easily. If you aren't looking for something specific, try using categories to drill down and narrow your search.

Searching the Internet

Web indexes are massive, computer-generated databases containing information on millions of webpages. By entering key words or phrases, you can retrieve lists of webpages that contain your search term. Once your query executes, the Web search site displays the list of hits as a page containing the Universal Resource Locators (URLs, or Internet addresses) that are hyperlinked. To move directly to any particular site, simply click its URL.

CONCEPT CHECK 9.4

Compose an Internet search statement that will locate sources of information about rock music but not about rocks in general.

The success of your Internet search depends on how skillfully you choose your key words (or search terms). Remember that the computer makes a literal search; it will find exactly what you ask for—and nothing more. If you use the search term *secretaries*, most search indexes will not find citations for the word *secretary* or *secretarial*. Some indexes have a feature known as truncation, which allows you to search for the root of a term. Thus, a search for *secre* would retrieve *secret, secretarial, secretaries, secretary, secretion*, and so on. You would then choose the entries appropriate for your purpose.

One of the most common mistakes people make is to use too few key words in their searches or to use the wrong kinds of key words. (Too many hits are just as unhelpful as too few.) Generally, try to identify three or four key words—and use nouns. The only time you generally need to use adjectives or adverbs is if the term itself contains one—such as *World Wide Web* (and don't forget to put phrases in quotation marks).

Evaluating the Quality of Electronic Information

Anyone with access to the Internet can post pretty much anything that he or she wants to online. There is no law, regulation, or Internet policy that states that the information posted on the Internet has to be true, objective, intelligent, or politically correct (recall that there is no central authority for managing the Internet).

Thus, the range of informational quality on the Internet is enormous. Information posted by governmental and educational institutions (typically, those sites that end in "gov" or "edu") is most often comprehensive, accurate, and up-to-date. Most pages sponsored by commercial organizations (typically, those sites that end in "com") are also of high quality, as long as you recognize the profit incentive for these pages. Personal homepages and those sponsored by advocacy organizations should be evaluated especially carefully for accuracy, fairness, and coverage.

The consequences of making decisions based on invalid data can range from minor inconvenience to jeopardizing the financial viability of your organization. You are responsible for the quality of the information you include in your correspondence, reports, and presentations. Avoid accepting something as fact just because you saw it on the Internet. Evaluate your sources critically, using the questions in Checklist 10, "Evaluating the Quality of Internet Resources," on page 213 as a guide.

COLLECTING DATA THROUGH QUESTIONNAIRES

5 ▶ *Develop an effective questionnaire and cover letter.*

Despite your best efforts, you will sometimes find that not enough high-quality secondary data is available to solve your problem. In such a situation, you will probably need to collect primary data.

A **survey** is a data-collection method that gathers information through questionnaires, telephone or e-mail inquiries, or interviews. The **questionnaire** is a written instrument containing questions designed to obtain information from the individual being surveyed. The advantages of conducting a survey are numerous:

▌ The researcher can economically get a representative sampling over a large geographical area. After all, it costs no more to mail a questionnaire across the country than across the street.

▌ The anonymity of a questionnaire increases the validity of some responses. Certain personal and economic data may be given more completely and honestly when the respondent remains unidentified.

▌ No interviewer is present to possibly bias the results.

▌ Respondents can answer at a time convenient for them, which is not always the case with telephone or interview studies.

The big disadvantage of mail questionnaires is the low response rate; also, those individuals who do respond may not be representative (typical) of the population.

Although different types of surveys (such as mail or telephone) are probably the most frequent type of business research, many organizations are now using focus groups to gather more in-depth information about opinions, attitudes, beliefs, and experiences.

Constructing the Questionnaire

Because the target audience's time is valuable, make sure that every question you ask is necessary—that it is essential to help you solve your problem and that you cannot acquire the information from other sources (such as through library or online research). Checklist 11 on page 214 provides guidelines for constructing a questionnaire. Some of the more important points are highlighted in the following paragraphs.

Your language must be clear, precise, and understandable so that the questionnaire yields valid and reliable data. Each question must also be neutral (unbiased).

NOT: Do you think our company should open an on-site child-care center as a means of ensuring the welfare of our employees' small children?
        ___ yes
        ___ no

BUT: Which one of the following possible additional fringe benefits would you most prefer?
        ___ a dental insurance plan
        ___ an on-site child-care center
        ___ three personal-leave days annually
        ___ other (please specify: _____)

survey   A data-collection method that gathers data through questionnaires, telephone or e-mail inquiries, or interviews.

questionnaire   The document containing questions designed to obtain information from the individual being surveyed.

The wording of the original question obviously favors the "pro" side, and thus it could bias the responses. A more neutral question is needed if valid responses are to result. Note several facts about the revised question. First, it is more neutral than the original version; no right answer is apparent. Second, the alternatives are arranged in alphabetical order. To avoid possibly biasing the responses, always present the alternatives in some logical order—alphabetical, numerical, chrono-logical, or the like.

Finally, note that the question provides an "other" category; this option always goes last and is accompanied by the request to "please specify." Suppose the one fringe benefit that the vast majority of employees wanted most was for the company to increase its pension contributions. If the "other" category were missing, the researcher would never learn that important information. Ensure that your categories are *exhaustive* (that is, that they include all possible alternatives) by including an "other" category if necessary.

Also, be certain that each question contains a single idea. Note the following question:

> **NOT:** Our company should spend less money on advertising and more money on research and development.
> ___ agree
> ___ disagree

Suppose the respondent believes that the company should spend more (or less) money on both advertising *and* research and development? How is he or she supposed to answer? The solution is to put each of the two ideas in a separate question.

Finally, ensure that your categories are *mutually exclusive*—that is, that no categories overlap.

> **NOT:** In your opinion, what is the major cause of high employee turnover?
> ___ lack of air conditioning in the factory
> ___ noncompetitive financial package
> ___ poor fringe benefits
> ___ poor working conditions
> ___ weak management

The problem with this item is that the "lack of air conditioning" category overlaps with the "poor working conditions" category, and "noncompetitive financial package" overlaps with "poor fringe benefits." And all four of these probably overlap with "weak management." Such intermingling of categories will thoroughly confuse the respondent and yield unreliable survey results.

Recognize that respondents may hesitate to answer sensitive questions (regarding age, salary, morals, and the like). Even worse, they may deliberately provide *inaccurate* responses. When it is necessary to gather such data, ensure that the respondent understands that the questionnaire is anonymous (by prominently discussing that fact in the cover letter). Respondents tend to be more cooperative in answering such questions when the survey uses broad categories. Accurate estimates provided by broad categories are preferable to precise but incorrect data.

> **NOT:** What is your annual gross salary? $_____
> **BUT:** Please check the category that best describes your annual salary:
> ___ Less than $15,000
> ___ $15,000–$30,000
> ___ $30,001–$60,000
> ___ More than $60,000

The use of the figure $30,001 in the third category is necessary to avoid overlap with the figure of $30,000 in the second category; remember that the categories must be mutually exclusive.

Even experienced researchers find it difficult to spot ambiguities or other problems in their own questionnaires. If time permits, administer the draft questionnaire to a small sample of potential respondents and then revise it as necessary. At a minimum, ask a colleague to edit your instrument with a critical eye. The sample questionnaire shown in Model 15 (on page 203) illustrates different question types, along with clear directions and efficient format.

Writing the Cover Letter

Unless you intend to distribute the questionnaires personally (in which case, you can explain the purpose and procedures in person), include a cover letter like the one shown in Model 16 (on page 204) with your questionnaire. The cover letter should be written as a regular persuasive letter (see Chapter 7). Your job is to convince the reader that it's worth taking the time to complete the questionnaire.

CONSTRUCTING TABLES AND CHARTS

 Construct effective tables and charts.

Preparing Tables

A **table** is an orderly arrangement of data into columns and rows (see Model 17 on page 206). It represents the most basic form of statistical analysis and is useful for showing a large amount of numerical data in a small space. A table presents numerical data more efficiently and in a more interesting way than narrative text and provides more information than a graph, albeit with less visual impact. Because of its orderly arrangement of information into vertical columns and horizontal rows, a table also permits easy comparison of figures. However, trends are more obvious when they are presented in graphs.

Your reader must be able to understand each table on its own, without having to read the surrounding text. Thus, at a minimum, each table should contain a table number, a descriptive but concise title, column headings, and body (the items under each column heading). If you need footnotes to explain individual items within the table, put them immediately below the body of the table, not at the bottom of the page. Similarly, if the table is based on secondary data, include a source note below the body, giving the appropriate citations. Common abbreviations and symbols are acceptable in tables. Once you have the data in hand, it is often helpful to the reader if you rearrange the data from high to low values.

In Figure 9.1, for example, the categories have been rearranged from their original *alphabetical* order in the questionnaire into *descending* order in the report table. Note also that the four smallest categories have been combined into a miscellaneous category, which always goes last, regardless of its size. Finally, note the position and format of the table footnote, which explains an entry in the table.

Preparing Charts

The appropriate use of well-designed charts can aid in reader comprehension, emphasize certain data, create interest, and save time and space because the reader can perceive immediately the essential meaning of large masses of statistical data.

CONCEPT CHECK 9.5

As president of the Marketing Club on campus, you want to know how much money students spend on off-campus entertainment during a typical week.

a. How would you define the term *entertainment* for the students?

b. Write an appropriate questionnaire item, including check-off responses.

table   An orderly arrangement of data in columns and rows.

CONCEPT CHECK 9.6

Assume that you surveyed 50 students in each class on campus and found that 42 freshmen purchased at least one music CD each week; the corresponding numbers for other students were 39 for sophomores, 29 for juniors, and 17 for seniors. Construct an appropriate table summarizing this information.

MODEL 15

Questionnaire

Uses a descriptive title.

Provides clear directions.

Uses check-off responses for Questions 1 to 3.

Lists alternatives in logical order (alphabetically, here).

Uses attitude-scale responses for Question 7, with both positive and negative statements.

Expresses appreciation and provides the name and address of the researcher.

① **STUDENT USE OF COMPUTERS AT PCC**

This survey is being conducted as part of a class research project. Please complete this questionnaire only if you are a full-time junior or senior student at PCC.

② 1. Grade level: 2. Gender: 3. Age:
   ___ junior   ___ female   ___ 20 or younger
   ___ senior   ___ male   ___ 21-24
                                        ___ 25 or older

4. Did you use a computer in a PCC computer lab last semester?
   ___ yes   *(Please continue with Question 5.)*
   ___ no   *(Please disregard the following questions and return the questionnaire in the enclosed campus envelope to Matt Jones, 105 Woldt Hall.)*

5. Which on-campus computer labs were most convenient for completing your computer assignments? Please rank the labs from 1 *(most convenient)* to 3 *(least convenient)* by writing in the appropriate number in each blank.
   ___ business lab
   ___ dormitory lab
   ___ library lab

6. Please check all of the types of computer software you used in a university lab last semester.
   ___ accounting/financial   ___ Internet
   ___ database   ___ programming
   ___ educational/tutorial   ___ spreadsheet
   ___ e-mail   ___ word processing
   ③ ___ graphics/presentation   ___ other *(please specify_____)*

7. Please check whether you agree with, have no opinion about, or disagree with each of the following statements.

	Agree	No Opinion	Disagree
a. I am receiving adequate training in the use of computers and software.	___	___	___
b. I have to wait an unreasonable length of time to get onto a computer in the lab.	___	___	___
c. The computer labs at PCC are up to date.	___	___	___
d. Lab attendants are not very helpful.	___	___	___
e. Most instructors provide adequate instruction in the use of the software they require.	___	___	___

④ *Thanks so much for your help. Please return the completed questionnaire in the enclosed campus envelope to Matt Jones, 105 Woldt Hall.*

Grammar and Mechanics Notes

1. Make the title and section heading stand out through the use of bold type and perhaps a larger font size.
2. If space is at a premium, group shorter questions on the same line (as in Questions 1 to 3).
3. Provide sufficient space for the respondent to fill in open-ended responses.
4. Provide a return name and address on the questionnaire itself in case the return envelope is misplaced.

Online Study Center college.hmco.com/pic/oberSASfund

MODEL 16

Questionnaire Cover Letter

This cover letter would accompany the questionnaire shown in Model 15.

Begins with a short attention-getter.

Provides a smooth transition to the purpose of the letter.

Provides reasons for cooperating.

Makes the requested action easy to take.

PEACE COMMUNITY COLLEGE

P.O. BOX 0049   FAIRBANKS, ALASKA 99701

February 28, 20—

① Dear Fellow Student:

"Oh no—not another computer project!"

Have you ever felt this way during the first day of class when the instructor makes course assignments? Or, instead, do you sometimes wonder, "Why is the instructor making us do this project manually when it would be so much
② easier to do on a computer?"

Either way, here is your chance to provide the PCC administration with your views on student computer and software use at Peace Community College. This research project is a class project for BEOA 249 (Business Communication), and the results will be shared with Dr. Dan Rulong, vice president for academic computing.

③ If you are a full-time junior or senior student, please take five minutes to complete this questionnaire. Then simply return it by February 19 in the enclosed envelope. You'll be doing yourself and your fellow students a big favor.

Sincerely,

Matt Jones

Matt Jones, Project Leader
105 Woldt Hall

Enclosures

*Training the mind,
body, and spirit*

Grammar and Mechanics Notes

1. *Dear Fellow Student:* Use a generic salutation for form letters that are not individually prepared.
2. *"on a computer?":* Position the question mark inside the closing quotation mark if the entire quoted matter is a question.
3. The word *questionnaire* contains two *n*'s and one *r*.

FIGURE 9.1

Arranging Data in Tables

Arrange the data in logical format—usually from high to low.

From This Survey Response:

6. In which of the following categories of clerical workers do you expect to hire additional workers within the next three years? (Check all that apply.)

211	bookkeepers and accounting clerks
31	computer operators
30	data-entry keyers
24	file clerks
247	general office clerks
78	receptionists and information clerks
323	secretaries/administrative assistants
7	statistical clerks
107	typists and word processors

To This Report Table:

Table 2. Companies Planning to Hire Additional Clerical Workers, by Category (*n* = 326)

Category	Pct.*
Secretaries/administrative assistants	99
General office clerks	76
Bookkeepers and accounting clerks	65
Typists and word processors	33
Receptionists and information clerks	24
Miscellaneous	28

*Answers total more than 100% because of multiple responses.

Because of their visual impact, charts receive more emphasis than tables or narrative text. Therefore, you should save them for presenting information that is important and that can best be grasped visually—for example, when the overall picture is more important than the individual numbers. Also, recognize that the more charts your report contains, the less impact each individual chart will have.

The cardinal rule for designing charts is this: keep them simple. Trying to cram too much information into one chart merely confuses the reader and lessens the effectiveness of the graphic. Well-designed charts have only one interpretation, and that interpretation should be clear immediately. The reader shouldn't have to study the chart at length or refer to the surrounding text to figure out its meaning.

Regardless of their type, label all your charts as *figures*, and assign them consecutive numbers, separate from table numbers. Although tables are captioned at the top, charts may be captioned at the top or the bottom. Charts used alone (for example, as an overhead transparency or slide) typically have a caption at the

MODEL 17

Table

Use tables to present a large amount of data clearly and concisely.

Table number and title

Subtitle (optional)

Column heading

Body

Source (optional)

Footnote (optional)

① the market leader for the past three years. As shown in Table 4, the Central Region led the company's sales force again in 2007.

Table 4. RECYCLED PAPER PRODUCTS				
Sales Through September 20, 2007				
Region	Year-to-Date Sales*		Percent Change	Goal Met?
	2007	2006		
Northeast	$ 20	17	15	No
Southeast	183	285	-56	No
Central	2,076	1,986	4	Yes
West	984	759	23	Yes
Totals	$3,263	3,047	7	No

② ③

Source: *Insurance Leaders DataQuest*, National Insurance Institute, New York, 2007, p. 663.

* Sales in thousands.

④ All regions but the Southeast experienced an increase in sales through September. According to Wanda Sánchez, regional manager, the main reason for the region's low performance during the past year was primarily the poor local economies in

Grammar and Mechanics Notes

1. Position the table below the first paragraph that includes a reference to the table. Many table formats are appropriate, but use a consistent format throughout the report.
2. Unless the column heading clearly indicates that the amounts represent dollars or percentages, insert the dollar sign before, or the percent sign after, the first number and before or after a total or average amount.
3. Align word columns at the left; align number columns either on the decimal points or on the numbers in the units position.
4. Leave the same amount of space (two to three blank lines) before and after the table.

top. Charts preceded or followed by text or containing an explanatory paragraph typically have a caption at the bottom. As with tables, you may use commonly understood abbreviations.

Today, many microcomputer software programs can generate special charts automatically from data contained in spreadsheets or from data entered at the keyboard. The professional appearance and ready availability of such charts often make up for the loss of flexibility in designing graphics that precisely match your wishes.

The main types of charts used in business reports and presentations are line charts, bar charts, and pie charts, as illustrated in Model 18 on page 208.

Line Charts

A **line chart** is a graph based on a grid of uniformly spaced horizontal and vertical lines. The vertical dimension represents values; the horizontal dimension represents time. Line charts are useful for showing changes in data over long periods of time and for emphasizing the *movement* of the data—that is, trends. Both axes should be marked off at equal intervals and clearly labeled. The vertical axis should begin with zero, even when all the amounts are quite large (in some situations, it may be desirable to show a break in the intervals by drawing in slash marks). Fluctuations of the line over time indicate variations in the trend; the distance of the line from the horizontal axis indicates quantity.

line chart A graph based on a grid, with the vertical axis representing values and the horizontal axis representing time.

Bar Charts

A **bar chart** is a graph whose horizontal or vertical bars represent values. Bar charts are one of the most useful, simple, and popular graphic techniques. They are particularly appropriate for comparing the magnitude or size of items, either at a specified time or over a period of time. The bars may be vertical or horizontal. The vertical bar chart (sometimes called a *column chart*) is typically used for portraying a time series when the goal is to emphasize the individual amounts rather than the trends.

All of the bars should be the same width, with the length changing to reflect the value of each item. The spacing between the bars should generally be about half the width of the bars themselves. As with tables, you should arrange the bars in some logical order. If space permits, include the actual value of each bar for quicker comprehension.

bar chart A graph with horizontal or vertical bars representing values.

Pie Charts

A **pie chart** is a circle graph whose area is divided into component wedges. It compares the relative parts that make up a whole. Some software charting programs permit you to "drag out" a particular wedge of the pie chart to give it special emphasis.

Although pie charts rank very high in popular appeal, graphics specialists hold them in somewhat lower esteem because of their lack of precision and because of the difficulty in differentiating more than a few categories and in comparing component values across several pie charts. However, pie charts are useful for showing how component parts add up to make a total when the whole contains three to five component parts. On the one hand, a chart is rarely needed for presenting only two component parts; on the other hand, more than five components can present visual difficulties in perceiving the relative value of each wedge.

It is customary to begin "slicing" the pie at the 12 o'clock position and move clockwise in some logical order (often in order of descending size). When used, a

pie chart A circle graph whose area is divided into component wedges.

MODEL 18

Charts

①

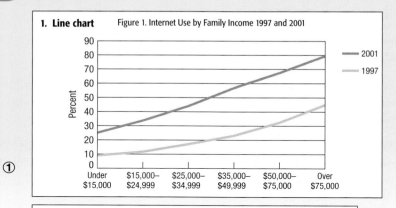

1. Line chart   Figure 1. Internet Use by Family Income 1997 and 2001

②

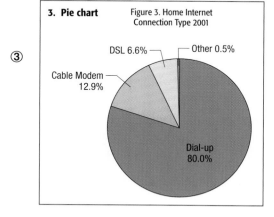

2. Bar chart   Figure 2. Internet Use by Sex 1997, 1998, 2000, and 2001

③

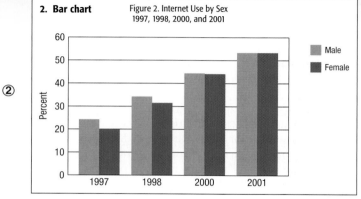

3. Pie chart   Figure 3. Home Internet Connection Type 2001

Source: "A Nation Online: How Americans Are Expanding Their Use of the Internet," National Telecommunications and Information Administration, n.d., retrieved from http://www.ntia.doc.gov/ntiamone/dn/ (December 21, 2004).

Grammar and Mechanics Notes

1. Start the vertical axis at the zero point. Clearly differentiate between the two trend lines, and label each.
2. Make all bars the same width; show value differences by varying the length or height. Position the bars either vertically or horizontally.
3. Begin slicing the pie at the 12 o'clock position and move clockwise in a logical order.

miscellaneous category goes last, regardless of its size. The labels should be placed either inside each wedge, directly opposite the wedge but outside the pie, or in a legend or key. It is also customary to include the percentages or other values represented by each wedge and to distinguish each wedge by shading, cross-hatched lines, different colors, or some similar device.

Three-dimensional graphics, although attention grabbing, are difficult to interpret because they typically display only two-dimensional data (horizontal and vertical), with the third dimension (depth) having no significance. Similarly, three-dimensional pie charts, which are shown slanted away from the viewer rather than vertically, can prove misleading because of perspective—the slices farthest away appear smaller than they actually are. Such graphics are effective for gaining attention and providing a general impression, but they are less effective for conveying the precise meanings needed in business communications. One laboratory experiment found that two-dimensional graphs communicated information more quickly and accurately than corresponding three-dimensional graphs.[1] Checklist 12 on page 215 summarizes the most important points to consider when constructing tables and charts.

A Word of Caution

As the name *visual aids* implies, charts act as a *help*—not a substitute—for the narrative presentation and interpretation. Never use visual aids simply to make your report "look prettier."

Research indicates that the format of the data (tables versus graphs) has little effect on the quality of the decisions made when the task requires a thorough analysis of financial data; both formats are judged to be equally effective. Managers appear to have more confidence in their decisions when such decisions are based on data from tables alone as opposed to data from graphs alone, but they have the most confidence when both formats are used.[2]

These research findings suggest that you should use graphic devices as an *adjunct* to your textual and tabular presentations. Although most numerical data can be presented more efficiently in tables, the competent business communicator uses charts to call attention to particular findings. Rarely should the same data be presented in both tabular and graphic formats.

In *The Visual Display of Quantitative Information*, Edward Tufte warns against *chartjunk*—charts that call attention to themselves instead of to the information they contain.[3] With the ready availability and ease of use of computer graphics, the temptation might be to "overvisualize" your report. Avoid using too many, too large, too garish, or too complicated charts. If the impact is not immediate or if interpretations vary, the chart loses its effectiveness. As with all other aspects of the report project, the visual aids must contribute directly to telling your story more effectively. Avoid chartjunk; strive to *express*—not to *impress*.

INTERPRETING THE DATA

7 ▶ *Interpret data for the report reader.*

At some point in the reporting process, you will have gathered enough data from your secondary and primary sources to enable you to solve your problem. (It is always possible, of course, that during data analysis and report writing, you

may find that you need additional information on a topic.) Your job at this point, then, is to convert your raw data, which might be represented by your notes, photocopies of journal articles, completed questionnaires, audiotapes of interviews, Internet and computer printouts, and the like, into *information*—meaningful facts, statistics, and conclusions—that will help the reader of your report make a decision.

Data analysis is not a step that can be accomplished in one sitting. The more familiar you become with the data and the more you pore over it, the more different things you will see. Data analysis is usually the part of the report process that requires the most time as well as the most skill. The more insight you can provide to the reader about the meaning of the data you've collected and presented, the more helpful your report will be.

The Three-Step Process of Analysis

When analyzing the data, you must first determine whether the data does, in fact, solve your problem. It would make no sense to prepare elaborate tables and other visual aids if your data is irrelevant, incomplete, or inaccurate. To help make this initial evaluation of your data, assume for the sake of simplicity that you have gathered only three bits of information—a paraphrase from a secondary source,

FIGURE 9.2

The Three Steps in Interpreting Data

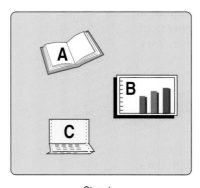
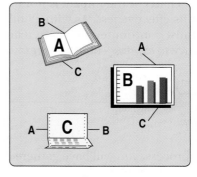
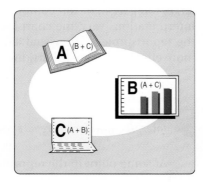

Step 1	Step 2	Step 3
Isolation	Context	Synthesis

FIGURE 9.3

Table for Analysis

Table 4. Response to Statement "Apex Company is an asset to our community." ($n = 271$; all figures in %)								
		Marital Status		**Sex**		**Age**		
	Total	**Married**	**Single**	**Male**	**Female**	**Under 21**	**21–50**	**Over 50**
Agree	80	82	77	83	57	69	77	90
No opinion	12	11	15	12	21	18	14	9
Disagree	8	7	8	5	22	13	9	1
Total	100	100	100	100	100	100	100	100

a chart you developed, and a computer printout, labeled Findings A, B, and C, respectively (see Figure 9.2). Now you are ready to analyze this data.

First, look at each piece of data in isolation (Step 1). If Finding A were the only piece of data you collected, what would it mean in terms of solving the problem? What conclusions, if any, could you draw from this one bit of data? Follow the same process for Findings B and C, examining each in isolation, without considering any other data.

Next, look at each piece of data in combination with the other pieces (Step 2). For example, by itself Finding A might lead to one conclusion, but when viewed in conjunction with Findings B and C, it might take on a different shade of meaning. In other words, does adding Findings B and C to your data pool reinforce your initial conclusion? If so, you can use stronger language in drawing your conclusion. Or does it weaken your initial conclusion? If so, you might wish to qualify your conclusion with less certain language or refrain from drawing any conclusion at all.

Finally, synthesize all the information you've collected (Step 3). When you consider all the facts and their relationships together, what do they mean? For example, if Findings A, B, and C all point in the same direction, you might be able to define a trend. More important, you must determine whether all the data taken together provide an accurate and complete answer to your problem statement. If so, you're then ready to begin the detailed analysis and presentation that will help the reader understand your findings. If not, you must backtrack and start the research process again.

Making Sense of the Data

As a report writer, you cannot simply present the raw data without interpreting it. The data in your tables and charts helps to solve a problem, and the report writer must make the connection between that data and the solution to the problem. In the report narrative, you need not discuss all the data in the tables and charts; that would be boring and insulting to the reader's intelligence. But you must determine what you think the important implications of your data are, and then you must identify and discuss them for the reader.

What types of important points do you look for? Almost always, the most important finding is the overall response to a question (rather than the responses of the subgroups). And almost always the category within the question that receives the largest response is the most important point. So discuss this question and this category first. Let's look at Table 4 shown in Figure 9.3.

In Table 4, the major finding is this: four-fifths of the respondents believe that Apex Company is an asset to their community. Note that if you give the exact figure given in the table (here, 80 percent), you can use less precise language in the narrative—"four-fifths" in this case, or in other cases "one in four," "a slight majority," and the like. Doing so helps you avoid presenting facts and figures too quickly. Pace your analysis because the reader will not be able to comprehend data that is presented too quickly or in too concentrated a format.

Once you've discussed the overall finding, begin discussing the data from the subgroups as necessary. Look for any of these features:

- Trends
- Unexpected findings
- Data that reinforces or contradicts other data
- Extreme values
- Data that raises questions

If any of these features are important, discuss them. In our example, there were no major differences in the responses by marital status, so you would probably not need to discuss them. However, you would need to discuss the big difference in responses between males and females. If possible, present data or draw any valid conclusions regarding the reasons for these differences.

Finally, point out the trend that is evident with regard to age: the older the respondent, the more positive the response. If it's important enough, you might display this trend in a graph for more visual effect.

By now, you probably know more about the topic on which you're writing than the reader knows. Assist the reader, then, by pointing out the important implications, findings, and relationships of your data. Help your reader reach the same conclusions you have reached.

Online Study Center
Improve Your Grade
Audio Chapter Review 9.4–9.7
Handouts

TEST PREPPER 9.4–9.7   ANSWERS CAN BE FOUND ON P. 412

True or False?

_____ 1. The terms *questionnaire* and *survey* may be used interchangeably.

_____ 2. Questionnaire categories should be either exhaustive or mutually exclusive.

_____ 3. The cover letter for a questionnaire is basically a persuasive letter.

_____ 4. Information on the Internet has generally been screened to ensure that it is accurate and objective.

_____ 5. Line charts are typically used to show changes in data over a period of time.

Vocabulary

Define the following terms in your own words.

6. Bar chart
7. Line chart
8. Pie chart
9. Table

Critical Thinking

10. Suppose the importance of the data contained in the table in Concept Check 9.6 merited a single sentence of interpretation. What is the most important thing you could tell the reader?

Online Study Center
ACE the Test
ACE Practice Tests 9.4–9.7

Online Study Center
Improve Your Grade
Audio Chapter Quiz 9.4–9.7
PowerPoint Review 9.4–9.7

CHECKLIST 10

Evaluating the Quality of Internet Resources

Criterion 1: Authority

✓ Is it clear who sponsors the page and what the sponsor's purpose is in maintaining the page?

✓ Is it clear who wrote the material and what the author's qualifications for writing on this topic are?

Criterion 2: Accuracy

✓ Are the sources for any factual information listed clearly so they can be verified in another source?

✓ Has the sponsor provided a link to outside sources (such as product reviews or reports filed with the Securities and Exchange Commission [SEC]) that can be used to verify the sponsor's claims?

✓ Is the information free of grammatical, spelling, and other typographical errors? (These kinds of errors not only indicate a lack of quality control but can actually produce inaccuracies in information.)

✓ Is the statistical data in graphs and charts clearly labeled and easy to read?

Criterion 3: Objectivity

✓ For any piece of information, is the sponsor's motivation for providing it clear?

✓ Is the information content clearly separated from any advertising or opinion content?

✓ Is the point of view of the sponsor presented in a clear manner, with well-supported arguments?

Criterion 4: Currentness

✓ Are there dates on the page to indicate when the page was written, first placed on the Web, and last revised?

✓ Are there any other indications that the material is kept current?

✓ If the material is presented in graphs or charts, is the date when the data was gathered clearly stated?

Source: Adapted from Jan Alexander and Marsha Ann Tate, "Evaluating Web Resources," July 25, 2001, http://muse.widener.edu/Wolfgram-Memorial-Library/ webevaluation/webeval.htm (accessed February 19, 2005).

CHECKLIST 11

Questionnaires

Content

✓ Do not ask for information that is easy to find elsewhere.

✓ Have a purpose for each question. Make sure that all questions help you to solve your problem directly. Avoid asking for unimportant or merely "interesting" information.

✓ Use precise wording so that no question can possibly be misunderstood. Use clear, simple language, and define any term that may be unfamiliar to the respondent or that you are using in a special way.

✓ Use neutrally worded questions and deal with only one topic per question. Avoid loaded, leading, or multifaceted questions.

✓ Ensure that the response choices are both exhaustive and mutually exclusive (that is, that there is an appropriate response for each one and that there are no overlapping categories).

✓ Be especially careful about asking sensitive questions, such as information about age, salary, or morals. Consider using broad categories for such questions (instead of narrow, more specific categories).

✓ Pilot-test your questionnaire on a few people to ensure that all questions function as intended. Revise as needed.

Organization

✓ Arrange the questions in a logical order. Group together questions that deal with a particular topic. If your questionnaire is long, divide it into sections.

✓ Arrange the alternatives for each question in a logical order—such as numerical, chronological, or alphabetical.

✓ Give the questionnaire a descriptive title, provide whatever directions are necessary, and include your name and return address somewhere on the questionnaire.

Format

✓ Use an easy-to-answer format. Check-off questions draw the most responses and are easiest to answer and tabulate. Use free-response items only when absolutely necessary.

✓ To increase the likelihood that your target audience will cooperate and take your study seriously, ensure that your questionnaire has a professional appearance.

✓ Use a simple and attractive format, allowing for plenty of white (blank) space.

✓ Ensure that the questionnaire is free from errors in grammar, spelling, and style.

✓ Use a high-quality printer and make high-quality photocopies.

CHECKLIST 12

Visual Aids

Tables

✓ Use tables to present a large amount of numerical data in a small space and to permit easy comparisons of figures.

✓ Number tables consecutively and use concise but descriptive table titles and column headings.

✓ Ensure that the table is understandable by itself—without reference to the accompanying narrative.

✓ Arrange the rows of the table in a logical order (most often, in descending numerical order).

✓ Combine smaller, less important categories into a miscellaneous category and put it last.

✓ Use only as much detail as necessary; for example, rounding figures off to the nearest whole increases comprehension. Align decimals (if used) vertically on the decimal point.

✓ Use easily understood abbreviations and symbols as needed.

✓ Ensure that the units (dollars, percentages, or tons, for example) are identified clearly.

Charts

✓ Use charts only when they will help the reader interpret the data better—never just to make the report "look prettier."

✓ Label all charts as *figures,* and assign them consecutive numbers (separate from table numbers).

✓ Keep charts simple. Strive for a single, immediate, correct interpretation, and keep the reader's attention on the *data* in the chart rather than on the chart itself.

✓ Choose two-dimensional charts; use three-dimensional charts only when generating interest is more important than precision.

✓ Use the most appropriate type of chart to achieve your objectives. Three of the most popular types of business charts are line, bar, and pie charts.

Line Charts: Use line charts to show changes in data over a period of time and to emphasize the movement of the data—the trends.

✓ Use the vertical axis to represent amount and the horizontal axis to represent time.

✓ Mark off both axes at equal intervals and clearly label them.

✓ Begin the vertical axis at zero; if necessary, use slash marks (//) to show a break in the interval.

✓ If you plot more than one variable on a chart, clearly distinguish between the lines and label each clearly.

Bar Charts: Use bar charts to compare the magnitude or relative size of items (rather than the trend over time), either at a specified time or over a period of time.

✓ Make all bars the same width; vary the length to reflect the value of each item.

✓ Arrange the bars in a logical order and clearly label each.

Pie Charts: Use pie charts to compare the relative parts that make up a whole.

✓ Begin slicing the pie at the 12 o'clock position, moving clockwise in a logical order.

✓ Label each wedge of the pie, indicate its value, and clearly differentiate the wedges.

> ## THREE PS
> ## PROBLEM, PROCESS, PRODUCT

A Questionnaire

Problem

You are Martha Halpern, assistant store manager for Just Pool Supplies, a small firm in San Antonio, Texas. You have been asked by Joe Cox, the store owner, to determine the feasibility of expanding into the spa supply business. To help determine whether there is a sufficient demand for spa (hot tub) supplies, you decide to develop and administer a short questionnaire to potential customers.

Process

1. What is the purpose of your questionnaire?

    To determine whether there are enough potential customers to make it profitable for us to expand into the spa supply business.

2. Who is your audience?

    The theoretical population for my study would be all spa owners in the San Antonio area. Because our major business will still be pool supplies, however, I'll assume that most of my spa supply business will come from my present pool supply customers.

    Thus, the real population for my survey will be the approximately 1,500 existing customers that I have on my mailing list. I don't need to contact every customer, only a representative sample. I'll have my database program generate address labels for every fifth customer.

3. What information do you need from these customers?

    a. Whether they presently own a spa or intend to purchase one in the near future
    b. Where they typically purchase their spa supplies
    c. How much money they typically spend on spa supplies each year
    d. How satisfied they are with their suppliers
    e. What the likelihood is that they'd switch their spa supply business to us
    f. How many spa supply firms are located in the area

4. Is all this information necessary? Can any of it be secured elsewhere?

    I can probably determine the number of spa supply firms and their volume of business from secondary data or from the local chamber of commerce, so I won't need to address that question (3f) in my survey. All of the other information is needed and none of it can be obtained elsewhere.

5. Do any of these questions ask for sensitive information, or are any of them difficult to answer?

    No. The question asking about the amount of money spent on spa supplies depends a little on memory because most people buy spa supplies only four or five times a year; however, respondents should be able to provide a fairly accurate estimate.

6. Is there any logical order to the questions in Item 3?

The question about spa ownership must come first because respondents cannot answer the other questions unless they own a spa. In reviewing the other questions, I think the logical order appears to be a, c, b, d, and e.

7. Will the questionnaire require a cover letter?

Yes, because it will be mailed to the respondents, instead of being administered personally. I'll use my word processing program to generate a personalized form letter to each of the customers selected.

Product

Cover Letter

JUST POOL SUPPLIES

P.O. Box 2277 San Antonio, TX 78298
Phone: (512) 555-0083 Fax: (512) 555-2994

February 22, 20—

Mr. Frederic J. Diehl
Rio Rancho Estates
1876 Anderson Road
San Antonio, TX 79299

Dear Mr. Diehl:

We miss you during the winter!

Although you're a frequent shopper at Just Pool Supplies during the summer months when you're using your pool, we miss having the opportunity to serve you during the rest of the year. Therefore, we're considering adding a complete line of spa supplies to our inventory.

Would you please help us make this decision by answering the enclosed five questions and then returning this form to us in the enclosed stamped envelope.

Thanks for sharing your views with us. We look forward to seeing you during our traditional Pool Party Sale in March.

Sincerely,

Martha Halpern

Martha Halpern
Assistant Manager

swm
Enclosures

THREE Ps (CONTINUED)

Questionnaire

SPA SUPPLIES

1. Do you presently own a spa?

    ____ yes

    ____ no (Please skip the remaining questions and return this form to us in the enclosed envelope.)

2. Considering the number of times you purchased spa supplies last year and the average amount of each purchase, how much do you estimate you spent on spa supplies last year (include all types of purchases—chemicals, accessories, decorative items, and the like).

    ____ less than $100

    ____ $100–$300

    ____ $301–$500

    ____ more than $500

3. Where did you purchase <u>most</u> of your spa supplies last year? (Please check only one.)

    ____ at a general-merchandise store (e.g., Kmart or Sears)

    ____ at a pool- or spa-supply store

    ____ from a mail-order firm

    ____ other (please specify: _____)

4. How satisfied were you with each of these factors at the store where you purchased most of your spa supplies?

Factor	Very Satisfied	Satisfied	Very Dissatisfied
Customer service	____	____	____
Hours of operation	____	____	____
Location of store	____	____	____
Prices	____	____	____
Quality of products	____	____	____
Quantity of products	____	____	____

5. If Just Pool Supplies were to sell spa supplies, how likely would you be to purchase most of your spa supplies there, assuming that the quality, selection, and pricing would be similar to those for its pool supplies?

    ____ very likely

    ____ somewhat likely

    ____ don't know

    ____ somewhat unlikely

    ____ very unlikely

Thanks for your cooperation. Please return the completed questionnaire in the enclosed envelope to Martha Halpern, Just Pool Supplies, P.O. Box 2277, San Antonio, TX 78298.

LEARNING OBJECTIVE REVIEW

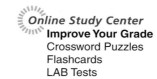

1 *Learn the guidelines to achieving report accuracy.*
- Report all relevant facts.
- Use emphasis and subordination appropriately.
- Give enough evidence to support your conclusions.
- Avoid letting personal biases and unfounded opinions influence your interpretation and presentation of the data.

2 *Identify the different purposes for writing reports.*
- At the outset, determine why you are writing the report.
  - To inform
  - To analyze
  - To recommend

3 *Evaluate the quality of data already available.*
- Determine what data is needed to solve the problem.
  - Primary data
  - Secondary data
- Determine how the data was collected.
- Consider how the data was analyzed and if it will work for your study.
- Determine if the data is consistent with that from other studies.

4 *Collect and evaluate data on the Internet.*
- Use web directories to find common information quickly.
- Use indexes to find specific information using search terms.
- Refine your searches with the effective use of key words.
- Evaluate the quality of electronic information.

5 *Develop an effective questionnaire and cover letter.*
- Collect primary data by conducting a survey using questionnaires, telephone or e-mail inquiries, or interviews.

- Develop an effective questionnaire.
  - Use clear, precise, and understandable language.
  - Avoid biased questions.
  - Be certain that each question contains a single idea.
  - Ensure that categories are mutually exclusive.
  - Recognize that respondents are hesitant to answer personal questions.
- Use a persuasive cover letter to convince the respondent to complete the survey.

6 *Construct effective tables and charts*
- Ensure that each table contains a table number, a descriptive title, column headings, and body.
  - Use footnotes at the bottom of the table to explain individual items.
  - Include a source for all secondary data.
  - Arrange the data from high to low values.
- Use charts for visual impact and to emphasize data.
  - Keep charts simple.
  - Label all charts as figures and assign them consecutive numbers.
  - Caption all charts.
  - Use line charts to graph changes in data over time or to emphasize movement.
  - Use bar charts to compare the magnitude or size of items.
  - Use pie charts to show parts of a whole.
  - Avoid chartjunk.

7 *Interpret data for the report reader.*
- Look at each piece of data in isolation.
- Look at each piece of information in combination with other pieces.
- Synthesize all information.
- Make the connection between the data and the solution to the problem.
- Discuss your findings.

EXERCISES

1. Gathering and Evaluating Secondary Data (▶9.3)

You have been asked to write a report on the feasibility of opening a frozen yogurt store in Tucson, Arizona. (Your instructor may substitute a different product or different city for these assignments.) Do some research on the Internet and use some printed sources. Identify at least eight *printed* sources of information on the topic. Evaluate the quality of these sources using the five questions presented on pages 197–198. Now prepare a memo to your instructor listing the good and poor qualities of your articles. Would you use them all in your report?

2. Locating Specific Facts (▶9.4)

You have been asked by your boss to help determine the feasibility of opening a frozen yogurt store in Tucson, Arizona. Answer the following questions, using the latest figures available. Print out the webpages that support your answers.

a. What are the number of establishments and the total sales last year for TCBY, a frozen yogurt franchise?
b. What is the population of Tucson, Arizona? What percentage of this population is between the ages of 18 and 24?
c. What is the per capita income of the residents of Tucson?
d. What is the address of Everything Yogurt, a frozen yogurt franchise?
e. What is the climate of Tucson, Arizona?
f. How many students are enrolled at the University of Arizona?
g. What is the market outlook for frozen yogurt stores nationwide?
h. What is the most current journal or newspaper article you can find on this topic?

3. The Quality of Internet Resources (▶9.4)

Select two Internet resources and evaluate them based on the four criteria—authority, accuracy, objectivity, and currentness—from Checklist 10 on page 213. Submit copies of the resources and a brief summary of their quality to your instructor.

4. Communication Skills (▶9.5)

The placement director at your institution has asked you, her assistant, to survey typical businesses in your state that have hired your business graduates within the past five years. The purpose of the survey is to determine whether your business graduates have competent communication skills. Draft, revise, format, and proofread a one-page questionnaire designed to elicit the needed information. Use the questionnaire model on page 203 as a formatting guide.

5. Yogurt Anyone? (▶9.5)

Because the student body at the University of Arizona would provide a major source of potential customers for your yogurt store (see Exercise 1), you decide to survey the students to gather relevant data. Working in a group of four or five, develop a two-

FIGURE 9.4

Survey Results

BROADWAY PRODUCTIONS SURVEY

1. Do you currently have an account at Tri-City Bank?
   58 yes
   170 no

2. At which of the following institutions do you currently have an account? (Please check all that apply.)
   201 commercial bank
   52 employee credit union
   75 savings and loan association
   6 other (please specify: ______)
   18 none

3. In terms of convenience, which one of the following bank locations do you consider most important in selecting your main bank?
   70 near home
   102 near office
   12 near shopping
   31 on way to and from work
   13 other (please specify: ______)

4. How important do you consider each of the following banking services?

	Very Important	Somewhat Important	Not Important
Bank credit card	88	132	8
Check-guarantee card	74	32	122
Convenient ATM machines	143	56	29
Drive-in service	148	47	33
Free checking	219	9	0
Overdraft privileges	20	187	21
Personal banker	40	32	156
Telephone transfer	6	20	202
Trust department	13	45	170

5. If you have changed banks within the past three years, what was the major reason for the change?
   33 relocation of residence
   4 relocation of bank
   18 dissatisfaction with bank service
   7 other (please specify: ______)

Thank you so much for your cooperation. Please return this questionnaire in the enclosed envelope to Customer Service Department, Tri-City Bank, P.O. Box 1086, Stamford, CT 06902.

page questionnaire and a cover letter that you will mail to a sample of these students. Ensure that the content and appearance of the questionnaire follow the guidelines given in Checklist 11 on page 214. Pilot-test your questionnaire and cover letter on a small sample of students; then revise it as necessary and submit it to your instructor.

6. **Constructing Tables (▶9.6)**

   a. Is a table needed to present the information in Question 1?
   b. Construct a table that presents the important information from Question 4 of the questionnaire in a logical, helpful, and efficient manner. Give the table an appropriate title and arrange it in final report format.

7. **Constructing Charts (▶9.6)**

   You decide to use a chart rather than a table to convey the data in Question 3 of the questionnaire shown in Figure 9.4.

   a. Should you use a line chart to present the data? Why or why not? If a line chart is appropriate, construct it and label the vertical and horizontal axes.
   b. Should you use a bar chart to present the data? Why or why not? If a bar chart is appropriate, construct it, arrange the bars in a logical order, and clearly label each bar as well as the vertical axis.
   c. Should you use a pie chart to present the data? Why or why not? If a pie chart is appropriate, construct it, label each wedge, and clearly differentiate the wedges.

   d. You want to construct a visual aid to emphasize the proportion of respondents who have changed banks within the past three years. Calculate this percentage using the survey results. Decide which type of chart would most effectively convey this information. Then construct the chart, using appropriate values and helpful labels.

8. **Interpreting a Table (▶9.7)**

   The following sentences interpret the table in Figure 9.3 on page 211. Analyze each sentence to determine whether it represents the data in the table accurately.

   a. Males and females alike believe Apex is an asset to the community.
   b. More than one-fifth of the females (22 percent) did not respond.
   c. Age and the generation gap bring about different beliefs.
   d. Married males over age 50 had the most positive opinions.
   e. Females disagree more than males—probably because most of the workers at Apex are male.
   f. Female respondents tend to disagree with the statement.
   g. Apex should be proud of the fact that four-fifths of the residents believe the company is an asset to the community.
   h. Thirteen percent of the younger residents have doubts about whether Apex is an asset to the community.
   i. More single than married residents didn't care or had no opinion about the topic.
   j. Overall, the residents believe that 8 percent of the company is not an asset to the community.

Additional exercises are available at the Online Study Center website: **college.hmco.com/pic/oberSASfund**.

Online Study Center **RESOURCES**

Prepare for Class, Improve Your Grade, and ACE the Test. Student Achievement Series resources include:

ACE Practice Tests	Ask Ober	Audio Chapter Reviews and Quizzes
Chapter Outlines	Communication Objectives	Crossword Puzzles
Flashcards	Glossaries	Handouts
LAB Tests	Portfolio Project Stationery	Sample Reports

To access these learning and study tools, go to **college.hmco.com/pic/oberSASfund**.

10 Writing the Business Report

Habitat for Humanity aims to convey more than just facts and figures about the program's success. In all of its business communication, Habitat for Humanity focuses on accuracy, thoroughness, and above all, showing how everyone involved is positively affected.

1 ▶ Determine an appropriate report structure and organization.

2 ▶ Draft the report body.

3 ▶ Use an effective writing style.

"We're not writing the reports just to give the information. Our readers are less interested in the statistics and more interested in what the facts really mean."

—Steve Messinetti, Director, Campus Chapters and Youth Programs, Habitat for Humanity International

Chapter Outline

Online Study Center
Prepare for Class
Chapter Outline

5 *Revise, format, and proofread the report.*

4 *Provide appropriate documentation of sources.*

The Right Tools to Build a Business Report

When Steve Messinetti writes a report, he wants to do more than simply inform, analyze, or recommend—he also wants to touch his readers in a very personal way. Messinetti is the director of campus chapters and youth programs at the Americus, Georgia, headquarters of Habitat for Humanity International, a nonprofit, ecumenical organization dedicated to eliminating poverty housing throughout the world.

Online Study Center college.hmco.com/pic/oberSASfund

on the job

STEVE MESSINETTI
Director,
Campus Chapters
and Youth Programs,
Habitat for Humanity
International
(Americus, Georgia)

Messinetti writes a variety of reports, including periodical management reports, progress reports, proposals for new programs, and one-time reports about special events. Whether writing for internal or external audiences, he brings his reports to life by including photos and quotes that capture the feelings of program participants. "We're not writing the reports just to give the information," he explains. "Our readers are less interested in the statistics and more interested in what the facts really mean."

One of Messinetti's longer reports summarizes the results of Habitat's Spring Break Collegiate Challenge. This 15-page report opens with a transmittal document bound directly into the report. Next comes the table of contents, comprising the report's generic headings, which helps readers quickly locate sections of particular interest. Throughout the report, graphs and charts interspersed with the narrative offer a visual snapshot of the program's success.

When Messinetti quotes from other documents, he is careful to provide a complete citation on the same page. "The documentation gives proper credit to the source and confirms the validity of the information," he says. ■

As we have seen throughout our study of business communication, the writing process consists of audience analysis, planning, drafting, revising, formatting, and proofreading. Follow this same process when writing a report.

Although much of the planning in the report process is, of necessity, done even before data collection begins, the written presentation of the results requires its own stage of planning. You need to make decisions about the structure of the report, the organization of the content, and the framework of the headings before and while you write.

DETERMINING THE REPORT STRUCTURE

1 ▷ *Determine an appropriate report structure and organization.*

The physical structure of the report and general traits such as complexity, degree of formality, and length depend on the audience for the report and the nature of the problem that the report addresses. The three most common formats for a report are the *manuscript, memorandum,* and *letter* formats.

Manuscript reports, the most formal of the three, are formatted in narrative (paragraph) style, with headings and subheadings separating the different sections. If the report addresses a complex problem that has serious consequences, it will likely follow a manuscript format and a formal writing style. A formal writing style typically avoids the use of first- and second-person pronouns, such as *I* and *you* (which keeps the emphasis on the report *data,* instead of on the writer or reader of the report). In addition, the more formal the report, the more supplementary parts are included (such as a table of contents, executive summary, and appendix) and, therefore, the longer the report.

Memorandum and letter reports contain the standard correspondence parts (for example, lines identifying the names of the sender and receiver). They use a more informal writing style and may or may not contain headings and subheadings. Compare the informal, simple, and short report in memo format shown in Model 19 on page 226 with the formal, complex, and long report (only the first page is shown) in manuscript format shown in Model 20 on page 227.

Organizing the Report

You may have organized the collection and analysis of data in a way that suited the investigation of various subtopics of the problem. Now that it is time to put the results of your work together into a coherent written presentation, however, you may need a *new* organization, one that integrates the whole and takes into account what you have learned through your research.

Planning your written presentation to show unity, order, and logic involves selecting an organizational basis for the *findings* (the data you've collected and analyzed) and developing an outline. You must decide what order to use to present each piece of the puzzle and when to present your overall *conclusions* (the answers to the research questions raised in the introduction) and any recommendations you may wish to make.

The four most common bases for organizing your findings are *time, location, importance,* and *criteria.* The purpose of the report (information, analysis, or recommendation), the nature of the problem, and your knowledge of the reader will help you select the most useful organizational framework.

Time

The use of chronology, or time sequence, is appropriate for agendas, minutes of meetings, programs, many status reports, and similar projects. Discussing events in the order in which they occurred or in the order in which they will or should occur is an efficient way to organize many informational reports—those whose purpose is simply to inform.

Despite its usefulness and simplicity, time sequence should not be overused. Because events *occur* one after another, chronology is often the most efficient way to *record* data, but it may not be the most efficient way to *present* that data to your readers. Assume, for example, that you are writing a progress report on a recruiting trip you made to four college campuses. Each day you interviewed candidates for the three positions you have open. The first passage, given in time sequence, requires too much work of the reader. The second version saves the reader time.

> **NOT:** On Monday morning, I interviewed one candidate for the budget-analyst position and two candidates for the junior-accountant position. Then, in the afternoon, I interviewed two candidates for the asset-manager position and another for the budget-analyst position. Finally, on Tuesday, I interviewed another candidate for budget analyst and two for junior accountant.

> **BUT:** On Monday and Tuesday, I interviewed three candidates for the budget-analyst position, four for the junior-accountant position, and two for the asset-manager position.

Obviously, a blow-by-blow description is not necessarily the most efficient means of communicating information to the reader—sometimes it forces the reader to do too much work. Organize your information chronologically only when it is important for the reader to know the sequence in which events occurred.

MODEL 19

Informal Memorandum Report

Weight Watchers International, Inc.
175 Crossways Park West
Woodbury, New York 11797-2055
516 390-1400
FAX 516 390-1445

The memo format indicates the reader is someone from within the firm.

MEMO TO:	Marketing Manager
FROM:	Barbara Novak, Sales Assistant
DATE:	August 9, 2007
SUBJECT:	Yellow Pages Advertising

Uses a direct organizational style: the recommendation and conclusions are given first, followed by the supporting evidence.

Uses informal language; makes extensive use of first- and second-person pronouns such as I, me, we, and you.

I recommend we continue purchasing a quarter-page ad in the Yellow Pages. My recommendation is based on the fact that Yellow Pages advertising has produced more inquiries than any other method of advertising and has increased net profits.

A Pilot Test Was Set Up

On March 1, you asked me to conduct a three-month test of the effectiveness of Yellow Pages advertising. I subsequently purchased a quarter-page ad for the edition of the Yellow Pages that was distributed the week of June 2 to 6. For six weeks thereafter, we queried all telephone and walk-in customers to determine how they had learned about our company. I also compared the percentage of signed contracts resulting from each source. Precise before-and-after sales data could not be generated because of other factors that affected sales for each period (for example, time of year and other promotional campaigns).

Uses talking headings to reinforce the direct plan.

Results Were Positive

My analysis of the data shows that 38 percent of the callers after June 2 to 6 first learned about our company from the Yellow Pages. The next highest source was referrals and repeat business, which accounted for 26 percent of the calls. In addition, 21 percent of the Yellow Pages inquiries resulted in signed contracts.

We Should Continue Advertising

Does not include the detailed statistical information but makes it available if needed.

Based on the $358 monthly cost of our quarter-page ad, each dollar of ad cost is producing $3.77 in sales revenue and $0.983 toward product margin. These results clearly support the continuation of our Yellow Pages advertising. I would be happy to discuss the results of this research with you in more detail and to provide the supporting statistical data if you wish.

jeo

Grammar and Mechanics Notes

See the Style Manual at the back of this text for guidance on how to format memorandums.

MODEL 20

Manuscript Report

The first page of a formal manuscript report is shown.

Uses an indirect organizational style: the conclusions and recommendations are given after the supporting data is presented.

Uses formal language; avoids first- and second-person pronouns.

Uses visual aids (such as tables and charts) and multilevel headings, which are typical of formal reports.

THE EFFECTIVENESS OF YELLOW PAGE ADVERTISING FOR ALL SYSTEMS GO COMPANY

Barbara Novak, Sales Assistant

According to Mountain Bell, display advertising typically accounts for 55 percent of total sales for a firm in the moving business.[1] Thus, Hiram Cooper, director of marketing, requested a three-month test be conducted of the effectiveness of Yellow Pages advertising for All Systems Go. This report describes the procedures used to gather the data and the results obtained. Based on the data, a recommendation is made regarding the continuation of Yellow Pages advertising.

A quarter-page ad was purchased in the edition of the Mountain Bell Yellow Pages that was distributed the week of June 2 to 6. For the six-week period encompassing June 9 through July 17, all telephone and walk-in customers were queried to determine how they had learned about the company.

One delimitation of this study was that precise before-and-after sales data could not be generated because of other factors that affected sales for each period (for example, time of year and other promotional campaigns).

Findings

The findings of this study are reported in terms of the sources of information for learning about All Systems Go, the amount of new business generated, and a cost-benefits comparison for Yellow Pages advertising.

Sources of Information

As shown in Table 1, 38 percent of the callers during the test period first learned about All Systems Go from the Yellow Pages display. The second highest source was referrals and repeat business, which together accounted for 26 percent of the calls. In addition, 21 percent of the Yellow Pages

---

[1] Joseph L. Dye <jldye@aol.com>, "Answers to Your Question," May 18, 2001, personal e-mail.

Grammar and Mechanics Notes

See the Style Manual at the back of this text for guidance on how to format manuscript reports.

Location

Like the use of time sequence, the use of location as the basis for organizing a report is often appropriate for simple informational reports. Discussing topics according to their geographical or physical location (for example, describing an office layout) may be the most efficient way to present the data. Again, be sure that such an organizational plan helps the reader process the information most efficiently and that it is not merely the easiest way for you to report the data. Decisions should be based on reader needs rather than on writer convenience.

Importance

For the busy reader, the most efficient organizational plan may discuss the most important topic first, followed in order by topics of decreasing importance. The reader then gets the major idea up-front and can skim the less important information as desired or needed.

For some types of reports, especially recommendation reports, the opposite plan might be used effectively. If you've analyzed four alternatives and will recommend the implementation of Alternative 4, you might first present each of the other alternatives in turn (starting with the least viable solution) and show why they're *not* feasible. Then, you save your trump card until last, thus making the alternative you're recommending the freshest in the reader's mind because it is the last one read. If you use this option, make sure that you effectively "slay all the dragons" except your own, so that the reader will agree that your recommendation is the most logical one.

Criteria

For reports whose purpose is to analyze the data and possibly recommend a solution, the most logical arrangement is to organize the data by criteria. One of the important steps in the reporting process is to develop hypotheses regarding causes of or solutions for the problem you're exploring. This process requires breaking down your problem into its component subproblems. These factors, or criteria, then become the basis for organizing the report.

If you're evaluating three sites for a new facility, for example, avoid the temptation to use the *locations* of these sites as the report headings. Such an organizational plan focuses attention on the sites themselves instead of on the criteria by which you evaluated them and on which you based your recommendation. Instead, use the criteria as the headings. Similarly, avoid using "Advantages" and "Disadvantages" as headings. Keep your reader in step with you by helping the reader focus on the same topics—the criteria—that you highlighted during the research and analysis phases of your project.

In actual practice, you might use a combination of these organizational plans. For instance, you might organize your first-level (major) headings by criteria but your second-level headings in simple-to-complex order. Or you might organize your first-level headings by criteria but present these criteria in their order of importance. Competent communicators select an organizational plan with a view toward helping the reader comprehend and appreciate the information and viewpoints being presented in the most efficient manner possible.

Presenting Conclusions and Recommendations

Once you've decided how to organize the findings of your study, you must decide where to present the conclusions and any recommendations that have resulted from these findings. The differences among findings, conclusions, and recommendations can be illustrated by the following examples:

Finding:	The computer monitor sometimes goes blank during operation.
Finding:	Nonsense data sometimes appears on the screen for no reason.
Conclusion:	The computer is broken.
Recommendation:	We should repair the computer before May 3, when payroll processing begins.
Finding:	Our Statesville branch has lost money four out of the past five years.
Conclusion:	Our Statesville branch is not profitable.
Recommendation:	We should close our Statesville branch.

Assume that in a survey of community residents, 212 out of 314 respondents indicated that the local police had been rude to them on at least one occasion. Compose a statement of finding, conclusion, and recommendation based on this data.

Academic reports and many business reports have traditionally presented the conclusions and recommendations of a study at the end of the report; the rationale is that conclusions cannot logically be drawn until the data has been presented and analyzed. Similarly, recommendations cannot be made until conclusions have been drawn. Models 19 and 20, presented on pages 226 and 227, illustrate these two approaches. The informal memo report presents the conclusions and recommendations in the first paragraph; the manuscript report delays such presentation until after the findings have been presented and analyzed.

Although no hard-and-fast rules exist regarding when to use the direct and indirect organizational plans in reports, some guidance can be given. Generally, it is better to use the direct organizational plan (in which the conclusions and recommendations are presented at the beginning of the report) when:

▌ The reader prefers the direct plan for reports (as is typically the case when preparing a business report for your superior).

▌ The reader will be receptive to your conclusions and recommendations.

▌ The reader can evaluate the information in the report more efficiently if the conclusions and recommendations are given up-front.

▌ You have no specific reason to choose the indirect pattern.

Similarly, the indirect plan (in which the evidence is presented first, followed by conclusions and recommendations) is more appropriate when:

▌ The reader prefers the indirect plan for reports.

▌ The reader will be initially uninterested in or resistant to your conclusions and recommendations.

▌ The topic is so complex that detailed explanations and discussions are needed for the conclusions and recommendations to be understood and accepted.

The decision isn't necessarily an either/or situation. Instead of putting all the conclusions and recommendations either first or last, you may choose to split them up, discussing each in the appropriate subsection of your report. Similarly, even though you write a report using an indirect plan, you may add an executive summary or letter of transmittal that communicates the conclusions and recommendations to the reader before the report itself has been read. The important point is that you consciously *plan* these aspects of the report.

Outlining the Report

Although we have not used the term *outlining* thus far, whenever we've talked about organizing, we've actually been talking about outlining as well. For example, early in the report process, you broke your problem statement into its logical component subproblems. Thus, your problem statement and subproblems served as your first working outline.

Many business writers find it useful at this point in the report process to construct a more formal outline. A formal outline provides an orderly visual representation of the report, showing clearly which points will be covered, in what order they will be covered, and how each relates to the rest of the report. The purpose of the outline is to guide you, the writer, in structuring your report logically and efficiently. Consider it a working draft, subject to being revised as you compose the report.

Use the working title of your report as the title of your outline. Use uppercase roman numerals for the major headings, uppercase letters for first-level subheadings, arabic numerals for second-level subheadings, and lowercase letters for third-level subheadings. Only rarely will you need to use all four levels of headings. Model 21 on page 231 shows an outline for a formal report.

As part of the process of developing a formal outline, you should compose the actual wording for your headings and decide how many headings you will need. Headings play an important role in focusing the reader's attention and in helping your report achieve unity and coherence, so plan them carefully, and revise them as needed as you work toward a final version of your report.

Talking Versus Generic Headings

talking headings Report headings that identify both the topic and the major conclusion of the section.

Talking headings identify not only the topic of the section but also the major conclusion. Talking headings, which are typically used in newspapers and magazines, are often useful for business reports as well. For example, they can serve as a preview or executive summary of the entire report. They are especially useful when directness is desired—the reader can simply skim the headings in the report (or in the table of contents) and get an overview of the topics covered and each topic's conclusions.

generic headings Report headings that identify only the topic of the section.

Generic headings, on the other hand, identify only the topic of the section, without giving the conclusion. Most formal reports and any report written in an indirect pattern use generic headings, similar to the headings used in Model 21 on page 231.

Parallelism

CONCEPT CHECK 10.2

Compose a report title for which it would be appropriate to use location as the basis for organizing the body of the report.

You have wide leeway in selecting the form of headings used in your report. Noun phrases are probably the most common form of heading, but you may also choose participial phrases, partial statements (in which a verb is missing—the kind often used in newspaper headlines), statements, or questions.

Regardless of the form of heading you select, be consistent within each level of heading. If the first major heading (a first-level heading) is a noun phrase, all first-level headings should be noun phrases. If the first major heading is a talking

MODEL 21

Report Outline

This report uses generic, not talking, headings.

Uses the working title of the report as the outline title.

Organizes the findings by criteria.

Contains at least two items in each level of subdivision.

Uses parallel structure (noun phrases are used for each heading and subheading).

STAFF EMPLOYEES' EVALUATION
OF THE BENEFIT PROGRAM
AT MAYO MEMORIAL HOSPITAL

Loretta J. Santorini

① **I. INTRODUCTION**
   A. Purpose and Scope
   B. Procedures

II. FINDINGS
② A. Knowledge of Benefits
      1. Familiarity with Benefits
      2. Present Methods of Communication
         a. Formal Channels
         b. Informal Channels
      3. Preferred Methods of Communication
   B. Opinions of Present Benefits
      1. Importance of Benefits
      2. Satisfaction with Benefits
   C. Desirability of Additional Benefits

III. SUMMARY, CONCLUSIONS, AND RECOMMENDATIONS
   A. Summary of the Problems and Procedures
   B. Summary of the Findings
   C. Conclusions and Recommendations

APPENDIX
③ A. Cover Letter
   B. Questionnaire

Grammar and Mechanics Notes

1. Align the Roman numerals vertically on the periods.
2. Type each entry in upper- and lowercase letters.
3. Identify each appendix item by letter.

heading, the others should be, too. As you move from level to level, you may switch to another form of heading if it is more appropriate. Again, however, the headings within the same level must be parallel.

Length and Number of Headings

Four to eight words is about the right length for most headings. Headings that are too long lose some of their effectiveness; the shorter the heading, the more emphasis it receives. Yet headings that are too short are ineffective because they do not convey enough meaning.

Similarly, choose an appropriate *number* of headings. Having too many headings weakens the unity of a report—they chop the report up too much, making it look more like an outline than a reasoned analysis. Having too few headings, however, confronts the reader with page after page of solid copy, without the chance to stop periodically and refocus attention on the topic. Often, having at least one heading or visual aid to break up each single-spaced page or each two consecutive, double-spaced pages makes a report attractive and easy to follow.

Balance

Maintain a sense of balance within and among sections. It would be unusual to give one section of a report five subsections (five second-level headings) and give the following section none. Similarly, it would be unusual to make one section ten pages long and another section only half a page long. Also, ensure that the most important ideas appear in the highest levels of headings. If you're discussing four criteria for a topic, for example, all four should be in the same level of heading—presumably in first-level headings.

When you divide a section into subsections, it must have at least two subsections. You cannot logically have just one second-level heading within a section because when you divide something, it divides into more than one "piece."

Online Study Center
Improve Your Grade
Audio Chapter Review 10.1

TEST PREPPER 10.1   ANSWERS CAN BE FOUND ON P. 412

True or False?

_____ 1. Conclusions are always based on the findings of a report.

_____ 2. The more headings a report contains, the easier it is for the reader to follow.

_____ 3. Conclusions and recommendations may be presented either at the beginning or at the end of the report, depending on the situation.

_____ 4. Formal reports should use talking headings.

Vocabulary

Define the following terms in your own words.

5. Generic headings

6. Talking headings

Critical Thinking

7. Why do you think most business reports are formatted with generic rather than talking headings?

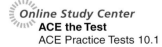

Online Study Center
ACE the Test
ACE Practice Tests 10.1

Online Study Center
Improve Your Grade
Audio Chapter Quiz 10.1
PowerPoint Review 10.1

DRAFTING

2 *Draft the report body.*

Although it is the last step of a long and sometimes complex process, the written presentation of your research is the only evidence your reader has of the effort you have invested in the project. The success or failure of your hard work depends on this physical evidence. Prepare the written report carefully to bring out the full significance of your data and to help the reader reach a decision and solve a problem.

The report body consists of the introduction; the findings; and the summary, conclusions, and recommendations. As stated earlier, the conclusions may go first or last in the report. Each part may be a separate chapter in long reports or a major section in shorter reports.

Introduction

The introduction sets the stage for understanding the findings that follow. In this section, present information such as the following:

▌ Background of the problem

▌ Need for the study

▌ Authorization for the report

▌ Hypotheses or problem statement and subproblems

▌ Purpose and scope (including definition of terms, if needed)

▌ Procedures used to gather and analyze the data

The actual topics and amount of detail presented in the introductory section depends on the complexity of the report and the needs of the reader. For example, if the procedures are extensive, you may want to place them in a separate section, with their own first-level heading. Model 22 on page 234 is an example of an introductory section for a formal report.

Findings

The findings of the study represent the major contribution of the report and make up the largest section of the report. Discuss and interpret any relevant primary and secondary data you gathered. Organize this section using one of the plans discussed earlier (for example, by time; location; importance; or, more frequently, criteria). Use objective language to present the information clearly, concisely, and accurately.

Many reports display numerical information in tables and figures (such as bar, line, or pie charts). The information in such displays should be self-explanatory; that is, readers should understand it without having to refer to the text. Nevertheless, all tables and figures must be mentioned and explained in the text so that the text, too, is self-explanatory. All text references should be by number (for example, "as shown in Table 4")—never by a phrase such as "as shown below"—because the table or figure might actually appear at the top of the following page in the final document.

Summarize the important information from the display (see Model 23 on page 235). Give enough interpretation to help the reader comprehend the table or figure,

MODEL 22

Report Introduction

Provides a citation for statistics, direct quotations, or paraphrases.

Identifies who authorized the report.

Provides the problem statement in the form of a question to be answered.

Identifies the subproblems that must be answered to resolve the problem statement.

Defines terms, as needed.

Provides a concise, but complete, discussion of the procedures used to answer the problem statement.

Ends with an appropriate sense of closure for this section.

① **INTRODUCTION**

Employee benefits are a rapidly growing and an increasingly important form of employee compensation for both profit and nonprofit organizations. According to a recent U.S. Chamber of Commerce survey, benefits now constitute 37 percent of all payroll costs, averaging $10,857 yearly for each employee (Ignatio, 2006, p. 812). Thus, on the basis of cost alone, an organization's benefits program must be carefully monitored and evaluated.

To ensure that the benefits program for Mayo Memorial Hospital's 2,500 staff personnel is operating as effectively as possible, David Riggins, director of personnel, authorized this report on February 15, 2006.

Purpose and Scope

Specifically, the following problem was addressed in this study: What are the opinions of staff employees at Mayo Memorial Hospital regarding their employee benefits? To answer this question, the following subproblems were addressed:

② 1. How knowledgeable are the employees about the benefits program?
2. What are the employees' opinions of the value of the benefits already available?
3. What benefits, if any, would the employees like to have added to the program?

This study attempted to determine employee preferences only. Whether or not these preferences are economically feasible is not within the scope of this study. As used in this study, employee benefits (also called fringe benefits) means an employment benefit given in addition to one's wages or salary.

Procedures

③ A list of the 2,489 staff employees eligible for benefits was generated from the January 15 payroll run. Using a 10 percent sample, 250 employees were selected for the survey. On March 3, each of these employees was sent the cover letter and questionnaire shown in Appendix A via campus mail. A total of 206 employees completed usable questionnaires, for a response rate of 82 percent.

In addition to the questionnaire data, personal interviews were held with three benefits managers. The primary data provided by the survey and personal interviews was then analyzed and compared with findings from secondary sources to determine the staff employees' opinions of the benefits program at Mayo.

Grammar and Mechanics Notes

1. If the heading *Introduction* immediately follows the report title, its use is optional.
2. In a single-spaced report, single-space numbered and bulleted lists if every item comprises a single line. Otherwise, single-space lines within an item but double-space between items.
3. Be consistent in using either the percent sign (%) or the word *percent*. Regardless, use figures for the actual percentage value.

Model 23

Report Findings

Refers to tables and charts by number.

Recent studies (Egan, 2003; Ignatio, 2006) have shown that employees' satisfaction with benefits is directly correlated with their knowledge of such benefits. Thus, the Mayo staff employees were asked to rate their level of familiarity with each benefit. As shown in Table 2, most staff employees believe that most benefits have been adequately communicated to them.

① **TABLE 2. LEVEL OF FAMILIARITY WITH BENEFITS PROGRAM**

Benefit	Level of Familiarity (%)				
	Familiar	Unfamiliar	Undecided	No Response	Total
Sick leave	94	4	1	1	100
Vacation	94	4	1	1	100
Paid holidays	92	4	3	1	100
Hospital/medical insurance	90	7	2	0	100
Life insurance	84	10	5	1	100
Retirement	84	11	4	1	100
Long-term disability insurance	55	33	12	1	100
Auto insurance	36	57	6	15	100

Discusses only the most important data from the table.

At least four-fifths of the employees are familiar with all major benefits except for long-term disability insurance, which is familiar to only a slight majority. The low level of knowledge about auto insurance (36 percent familiarity) may be explained by the fact that this benefit started just six weeks before the survey was taken.

Subordinates the reference to tables and charts by placing it in a dependent clause ("As shown in Figure 1").

In general, benefit familiarity is not related to length of employment at Mayo. Most employees are familiar with most benefits regardless of their length of employment. However, as shown in Figure 1, the only benefit for which this is not true is life insurance. The longer a person has been employed at Mayo, the more likely he or she is to know about this benefit.

② **FIGURE 1. KNOWLEDGE OF LIFE INSURANCE BENEFIT**

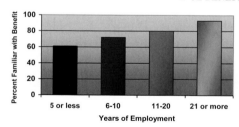

Grammar and Mechanics Notes

1. Position tables and charts immediately below the paragraph that introduces them.
2. Label charts as "figures" and number them independently of table numbers.

MODEL 24

Summary, Conclusions, and Recommendations

Quickly summarizes the need for the study.

Summarizes the problem and procedures used to solve the problem.

Summarizes the findings.

Presents the recommendations based on the findings and conclusions.

Provides an appropriate concluding statement.

① **SUMMARY, CONCLUSIONS, AND RECOMMENDATIONS**

Nationwide, employee benefits now account for more than one-third of all payroll costs. Thus, on the basis of cost alone, an organization's benefits program must be carefully monitored and evaluated.

The problem in this study was to determine the opinions of the nearly 2,500 staff employees at Mayo Memorial Hospital regarding the employee benefits program. Specifically, the investigation included determining the employees' present level of knowledge about the program, their opinions of the benefits presently offered, and their preferences for additional benefits. A survey of 206 staff employees and interviews with three managers familiar with the Metro employee benefits program provided the primary data for this study.

② The findings show that staff employees at Mayo Memorial Hospital are extremely knowledgeable about all benefits except long-term disability and automobile insurance; however, a majority would prefer to have an individualized benefits statement instead of the brochures now used to explain the benefits program. They consider paid time off the most important benefit and automobile insurance the least important. A majority are satisfied with all benefits, although retirement benefits generated substantial dissatisfaction. The only additional benefit desired by a majority of the employees is compensation for unused sick leave.

The following recommendations are based on these conclusions:

1. Determine the feasibility of generating an annual individualized benefits statement for each staff employee.

③ 2. Reevaluate the attractiveness of the automobile insurance benefit in one year to determine staff employees' knowledge about, use of, and desire for this benefit. Consider the feasibility of substituting compensation for unused sick leave for the automobile insurance benefit.

3. Conduct a follow-up study of the retirement benefits at Mayo to determine how competitive they are with those offered by comparable public and private institutions.

These recommendations, as well as the findings of this study, should help the hospital administration ensure that its benefits program is accomplishing its stated objectives of attracting and retaining high-quality employees and meeting their needs once employed.

Grammar and Mechanics Notes

1. If necessary, break a long heading at a logical point and single-space the lines of the heading. Try to make the second line shorter than the first.
2. Note the use of the present tense when summarizing the findings.
3. Leave a blank line between multiline numbered items.

but don't repeat all the information it contains. Discussing displayed information in the narrative *emphasizes* that information, so discuss only what merits such emphasis.

The table or figure should appear immediately *below* the first paragraph of text in which the reference to it occurs. Avoid splitting a table or figure between two pages. If not enough space is available on the page for the display, continue with the text to the bottom of the page and then place the table or figure at the top of the following page.

For all primary and secondary data, point out important items, implications, trends, contradictions, unexpected findings, similarities and differences, and the like. Use emphasis, subordination, preview, summary, and transition to make the report read clearly and smoothly. Avoid presenting facts and figures so fast that the reader becomes overwhelmed with data. Always keep the reader's needs and desires uppermost in mind as you organize, present, and discuss the information.

Summary, Conclusions, and Recommendations

A one- or two-page report may need only a one-sentence or one-paragraph summary. Longer or more complex reports, however, should include a more extensive summary. Briefly review the problem and the procedures used to solve the problem, and provide an overview of the major findings. Repeating the main points or arguments immediately before presenting the conclusions and recommendations reinforces the reasonableness of those conclusions and recommendations. To avoid monotony when summarizing, use wording that differs from the original presentation.

If your report merely analyzes the information presented but does not make recommendations, you might label the final section of the report "Summary" or "Summary and Conclusions," as appropriate. If your report includes both conclusions and recommendations, ensure that the conclusions stem directly from your findings and that the recommendations stem directly from the conclusions. Provide ample evidence to support all your conclusions and recommendations. Model 24 on page 236 shows an example of a closing section of a report. As shown in the model, you should end your report with an overall concluding statement that provides a definite sense of project completion. Don't leave your reader wondering if additional pages will follow.

DEVELOPING AN EFFECTIVE WRITING STYLE

3 ▶ *Use an effective writing style.*

You can enhance the effectiveness of your written reports by paying attention to your writing style, including tone, use of pronouns, verb tense, emphasis and subordination, and coherence.

Tone

Regardless of the structure of your report, the writing style used is typically more objective and less conversational than, for example, the style of an informal memorandum. Avoid colloquial expressions, attempts at humor, subjectivity, bias, and exaggeration.

NOT: The company *hit the jackpot* with its new system.

BUT: The new system saved the company $125,000 the first year.

NOT: He *claimed* that half of his projects involved name-brand advertising.

BUT: He stated that half of his projects involved name-brand advertising.

Pronouns

For many business reports, the use of first- and second-person pronouns is not only acceptable but also quite helpful for achieving an effective writing style. Formal language, however, focuses attention on the information being conveyed instead of on the writer; reports written in the formal style should use third-person pronouns and avoid using *I, we,* and *you.* You can avoid the awkward substitute "the writer" by revising the sentence. Most often, it is evident that the writer is the person doing the action communicated.

Informal: I recommend that the project be canceled.

Awkward: The writer recommends that the project be canceled.

Formal: The project should be canceled.

Using the passive voice is a common device for avoiding the use of *I* in formal reports, but doing so weakens the impact. Instead, revise the sentence to avoid undue use of the passive voice.

Informal: I interviewed Jan Smith.

Passive: Jan Smith was interviewed.

Formal: In a personal interview, Jan Smith stated . . .

You will probably also want to avoid using *he* as a generic pronoun when referring to an unidentified person. Chapter 5 discusses many ways to avoid such discriminatory language.

Verb Tense

Use the verb tense (past, present, or future) that is appropriate at the time the reader *reads* the report—not necessarily at the time that you *wrote* the report. Use past tense to describe procedures (because they have already been completed at the time the reader reads the report) and to describe the findings of other studies already completed, but use present tense for conclusions from those studies (because we assume they continue to be true).

When possible, use the stronger present tense to present the data from your study. The rationale for doing so is that we assume our findings continue to be true; thus, the use of the present tense is justified. (If we cannot assume the continuing truth of any findings, we should probably not use them in the study.)

NOT: These findings *will be discussed* later in this report.

BUT: These findings *are discussed* later in the report. (*But:* These findings *were discussed* earlier in this report.)

NOT: Three-fourths of the managers *believed* that quality circles *were* effective at the plant.

BUT: Three-fourths of the managers *believe* that quality circles *are* effective at the plant.

Procedure:	Nearly 500 people *responded* to this survey.
Finding:	Only 11 percent of the managers *received* any specific training on any new procedure.
Conclusion:	Most managers *do not receive* any specific training on any new procedure.

Emphasis and Subordination

Only rarely does all of the data consistently point to one conclusion. More likely, you will have a mixed bag of data from which you will have to evaluate the relative merits of each point. For your report to achieve its objective, the reader must evaluate the importance of each point in the same way that you did. At the very least, your reader must be *aware* of the importance you attached to each point. To ensure this outcome, employ the emphasis and subordination techniques you learned in Chapter 5 when discussing your findings. By (a) making sure that the amount of space devoted to a topic reflects the importance of that topic, (b) carefully positioning your major ideas, and (c) using language that directly tells what is more and less important, you can help ensure that you and your reader share the same perspective when your reader analyzes the data.

Use emphasis and subordination to let the reader know what you consider most and least important—but *not* to unduly sway the reader. If the data honestly leads to a strong, definite conclusion, then by all means make your conclusion strong and definite. But if the data permits only a tentative (or no) conclusion, then say so.

Coherence

One difficulty in writing any long document—especially when the document is drafted in sections and then put together—is making the finished product read smoothly and coherently, like a unified presentation rather than a cut-and-paste job. This problem is even more challenging for team-written reports (see "Team Writing" on page 23 of Chapter 2).

One effective way to achieve coherence in a report is to use previews, summaries, and transitions regularly. At the beginning of each major section, preview what will be discussed in that section. At the conclusion of each section, summarize what was presented and provide a smooth transition to the next topic. For long sections, the preview, summary, and transition might each be a separate paragraph; for short sections, a single sentence might suffice. Note how preview, summary, and transition are used in the following example of a report section opening and closing:

> *Training of System Users*
>
> The training program can be evaluated in terms of the opinions of the users and in terms of the cost of training in proportion to the cost of the system itself. . . . *(After this topic preview, several paragraphs follow that discuss the opinions of the users and the cost of the training program.)*
>
> Even though a slight majority of users now feel competent in using the system, the training provided falls far short of the 20 percent of the total system cost recommended by experts. This low level of training may have affected the precision of the data generated by the system. *(The first sentence contains the summary of this section; the second sentence provides the transition to the next section.)*

Always introduce a topic before dividing it into subtopics. Thus, you should never have one heading following another without some intervening text. (The exception to this guideline is that the heading "Introduction" may be used immediately after the report title or subtitle.) Preview for the reader how the topic will be divided before you actually make the division.

DOCUMENTING YOUR SOURCES

4 ▸ *Provide appropriate documentation of sources.*

When including the ideas of another person in your report, avoid the temptation to become lazy and simply repeat everything in the author's exact words. It is unlikely that the problem you're trying to solve and the problem discussed by the author mesh exactly. More than likely, you'll need to take bits and pieces of information from numerous sources and integrate them into a context appropriate for your specific purposes.

paraphrase   A summary or restatement of a passage in one's own words.

direct quotation   The exact words of another.

A **paraphrase** is a summary or restatement of a passage in your own words. A **direct quotation**, on the other hand, contains the exact words of another. Use direct quotations (always enclosed in quotation marks) only for definitions or for text that is so precise, clear, or otherwise noteworthy that it cannot be improved upon. Most of your references to secondary data should take the form of paraphrases. Paraphrasing involves more than just rearranging the words or leaving out a word or two, however. It requires that you understand the writer's idea and then restate it in your own language.

documentation   Giving credit to another person for his or her words or ideas that are used in a report.

Documentation is the identification of sources by giving credit to another person, either in the text or in the reference list, for using his or her words or ideas. You may, of course, use the words and ideas of others, provided such use is properly documented; in fact, for many business reports, such secondary information may be the *only* data you use. You must, however, provide appropriate documentation whenever you quote, paraphrase, or summarize someone else's work.

plagiarism   Using another person's words or ideas without giving proper credit.

Plagiarism is the use of another person's words or ideas without giving proper credit. Writings are considered the writer's legal property; someone else who wrongfully uses such property is guilty of theft. Plagiarism, therefore, carries stiff penalties. In the classroom, the penalty ranges from failure in a course to expulsion from school. On the job, the penalty for plagiarism ranges from loss of credibility to loss of employment.

You must document all material in your report that comes from secondary sources; that is, you must give enough information about the original source to enable the reader to locate the source if he or she so desires. If the secondary source is published (for example, a journal article), the documentation should appear as a reference citation. If the source is unpublished, sufficient documentation can generally be given in the narrative, making a formal citation unnecessary, as illustrated here:

> According to Board Policy 91-18b, all position vacancies above the level of C-3 must be posted internally at least two weeks prior to being advertised.

> The contractor's letter of May 23, 2003, stated, "We agree to modify Blueprint 3884 by widening the southeast entrance from 10 feet to 12 feet 6 inches for a total additional charge of $273.50."

If your report (for example, an informal memorandum report) contains only one or two citations, you can include them in the report narrative itself:

> Writing in the November 2006 issue of *Economics Today* (page 274), John Willard argued that "location is *not* the most important factor in selling a home."

Once a study has been cited once, it may be mentioned again in continuous discussion on the same page or even on the next pages without further citation if no ambiguity results. If several pages intervene or if ambiguity might result, give the citation again.

The three major forms for documenting the ideas, information, and quotations of other people in a report are endnotes, footnotes, and author-date references (see the Style Manual at the end of this text for examples and formatting conventions). Let the nature of the report and the needs of the reader dictate the documentation method used. Regardless of which method you select, ensure that the citations are accurate, complete, and consistently formatted and that your bibliography format is consistent with your documentation format.

■ *Footnotes:* For years, footnotes were the traditional method of citing sources. A bibliographic footnote provides the complete reference at the bottom of the page on which the citation occurs in the text. Thus, a reader interested in exploring the source does not have to turn to the back of the report. Today's word processors can format footnotes (and endnotes) almost painlessly—automatically numbering and positioning each note correctly. Some readers, however, find the presence of footnotes on the text page distracting.

■ *Endnotes:* The endnote format uses superscript (raised) numbers to identify secondary sources in the text and then provides the actual citations in a numbered list entitled "Notes" or "Endnotes" at the end of the report. The endnotes are numbered consecutively throughout the report. Some readers prefer the endnote format because it avoids the clutter of footnotes and because it's easy to use.

■ *Author-Date Format:* Some report readers prefer the author-date format of documentation, regarding the method as a reasonable compromise between endnotes (which provide *no* reference information on the text page) and footnotes (which provide *all* the reference information on the text page). In the author-date format, the writer inserts at an appropriate point in the text the last name of the author and the year of publication in parentheses. Complete bibliographic information is then included in the Notes or References section at the end of the report.

REFINING YOUR DRAFT

5 ▶ *Revise, format, and proofread the report.*

Once you have produced a first draft of your report, put it away for a few days. Doing so will enable you to view the draft with a fresh perspective and perhaps find a more effective means of communicating your ideas to the reader. Don't try to correct all problems in one review. Instead, look at this process as having three steps—revising first for content, then for style, and finally for correctness.

"Richard, let's have a talk about margins and report lengths."

© NAS. North America Syndicate.

Revising

Revise first for content. Make sure you've included sufficient information to support each point, you've included no extraneous information (regardless of how interesting it might be or how hard you worked to gather the information), all information is accurate, and the information is presented in an efficient and logical sequence. Keep the purpose of the report and the reader's needs and desires in mind as you review for content.

Once you're satisfied with the content of the report, revise for style. Ensure that your writing is clear and that you have used short, simple, vigorous, and concise words. Check whether you have used a variety of sentence types and have relied on active and passive voice appropriately. Do your paragraphs exhibit unity and coherence, and are they of reasonable length? Have you maintained an overall tone of confidence, courtesy, sincerity, and objectivity? Finally, review your draft to ensure that you have used nondiscriminatory language and appropriate emphasis and subordination.

After you're confident about the content and style of your draft, revise once more for correctness. This revision step, known as *editing*, identifies and resolves any problems with grammar, spelling, punctuation, and word usage. Do not risk losing credibility with the reader by careless English usage. If possible, have a colleague review your draft to catch any errors you may have overlooked.

Formatting

The physical format of your report (margins, spacing, and the like) depends to a certain extent on the length and complexity of the report and the format preferred by either the organization or the reader.

Consistency and readability are the hallmarks of an effective format. For example, be sure that all of your first-level headings are formatted consistently; if they are not, the reader may not be able to tell which headings are superior or subordinate to other headings. Regardless of the format used, make sure the reader can instantly tell which are major headings and which are minor headings. You can differentiate the different levels of headings by using different fonts, font sizes, styles (such as bold or italic), and horizontal alignment.

If the organization or reader has a preferred format style, use it. Otherwise, follow the report formatting guidelines provided in the Style Manual.

Proofreading

First impressions are important. Even before reading the first line of your report, the reader will have formed an initial impression of the report—and of *you*. Make this impression a positive one by ensuring that the report bears a professional appearance.

After making all your revisions and formatting the various pages, give each page one final proofreading. Check closely for typographical errors. Assess the appearance of the page. Have you arranged the pages in correct order and stapled them neatly? If you're submitting a photocopy, are all copies legible and of even darkness? Is each page free of wrinkles and smudges?

In short, let your pride of authorship shine through in every facet of your report. Appearances and details count. Review your entire document to ensure that you can answer "yes" to every question found in Checklist 13 on page 244.

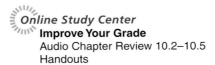

Online Study Center
Improve Your Grade
Audio Chapter Review 10.2–10.5
Handouts

True or False?

_____ 1. The procedures used to gather the data represent the major contribution of the report.

_____ 2. Conclusions must stem directly from the findings, and recommendations must stem directly from the conclusions.

_____ 3. Most business reports should not use first- or second-person pronouns.

_____ 4. You should prefer the present tense when discussing findings and conclusions from your study.

_____ 5. You do not need to provide reference citations for using another person's statements if you present the information in your own words.

Vocabulary

Define the following terms in your own words.

6. Direct quotation
7. Documentation
8. Paraphrase
9. Plagiarism

Critical Thinking

10. This chapter emphasizes the importance of documenting sources of data that are not your own words or ideas. Can you think of any instances in which documentation of such sources would *not* be necessary—or even appropriate?

Online Study Center
ACE the Test
ACE Practice Tests 10.2–10.5

Online Study Center
Improve Your Grade
Audio Chapter Quiz 10.2–10.5
PowerPoint Review 10.2–10.5

Online Study Center *college.hmco.com/pic/oberSASfund*

CHECKLIST 13

Reviewing Your Report Draft

Introduction

✓ Is the report title accurate, descriptive, and honest?

✓ Is the research problem or the purpose of the study stated clearly and accurately?

✓ Is the scope of the study identified?

✓ Are all technical terms, or any terms used in a special way, defined?

✓ Are the procedures discussed in sufficient detail?

✓ Are any questionable decisions justified?

Findings

✓ Is the data analyzed completely, accurately, and appropriately?

✓ Is the analysis free of bias and misrepresentation?

✓ Is the data *interpreted* (its importance and implications discussed) rather than just presented?

✓ Are all calculations correct?

✓ Is all relevant data included and all irrelevant data excluded?

✓ Are visual aids correct, necessary, clear, appropriately sized and positioned, and correctly labeled?

Summary, Conclusions, and Recommendations

✓ Is the wording used in the summary different from that used earlier to present the data initially?

✓ Are the conclusions supported by ample, credible evidence?

✓ Do the conclusions answer the questions or issues raised in the introduction?

✓ Are the recommendations reasonable in light of the conclusions?

✓ Does the report end with a sense of completion and convey an impression that the project is important?

Writing Style and Format

✓ Does the overall report take into account the needs and desires of the reader?

✓ Is the material organized appropriately?

✓ Are the headings descriptive, parallel, and appropriate in number?

✓ Are emphasis and subordination used effectively?

✓ Does each major section contain a preview, summary, and transition?

✓ Has proper verb tense been used throughout?

✓ Has an appropriate level of formality been used?

✓ Are all references to secondary sources documented properly?

✓ Is each needed report part included and in an appropriate format?

✓ Is the length of the report appropriate?

✓ Are the paragraphs of an appropriate length?

✓ Is the report free from spelling, grammar, and punctuation errors?

✓ Does the overall report provide a positive first impression and reflect care, neatness, and scholarship?

THREE PS
PROBLEM, PROCESS, PRODUCT

A Section of a Report

Problem

You are a manager at a software-development house that publishes communication software for the HAL and Pear microcomputers. Together, these two computers account for about 90 percent of the business market. You were asked in 2006 to survey users of communication software—a repeat of a similar study you undertook in 2001.

You conducted the survey using the same questionnaire and same procedures from the 2001 study. Now you've gathered the data, along with the comparable data collected in 2001, and have organized it roughly into draft tables, one of which is shown in Figure 10.1. You're now ready to put this table into final report format and analyze its contents.

FIGURE 10.1

Draft Table

Q. From what source did you obtain your last software program?												
	2001						**2006**					
	Total		**HAL**		**Pear**		**Total**		**HAL**		**Pear**	
Source	***n***	**%**	***n***	**%**	***n***	**%**	***n***	**%**	***n***	**%**	***n***	**%**
Online	28	21.2	24	26.1	4	10.0	60	41.1	25	30.9	35	53.9
Mail-order company	3	2.3	2	2.2	1	2.5	4	2.7	2	2.5	2	3.1
Retail outlet	70	53.0	46	50.0	24	60.0	63	43.2	44	54.3	19	29.2
Software publisher	9	6.8	4	4.3	5	12.5	10	6.8	4	4.9	6	9.2
Unauthorized copy	21	15.9	15	16.3	6	15.0	6	4.1	3	3.7	3	4.6
Other	1	.8	1	1.1	0	0.0	3	2.1	3	3.7	0	0.0
Total	132	100.0	92	100.0	40	100.0	146	100.0	81	100.0	65	100.0

Process

1. Table Format

a. Examine the format of your draft table—the arrangement of columns and rows. Should you change anything for the final table?

> First, the year columns (2001 and 2006) should be reversed. The new data is more important than the old data, so putting it first will emphasize it.
>
> Second, the rows need to be rearranged. They should be rearranged in descending order according to the first amount column—the 2006 total column. This new arrangement will put the most important data first in the table.

b. Assuming that you will have many tables in your final report, is there some way to condense the information in this table without undue loss of precision or detail?

> Although the number of respondents is important, the readers of my report will be much more interested in the percentages. Therefore, I'll give only the total number of respondents for each column and put that figure immediately under each column heading.
>   Also, I see immediately that very few people obtained their software from online bulletin boards either in 2001 or 2006, so I'll combine that category with the "Other" category.
>   These changes are shown in Figure 10.2.

Product

FIGURE 10.2

Revised Table

Source	2006			2001		
	Total ($n = 146$)	HAL ($n = 81$)	Pear ($n = 65$)	Total ($n = 132$)	HAL ($n = 92$)	Pear ($n = 40$)
Retail outlet	43	54	29	53	50	60
Online	41	31	54	21	26	10
Software publisher	7	5	9	7	4	13
Unauthorized copy	4	3	5	16	17	15
Other	5	7	3	3	3	2
Total	100	100	100	100	100	100

---

2. **Table Interpretation**

   a. Study the table in Figure 10.2. If you had space to make only one statement about this table, what would it be?

   > Retail outlets and mail-order companies are equally important sources for obtaining software, together accounting for more than four-fifths of all sources.

   b. What other 2006 data should you discuss in your narrative?

   > HAL and Pear users obtain their software in different ways: the majority of HAL users obtain theirs from retail outlets, whereas the majority of Pear users obtain theirs from mail-order firms.

c. What should you point out in comparing 2006 data with 2001 data?

> The market share for retail outlets decreased by almost 20 percent from 2001 to 2006, while the market share for mail-order companies almost doubled. Also, the use of unauthorized copies appears to be decreasing (although the actual figures for both years are probably somewhat higher than these self-reported figures).

3. **Report Writing**

   a. Develop an effective generic heading and an effective talking heading for this section of the report. Which one will you use?

   > *Generic Heading*: SOURCES OF SOFTWARE PURCHASES
   >
   > *Talking Heading*: MAIL ORDERS CATCHING UP WITH RETAIL SALES
   >
   > Because I do not know personally the readers of the report and their preferences, I'll make the conservative choice and use a generic heading.

   b. Compose an effective topic (preview) sentence for this section.

   > Respondents were asked to indicate the source of the last software program they purchased.

   c. Where will you position the table for this section?

   > At the end of the first paragraph that refers to the table.

   d. What verb tense will you use in this section?

   > Past tense for the procedures; present tense for the findings.

   e. Assume that the next report section discusses the cost of software. Compose an effective summary/transition sentence for this section of the report.

   > Perhaps the increasing reliance on mail-order purchases is one reason that the cost of communication software has decreased since 2001.

Product

SOURCES OF SOFTWARE PURCHASES

Respondents were asked to indicate the source of the last software program they purchased. As shown in Table 8, retail outlets and online companies are now equally important sources for obtaining software, together accounting for more than four-fifths of all sources. HAL and Pear users obtain their software in different ways: the majority of HAL users obtain theirs from retail outlets, whereas the majority of Pear users obtain theirs online.

TABLE 8. SOURCE OF LAST SOFTWARE PROGRAM
(in Percentages)

Source	2006			2001		
	Total (*n* = 146)	HAL (*n* = 81)	Pear (*n* = 65)	Total (*n* = 132)	Hal (*n* = 92)	Pear (*n* = 40)
Retail outlet	43	54	29	53	50	60
Online	41	31	54	21	26	10
Software publisher	7	5	9	7	4	13
Unauthorized copy	4	3	5	16	17	15
Other	5	7	3	3	3	2
Total	100	100	100	100	100	100

Retail outlets have decreased in popularity (down 10 percent) since 2001, while online sources have dramatically increased in popularity (up 20 percent). Also, the use of unauthorized copies appears to be decreasing (although the actual figure is probably somewhat higher than these self-reported figures).

Perhaps the increasing reliance on online purchases is one reason that the cost of communication software has declined since 2001.

COST OF SOFTWARE

...

PORTFOLIO PROJECT 5

Writing a Business Report

Online Study Center
Prepare for Class
Portfolio Stationery

Problem

The manufacturing facility where you work employs three data-entry operators who work full-time keyboarding production, personnel, and inventory data into a computer. This data is then sent via secure Internet connection to the headquarters minicomputer, where it becomes part of the corporate database for financial, production, and personnel management.

Last year, one of the operators was absent from work for two weeks for a condition diagnosed as carpal tunnel syndrome, a neuromuscular disorder of the tendons and tissue in the wrists caused by repeated hand motions. Her symptoms included a dull ache in the wrist and excruciating pain in the shoulder and neck. Her doctor treated her with anti-inflammatory medicine and a cortisone injection, and she has had no further problems. However, just last week a second data-entry operator experienced similar symptoms; her doctor diagnosed her ailment as "repeated-motion illness," or repetitive stress injury (RSI).

Because the company anticipates further automation in the future, with more data-entry operators to be hired, your boss has asked you to gather additional information on this condition. Once the extent of the problem is known, she wants you to make any appropriate recommendations regarding the work environment—posture, furniture, work habits, rest breaks, and the like —that will alleviate this problem.

Process

Compose a few paragraphs describing how you solved this problem. In narrative form, provide information such as the following:

1. The problem statement and subproblems for your report
2. How you gathered the needed secondary data
3. How you evaluated the quality and relevance of any data you collected from online searching
4. How you decided whether to use a direct or an indirect organizational plan
5. The degree of formality you decided to use
6. Factors you used to determine whether to include any visual aids

Product

Compose your five- to seven-page, double-spaced report, following the steps of the writing process (audience analysis, planning, drafting, revising, formatting, and proofreading). Include a title page and bibliography or reference list. Format the final version in appropriate style (refer to the Style Manual at the back of the book for formatting guidelines).

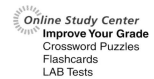

LEARNING OBJECTIVE REVIEW

 Determine an appropriate report structure and organization.

- Choose the report format—manuscript, memorandum, or letter—based on the audience and purpose of the report.
- Plan your report so information will be presented in a unified, ordered, and logical way by:
  - Selecting an organizational basis for the findings
  - Developing an outline
- When organizing your findings:
  - Choose a chronological method when discussing events with a time sequence.
  - Use a location method when topics relate to a geographical or physical location.
  - Organize by order of importance for busy readers.
  - Organize by the criteria used in compiling the data.
  - Use a direct organizational plan if the reader prefers it, will be receptive to your conclusions and recommendations, and can evaluate the material easily.
  - Use an indirect organizational plan if the reader prefers it, will be initially uninterested, or cannot evaluate the material easily.

2 *Draft the report body.*

- Use the introduction to give needed background and provide the purpose and scope of the report.
- Present and summarize findings in the body of your report, using visuals for emphasis.

- Include a summary section that reviews the problem, repeats the main points of the argument, and provides conclusions and recommendations.

3 *Use an effective writing style.*

- Use an objective tone.
- Use third-person pronouns for formal reports.
- Use past tense to describe procedures and findings of other studies already completed; use present tense when presenting conclusions.
- Make your reader aware of the importance you attach to your points.
- Create a unified presentation that is smooth and coherent.

4 *Provide appropriate documentation of sources.*

- Paraphrase secondary source information.
- Provide documentation to identify sources.
- Avoid plagiarism.

5 *Revise, format, and proofread the report.*

- Revise for content to make sure you've included all necessary information, the information is correct, and it is presented in a logical manner.
- Format for consistency and readability.
- Proofread after revising.

1. Generic Products (▶ 10.1–10.5)

North Star is a producer of consumer products with annual sales of $847.2 million. It has 4.5 percent of the consumer market for its six consumer products (soap, deodorant, ammonia, chili, canned ham, and frozen vegetables).

On July 8 of this year, Paul Gettisfield, sales manager, asked you, a product manager, to study the feasibility of North Star's entering the generic products market. Generic products are products that do not have brand names but instead carry a plain generic label, such as "Paper Towels." Generic products are typically not advertised; they involve less packaging, less processing, and cheaper ingredients than brand names; and they compete both with private brands (those distributed solely by individual store chains such as A&P and Kroger) and with national brands (those available for sale at all grocery stores and advertised nationally). At the present time, North Star produces only national brands.

Paul specifically asked you *not* to explore whether North Star had the necessary plant capacity. He wanted you only to provide up-to-date information on the generic market in general and to explore likely consumer acceptance of generic brands for the products that North Star produces. He is quite interested in learning the results of your research.

In August, you conducted a mail survey of 1,500 consumers in the three states (California, Texas, and Arizona) that constitute your largest market. Responses were received from 832 consumers to the following questions; responses are provided for all 832 consumers and for the 237 largest consumers (those who indicated that they did 51 percent to 100 percent of their household shopping).

> Have you purchased a food generic product (such as canned fruit or vegetables) in the last month?
>
> > All consumers: 36 percent yes, 64 percent no
> > Largest consumers: 29 percent yes,
> >   71 percent no
>
> Was this the first time you had purchased a food generic product?
>
> > All consumers: 18 percent yes, 82 percent no
> > Largest consumers: 20 percent yes,
> >   80 percent no

> Have you purchased a nonfood generic product (such as paper towels or soap) in the last month?
>
> > All consumers: 60 percent yes, 40 percent no
> > Largest consumers: 59 percent yes,
> >   41 percent no
>
> Was this the first time you had purchased a non-food generic product?
>
> > All consumers: 5 percent yes, 95 percent no
> > Largest consumers: 7 percent yes,
> >   93 percent no
>
> If you could save at least 30 percent by purchasing a generic brand rather than a national brand, would you purchase a generic brand of any of the following products?
>
> > Bar of soap: 43 percent yes, 57 percent no,
> >   0 percent don't use this product
> > Deodorant: 31 percent yes, 67 percent no,
> >   2 percent don't use this product
> > Ammonia: 80 percent yes, 10 percent no,
> >   10 percent don't use this product
> > Chili: 34 percent yes, 52 percent no,
> >   14 percent don't use this product
> > Canned ham: 19 percent yes, 44 percent no,
> >   37 percent don't use this product
> > Frozen vegetables: 54 percent yes, 30 percent no, 16 percent don't use this product

You also asked the local North Star sales representatives to audit 20 randomly selected chain supermarkets in each of these three states in August. Personal observation showed that 39 of the stores stocked generic brands, 37 of these 39 stocked 100 or more generic items, and 15 had separate generic product sections. All but three of the 60 stores stocked all six products that North Star now produces.

In gathering your data, you also made the following notes from three secondary sources:

1. *Hammond's Market Reports*, Gary, IN, 2007, pp. 1027–1030. This annual index lists various types of information for more than 2,000 consumer products. The percentages of market share for the six products North Star produces are as follows:

	2000	2003	2006
Generic brands	1.5%	2.6%	7.3%
Private labels	31.6%	30.7%	27.8%
National brands	66.9%	66.7%	64.9%

2. H. R. Nolan, "No-Name Brands: An Update," *Supermarket Management*, April 2006, pp. 31–37.

   a. Generic brands are typically priced 30 percent to 50 percent below national brands. (p. 31)
   b. Consumers require a 36 percent saving on a bar of soap and 40 percent savings on deodorant to motivate them to switch to a generic. (p. 32)
   c. Consumer awareness of generics has tripled since 1982. (p. 33)
   d. "The easiest way to become a no-name store is to ignore no-name brands." (direct quotation from p. 33)
   e. Many leading brand manufacturers feel compelled to produce the lower-profit generic brands because either the market has grown too big to ignore or the inroads that generic brands have made on their own brands have left them with idle capacity. (p. 35)

3. Edward J. Rauch and Pamela G. McCleary, "National Brands to Play a Bit Part in the Future," *Grocery Business*, Fall 2005, pp. 118–120.

   a. Eight out of ten food chains believe their costs will rise more than their prices this year. (p. 118)
   b. Generics are now available in 84 percent of the stores nationwide and account for about 4 percent of the store space. (p. 118)
   c. "Supermarket executives foresee a drop in shelf space allocated to brand products and an increase in the space allocated to generics and private labels. Many experts predict that supermarkets will ultimately carry no more than the top two brands in a category plus a private label and a generic label." (p. 119)
   d. Today, 37 percent of the grocery stores have switched from paper bags to the less expensive plastic bags for packaging customer purchases, even though the plastic bags are nonbiodegradable. (p. 119)
   e. Starting from nearly zero in 1982, generics have acquired 7 percent of the $275 billion grocery market. Many observers predict they will go up to 25 percent within the next five years. (p. 120)

Analyze the data, prepare whatever visual aids would be helpful, and then write a formal report for Gettisfield.

2. **Career Choices (▶10.1–10.5)**

Explore a career in which you are interested. Determine the job outlook, present level of employment, salary trends, typical duties, working conditions, educational or experience requirements, and the like. Interview someone holding this position to gain firsthand impressions. Then write up your findings in a report to your instructor. Include at least five secondary sources and at least one table or visual aid in your report.

3. **Intercultural Dimensions (▶10.1–10.5)**

To what extent do network and cable television accurately portray members of cultural, ethnic, and racial minorities? To what extent are they portrayed at all during prime time (8 p.m. to 11 p.m.)? In what types of roles are they shown, and what is their relationship with nonminority characters? As assistant to the director of public relations of the National Minority Alliance, you are interested in such questions.

Locate and review at least three journal articles on this topic. Then develop a definition of the term *minority*. Randomly select and view at least ten prime-time television shows, and develop a form for recording the needed data on minority representation in these shows. As part of your research, compare the proportion of minority members in this country with their representation on prime-time television. Integrate your primary and secondary data into a report. Use objective language, and be careful to present ample data to support any conclusions or recommendations you may make.

4. **Frozen Yogurt (▶10.1–10.5)**

Assume that you have been asked by Jim Miller, executive vice president of Jefferson Industries, to write an exploratory report on the feasibility of Jefferson opening a frozen yogurt store in Tucson, Arizona. If the preliminary data you gather warrants further exploration of this project, a professional venture-consultant group will be hired to conduct an in-depth, dollars-and-cents study. Your job, then, is to recommend whether such an expensive follow-up study is justified. Assume that Jefferson has the financial resources to support such a venture if it looks promising.

You can immediately think of several areas you want to explore: the general market outlook for frozen yogurt stores, the demographic makeup of Tucson (home of the University of Arizona), the local economic climate, franchise opportunities in the industry, and the like. Undoubtedly, other topics (or criteria) will surface as you brainstorm the problem.

Carry through the entire research process for this project—planning the study, collecting the data, organizing and analyzing the data, and writing the report. Write the body of the report using formal language, organize the study by criteria, and place the conclusions and recommendations at the end. (*Note:* If you gathered any data by completing the exercises at the end of Chapter 9, integrate that data into your study as needed.)

5. Student Living Arrangements (▶ 10.1–10.5)

Darlene Anderson, a real estate developer and president of Anderson and Associates, is exploring the feasibility of building a large student apartment complex on a lot her firm owns two blocks from campus. Even though the city planning commission believes there is already enough student housing, Anderson thinks she can succeed if she addresses specific problems of present housing. She has asked you, her executive assistant, to survey students to determine their views of off-campus living. Specifically, she wants you to

develop a ranked listing of the most important attributes of student housing. How important to students are such criteria as price, location (access to campus, shopping, public transportation, and the like), space and layout, furnishings (furnished versus unfurnished), social activities, parking, pets policy, and the like?

In addition, the architect has drawn a plan that features the following options: private hotel-like rooms (sleeping and sitting area and private bath but no kitchen); private one-room efficiency apartments; one-bedroom, two-person apartments; and four-bedroom, four-person apartments. Which of these arrangements would students most likely rent, given their present economic situation? Would another alternative be more appealing to them?

Develop a questionnaire and administer it to a sample of students. Then analyze the data and write a report for Anderson.

6. Speech Recognition Software (▶ 10.1–10.5)

Speech recognition software enables the user to dictate a passage into a microphone and it is displayed immediately on the computer. You can even format documents by speaking the correct commands. Such software would be helpful, of course, to disabled users, those who have not learned to type, and people (like physicians) who need to be doing other things with their hands while entering information. Research this new data-entry tool and write a six-to-eight-page report giving your conclusions about whether this type of software can be used instead of, or in addition to, the computer keyboard for your business office.

Additional exercises are available at the Online Study Center website: **college.hmco.com/pic/oberSASfund**.

Online Study Center   RESOURCES

Prepare for Class, Improve Your Grade, and ACE the Test. Student Achievement Series resources include:

ACE Practice Tests	Ask Ober	Audio Chapter Reviews and Quizzes
Chapter Outlines	Communication Objectives	Crossword Puzzles
Flashcards	Glossaries	Handouts
LAB Tests	Portfolio Project Stationery	Sample Reports

To access these learning and study tools, go to **college.hmco.com/pic/oberSASfund**.

11 **Making Oral Presentations**

Almost everyone in business will give at least one major presentation a year.

1 ▶ *Determine the purpose of the presentation, analyze the audience, and select a delivery method.*

2 ▶ *Analyze and organize your presentation material into an opening, body, and ending.*

3 ▶ *Plan a team and video presentation.*

I prefer to make my presentations interactive rather than following a formal script, and I make a point of following up on audience questions."
—Sara González, President and CEO, Georgia Hispanic Chamber of Commerce

Chapter Outline

▶ **PLANNING THE PRESENTATION**
Purpose
Audience Analysis
Delivery Method

▶ **ORGANIZING THE PRESENTATION**
The Opening
The Body
The Ending
The Use of Humor in Business Presentations

▶ **PLANNING TEAM AND VIDEO PRESENTATIONS**
Work-Team Presentations
Video Presentations

▶ **VISUAL AIDS FOR BUSINESS PRESENTATIONS**
Transparencies and Electronic Presentations
Preparing Visual Aids
Using Visual Aids

▶ **PRACTICING AND DELIVERING THE PRESENTATION**
Practicing the Presentation
Delivering the Presentation
Post-Presentation Activities

Online Study Center
Prepare for Class
Chapter Outline

5 ▶ *Practice and deliver a presentation.*

4 ▶ *Develop effective visual aids.*

(Ad)dressing to Impress

W hen Sara González makes a presentation, she starts with the past and ends with the future. González is president and chief executive officer (CEO) of the Georgia Hispanic Chamber of Commerce. This Atlanta-based nonprofit organization promotes and supports the economic development of Georgia's Hispanic business community.

González receives invitations to address all kinds of audiences, from graduate students to international women's groups, about

Online Study Center college.hmco.com/pic/oberSASfund

SARA GONZÁLEZ
President and CEO,
Georgia Hispanic
Chamber of Commerce
(Atlanta, Georgia)

the chamber's background, achievements, and goals. "I prefer to make my presentations interactive rather than following a formal script, and I make a point of following up on audience questions. I love questions. I always invite people to ask me questions. Usually I know the answer because I know my topic so well. If by chance I don't have an answer, I say that I don't know but I'll find out." After taking the questioner's business card or noting the name and phone number, she heads back to the office, researches the answer, and calls the questioner right away.

The chamber sponsors a "How to Open Your Own Business" presentation every month, and several attendees have founded businesses. González invites these entrepreneurs to join her for future presentations as a way of inspiring and informing others. "I want to include someone with a success story," she explains. "What better example?"

Anyone who plans a career in sales, training, or education expects to make many oral presentations to customers, employees, or students each week. What you may not realize, though, is that almost *everyone* in business will give at least one major presentation and many smaller ones each year, to customers, superiors, subordinates, or colleagues—not to mention presentations at PTA meetings, homeowners' association meetings, civic clubs, and the like.

A presentation that discusses ideas incompletely and inefficiently wastes time and money. Sales are lost, vital information is not communicated, training programs fail, policies are not implemented, and profits fall.

Technology is undoubtedly changing the physical characteristics of oral presentations in business—for example, by making presentations possible via interactive computer or television rather than in person. However, the verbal and nonverbal communication strategies present in oral presentations can make any communicator a key competency in a modern business organization.

PLANNING THE PRESENTATION

1 ▶ *Determine the purpose of the presentation, analyze the audience, and select a delivery method.*

When assigned the task of making a business presentation, your first impulse might be to sit down at your desk or computer and begin writing. Resist the temptation. As in written communications, several important steps precede the actual writing. These steps involve determining the purpose of the presentation, analyzing the audience, and selecting a delivery method.

Purpose

Keeping your purpose uppermost in mind helps you decide what information to include and what to omit, in what order to present this information, and which points to emphasize and which to subordinate. (See Figure 11.1 for a look at the most popular topics of professional speakers.)

Most business presentations have one of these four purposes:

▌ *Reporting:* Updating the audience on some project or event

▌ *Explaining:* Detailing how to carry out a procedure or how to operate a new piece of equipment

▌ *Persuading:* Convincing the listeners to purchase something or to accept an idea you're presenting

▌ *Motivating:* Inspiring the listeners to take some action

After your presentation is over, your purpose provides a criterion—the *only* important criterion—by which to judge the success of your presentation. No matter how well or how poorly you spoke and no matter how impressive or ineffective your visual aids were, the most important question that remains is whether you accomplished your purpose.

Audience Analysis

In addition to identifying demographic factors such as the size, age, and organizational status of your audience, you need to determine the audience members' level of knowledge about your topic and their psychological needs (values, attitudes, and beliefs). These factors provide clues about everything from the overall content, tone, and types of examples you should use to the types of questions to expect and even the way you should dress.

The principles by which you analyze your audience are the same as those discussed in the chapters on writing letters, e-mails, memos, and reports. Consider the effect of your message on your audience and your credibility with them. The key is to put yourself in your audience's place so that you can anticipate their questions and reactions. The "you" attitude applies to oral as well as to written communication.

The larger your audience, the more formal your presentation will be. When you speak to a large group, you should speak more loudly and more slowly and use more emphatic gestures and larger visuals. Usually, you should allow questions only at the end of your talk. If you're speaking to a small group, you can be more flexible about questions, and your tone and gestures will be more like those used in normal conversation. Furthermore, when presenting to small groups, your options in terms of visual aids increase.

If your audience is unfamiliar with your topic, you need to use clear, easy-to-understand language, with extensive visual aids and many examples. If the audience is more knowledgeable, you can proceed at a faster pace.

The audience's psychological needs also affect your presentation. If, for example, you think your listeners will be hostile—either to you personally or to your message—then you may have to oversell yourself or your idea. Instead of giving one or two examples, you may need to give several. In addition to establishing your own credibility, you may need to cite other experts to bolster your case.

Delivery Method

By far the most common (and generally the most effective) method for business presentations is speaking from prepared notes. The notes contain key phrases rather than complete sentences, and you compose the

---

CONCEPT CHECK 11.1

Give an original example of a presentation whose purpose is:

a. Reporting
b. Explaining
c. Persuading
d. Motivating

FIGURE 11.1

Popular Topics

The chart illustrates that the topics of motivation, leadership, and communication are favorites among professional speakers.

Most popular topics of professional speakers

exact wording as you speak. The notes help ensure that you cover all the material and do so in a logical order.

The specific content and format of the notes is not important; choose whatever works best for you. Some people use a formal outline on full sheets of paper; others prefer notes typed or jotted on index cards. Some use complete sentences; others, short phrases. Figure 11.2 shows outline notes for an oral presentation.

Some speakers insert delivery cues, indicating when to pause, smile, make a gesture, display a visual aid, slow down, and the like. Inexperienced speakers may start off by writing out the entire speech and then practicing extensively from the prepared script. Only after they are thoroughly familiar with their verbatim script do they condense it into an outline and then speak from the outline. Whichever method you use, the key to a successful delivery is practice, practice, practice.

ORGANIZING THE PRESENTATION

 Analyze and organize your presentation material into an opening, body, and ending.

For most presentations, the best way to begin is simply to brainstorm: write down every point you can think of that might be included in your presentation. Don't worry about the order or format—just get it all down.

Later, separate your notes into three categories: opening, body, and ending. As you begin to analyze and organize your material, you may find that you need additional information. You may need to retrieve records from files, consult with a colleague, visit your corporate or local library to fill in the gaps, or go online to retrieve data from the World Wide Web.

The Opening

The purpose of the opening is to capture the interest of your audience, and the first 90 seconds of your presentation are crucial in that regard. The audience will be observing every detail about you—your dress, posture, facial features, and voice qualities, as well as what you're actually saying—for clues about you and your topic, and they will be making preliminary judgments accordingly.

Begin immediately to establish rapport and build a relationship with your audience—not just for the duration of your presentation but for the long term. Because the opening is so crucial, some speakers write out the entire opening and practice it word for word until they almost know it by heart.

The kind of opening that will be effective depends on what your topic is, how well you know the audience, and how well they know you. If, for example, you're giving a status report on a project about which you've reported before, you can immediately announce your main points (for example, that the project is on schedule and proceeding as planned) and go immediately to the body of your remarks. If, however, you're presenting a new proposal to your superiors, you'll first have to introduce the topic and provide background information.

FIGURE 11.2

Outline Notes for an Oral Presentation
Note the incomplete sentences and abbreviations used in these notes.

FAMILIARITY WITH BENEFITS—<u>SLIDE 1</u>
• Most know about most benefits
• + 3/4 know about all but 2 benefits:
—Long-term disability = slight majority
—Auto insur = +1/3 (begun 6 wks before survey)
• No correlation between employment length & familiarity
—Not true for life insur—<u>SLIDE 2</u>
—Life insur: Longer employment = more familiarity

If most of the listeners don't know you, you'll need to gain their attention with a creative opening. The following types of attention-getting openings have proven successful for business presentations. The examples given are for a presentation to union employees with the purpose of motivating them to decrease absenteeism.

- *Quote a well-known person:* "Comedian Woody Allen once noted that 90 percent of the job is just showing up."

- *Ask a question:* "If we were able to cut our absenteeism rate by half during the coming six months, exactly how much do you think that would mean for each of us in our end-of-year bonus checks?"

- *Present a hypothetical situation:* "Suppose that, as you were leaving home this morning to put in a full day at work, your son came up to you and said he was too tired to go to school because he had stayed up late last night watching 'Wrestle Mania.' What would be your reaction?"

- *Relate an appropriate anecdote, story, joke, or personal experience:* "George, a friend of mine who had recently changed jobs, happened to meet his former boss and asked her whom she had hired to fill his vacancy. 'George,' his former boss said, 'when you left, you didn't *leave* any vacancy!' Perhaps the reason George didn't leave any vacancy was that. . . ."

- *Give an unusual fact:* "During the next 24 hours, American industry will lose $136 million because of absenteeism."

- *Use a dramatic prop or visual aid:* Holding up a paper clip, say, "What do you think is the true cost of this paper clip to our company?"

Don't apologize or make excuses (for example, "I wish I had had more time to prepare my remarks today" or "I'm not really much of a speaker"). The audience may agree with you! At any rate, you'll turn them off immediately and weaken your credibility. Your opening should lead into the body of your presentation by previewing your remarks: "Today, I'll cover four main points. First, ..." For most business presentations, let the audience know up front what you expect of them. Are you simply presenting information for them to absorb, or will audience members be expected to react to your remarks? Are you asking for their endorsement, their resources, their help, or what? Let the audience know what their role will be so that they can then place your remarks in perspective.

CONCEPT CHECK 11.2

Assume you are preparing a motivational presentation to your classmates on the importance of drinking responsibly (or not at all). Create an attention-getting opening for your presentation.

The Body

The body of your presentation conveys the real content. Here, you'll develop the points you introduced in the opening, giving background information, specific evidence, examples, implications, consequences, and other needed information.

Choose a Logical Sequence

Just as you do when writing a letter or report, choose an organizational plan that suits your purpose and your audience's needs. The most commonly used organizational plans are the following:

- *Criteria:* Introduce each criterion in turn and show how well each alternative meets that criterion (typically used for presenting proposals).

- *Direct sequence:* Give the major conclusions first, followed by the supporting details (typically used for presenting routine information).

Online Study Center college.hmco.com/pic/oberSASfund

During his 2004 presidential campaign, Senator John Kerry of Massachusetts gave hundreds of speeches. Yet he spent hours revising drafts of each new speech. "Polishing and polishing and polishing until he's satisfied," is how one aide described the process.

▌ *Indirect sequence:* Present the reasons first, followed by the major conclusion (typically used for persuasive presentations).

▌ *Chronology:* Present the points in the order in which they occurred (typically used in status reports or when reporting on some event).

▌ *Cause/effect/solution:* Present the sources and consequences of some problem and then propose a solution.

▌ *Order of importance:* Arrange the points in order of importance, then pose each point as a question and answer it (an effective way of ensuring that the audience can follow your arguments).

▌ *Elimination of alternatives:* List all alternatives and then gradually eliminate each one until only one option remains—the one you're recommending.

Whatever organizational plan you choose, make sure that your audience knows at the outset where you're going and can follow your organization. In a written document, signposts such as headings tell the reader how the parts fit together. In an oral presentation, you must compensate for the lack of such aids by using frequent and clear transitions that tell your listeners where you are. Pace your presentation of data so that you do not lose your audience.

Establish Your Credibility

Convince the listener that you've done a thorough job of collecting and analyzing the data and that your points are reasonable. Support your arguments with credible evidence—statistics, actual experiences, examples, and support from experts. Use objective language; let the data—not exaggeration or emotion—persuade the audience. Be guided by the same principles you use when writing a persuasive letter or report.

Avoid saturating your presentation with so many facts and figures that your audience won't be able to absorb them. Regardless of their relevance, statistics will not strengthen your presentation if the audience cannot digest all the data. A more effective tactic is to prepare handouts of detailed statistical data to distribute for review at a later time.

Deal with Negative Information

It would be unusual if *all* the data you collected and analyzed supported your proposal. (If that were the case, persuasion would not be necessary.) What should you do, then, about negative information, which might weaken your argument if you presented it? You cannot simply ignore it. To do so would surely open up a host of questions and subsequent doubts that would seriously undermine your position.

Think about your own analysis of the data. Despite the negative information, you still concluded that your solution has merit. Your tactic, then, is to present the important information—both pro and con—and to show, through your analysis and discussion, that your recommendations are still valid despite the disadvantages and drawbacks. Use the techniques you learned in Chapter 5 about emphasis and subordination to let your listeners know which points you considered major and which you considered minor.

Although you should discuss the important negative points, you may safely omit minor ones. You should be prepared, however, to discuss these issues if any questions about them arise at the conclusion of your presentation.

The Ending

The ending of your presentation is your last opportunity to achieve your objective. Don't waste it. A presentation without a strong ending is like a joke without a punch line.

Your closing should summarize the main points of your presentation, especially if it has been a long one. Even if the members of your audience have had an easy time following the structure of your talk, they won't necessarily remember all your important points. Let them know the significance of what you've said. Draw conclusions, make recommendations, or outline the next steps to take. Leave the audience with a clear and simple message.

To add punch to your ending, you may want to use one of the same techniques discussed for opening a presentation. You might tell a story, make a personal appeal, or issue a challenge. However, resist the temptation to end with a quotation. It won't sound dramatic enough. Besides, you want your listeners to remember *your* words and thoughts—not someone else's. Also avoid fading out with a weak "That's about all I have to say" or "I see that our time is running out."

Practice your presentation with a stopwatch. If necessary, insert reminders at critical points in your notes indicating where you should be at what point in time. Avoid having to drop important sections or rush through the conclusion of your presentation because you misjudged your timing.

Your audience will remember best what they hear last, so think of your ending as one of the most important parts of your presentation. Finish on a strong, upbeat note. If you've used a projector during your presentation, turn it off and turn the room lights on so that *you* are the center of attention. Also remember that no one ever lost any friends by finishing a minute or two ahead of schedule. As Toastmasters International puts it, "Get up, speak up, shut up, and sit down."

The Use of Humor in Business Presentations

Memory research indicates that when ideas are presented with humor, the audience not only can recall more details of the presentation but can also retain the information longer.[1]

Jokes, puns, satire, and especially amusing real-life incidents are just a few examples of humor, all of which serve to form a bond between speaker and

CONCEPT CHECK 11.3

Assume you're giving a 15-minute presentation to a campus group about the effective use of e-mail. Do research to locate a humorous story you might use in your presentation. Then personalize it for your particular situation.

audience. Humor can be used anywhere in a presentation—in the opening to get attention, in the body to add interest, or in the closing to drive home a point. Humor should, of course, be avoided if the topic is very serious or has negative consequences for the audience.

If you tell an amusing story, it must always be appropriate to the situation and in good taste. Never tell an off-color or sexist joke; never use offensive language; never single out an ethnic, racial, or religious group; and never use a dialect or foreign accent in telling a story. Such tactics are always in bad taste. The best stories are directed at yourself; they show that you are human and can laugh at yourself.

Regardless of your expertise as a joke teller, do not use humor too frequently. Humor is a means to an end—not an end in itself. When all is said and done, you don't want your audience to remember that you were funny. You want them to remember that what you had to say was important and made sense.

Online Study Center
Improve Your Grade
Audio Chapter Review 11.1, 11.2

TEST PREPPER II.1, II.2   ANSWERS CAN BE FOUND ON P. 412

True or False?

_____ 1. Audience analysis for oral presentations is similar to that used for written presentations.

_____ 2. The most effective method of delivery for most business presentations is to speak from brief, prepared notes.

_____ 3. Your speech notes should consist of a formal outline using phrases rather than complete sentences.

_____ 4. All business presentations need not begin with an attention-getting opening.

_____ 5. You should avoid discussing negative aspects of your oral proposal.

_____ 6. It is inappropriate to use humor in most business presentations.

Critical Thinking

7. Assume that because of your so-so grades, you were initially denied admission to graduate school at your institution. You have been given the chance, however, to present your case formally to the graduate council. What are some ways that you might establish your personal credibility with them?

Online Study Center
ACE the Test
ACE Practice Tests 11.1, 11.2

Online Study Center
Improve Your Grade
Audio Chapter Quiz 11.1, 11.2
PowerPoint Review 11.1, 11.2

PLANNING TEAM AND VIDEO PRESENTATIONS

 Plan a team and video presentation.

If you're typical, most of the business presentations you make will be solo performances—before a live audience. However, sometimes you will be a member of a work-group presentation team, and sometimes you may be asked to prepare a video on tape instead of a speech in front of a live audience.

Work-Team Presentations

Work-team presentations are common strategies for communicating about complex projects. Such presentations require extensive planning, close coordination, and a measure of maturity and goodwill. If you are responsible for coordinating such efforts, allow enough time and assign responsibilities on the basis of individual talents and time constraints.

Your major criterion for making assignments is the division of duties that will result in the most effective presentation. Tap into each team member's strengths. Some individuals may be better at collecting and analyzing the information to be presented, others may be better at developing the visual aids, and still others may be better at delivering the presentation. Does any work-team member have a knack for telling good stories or connecting with strangers? Perhaps he or she should begin the presentation. Consider picking a "diplomat" to moderate the question-and-answer session.

Everyone need not share equally in each aspect of the project. As coordinator, ensure that all efforts are recognized publicly and equally during the actual presentation, regardless of how much podium time is assigned to each person.

Achieving Coherence

Just as people have different writing styles, they also have different speaking styles. You must ensure that your overall presentation has coherence and unity—that is, that it sounds as if it were prepared and given by one individual. Thus, the group members should decide beforehand the most appropriate tone, format, organization, style for visual aids, manner of dress, method of handling questions, and similar factors that will help the presentation flow smoothly from topic to topic and from speaker to speaker.

Use one of the presentation templates that came with your software presentation program to maintain a consistent look and feel to everyone's slides. These templates define backgrounds and colors, slide heading formats, and font styles and sizes. Someone must also monitor the presentation for semantic consistency—both in the visual aids and in the verbal portion. Do you refer to people by first and last names, last names only, or a personal title and last name? Do you refer to your visual aids as charts, slides, overheads, graphics, or something else? If an unfamiliar term is used, ensure that the first person using the term (and only the first person) defines it.

Practicing the Team Presentation

At least one full-scale rehearsal—in the room where the presentation will take place, if possible, and using all visual aids—is crucial for work-team presentations. If possible, videotape this rehearsal for later analysis by the entire group. Schedule your final practice session early enough that you will have time to make any changes needed—and then to practice the presentation once more, if necessary.

Critiquing the performance of a colleague requires tact, empathy, and goodwill; accepting such feedback requires grace and maturity. For the entire presentation to succeed, each individual element must succeed. If it does, each contributor shares in the success and any rewards that may result.

The failure to plan and coordinate introductions and transitions is a frequently encountered dilemma. Will the first speaker introduce all team members at the beginning, or will each one introduce himself or herself as he or she gets up to speak?

Finally, consider yourself to be on stage during the entire team presentation—no matter who is presenting. If you're on the sidelines for the moment, stand erect; pay attention to the presenter (even though you may have heard the content a dozen times); and try to read the audience for nonverbal signs of confusion, boredom, disagreement, and the like.

Video Presentations

Most of the same principles mentioned earlier apply equally to video presentations. In addition, unique effects may result when the presenter faces the camera because gazing into the eye of the camera for a long time is an unnatural, artificial situation. The only solution is to practice. Fortunately, handheld video cameras and VCRs are now so common that you can practice easily in the comfort of your own home or office.

The best colors to wear when participating in a video presentation are shades of blue; a light blue shirt or blouse with a blue jacket or blazer is ideal. Avoid contrasting colors and stripes. Makeup is recommended for both men and women to reduce sweat and even out skin tone. When recording, sit or stand straight and look into the camera as long as possible while talking. Always focus your eyes on one of two places—either directly at the camera or at your notes; never gaze off to the side or over the camera. Because television exaggerates movements, stand or sit as still as possible and keep gestures to a minimum. Also, stay within an established area of movement (determined beforehand with the person who will be videotaping).

If possible, use actual color printouts of your visuals instead of an overhead or computer projection; the camera will pick up the image much better. Use lettering that is at least 1 inch in size and printed on a light blue or pastel background rather than on white. Try to group your visuals so that the camera is not zooming in and out too much because such movement can be distracting to the audience.

The increasing use of video presentations also means that you may be called on to operate the video camera. As a camera operator:

▮ Control the noise level in the room; even an air conditioner can add distracting background noise. Also, make sure that the room has good overall lighting, although it does not have to be "spotlights."

▮ Check your camera batteries beforehand and perhaps have a spare battery on hand.

▮ Use a tripod for stability. If you do not have access to a tripod, use your body as a brace for the camera, tucking it in against your body to steady it.

▮ Zoom in on the visual when the speaker mentions it.

▮ Minimize camera movement, but don't be afraid to move the camera. Use smooth, slow movement rather than fast, jerky movement.

▮ Try to "frame" or block the person in the camera (waist up, for example); don't get a shot that is too wide, covering too much area. A good rule of thumb is to provide a 1-inch border around the subject. If the presenter plans to move around, establish the area for movement with him or her before filming. Then let the person move within this frame instead of always following the person with the camera.

▮ Think in terms of what will be viewed by the audience rather than what will be filmed by the camera operator (that is, think in terms of showing, not shooting). Rarely will you use all of the footage shot; consider it the raw material from which to select and organize an effective presentation.

Contemporary businesspeople need to become not only computer literate but also "video literate." If you're unfamiliar with videotaping procedures, visit a local video studio and observe a shoot to see how the process is handled and how directors and camera crews work with the presenter.

VISUAL AIDS FOR BUSINESS PRESENTATIONS

4 ▶ *Develop effective visual aids.*

Today's audiences are accustomed to multimedia events that bombard the senses with information. They often assume that any formal presentation must be accompanied by some visual element, whether it is a flipchart, overhead transparency, slide, film, videotape, or actual model.

Visual aids are relatively simple to create and help the audience understand the presentation, especially if it includes complex or statistical material. A University of Pennsylvania study found that presenters who used visual aids successfully persuaded 67 percent of their audience, whereas those who did not use such aids persuaded only 50 percent of their audience. In addition, meetings in which visual aids were used were 28 percent shorter than those that lacked such aids. Similarly, a University of Minnesota study found that the use of graphics increased a presenter's persuasiveness by 43 percent. Presenters who used visual aids were also perceived as being more professional, better prepared, and more interesting than those who didn't use visual aids.[2]

Transparencies and Electronic Presentations

Inexpensive, easy to produce, and simple to update, transparencies for overhead projection can be used without darkening the room and while you are facing the audience. Thus, your audience can see to take notes, and you can maintain eye contact with them. Thanks to presentation software, overhead transparencies can readily take advantage of color, designed fonts, charts, artwork, and preplanned layouts (called *templates*). Despite the convenience and ease of use of transparencies, however, the availability and low cost of computer projectors, combined with growing sales of notebook computers, has caused the use of transparencies to drop significantly in recent years.

Electronic presentations are the newest medium for visual aids. They consist of slides or video shown directly from a computer and projected onto a screen via a projector. Because the slide images come directly from the computer file, actual transparencies do not have to be made. Electronic presentations enable you to add multimedia effects easily to your presentation—if doing so helps you tell your story more effectively. You could, for example, show a short video, move text across the screen, or play background sound effects. Electronic slide presentations offer greater flexibility than traditional slide presentations do, but they require the use of high-powered projectors to obtain the best results.

When giving an electronic presentation, follow these guidelines:

▌ Check colors for accuracy. If precise color matching is important (for example, with the color of your corporate logo), ensure that the color projected on the computer on which you designed the presentation matches the color shown on the projection system on which you will display it.

▌ Keep special effects simple. Elaborate or random transition effects, for example, are distracting. Nevertheless, consider using builds to reveal one bullet point at a time; doing so helps focus the audience's attention. Avoid sound effects unless essential for understanding.

When showing slides, be sure to avoid walking in front of the projector. Also, avoid including too much information on each slide. Here, Attorney Philip Beck violates these guidelines as he testifies at a court hearing on the contested presidential election results in Florida.

▌ Disable any screen savers and energy-saving automatic shutdown features of your computer. You don't want your screen to begin displaying a screen saver or to go blank in the middle of your presentation.

▌ Be seen and heard. Stand on the left side of the screen from the audience's point of view—in the light and away from the computer—using a remote mouse. Make sure that you're still clearly visible when the projection screen is dark.

Preparing Visual Aids

Avoid using too many visual aids. Novice presenters sometimes employ them as a crutch. Such overuse keeps the emphasis on the visual aid rather than on the presenter. Instead, use visual aids only when they will help the audience grasp an important point, and remove them when they're no longer needed. One or two relevant, helpful visual aids are better than an armload of irrelevant ones—no matter how attractive they are.

If you do not keep your visual aids clear and simple, your audience can easily become overwhelmed, with their attention drawn to the technology rather than to the content. As always, seek to *express*—not to *impress*. With visual aids, less is more. According to Joan Detz, speaker, trainer, and author of *How to Write and Give a Speech*:

> A successful presentation has little to do with technical wizardry. The single biggest mistake I see is overusing technology. Most of the time, visuals are used as a security blanket for people who haven't thought through a presentation. It's easier to have an audience look at a slide or other visual rather than at you.[3]

Do not simply photocopy tables or illustrations from reports, printouts, or journals and project them on a screen. Print graphics usually contain far too much information to serve effectively as presentation graphics. Using such graphics in a presentation will often do more to hinder your presentation than to help it.

As a general rule, each slide or transparency should contain no more than 40 characters per line, no more than six or seven lines per visual, and no more than three columns of data (think of your slide as a highway billboard rather than a memo). Use upper- and lowercase letters (rather than all capitals) in a large, simple typeface and plenty of white (empty) space. Use bulleted lists to show a group of related items that have no specific order and numbered lists to show related items in a specific order. Establish a color scheme and stick with it for all your visual aids; that is, use the same background color for each slide or transparency. Ensure that your visual aids are readable by testing them beforehand; look at them from the back seat of the room in which you will be presenting.

Another form of visual aid, of course, is the audience handout. Handouts are a standard part of most business presentations because they provide a review or new information for the audience long after your presentation is over.

The quality of your visual aids sends a nonverbal message about your competence and your respect for your audience. Just as you don't want your audience's attention distracted by the razzle-dazzle of your slides, neither do you want their attention distracted by poor quality. If the visual aid isn't readable or attractive, don't use it.

Using Visual Aids

Even the best visual aid will not be effective if it is used improperly during the presentation or if the equipment doesn't work. Operating equipment smoothly does not come naturally; it takes practice and a keen awareness of audience needs, especially when using a slide or overhead projector.

Confirm that your equipment is in top working order, you know how to operate it, and you know how to secure a spare bulb or spare machine quickly if one becomes necessary. Adjust the projector and focus the image so that it is clearly readable from the farthest seat. However, do not make the image larger than necessary; the presenter should be the center of attention. The image should be a square or rectangle. Avoid the common keystoning effect (where the top of the image is wider than the bottom) by tilting the top of the screen forward slightly toward the projector. Also, avoid walking in front of the projected image.

Prepare for potential problems. Number your transparencies so that they can be reorganized quickly if they are dropped. Clean the overhead projector glass before using it. Have an extra bulb handy and know how to insert it. Finally, be prepared to give your presentation without visual aids if that should become necessary.

With practice, you can learn to stand to the side of the screen, facing the audience with your feet pointed toward them. Then, when you need to refer to an item on the screen, point with either a finger, pointer, or pen. (Many people find the use of laser pointers distracting.) Turn your body from the waist, keeping your feet pointed toward the audience. Doing so enables you to maintain better eye contact with the audience as well as better control of the presentation.

Online Study Center
Improve Your Grade
Audio Chapter Review 11.3, 11.4

TEST PREPPER 11.3, 11.4   ANSWERS CAN BE FOUND ON P. 412

True or False?

_____ 1. Each member of a work-team presentation should use the same software template to format his or her slides.

_____ 2. The best colors to wear when giving a video presentation are shades of blue.

_____ 3. Generally, the more visual aids you use, the more effective your presentation.

_____ 4. The screen should be on the speaker's left as he or she faces the audience.

Critical Thinking

5. What has been the major problem in work-team presentations (or other group projects) in which you have personally participated? How did your group solve it?

Online Study Center
ACE the Test
ACE Practice Tests 11.3, 11.4

Online Study Center
Improve Your Grade
Audio Chapter Quiz 11.3, 11.4
PowerPoint Review 11.3, 11.4

PRACTICING AND DELIVERING THE PRESENTATION

 5 ▶ *Practice and deliver a presentation.*

Now that you have prepared your presentation, you should practice it before the actual delivery.

Practicing the Presentation

The language of oral presentations must be simple. Because the listener has only one chance to comprehend the information presented, shorter sentences and

CONCEPT CHECK 11.4

What are some ways in which effective spoken language differs from effective written language?

Online Study Center college.hmco.com/pic/oberSASfund

simpler vocabulary should be used for oral presentations than for written presentations. Presenters have trouble articulating long, involved sentences with complex vocabulary, and listeners have trouble understanding them. A long sentence that reads easily on paper may leave the speaker breathless when he or she says it aloud. Avoid such traps. Use short, simple sentences and a conversational style. Use contractions freely, and avoid using words that you may have trouble pronouncing.

Begin practicing by simulating the conditions of the meeting room as closely as possible. Always practice standing, with your notes at the same level and angle as at a podium, and use any visual aids that will be part of your presentation.

Remember that 55 percent of your credibility with an audience comes from your body language, 38 percent comes from your voice qualities, and only 7 percent comes from the actual words you use.[4]

For important presentations, plan on a minimum of three run-throughs. Record how much time it takes on each section of your outline. If necessary, cut out a minor point or two so that you have time for a solid, well-rehearsed, and unrushed summary and conclusion. Schedule your practice sessions far enough ahead to allow you to make any needed changes. Become familiar enough with your message that a few notes or a graphic will keep you on track. Practice the most important parts (introduction, summary of key points, and conclusion) the most number of times.

Speak in a conversational tone, but at a slightly slower rate than normally used in conversation. For interest and to fit the situation, vary both your volume and your rate of speaking, slowing down when presenting important or complex information and speeding up when summarizing. Use periodic pauses to emphasize important points. Use correct diction, avoid slurring or dropping off the endings of words, and practice pronouncing difficult names.

Occasional hand and arm gestures are important for adding interest and emphasis, but only if they are appropriate and appear natural. If you never "talk with your hands" in normal conversation, it is unlikely you will do so naturally while presenting. Generally, one-handed gestures are more effective and less distracting than two-handed ones. Avoid annoying and distracting mannerisms and gestures, such as jingling coins or keys in your pocket; coughing or clearing your throat excessively; wildly waving your hands; gripping the lectern tightly; nervously swaying or pacing; playing with jewelry, pens, or paper clips; or peppering your remarks with "and uh" or "you know."

Practice smiling occasionally, standing tall and naturally, with the body balanced on both feet. Rest your hands on the podium; by your side; or in any natural, quiet position. Your voice and demeanor should reflect professionalism, enthusiasm, and self-confidence.

Delivering the Presentation

You should know your presentation well enough that you can maintain eye contact easily with your audience, taking care to include members in all corners of the room. Lock in on one person and maintain eye contact for at least three seconds—or until you have completed a thought.

If you lose your place in your notes, relax and take as much time as you need to regroup. If your mind actually does go blank, try to keep talking—even if you repeat what you've just said. The audience will probably think you intentionally repeated the information for emphasis, and the extra time may jog your memory. If this trick doesn't work, simply skip ahead to another part of your presentation that you do remember; then come back later to the part you omitted.

Stage Fright

According to author Mark Twain, "There are two types of speakers—those who are nervous and those who are liars." If you've ever experienced stage fright, take comfort in the fact that you're not alone. Fear of giving a speech is the number one fear of most Americans. In a national poll of 3,000 people, 42 percent said the one thing they're most afraid of in life—even more than having cancer or a heart attack—is giving a speech.[5] Fortunately, behavior-modification experts have found that of the full range of anxiety disorders, people can most predictably overcome their fear of public speaking.[6]

Recognize that you have been asked to make a presentation because someone obviously thinks you have something important to say. You should feel complimented by the request. Unless you are an exceptionally good or exceptionally bad speaker, the audience will more likely remember *what* you say rather than *how* you say it. Most of us fall somewhere between these two extremes as presenters. Recognize also that some nervousness, of course, is good. It gets the adrenaline flowing and gives your speech an edge.

The best way to minimize any lingering anxiety is to overprepare. For the anxious presenter, there is no such thing as overpractice. The more familiar you are with the content of your speech and the more trial runs you've made, the better you'll be able to concentrate on your delivery once you're actually in front of the group. You may want to memorize the first few sentences of your presentation just so you can approach those critical first moments (when anxiety is highest) with more confidence.

Practice mental imagery. Several times before your big presentation, sit in a comfortable position, close your eyes, and visualize yourself giving your speech. Picture yourself speaking confidently, loudly, and clearly in an assured voice. If you can imagine yourself giving a successful speech, you will be able to do so.

Before your presentation, take a short walk to relax your body. While waiting for your presentation to begin, let your arms drop loosely by your sides, shake your wrists gently, and breathe deeply several times. As you begin to speak, look for friendly faces in the crowd, and concentrate on them initially.

Finally, businesspeople who are anxious about speaking in public should consider taking a public-speaking course or joining Toastmasters International, the world's oldest and largest nonprofit educational organization. The purpose of Toastmasters is to improve the speaking skills of its members. Members meet

CONCEPT CHECK 11.5

Use the Internet to locate the nearest Toastmasters International chapter (www.toastmasters.org). Give the name of the chapter and tell when and where it meets.

© Grantland Enterprises; www.grantland.net

weekly or monthly and deliver prepared speeches, evaluate one another's oral presentations, give impromptu talks, develop their listening skills, conduct meetings, and learn parliamentary procedure.

Answering Questions

One advantage that oral presentations have over written reports is the opportunity to engage in two-way communication. The question-and-answer session is a vital part of your presentation, and you should plan for it accordingly.

Normally, you should announce at the beginning of your presentation that you will be happy to answer any questions when you're through. Holding questions until the end prevents you from being interrupted and losing your train of thought, or possibly running out of time and not being able to complete your prepared remarks. Also, there is always the possibility that the listener's question will be answered later in the course of your presentation.

The exception to a questions-at-the-end policy occurs when your topic is so complex that a listener's question must be answered immediately if he or she is to follow the rest of the presentation. Another exception is informal (and generally small) meetings, where questions and comments naturally occur throughout the presentation.

Always listen carefully to the question; repeat it, if necessary, for the benefit of the entire audience; and look at the entire audience as you answer—not just at the questioner. Treat each questioner with unfailing courtesy. If the question is antagonistic, be firm but fair and polite.

If you don't know the answer to a question, freely say so and promise to have the answer within a specific period. Then write down the question (and the name of the questioner) to remind yourself to find the answer later. Do not risk embarrassing another member of the audience by referring the question to him or her.

Post-Presentation Activities

After the presentation ends and you're back in your office, evaluate your performance using the guidelines presented in Checklist 14 on page 271 so that you can benefit from the experience. What seemed to work well and what not so well? Analyze each aspect of your performance—from initial research through delivery. Regardless of how well the presentation went, vow to improve your performance next time.

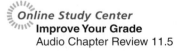
Online Study Center
Improve Your Grade
Audio Chapter Review 11.5

TEST PREPPER 11.5
ANSWERS CAN BE FOUND ON P. 412

True or False?

_____ 1. Behavior modification experts have found that fear of public speaking is almost impossible to overcome.

_____ 2. Unless you're talking about a rather complex topic or speaking to a small group, it is generally better to hold questions until the end of your presentation.

_____ 3. After your presentation, you should evaluate your presentation performance even if you achieved your objective.

_____ 4. Most of your credibility with the audience comes from the information you deliver.

Critical Thinking

5. Which would you find less stressful—giving a presentation to a live audience or giving a presentation in front of a video camera? Why?

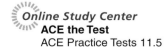
Online Study Center
ACE the Test
ACE Practice Tests 11.5

Online Study Center
Improve Your Grade
Audio Chapter Quiz 11.5
PowerPoint Review 11.5

CHECKLIST 14

The Oral Presentation Process

Planning

✓ Determine your purpose: What response do you want from your audience?

✓ Analyze your audience in terms of demographic factors, level of knowledge, and psychological needs.

✓ Select an appropriate delivery method.

Organizing

✓ Brainstorm. Write down every point you think you might cover in the presentation.

✓ Separate your notes into the opening, body, and ending. Gather additional data if needed.

✓ Write an effective opening that introduces the topic, discusses the points you'll cover, and tells the audience what you hope will happen as a result of your presentation.

✓ In the body, develop the points fully, giving background data, evidence, and examples.

- Organize the points logically.
- To maintain credibility, discuss any major negative points and be prepared to discuss any minor ones.
- Pace the presentation of data to avoid presenting facts and figures too quickly.

✓ Finish on a strong, upbeat note by summarizing your main points, adding a personal appeal, drawing conclusions and making recommendations, discussing what needs to be done next, or using some other logical closing.

✓ Use humor only when appropriate and only if you are effective at telling amusing stories.

✓ Ensure that your visual aids are necessary, simple, easy to read, and of the highest quality.

Practicing

✓ Rehearse your presentation extensively, simulating the actual speaking conditions as much as possible and using your visual aids.

✓ Use simple language and short sentences, with frequent preview, summary, transition, and repetition.

✓ Stand tall and naturally, and speak in a loud, clear, enthusiastic, and friendly voice. Vary the rate and volume of your voice.

✓ Use correct diction and appropriate gestures.

Delivering

✓ Dress appropriately—in comfortable, businesslike, conservative clothing.

✓ Maintain eye contact with the audience, including all corners of the room in your gaze.

✓ To avoid anxiety, practice extensively, develop a positive attitude, and concentrate on the friendly faces in the audience.

✓ Plan your answers to possible questions ahead of time. Listen to each question carefully and address your answer to the entire audience.

THREE Ps
PROBLEM, PROCESS, PRODUCT

Visual Aids for a Business Presentation

Problem

You are Matt Kromer, an administrative assistant at Lewis & Smith. Your company publishes three major external documents—a quarterly customer newsletter, a semiannual catalog, and an annual report. All three are currently prepared by an outside printing company. However, the company recently decided to switch to some form of in-house publishing to produce these publications.

Your superior asked you to research the question of whether your firm should use word processing or desktop publishing software to create these documents. You have completed your research and drafted a formal 20-minute presentation of your findings and recommendations to the firm's administrative committee. You are now ready to develop some visual aids.

Process

1. What types of visual aids will you use?

   Slides (in the form of an electronic presentation)
   a. Two slides at the beginning—to preview the topic and to illustrate our three publications
   b. Two in the middle—to compare the costs and features of the two programs
   c. Two at the end—to give my recommendations and to show what needs to be done next

2. Will you develop an audience handout?

   I could, of course, easily develop a one-page handout showing miniature copies of the six slides—as a summary of my important points and for future reference. Because the purpose of my presentation is to get a decision made today and I have no supplementary information to present, however, a handout isn't necessary.

3. How will you practice your presentation?

   I'll do a dry run in the conference room where I'll be speaking. I'll stand where I'll actually be giving the presentation and use my computer and projector. I'll also set up a cassette recorder at the far end of the conference table to tape my practice presentation to ensure that I can be heard, to check for clarity and voice qualities, and to time my presentation. In addition, I'll practice answering any questions I think the managers might ask.

4. Afterward, how will you determine whether your presentation was a success?

   If the administrative committee votes to accept my recommendation and schedule, I will have achieved my purpose and the presentation will have been successful.

Product

Actual documents can be scanned into the computer, sized to fit, and positioned as desired.

Slide 1

Slide 2

Tables and charts are created easily using presentation software.

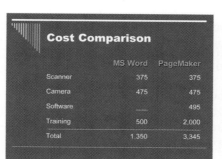

Slide 3

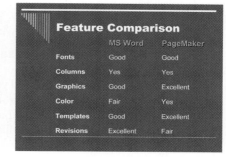

Slide 4

During the presentation, each bulleted point and each schedule line is projected one at a time— for emphasis.

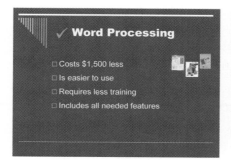

Slide 5

Slide 6

Grammar and Mechanics Notes

This presentation uses a standard template in Microsoft PowerPoint. All font typefaces, sizes, and locations are preselected for you. Do not try to crowd too much information on each slide.

PORTFOLIO PROJECT 6

Making a Business Presentation

Online Study Center
Prepare for Class
Portfolio Stationery

Problem

You are a legal assistant in the corporate law department of a large business firm. The five attorneys for whom you work are interested in learning more about the topic of speech-recognition software and finding out which program is the best. Use the Internet and any printed resources available to locate at least five articles on speech-recognition software. Use these articles to develop a ten-minute videotaped presentation to an audience comprising these five attorneys.

Process

Compose a few paragraphs describing how you solved this problem. In narrative form, provide information such as the following:

1. What is the purpose of your presentation?
2. Describe your audience.
3. What kind of presentation notes will you prepare?
4. How will you organize your presentation?
5. What kind of visual aids will you prepare?
6. What kind of opening and closing will you use?
7. Describe how you decided what to wear for this videotaped presentation.
8. How will you secure a video camera and operator? Will you act as operator for another person's presentation?
9. How many times did you videotape your presentation?

Product

Have your presentation videotaped as many times as you feel necessary to ensure a competent and professional presentation.

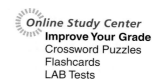

LEARNING OBJECTIVE REVIEW

1 *Determine the purpose of the presentation, analyze the audience, and select a delivery method.*

- Identify your presentation's purpose: reporting, explaining, persuading, or motivating.
- Determine your audience's demographics as well as the audience members' level of knowledge and psychological needs.
- Prepare notes to use as a guide during the presentation.

2 *Analyze and organize your presentation material into an opening, body, and ending.*

- Create an opening that will gain the attention of the audience.
- Present the body of your presentation in a logical way, convincing the audience of your credibility.
- Deal with negative information.
- End your presentation with a summary of your main points.
- Use humor when appropriate.

3 *Plan a team and video presentation.*

- Make individual assignments based on the strengths of team members.
- Achieve a unified and coherent presentation by having all team members use a similar format, organization, and style.

- Rehearse as a team to ensure a smooth presentation.
- Make video presentations effective by:
  - Dressing appropriately for the camera
  - Talking directly to the camera
  - Using color visuals
  - Using video equipment appropriately

4 *Develop effective visual aids.*

- Use transparencies and electronic media to produce inexpensive, professional presentations.
- Avoid the overuse of visual aids.
- Limit the amount of information on individual slides.
- Prepare audience handouts that will help the audience recall information later.

5 *Practice and deliver a presentation.*

- Rehearse presentations until a smooth delivery is achieved.
- Dress appropriately for a business presentation.
- Overcome stage fright by preparing.
- Plan an effective question-and-answer session as part of your presentation.

EXERCISES

1. Work-Team Presentation (▶ 11.3)

Divide into teams of four or five students. Your instructor will assign you to either the pro or the con side of one of the following topics:

- Drug testing should/should not be mandatory for all employees.
- All forms of smoking should/should not be banned completely from the workplace—including outside the building.
- Employers should/should not provide flextime (flexible working hours) for all office employees.
- Employers should/should not provide on-site child-care facilities for the preschool-age children of their employees.
- Employees who deal extensively with the public should/should not be required to wear a company uniform.
- Employers should/should not have the right to hire the most qualified employees without regard to affirmative action guidelines.

Assume that your employee group has been asked to present its views to a management committee that will make the final decision regarding your topic. The presentations will be given as follows:

a. Each side (beginning with the pro side) will have ten minutes to present its views.
b. Each side will then have three minutes to confer.
c. Each side (beginning with the con side) will deliver a two-minute rebuttal—to refute the arguments and answer the issues raised by the other side.
d. Each side (beginning with the pro side) will give a one-minute summary of its argument.
e. The management committee (the rest of the class) will then vote by secret ballot regarding which side (pro or con) presented its case more effectively.

Gather whatever data you think will be helpful to your case, organize it, divide the speaking roles as you deem best, and prepare speaker notes. (*Hint:* It might be helpful to gather information on both the pro and the con sides of the issue in preparation for the rebuttal session, which will be given impromptu.)

2. International Presentation (▶ 11.3)

Working in teams of three or four people, prepare and make a presentation to the class. Each member of the group should take approximately the same amount of time in the presentation. The presentation should be at least 9 minutes but no more than 12 minutes long.

The audience is comprised of wealthy individuals from a foreign country who are being persuaded to invest in a new product to be sold in their country. The product being sold and the country should be selected by the students.

You should plan the presentation—determine the timing and method of delivery (the purpose and audience have already been determined). Provide evidence of data collected regarding the presentation. Visual aids should be used in the presentation. Evidence of rehearsing should be included—videotaped if possible. The final presentation to the class should also be videotaped for critiquing the presentation.

Submit your notes for the presentation to the instructor after making the presentation. In addition to the notes, discuss why particular things were done regarding cultural differences.

3. Video Presentation (▶ 11.3)

Locate two journal articles on some aspect of business communication (the topics in this book's Table of Contents provide clues for searching). The two articles should be about the same topic. Integrate the important information from both articles, and present your findings to the class in a five-minute videotaped presentation.

4. Planning the Visual Element (▶ 11.4)

You are the trainer for an in-house, introductory course in effective advertising techniques that is being offered to franchise owners of your Mexican fast-food chain. As part of the course, you are scheduled to present a 30-minute session on writing effective bad-news letters. You decide to use Chapter 7 in this text as the basis for your presentation. Prepare four to six slides that you might use for your presentation to the 25 participants in the course. Submit full-size color copies of the transparencies to your instructor.

5. Presenting Research Data (▶ 11.4)

Review a report you prepared in Chapter 10. Assume that you have been given ten minutes to present the important information from your written report to a committee of your superiors who will not have an opportunity to read the written report. Prepare your presentation notes, using either full sheets of paper or note cards. Also, develop at least four visual aids using Microsoft PowerPoint or some other software presentation program. Submit your notes along with a handout (four to a page) of your visual aids.

6. Stage Fright (▶ 11.5)

Working in groups of three or four, develop at least five slides for an electronic presentation on how to overcome stage fright. The presentation would be to ten people in a small boardroom. Use the Internet and other outside sources as well as information from the textbook for your slides. Remember to use an appropriate background color and to keep the special effects simple. Submit the slides to your instructor for evaluation.

7. Presenting Research Data (▶ 11.5)

Review a report that you prepared in Chapter 10 and the presentation notes and visual aids that you prepared for the ten-minute oral presentation in Exercise 5 of this chapter. Practice your presentation several times—including at least once in the classroom where you will actually give it. Give your presentation to the class. (Your instructor may ask the audience to evaluate each presentation in terms of the effectiveness of its content, use of visual aids, and delivery.)

Additional exercises are available at the Online Study Center website: **college.hmco.com/pic/oberSASfund**.

Online Study Center   **RESOURCES**

Prepare for Class, Improve Your Grade, and ACE the Test. Student Achievement Series resources include:

ACE Practice Tests	Ask Ober	Audio Chapter Reviews and Quizzes
Chapter Outlines	Communication Objectives	Crossword Puzzles
Flashcards	Glossaries	Handouts
LAB Tests	Portfolio Project Stationery	Sample Reports

To access these learning and study tools, go to **college.hmco.com/pic/oberSASfund**.

12 The Job Search, Resumes, and Job-Application Letters

With the job market more competitive than ever, employers are on the lookout for candidates who stand above the crowd. Résumés that use descriptive words are distinguished from others.

3 Compose a job-application letter.

2 Compose and format a résumé.

1 Perform a self-analysis and research possible employers.

"If the applicant's background has little relation to an employer's business, the résumé should stress communication skills . . . ."

—Paul Orvos, Corporate Manager of Employment, Computer Sciences Corporation

Chapter Outline

- **Planning Your Career**
  - Self-Analysis
  - Research
- **Preparing Your Résumé**
  - Résumé Length
  - Résumé Format
  - Résumé Content
  - Electronic Résumé
- **Writing Job-Application Letters**
  - Address and Salutation
  - Opening
  - Body
  - Closing

Online Study Center
Prepare for Class
Chapter Outline

Selling Yourself: The Basics

Before electronic résumés, Paul Orvos used to receive mailbags full of résumés and job-application letters. Orvos is the corporate manager of employment for Computer Sciences Corporation (CSC), a $5.6 billion company that provides management consulting and information solutions to businesses and government agencies. With nearly 44,000 employees and aggressive plans for expansion, CSC is growing so fast that Orvos and his colleagues can no longer read each of the thousands of résumés they receive every year—many from college graduates starting their careers. Instead, CSC has gone paperless—requesting that applicants submit electronic résumés directly to the company's database, which stores tens of thousands of résumés for screening and consideration when openings arise.

Online Study Center *college.hmco.com/pic/oberSASfund*

on the job

PAUL ORVOS
Corporate Manager of
Employment,
Computer Sciences
Corporation
(Falls Church, Virginia)

KEY TERMS

application letter   *p. 297*
electronic résumé   *p. 292*
reference   *p. 289*
résumé   *p. 283*

Orvos recommends that job-seekers use appropriate descriptive nouns in their electronic résumés. "The keywords vary from employer to employer and from industry to industry," he says. He believes every experience is a learning experience. "If the applicant's background has little relation to an employer's business, the résumé should stress communication skills, mediation skills, organizational skills, or time-management skills, as well as other skills that translate across business lines." ■

PLANNING YOUR CAREER

1 ▸ *Perform a self-analysis and research possible employers.*

Although we've stressed throughout this text the importance of communication skills for success on the job, one of your first professional applications of what you've learned may be in actually securing a job. Think for a moment about some of the important communication skills you've developed thus far—for example, how to analyze your audience, write effective letters, research and analyze data, speak persuasively, and use nonverbal communication to achieve your objectives.

All these communication skills will serve you well when you apply for an internship or begin your job search—from researching career, industry, and company information, to writing effective résumés and application letters, to conducting yourself effectively during the job interview. To refine these skills further, in this chapter you will learn how to plan your career, develop a résumé, and write application letters. Chapter 13 covers interviewing and post-interview activities.

You must put considerable time, effort, and thought into getting a job if you want to have a rewarding and fulfilling work life. The process is the same whether you're applying for an internship, beginning your first job, changing careers, or returning to the workplace after an extended absence; and it begins with a self-analysis.

Self-Analysis

When it is time to decide how to use your college education, you must do some soul-searching to decide exactly how you wish to spend the working hours of your life. Recognize that during the typical week you will probably spend as many of your waking hours at the workplace as at home.

Think about your life, your interests, things you're good at (and those you're not), and the experiences that have given you the most satisfaction. Such introspection will help you make sound career decisions. Take a few moments to answer these questions:

1. Which courses have you enjoyed most and least in school?
2. Recalling projects on which you've worked in class, in organizations you belong to, or at work, which kinds have you been most successful at and enjoyed the most? Which have you disliked?
3. Do you enjoy working most with records (reports, correspondence, and forms), people, ideas, or things?
4. Do you enjoy working more with your mind or with your body?

5. Do you prefer working independently on a project or with a team?
6. How important is it to you to be your own boss?
7. What is important about the geographical location of your job in terms of climate, size of metropolitan area, and location?
8. For what kind of organization would you like to work: large or small? established or new? commercial, government, or nonprofit?
9. How would you like to dress for work?
10. What types of material rewards are important for you in terms of salary, commissions, fringe benefits, job security, and the like?
11. How willing or eager are you to participate in an extensive on-the-job training program?
12. What are your career goals five years after graduating from college?

Your answers to these questions will help you identify the type of career that would offer you the most satisfaction and success. Remember that for any particular college major, many jobs are available. One of them will likely meet your needs and desires.

Research

Many job seekers begin their search for occupational information by interviewing one or more people currently employed in the career or industry that interests them. Such sources can provide current and detailed information and are likely to be more objective than a recruiter.

Occupational Information

One of the most comprehensive sources of up-to-date information about jobs is the *Occupational Outlook Handbook*, published by the U.S. Department of Labor. The handbook is available both in print and online (http://www.bls.gov/oco/). This handbook describes in detail the 250 occupations that account for seven out of every eight jobs in the U.S. economy. Other sources of job information are your college career services office, professional associations, and business periodicals, such as *The Wall Street Journal, Business Week*, and *Forbes*.

Demographic Information

Smart career choices are dictated not only by personal interest but also by demographic characteristics. For example, no matter how much you might enjoy handwriting and no matter how clear and lovely your lettering is, it is unlikely that you would be able to make a good living today as a scribe (a copier of manuscripts) because technology has preempted that occupation.

Some of the demographic trends that the U.S. Department of Labor projects for the ten-year period from 2002 until 2012 are as follows:[1]

▮ The civilian labor force is expected to grow 12 percent.

▮ For all but one of the 50 highest-paying occupations, a college degree or higher is required.

▮ Nine of the ten fastest-growing occupations are health or computer (information technology) occupations.

▮ Education and health services will add more jobs than any other industry sector.

▌ The three occupations with the greatest numerical increase in employment are, in order, registered nurses, postsecondary teachers, and retail salespeople.

▌ The three occupations with the greatest numerical decrease in employment are, in order, farmers and ranchers, sewing machine operators, and word processors and typists.

▌ Office and administrative support occupations are projected to grow much more slowly than average.

Industry and Company Information

No organization exists in a vacuum. Each is affected by the economic, political, and social environment in which it operates. Start with the Standard Industry Classification (SIC) code for the industry in which you're interested. Also helpful are the *U.S. Industrial Outlook*, published by the U.S. Department of Commerce, and *Standard and Poor's Industry Surveys*.

After learning about the industry, pick out a few companies to explore further. Be guided by your interests—large versus small firms, geographical constraints, and so forth. This research will give you a better framework for evaluating the specific companies with whom you will be interviewing.

Go online to visit the homepage of prospective employers. These sources may not contain completely objective information because companies use them to market themselves, but that information can still reveal how a firm likes to see itself and can provide key details about the company.

Networking

In the job-search process, *networking* refers to developing a group of acquaintances who might provide job leads and career guidance. Everyone—from the most recent college graduate to the president of a *Fortune* 500 firm—has a network on which to draw.

Your initial network might include the following:

▌ Friends

▌ Family

▌ Professors

▌ Former employers

▌ Social acquaintances

▌ College alumni

▌ Your dentist, doctor, insurance agent, and the like

Ideally, your network will combine both personal and professional connections. That's one benefit of belonging to professional associations, and college isn't too early to start. Most professional organizations either have student chapters of their associations or provide reduced-rate student memberships in the parent organization.

Don't forget to expand your networking efforts into cyberspace. Sign up for online mailing lists, bulletin boards, and newsgroups targeted to your particular interest. You can gain new contacts from around the world.

CONCEPT CHECK 12.1

What is meant by *networking* as it relates to the job-search process?

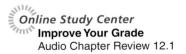

Online Study Center
Improve Your Grade
Audio Chapter Review 12.1

TEST PREPPER 12.1

ANSWERS CAN BE FOUND ON P. 412

True or False?

_____ 1. Identifying the projects and courses you enjoy most in college is part of your self-analysis for determining a career.

_____ 2. A recruiter usually provides more objective information about a company than does a person currently employed in the industry in which you are interested.

_____ 3. The U.S. Department of Labor forecasts that by the year 2012, most new jobs will not require a college degree.

_____ 4. The first step in a job campaign should be preparing a résumé.

_____ 5. The homepage of a company doesn't necessarily contain objective information.

Critical Thinking

6. Which 2 of the 12 questions identified on pages 280–281 are most important to you personally? Why?

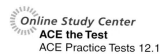

Online Study Center
ACE the Test
ACE Practice Tests 12.1

Online Study Center
Improve Your Grade
Audio Chapter Quiz 12.1
PowerPoint Review 12.1

PREPARING YOUR RÉSUMÉ

2 ▶ *Compose and format a résumé.*

A **résumé** is a brief record of one's personal history and qualifications that is typically prepared by an applicant for a job. The emphasis in the résumé should be on the future rather than on the past: you must show how your education and work experience prepared you for future jobs—specifically, the job for which you are applying.

Right from the start, be realistic about the purpose of your résumé. Few people are hired on the basis of their résumés alone. (On the other hand, many people are *not* hired because of their poorly written or poorly presented résumés.) Instead, applicants are generally hired on the basis of their performance during one or more job interviews.

Thus, the purpose of the résumé is to get you an interview, and the purpose of the interview is to get you a job. Remember, however, that the résumé and accompanying application letter (cover letter) are crucial in advancing you beyond the mass of initial applicants and into the much smaller group of potential candidates invited to an interview. (See Figure 12.1 on page 285 for more information on how workers typically find their jobs.)

résumé A brief record of one's personal history and qualifications, usually prepared by a job applicant.

Résumé Length

Decisions about résumé length become much easier when you consider what happens on the receiving end: recruiters typically spend no more than 35 seconds looking at each résumé during their initial screening to pare down the perhaps hundreds of applications for a position into a manageable number to study in more detail.[2] How much information can the recruiter be expected to read in less than a minute? It won't matter how well qualified you are if no one ever reviews those qualifications.

How much is too much? Surveys of employment and human resources executives consistently show that most managers prefer a one-page résumé for the entry-level positions typically sought by recent college graduates, with a two-page résumé being reserved for unusual circumstances or for higher-level positions.[3] True or not, take note of the old placement-office adage, "The thicker the résumé, the thicker the applicant."

Note, however, that a recent survey of personnel recruiters from Big Five accounting firms found that recruiters ranked candidates with two-page résumés more favorably than candidates with one-page résumés. The researchers recommended that graduating seniors with accounting majors *and outstanding credentials* consider writing two-page résumés when applying for entry-level Big Five accounting positions.[4]

According to one survey of 200 executives from major U.S. firms, the most serious mistake job candidates make is including too much information in their résumés. Their ranking (in percentages of the whole) of the most serious résumé errors is as follows:[5]

Too long	32%
Typographical or grammatical errors	25%
No description of job functions	18%
Unprofessional appearance	15%
Achievements omitted	10%
Total	100%

A one-page résumé is *not* the same as a two-page résumé crammed onto one page by means of small type and narrow margins. Your résumé must be attractive and easy to read. Shorten it by making judicious decisions about what to include and then by using concise language to communicate what is important.

But do not make your résumé *too* short, either. A résumé that does not fill one page may tell the prospective employer that you have little to offer. It has been estimated that one page is ideal for 85 percent of all résumés, and that is the length you should target.[6]

Résumé Format

Although the content of your résumé is obviously more important than its format, remember that first impressions are lasting. As pointed out earlier, those first impressions are formed during the half-minute that is typically devoted to the initial screening of each résumé. For this reason, even before you begin writing your résumé, think about the format because some format decisions will affect the amount of space available to discuss your qualifications and background.

Choose a simple, easy-to-read typeface, and avoid the temptation to use a lot of "special effects" just because they're available on your computer. One or two typefaces in one or two different sizes should be enough. Use a simple format, with lots of white space, short paragraphs, and a logical organization. Through the use of type size and style, indentation, bullets, and the like, make clear which parts are subordinate to main features. One of your word processor's built-in résumé templates is a good place to start.

Format your résumé on standard-size paper (8½ by 11 inches) so that it can be filed easily. Avoid brightly colored papers: they'll get attention but perhaps the wrong kind. Dark colors do not photocopy well, and you want photocopies of your résumé (whether made by you or by the potential employer) to look professional. Choose white or an off-white (cream or ivory) paper of good quality—at least 20-pound bond.

If you are applying for the typical business position, the overall appearance of your résumé should present a professional, conservative appearance—one that adds to your credibility. Don't scare off your readers before they have a chance to meet you.

Finally, your résumé and application letter must be 100 percent free from error—in content, spelling, grammar, and format. Ninety-nine percent accuracy is simply not good enough when seeking a job. One survey of executives in large companies showed that 80 percent of them had decided against interviewing a job seeker simply because of poor grammar, spelling, or punctuation in his or her résumé.[7]

Résumé Content

Fortunately, perhaps, there is no such thing as a standard résumé; each is as individual as the person it represents. There are, however, standard parts of the résumé—those parts recruiters expect and need to see to make valid judgments. For example, one survey of 152 *Fortune* 500 company personnel indicated that 90 percent or more wanted the following information on a résumé:[8]

▎ Name, address, and telephone number

▎ Job objective

▎ College major, degree, name of college, and date of graduation

▎ Jobs held, employing company or companies (but not complete mailing address or the names of your supervisors), dates of employment, and job duties

▎ Special aptitudes and skills

Similarly, items *not* wanted on the résumé (items rated unimportant by more than 90 percent of those surveyed) related primarily to bases for possible discrimination: religion, ethnicity, age, gender, photograph, and marital status. Additionally, most of the employers questioned thought high school activities should not be included on the résumés of college graduates.

The standard and optional parts of the résumé are discussed in the following subsections in the order in which they typically appear on the résumé of a recent (or soon-to-be) college graduate.

Identifying Information

It doesn't do any good to impress a recruiter if he or she cannot locate you easily to schedule an interview. Your name should appear as the very first item on the résumé, arranged attractively at the top. Use whatever form you typically use for signing your name (for example, with or without initials). Give your complete name, avoiding nicknames, and do not use a personal title such as *Mr.* or *Ms.*

It is not necessary to include the heading "Résumé" at the top. The purpose of the document will be evident to the recruiter. Besides, you want your name to be the main heading—where it will stand out in the recruiter's mind. If you will soon be changing your address (for example, from a college address to a home address), include both, along with the relevant dates for each. If you are away from your telephone most of the day and no one is at home to answer it and take a message,

FIGURE 12.1

How Workers Found Their Jobs
The pie chart illustrates how and where job seekers located job postings.

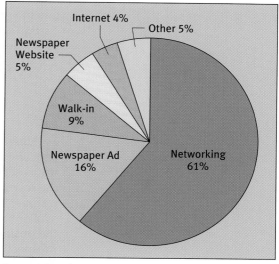

Source: *USA Today*, 2003.

you would be wise to secure a voice-mail service or invest in an answering machine. The important point is to be available for contact.

Job Objective

The job objective is a short summary of your area of expertise and career interest. Most recruiters want the objective stated so that they will know where you might fit into their organization. Don't force the employer to guess about your career goals.

Furthermore, don't waste the prominent spot for your objective at the top of your résumé by giving a weak, overgeneral goal like one of the following:

> NOT: "A position that offers both a challenge and an opportunity for growth."
>
> "Challenging position in a progressive organization."
>
> "A responsible position that lets me use my education and experience and that provides opportunities for increased responsibilities."

The problem with such goals is not that they're unworthy objectives; they are *very* worthwhile. That is why everyone—including the recruiter presumably—wants such positions. The problem is that such vague, high-flown goals don't help the recruiter find a suitable position for *you*. They waste valuable space on your résumé.

For your objective to help you, it must be personalized—both for you and for the position you're seeking. Also, it must be specific enough to be useful to the prospective employer but not so specific as to exclude you from many types of similar positions. The following job objectives meet these criteria:

> BUT: "A paid, one-semester internship in marketing or advertising."
>
> "Position in personal sales in a medium-size manufacturing firm."
>
> "Opportunity to apply my accounting education and Spanish-language skills outside the United States."
>
> "A public relations position requiring well-developed communication, administrative, and computer skills."

Note that, after reading these objectives, you feel you know a little about each candidate, a feeling you did not get from reading the earlier, too-general objectives.

You should be aware that most large corporations now scan the résumés they receive into their computer systems and then search this computerized database by key word. For this reason, make certain that your résumé includes the title of the actual position you desire and other relevant terms. (Later in this chapter, we discuss electronic résumés.)

Education

CONCEPT CHECK 12.2

For your own résumé, will you list education or work experience first? Why?

Unless your work experience has been extensive, at a fairly high level, and directly related to your job objective, your education is probably a stronger job qualification than your work experience and should therefore come first on the résumé. List the title of your degree, the name of your college (and its location if needed), your major and (if applicable) minor, and your expected date of graduation (month and year).

List your grade-point average if it will set you apart from the competition (generally, at least a 3.0 on a 4.0 scale). If you've made the dean's list or have financed any substantial portion of your college expenses through part-time work, savings, or scholarships, mention these facts. Unless your course of study provided distinctive experiences that uniquely qualify you for the job, avoid including a lengthy list of college courses.

Work Experience

Most students have had at least some work experience—for example, part-time or summer jobs. Thus, most students will have some work experience to bring to their future jobs.

Work experience—*any* work experience—is a definite plus. It shows the employer that you've had experience in satisfying a superior, following directions, accomplishing objectives through team effort, and being rewarded for your labors. If your work experience has been directly related to your job objectives, consider putting it ahead of the education section, where it will receive more emphasis.

In relating your work experience, use either a chronological or a functional organizational pattern:

▌ *Chronological:* In a chronological arrangement, organize your experience by date, describing your most recent job first and working backward. This format is most appropriate when you have had a strong continuing work history and much of your work has been related to your job objective (see Model 25 on page 290). Approximately 95 percent of all résumés are chronological, beginning with the most recent information and working backward.[9]

▌ *Functional:* In a functional arrangement, organize your experience by type of function performed (such as *supervision* or *budgeting*) or by type of skill developed (such as *human relations* or *communication skills*). Then, under each, list specific examples (evidence) as illustrated in Model 26 on page 291. Functional résumés are most appropriate when you're changing industries, moving into an entirely different line of work, or reentering the work force after a long period of unemployment because they emphasize your *skills* rather than your employment history and let you show how these skills have broad applicability to other jobs.

CONCEPT CHECK 12.3

For your own personal situation, will you use a chronological or functional arrangement for your work experience? Why?

In actual practice, these patterns are not mutually exclusive; you can use a combination of the two. And regardless of which arrangement you ultimately select, remember that more than 90 percent of the employers in the survey cited earlier indicated that they want to see on a résumé the jobs held, employing company or companies, dates of employment, and job duties.

Remember that the purpose of describing your work history is to show the prospective employer what you've learned *that will benefit the organization.* No matter what your previous work, you've developed certain traits or had certain experiences that can be transferred to the new position. On the basis of your research into the duties of the job you are seeking, highlight those transferable skills.

If you can honestly do so, show in your résumé that you have developed as many of the following characteristics as possible:

▌ Ability to work well with others

▌ Communication skills

▌ Competence and good judgment

▌ Innovation

▌ Reliability and trustworthiness

▌ Enthusiasm

▌ Honest and moral character

▌ Increasing responsibility

Complete sentences are not necessary. Instead, start your descriptions with action verbs, using present tense for current duties and past tense for previous job duties or accomplishments. Concrete words such as those shown below make your work experience come alive:

accomplished	created	negotiated
achieved	delegated	operated
administered	designed	organized
analyzed	developed	oversaw
applied	directed	planned
approved	edited	presented
assisted	established	presided
budgeted	evaluated	purchased
built	hired	recommended
changed	implemented	researched
collected	increased	revised
communicated	interviewed	sold
completed	introduced	supervised
conceived	led	taught
conducted	managed	trained
controlled	marketed	updated
coordinated	motivated	wrote

Avoid weak verbs such as *attempted, endeavored, hoped,* and *tried,* and avoid sexist language such as *manpower* (use *labor* instead) and *chairman* (use *chair* or *chairperson* instead). When possible, ensure credibility by listing specific accomplishments, giving numbers or dollar amounts. Highlight especially those accomplishments that have direct relevance to the desired job. Here are some examples:

NOT: I was responsible for a large sales territory.

BUT: Managed a six-county sales territory; increased sales 13 percent during first full year.

NOT: I worked as a clerk in the cashier's office.

BUT: Balanced the cash register every day; was the only part-time employee entrusted to make nightly cash deposits.

NOT: Worked as a bouncer at a local bar.

BUT: Maintained order at Nick's Side-Door Saloon; learned firsthand the importance of compromise and negotiation in solving problems.

NOT: Worked as a volunteer for Art Reach.

BUT: Personally sold more than $1,000 worth of tickets to annual benefit dance; introduced an "Each one, reach one" membership drive that increased membership every year during my three-year term as membership chairperson.

As illustrated in the last example above, if you have little or no actual work experience, show how your involvement with professional, social, or civic organizations has helped you develop skills that are transferable to the workplace. Volunteer work, for example, can help develop valuable skills in time management, working with groups, handling money, public speaking, accepting responsibility, and the like. In addition, most schools offer internships in which a student receives course credit and close supervision while holding down a temporary job.

Employers recognize your right to put your best foot forward in your résumé—that is, to highlight your strengths and minimize your weaknesses. However, you must never lie about anything and must never take credit for anything you did not do. A simple telephone call can verify any statement on your résumé. A recent study by Automatic Data Processing found that more than 40 percent of applicants misrepresented their education or employment history.[10] Don't risk destroying your credibility before being hired, and don't risk the possibility of being dismissed later for misrepresenting your qualifications.

Other Relevant Information

If you have special skills that might give you an edge over the competition (such as knowledge of a foreign language or webpage-creation competence), list them on your résumé. Although employers assume that college graduates today have competence in word processing, you should specify any other particular software skills you possess.

Include any honors or recognitions that have relevance to the job you're seeking. Memberships in business-related organizations demonstrate your commitment to your profession, and you should list them if space permits. Likewise, involvement in volunteer, civic, and other extracurricular activities gives evidence of a well-rounded individual and reflects your values and commitment.

Avoid including any data that can become grounds for a discrimination suit—such as information about age, gender, race, religion, handicaps, marital status, and the like. Do not include a photograph with your application papers. Some employers like to have the applicant's social security number included as an aid in verifying college or military information. If you have military experience, include it. If your name stereotypes you as a possible noncitizen and citizenship is important for the job you want, you may want to state your citizenship explicitly.

Other optional information includes hobbies and special interests, travel experiences, willingness to travel, and health status. (A health statement may be meaningless, however, because it is unlikely that anyone has ever written "Health—Poor" on a résumé.) Such information may be included if it has direct relevance to your desired job and if you have space for it, but it may be safely omitted if you need space for more important information.

References

A **reference** is a person who has agreed to provide information to a prospective employer regarding a job applicant's fitness for a job. As a general rule, the names and addresses of references need not be included on the résumé itself. Instead, give a general statement that references are available. This policy ensures that you will be contacted before your references are called. The exception to this practice occurs when the person reading the résumé is likely to know your references; in this case, list their names.

CONCEPT CHECK 12.4

Identify two professional associations in the field in which you're interested. Do they offer reduced membership fees to students or have a student chapter?

reference A person who provides information to a prospective employer about an applicant's qualifications.

MODEL 25

Résumé in Chronological Format

Provides specific enough objective to be useful.

Places work experience before education because applicant considers it to be her stronger qualification.

Uses action words like assisted *and* conducted; *uses incomplete sentences to emphasize the action words and to conserve space.*

Provides degree, institution, major, and graduation date.

Provides additional data to enhance her credentials.

Omits actual names and addresses of references.

225 West 70 Street
New York, NY 10023
Phone: 212-555-3821
Email: agomez@nyu.edu

① **Aurelia Gomez**

②

Objective	Entry-level staff accounting position with a public accounting firm	
③ **Experience**	Summer 2005	***Accounting Intern***: Coopers & Lybrand, New York City • Assisted in preparing corporate income tax returns • Attended meetings with clients • Conducted research in corporate tax library and wrote research reports
④	Nov. 2001-Aug. 2003	***Payroll Specialist:*** City of New York • Worked in civil service position in Department of Administration • Used payroll software on both DEC 1034 minicomputer and on personal computers • Audited all overtime billing • Developed two new forms for requesting independent-contractor status that are now used city-wide • Represented 28-person work unit on the department's management-labor committee • Left job to pursue college degree full-time
Education	Jan. 1999-Present	Pursuing a 5-year bachelor of business administration degree (major in accounting) from New York University • Will graduate June 2006 • Attended part-time from 1999 until 2003 while holding down a full-time job • Have financed 100% of all college expenses through savings, work, and student loans • Plan to sit for the CPA exam in May 2007
Personal Data	• Helped start the Minority Business Student Association at NYU and served as program director for two years • Have traveled extensively throughout the Caribbean • Am a member of the Accounting Society • Am willing to relocate	
References	Available upon request	

Grammar and Mechanics Notes

1. The name is formatted in larger type for emphasis.
2. Horizontal and vertical rules separate the heading information from the body of the résumé.
3. The major section headings are parallel in format and in wording.
4. The side headings for the dates are formatted in a column for ease of reading. Note that abbreviations may be used.

MODEL 26

Résumé in Functional Format

Objective introduces three skill areas and résumé expands on each with bulleted examples.

Relates each listed item directly to the desired job.

Provides specific evidence to support each skill.

Weaves work experiences, education, and extracurricular activities into the skill statements.

Avoids repeating the duties given earlier.

① ② ③ ④

RAYMOND J. ARNOLD

OBJECTIVE

Labor relations position in a large multinational firm that requires well-developed labor relations, management, and communication skills

SKILLS

LABOR RELATIONS
- Majored in labor relations; minored in psychology
- Belong to Local 463 of International Office Workers Union
- Was crew chief for the second-shift work team at Wainwright Bank

MANAGEMENT
- Learned time-management skills by working 30 hours per week while attending school full-time
- Was promoted twice in three years at Wainwright Bank
- Practiced discretion while dealing with the financial affairs of others; treated all transactions confidentially

COMMUNICATION
- Developed a webpage for Alpha Kappa Psi business fraternity
- Ran for senior class vice president, making frequent campaign speeches and impromptu remarks
- Took elective classes in report writing and business research
- Am competent in Microsoft Office 2003 and Internet research

EDUCATION

B.S. Degree from Boston University to be awarded June 2006
Major: Labor Relations; Minor: Psychology

EXPERIENCE

Bank teller, Wainwright Bank, Boston, Massachusetts: 2003-Present
Salesperson, JC Penney, Norfolk, Nebraska: Summer 2001

REFERENCES

Available from the Career Information Center
Boston University, Boston, MA 02215; phone: 617-555-2000

15 TURNER HALL, BOSTON UNIVERSITY, BOSTON, MA 02215 • PHONE: 617-555-9833 • E-MAIL: RJARN@BU.EDU

Grammar and Mechanics Notes

1. Putting the headings along the side and indenting the copy opens up the résumé, providing more white space. (This document is based on the "Elegant" résumé template in Microsoft Word.)
2. Bullets are used to highlight the individual skills; asterisks would have worked just as well.
3. All items are in parallel format.
4. More space is left *between* the different sections than *within* sections (to separate each section clearly).

Your references should be professional references rather than character references. The best references are employers, especially your present employer. College professors with whom you have had a close and successful relationship are also valuable references. When asking for references, be prepared to sign a waiver stating that you forgo your right to see the recommendation or that you won't claim that a reference prevented you from getting a job. Many firms are becoming reluctant to authorize their managers to provide reference letters because of the possibility of being sued.

Study the two résumés shown earlier in Models 25 and 26. Note the different formats that can be used to present the data. As stated earlier, there is no standard résumé format. Use these résumés or others to which you have access (available from your college career-center office, from job-hunting books, or on the Internet) to glean ideas for formatting your own.

Note also the different organizational patterns used to convey work experience. The résumé in Model 25 is arranged in a chronological pattern (with the most recent work experience listed first), whereas the one in Model 26 is arranged in a functional pattern that stresses the skills learned rather than the jobs held. Note how job descriptions and skills are all geared to support the applicant's qualifications for the desired job. Note also the concise, concrete language used and the overall tone of quiet confidence.

Electronic Résumé

electronic résumé   A résumé stored in a computer database.

An **electronic résumé** is a résumé that is stored in a computer database designed to help manage and initially screen job applicants. These résumés come from various sources. Applicants may:

- Mail or fax a paper copy of their standard résumé, which is then scanned into a database.
- Fill out (type in) an online résumé form and submit it.
- Send the résumé as an e-mail message.
- Post their résumé on the Internet, using a bulletin board system, a newsgroup, or a personal homepage on the World Wide Web.

Note the directions (see Figure 12.2 on page 293) provided by Eli Lilly and Company for copying and pasting a résumé directly into an online form. Electronic résumés provide benefits to the recruiter and to the job seeker:

- The job seeker's résumé is potentially available to many employers.
- The job seeker may be considered for positions of which he or she wasn't even aware.
- The initial screening is done by a bias-free computer.
- Employers are relieved of the drudgery of having to manually screen and acknowledge résumés.
- A focused search can be conducted quickly.
- Information is always available until the individual résumé is purged from the system (often in six months).

When jobs need to be filled, company personnel feed the computer a list of key words and phrases. The computer then looks through the database and prints out a list of candidates with the most key-word matches. A person picks the process up from there, manually studying each selected résumé to determine whom to invite for an interview. (So far, electronic tools alter only the screening—not the selection—process. People are still hired by people.)

Building appropriate key words into your résumé is essential to successfully using automated résumé systems. Key words are the descriptive terms for which employers search when trying to fill a position. They are the words and phrases employers believe best summarize the characteristics that they are seeking in candidates for particular jobs, such as college degree, foreign language skills, job titles, specific job skills, software packages, or names of competitors for whom applicants may have worked. Examples of key terms include *human resources manager, Hughes Aircraft, Windows XP, teamwork,* and *ISO 9000.*

Electronic résumés must be picked up by a computer search before they are seen by human eyes. Optical character recognition (OCR) software creates an ASCII (text) file of your résumé, and artificial intelligence software then "reads" the text and extracts important information about you. Thus, your first hurdle is to be selected by the computer.

Because you can never be sure how your résumé will be treated, you should prepare two résumés—one for the computer to read and one for people to read. When mailing a résumé, you may wish to include both versions, making note of that fact in your cover letter. Differences between the two versions concern both content and format.

FIGURE 12.2

Directions for Submitting an Electronic Résumé

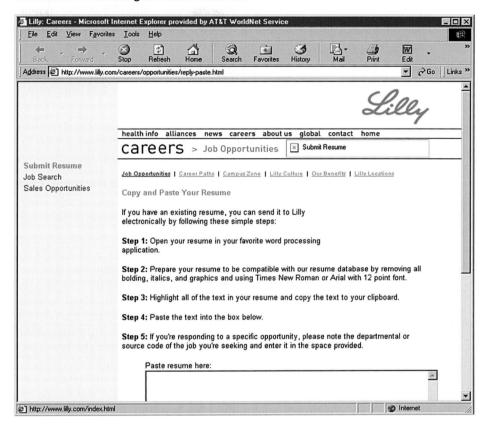

Content Guidelines for Electronic Résumés

Using your standard résumé as a starting point, make these modifications to ensure that your résumé is computer-friendly and to maximize the chance that your résumé will be picked by the computer for further review by humans.

1. Think "nouns" instead of "verbs" (users rarely search for verbs). Use concrete words rather than vague descriptions. Include industry-specific descriptive nouns that characterize your skills accurately and that people in your field use and commonly look for. (Browse other online résumés, newspaper ads, and industry publications to see what terms are currently being used.)

2. Put key words in the proper context, weaving them throughout your résumé. (This strategy is considered a more polished and sophisticated approach than listing them in a block at the beginning of the résumé.)
3. Use different words to describe your skills, and don't overuse important words. In most searches, each word counts once, no matter how many times it is used.
4. Because your résumé will look very bland in plain ASCII text, stripped of all formatting, consider adding a sentence such as this to the end of your posted résumé: "An attractive and fully formatted hard-copy version of this résumé is available upon request."

These guidelines are illustrated in Model 27 on page 295, which is an electronic version of the standard résumé shown in Model 25. The savvy job seeker would probably send both versions to a prospective employer.

Formatting Guidelines for Electronic Résumés

The following guidelines will ensure that your résumé is in a format that can be scanned accurately and transmitted accurately as an e-mail message:

1. Create a traditionally formatted résumé following the guidelines discussed earlier in this chapter, and save it as you normally would (so that you will always have the formatted version available).
2. Save the résumé a second time as a text-only file. Most word processors allow you to save a file as an ASCII or DOS file, which has a file name with a .txt extension. Special formatting, fonts, tabs, margin changes, and the like, are lost in a text file. By saving your scannable résumé as a text file, you can view a printout of your résumé pretty much as it will look after it has been scanned by the prospective employer.
3. Reopen the text file and make any needed changes to your résumé (see the remaining guidelines). Make sure you always save the document as a text file—not as a word processing document.
4. Do not change typefaces, justification, margins, tabs, font sizes, and the like; do not insert underlines, bold, or italic; and do not use horizontal or vertical rules, graphics, boxes, tables, or columns. None of these items will show up in a printout or scan of a text file.
5. Do not divide (hyphenate) words at the end of a line.
6. Change bullets to * (asterisks) or + (plus) signs at the beginning of the line; then insert spaces at the beginning of runover lines to make all lines of a bulleted paragraph begin at the same point.
7. Type your name on the first line by itself, use a standard address format below your name, and type each phone number on its own line. Include an e-mail address, also on its own line.
8. Make the résumé as long as necessary (most electronic résumés average two to three pages).
9. Use white 8½-by-11-inch paper, printed on one side only. Do not use textured paper.
10. Submit a clean, laser-printed original copy; do not fold or staple it.
11. If responding to an employment advertisement via e-mail, use the job title or reference number as the subject of your message. Always send the résumé in the body of the e-mail message. Don't assume that you can attach a word-processed document to an e-mail message; it may or may not be readable.
12. Whenever you update your résumé, remember to update both versions.

CONCEPT CHECK 12.5

Why is it important to make your electronic résumé attractive as well as machine-readable?

MODEL 27

Electronic Résumé

Runs longer than one page (acceptable with electronic résumés).

Includes notice of availability of a fully formatted version.

Begins with name at the top, followed immediately by addresses (both an e-mail address and a home address).

Emphasizes, where possible, nouns as key words.

```
PERSONAL DATA
     * Helped start the Minority Business Student
       Association at New York University and served as
       program director for two years
     * Have traveled extensively throughout the Caribbean
     * Am a member of the Accounting Society
     * Am willing to relocate

REFERENCES
     Available upon request

NOTE
     An attractive and fully formatted hard-copy version of
     this resume is available upon request.
```

```
AURELIA GOMEZ

225 West 70 Street
New York, NY 10023
Phone: 212-555-3821
E-mail: agomez@nyu.edu

OBJECTIVE
     Entry-level staff accounting position with a public
     accounting firm

EXPERIENCE
     Summer 2005
     Accounting Intern: Coopers & Lybrand, NYC
     * Assisted in preparing corporate tax returns
     * Attended meetings with clients
     * Conducted research in corporate tax library and
       wrote research reports

     Nov. 2001-Aug. 2003
     Payroll Specialist: City of New York
     * Full-time civil service position in the Department
       of Administration
     * Proficiency in payroll and other accounting software
       on DEC 1034 minicomputer and on personal computers
     * Representative for a 28-person work unit on the
       department's management-labor committee
     * Reason for leaving job: To pursue college degree
       full-time

EDUCATION
     Jan. 1999-Present
     Pursuing a 5-year bachelor of business administration
     degree (major in accounting) from NYU
     * Will graduate June 2006
     * Attended part-time from 1999 until 2003 while
       holding down a full-time job
     * Have financed 100% of all college expenses through
       savings, work, and student loans
     * Plan to sit for the CPA exam in May 2007
```

Grammar and Mechanics Notes

Only ASCII characters are used; all text is one size with no special formatting; no rules, graphics, columns, tables, and the like are used. Vertical line spaces (Enter key) and horizontal spacing (space bar) show relationship of parts. Lists are formatted with asterisks instead of bullets.

As illustrated in Figure 12.3, when formatted in plain ASCII text, an electronic résumé can be sent as an e-mail message with the assurance that it will arrive in readable format.

One type of electronic résumé that *is* designed to look attractive is the online résumé, which can be viewed on your homepage on the Web. Many providers, such as Yahoo! Geocities, will host your homepage for free or little cost. (To locate other websites with free web-space hosting, log on to http://freewebspace.net). Online résumés offer these advantages:

▌ Potential employers can access your résumé at any time. Assume, for example, you're talking to a potential employer who expresses an interest in your qualifications. You can simply refer him or her to your web address for instant reviewing.

▌ You can include hypertext links to work samples you've completed. For example, instead of merely saying that you wrote extensive reports in your job or that you have top-level communication skills, you can prove it by providing links to actual documents you have created.

▌ You can highlight your creativity because the online language (HTML or XML) provides enough formatting options to enable you to produce a very attractive page (your online résumé also provides evidence of your technical expertise).

Note the attractive appearance and numerous links in the online résumé shown in Model 28 on pages 298 and 299. Pay particular attention to the marginal notations and mechanics notes at the bottom.

Because your résumé is about you, it is perhaps the most personal business document you'll ever write. Use everything you know about successful communication techniques to ensure that you tell your story in the most effective manner possible. After you're satisfied with the content and arrangement of your résumé, proofread the document carefully and have several others proofread it as well. Then have your résumé printed on high-quality white or off-white 8½-by-11-inch paper, and turn your attention to your cover letters.

Checklist 15 on page 304 summarizes the guidelines for developing a résumé.

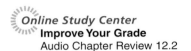
Online Study Center
Improve Your Grade
Audio Chapter Review 12.2

FIGURE 12.3

An Electronic Résumé in an E-mail Message

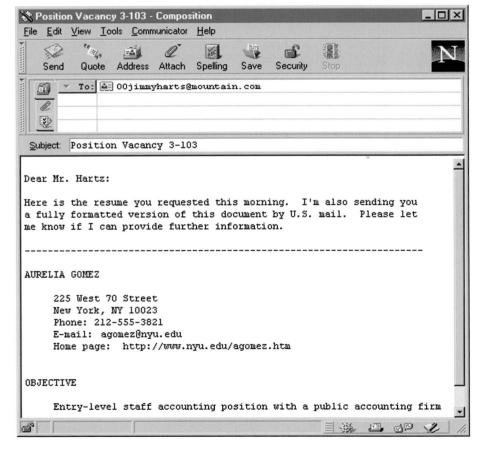

TEST PREPPER 12.2

ANSWERS CAN BE FOUND ON P. 412

True or False?

_____ 1. The purpose of a well-written résumé is to get you a good job.

_____ 2. There is no such thing as a standard format for résumés.

_____ 3. Most traditional college graduates should use a chronological arrangement for their work experience.

_____ 4. Electronic résumés for most graduates should be no longer than one page.

_____ 5. You should send your electronic résumé in the body of an e-mail message instead of as a separate attachment.

Vocabulary

Define the following terms in your own words.

6. Electronic résumé

7. Reference

8. Résumé

Critical Thinking

9. Think about a specific volunteer job you have held. Identify that job and list the skills you learned that can transfer to a professional career.

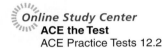

Online Study Center
ACE the Test
ACE Practice Tests 12.2

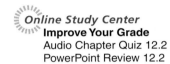

Online Study Center
Improve Your Grade
Audio Chapter Quiz 12.2
PowerPoint Review 12.2

WRITING JOB-APPLICATION LETTERS

3 ▶ *Compose a job-application letter.*

A résumé itself is all that is generally needed to secure an interview with an on-campus recruiter. However, you will likely not want to limit your job search to those employers who interview on campus. Campus recruiters typically represent large organizations or regional employers. Thus, if you want to work in a smaller organization or in a distant location, you will need to contact those organizations by writing application letters.

An **application letter** communicates to the prospective employer your interest in and qualifications for a position within the organization. The letter is also called a *cover letter* because it introduces (or "covers") the major points in your résumé, which you should include with the application letter. A *solicited application letter* is written in response to an advertised vacancy, whereas an *unsolicited application letter* (also called a *prospecting letter*) is written to an organization that has not advertised a vacancy. Most job applicants use the same résumé when applying for numerous positions and then use their application letters to personalize their qualifications for the specific job for which they are applying.

Because the application letter is the first thing the employer will read about you, it is of crucial importance. Make sure the letter is formatted appropriately, looks attractive, and is free from typographical, spelling, and grammatical errors. Don't forget to sign the letter and enclose a copy of your résumé (or perhaps both versions—formatted and plain-text—of your résumé).

Your cover letter is a sales letter—you're selling your qualifications to the prospective employer. You should use the same persuasive techniques you learned earlier: provide specific evidence, stress reader benefits, avoid exaggeration, and show confidence in the quality of your product.

application letter A letter that communicates to a prospective employer an applicant's interest in and qualifications for a position.

MODEL 28

Online Résumé

Provides appropriate identification information in an attractive heading.

Allows the reader to view, download, and print the résumé in different formats.

Provides links to make it easy to navigate the page.

Links to a copy of her transcript for viewing courses taken and grades.

Contains underlined links throughout the page that bring up copies of the actual documents for viewing.

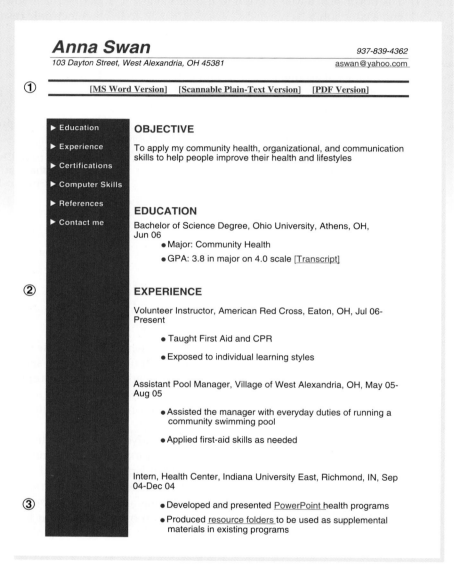

① **Anna Swan**   937-839-4362
103 Dayton Street, West Alexandria, OH 45381   aswan@yahoo.com

[MS Word Version]   [Scannable Plain-Text Version]   [PDF Version]

► Education
► Experience
► Certifications
► Computer Skills
► References
► Contact me

OBJECTIVE

To apply my community health, organizational, and communication skills to help people improve their health and lifestyles

EDUCATION

Bachelor of Science Degree, Ohio University, Athens, OH, Jun 06
- Major: Community Health
- GPA: 3.8 in major on 4.0 scale [Transcript]

② **EXPERIENCE**

Volunteer Instructor, American Red Cross, Eaton, OH, Jul 06-Present
- Taught First Aid and CPR
- Exposed to individual learning styles

Assistant Pool Manager, Village of West Alexandria, OH, May 05-Aug 05
- Assisted the manager with everyday duties of running a community swimming pool
- Applied first-aid skills as needed

Intern, Health Center, Indiana University East, Richmond, IN, Sep 04-Dec 04
③
- Developed and presented PowerPoint health programs
- Produced resource folders to be used as supplemental materials in existing programs

Grammar and Mechanics Notes

1. Use color—but in moderation; ensure that your webpage projects a professional image.
2. Avoid the temptation to include a photograph of yourself on your webpage.
3. Do not underline any part of your webpage. Save underlining to indicate links.

Anna Swan • 937-839-4362 • aswan@yahoo.com

④

- Assisted in conducting corporate health appraisals

Nursing Assistant, Hudson Center, Ohio University, Athens, OH, Jan 03-Aug 04
- Assisted physicians and nurses in performing medical exams and charting
- Wrote Procedures Handbook for the staff

Provides links to a sample of her report-writing skills.

CERTIFICATIONS
- First Aid and CPR Instructor
- Professional Rescuer Instructor

Provides links to actual copies of the certification documents.

COMPUTER SKILLS
- Microsoft Word, PowerPoint, and Excel (Ver. 2003)
- Microsoft Publisher
- Print Shop
- All aspects of Internet research

⑤

REFERENCES

Available on request

CONTACT ME

Please contact me by e-mail at aswan@yahoo.com or by phone at 937-839-4362.

Created on April 3, 2006
Last updated on April 21, 2006

Shows the currency of the information.

Return to Top • Education • Experience

Repeats the navigation links.

Certifications • Computer Skills • References

Grammar and Mechanics Notes

4. Use Google or some other search engine to search the Web for "resumes + online." You'll find a wide variety of actual online résumés to review. When you see one you like, download it and adjust it to fit your own needs.
5. Leave plenty of white space and make your section headings stand out.

An application letter should be no longer than one page. Let's examine each part of a typical letter. Model 29 on page 301 shows a solicited application letter, written to accompany the résumé presented in Model 25 on page 290. (An unsolicited application letter appears in the 3Ps model on page 307.)

Address and Salutation

Your letter should be addressed to an individual rather than to an organization or department. Remember, the more hands your letter must go through before it reaches the right person, the more chances exist for something to go wrong. Ideally, your letter should be addressed to the person who will actually interview you and who will likely be your supervisor if you get the job.

If you do not know enough about the prospective employer to know the name of the appropriate person (the decision maker), you have probably not gathered enough data. If necessary, call the organization to make sure you have the right name—including the correct spelling—and position title. In your salutation, use a courtesy title (such as *Mr.* or *Ms.*) along with the person's last name.

Some job-vacancy ads are blind ads; they do not identify the hiring company by name and provide only a box number address, often in care of the newspaper or magazine that contains the ad. In such a situation, you (and all others responding to that ad) have no choice but to address your letter to the newspaper and to use a generic salutation, such as "Dear Human Resources Manager." Insert a subject line to identify immediately the purpose of this important message.

Opening

The opening paragraph of a solicited application letter is fairly straightforward. Because the organization has advertised an opening, it is eager to receive quality applications, so use a direct organization: state (or imply) the reason for your letter, identify the particular position for which you're applying, and indicate how you learned about the opening.

Gear your opening to the job and to the specific organization. For positions that are widely perceived to be somewhat conservative (such as in finance, accounting, and banking), use a restrained opening. For more creative work (such as sales, advertising, and public relations), you might start out on a more imaginative note. Here are two examples:

> *Conservative:*
>
> Mr. Adam Storkel, manager of your Fleet Street branch, has suggested that I submit my qualifications for the position of assistant loan officer that was advertised in last week's *Indianapolis Business*.

> *Creative:*
>
> If quality is Job 1 at Ford, then Job 2 must surely be communicating that message effectively to the public. My degree in journalism and work experience at the Kintzell Agency will enable me to help you achieve that objective. The enclosed résumé further describes my qualifications for the position of advertising copywriter posted in the June issue of *Automotive Age*.

> **CONCEPT CHECK 12.6**
>
> Assume that you are applying for a full-time position as an admissions representative at your institution upon graduation. Compose an effective opening sentence for your unsolicited application letter.

For unsolicited application letters, you must first get the reader's attention. You can gain that attention most easily by talking about the company rather than about yourself. One effective strategy is to show that you know something about the organization—its recent projects, awards, changes in personnel, and the like—and then show how you can contribute to the corporate effort.

MODEL 29

Job-Application Letter

This model is an example of a solicited application letter; it accompanies the résumé in Model 25 on page 290.

Begins by identifying the job position and the source of advertising.

Emphasizes a qualification that might distinguish her from other applicants.

Relates her work experience to the specific needs of the employer.

Provides a telephone number (may be given either in the body of the letter or in the last line of the address block).

March 13, 20—

Mr. David Norman, Partner
Ross, Russell & Weston
452 Fifth Avenue
New York, NY 10018

① Dear Mr. Norman:

Subject: EDP Specialist Position (Reference No. 103-G)

② My varied work experience in accounting and payroll services, coupled with my accounting degree, has prepared me for the position of EDP specialist that you advertised in the March 9 *New York Times*.

③ In addition to taking required courses in accounting and management information systems as part of my accounting major at New York University, I also took an elective course in EDP auditing and control. The training I received in this course in applications, software, systems, and service-center records would enable me to immediately become a productive member of your EDP consulting staff.

My college training has been supplemented by an internship in a large accounting firm. In addition, my two and one-half years of experience as a payroll specialist for the city of New York have given me firsthand knowledge of the operation and needs of nonprofit agencies. This experience should help me to contribute to your large consulting practice with governmental agencies.

④ After you have reviewed my enclosed résumé, I would appreciate having the opportunity to discuss with you why I believe I have the right qualifications and personality to serve you and your clients. I can be reached by phone after 3 p.m. daily.

Sincerely,

Aurelia Gomez

⑤ Aurelia Gomez
225 West 70 Street
New York, NY 10023
Phone: 212-555-3821
Email: agomez@nyu.edu

Enclosure

Grammar and Mechanics Notes

1. This letter is formatted in modified-block style with standard punctuation (colon after the salutation and comma after the complimentary closing).
2. *New York Times:* Italicize the names of newspapers.
3. *accounting and management information systems:* Do not capitalize the names of college courses unless they include a proper noun.
4. *résumé:* This word may also properly be written without the accent marks: *resume.*
5. Putting the writer's name and address together at the bottom of the letter makes it convenient for the reader to respond.

Now that Russell Industries has expanded operations to Central America, can you use a marketing graduate who speaks fluent Spanish and who knows the culture of the region?

Your opening should be short, interesting, and reader-oriented. Avoid tired openings such as "This is to apply for . . ." or "Please consider this letter my application for . . . ." Maintain an air of formality by using a personal title and last name when addressing the reader.

Body

In a paragraph or two, highlight your strongest qualifications and show how they can benefit the employer. Show—don't tell; that is, provide specific, credible evidence to support your statements, using wording different from that used in the résumé. Tell an anecdote about yourself ("For example, recently I . . ."). Your discussion should reflect modest confidence rather than a hard-sell approach. Avoid starting too many sentences with *I*.

NOT: I am an effective supervisor.

BUT: Supervising a staff of five counter clerks taught me . . . .

NOT: I am an accurate person.

BUT: In my two years of experience as a student secretary, none of the letters, memorandums, and reports I typed were ever returned with a typographical error marked.

NOT: I took a course in business communication.

BUT: The communication strategies I learned in my business communication course will enable me to solve customer problems as a customer service representative at Allegheny Industries.

Refer the reader to the enclosed résumé. Subordinate the reference to the résumé, and emphasize instead what the résumé contains.

NOT: I am enclosing a copy of my résumé for your review.

BUT: As detailed in the enclosed résumé, my extensive work experience in records management has prepared me to help you "take charge of this paperwork jungle," as headlined in your classified ad.

Closing

You are not likely to get what you do not ask for, so close by asking for a personal interview. Indicate flexibility regarding scheduling and location. Provide your phone number and e-mail address, either in the last paragraph or immediately below your name and address in the closing lines.

After you have reviewed my qualifications, I would appreciate your letting me know when we can meet to discuss further my employment with Connecticut Power and Light. I will be in the Hartford area from December 16 through January 4 and could come to your office at any time that is convenient for you.

or

I will call your office next week to see if we can arrange a meeting at your convenience to discuss my qualifications for working as a paralegal with your firm.

CONCEPT CHECK 12.7

Rewrite the following sentences of an application letter to make them more effective.

a. I am a hard worker.
b. I am good at sales.
c. I can be trusted.

Use a standard complimentary closing (such as "Sincerely"), leave enough space to sign the letter, and then type your name, address, phone number, and e-mail address. Even though you may be sending out many application letters at the same time, take care with each individual letter. You never know which one will be the letter that actually gets you an interview. Sign your name neatly in blue or black ink, fold each letter and accompanying résumé neatly, and mail them.

Checklist 16 on page 305 summarizes the guidelines for writing an application letter.

Online Study Center
Improve Your Grade
Audio Chapter Review 12.3
Handouts

TEST PREPPER 12.3

ANSWERS CAN BE FOUND ON P. 412

True or False?

_____ 1. All advertised job vacancies require the applicant to write a job-application letter.

_____ 2. Most applicants will submit a unique application letter for every job for which they apply.

_____ 3. "Please consider this letter my application for . . ." would be an appropriate opening for an unsolicited letter of application.

_____ 4. In the body of your application letter, you should highlight each of your qualifications for the job.

_____ 5. You should not directly ask for a personal interview in your first application letter.

Vocabulary

Define the following term in your own words.
6. Application letter

Critical Thinking

7. Do you think it is savvy to include an attention-grabbing gimmick in your application letter, such as sending a worn, once-white running shoe with the note "Now that I have one foot in the door, I hope you'll let me get the other one in" or writing the application letter beginning at the bottom of the page and working upward (to indicate a willingness to start at the bottom and work one's way up)?

Online Study Center
ACE the Test
ACE Practice Tests 12.3

Online Study Center
Improve Your Grade
Audio Chapter Quiz 12.3
PowerPoint Review 12.3

CHECKLIST 15

Résumés

Length and Format

✓ Use a one-page résumé when applying for most entry-level positions.

✓ Use a simple format, with lots of white space and short blocks of text. Use type size, indenting, bullets, boldface, and the like, to show which parts are subordinate to other parts.

✓ Print your résumé on standard-size (8½-by-11-inch), good-quality, white or off-white paper.

✓ Make sure the finished document looks professional and attractive and that it is 100 percent error-free.

Content

✓ Type your complete name without a personal title at the top of the document (omit the word *résumé*), followed by an address, a daytime phone number, and an e-mail address.

✓ Include a short job objective that is specific enough to be useful to the employer but not so specific as to preclude consideration for similar jobs.

✓ Decide whether your education or work experience is your stronger qualification, and list it first. For education, list the title of your degree, the name of your college and its location, your major and minor, and your expected date of graduation (month and year). List your grade-point average if it is impressive and list any academic honors. Avoid listing college courses that are part of the normal preparation for your desired position.

✓ For work experience, determine whether to use a chronological (most recent job first) or a functional (list of competencies and skills developed) organizational pattern. For either, stress those duties or skills that are transferable to the new position. Use short phrases and action verbs, and provide specific evidence of the results you achieved.

✓ Include any additional information that will help to distinguish you from the competition. Avoid including personal information such as age, gender, ethnicity, religion, disabilities, or marital status.

✓ Provide a statement that references are available on request.

✓ Throughout, highlight your strengths and minimize any weaknesses, but always tell the truth.

Electronic Résumés

✓ In general, describe your qualifications and experiences in terms of nouns rather than verbs. Weave these key words throughout your résumé.

✓ Save the electronic résumé in plain ASCII text. Do not include any special formatting.

✓ Include a note at the end of your electronic résumé that a fully formatted version is available upon request.

✓ Print your résumé on plain 8½-by-11-inch, smooth white paper (print on one side only) and mail it unfolded and unstapled.

✓ For online résumés, choose an open, attractive design and create links to your actual work samples.

CHECKLIST 16

Job-Application Letters

✓ Use your job-application letter to show how the qualifications listed in your résumé have prepared you for the specific job for which you're applying.

✓ If possible, address your letter to the individual in the organization who will interview you if you're successful.

✓ When applying for an advertised opening, begin by stating (or implying) the reason for the letter, identify the position for which you're applying, and tell how you learned about the opening.

✓ When writing an unsolicited application letter, first gain the reader's attention by showing that you are familiar with the company and can make a unique contribution to its efforts.

✓ In one or two paragraphs, highlight your strongest qualifications and relate them directly to the needs of the specific position for which you're applying. Refer the reader to the enclosed résumé.

✓ Treat your letter as a persuasive sales letter: provide specific evidence, stress reader benefits, avoid exaggeration, and show confidence in the quality of your product.

✓ Close by tactfully asking for an interview.

✓ Maintain an air of formality throughout the letter.

✓ Make sure the finished document presents a professional, attractive, and conservative appearance and that it is 100 percent error-free.

THREE PS
PROBLEM, PROCESS, PRODUCT

An Application Letter

Problem

You are Ray Arnold, a senior and labor relations major at Boston University. You have analyzed your interests, strengths and weaknesses, and preferred lifestyle and have decided you would like to work in some area of labor relations for a large multinational firm in southern California. Because you attend a school in the East, you decide not to limit your job search to on-campus interviewing.

In your research you learned that Precision Systems, Inc. (PSI) has recently been awarded a $23 million contract by the U.S. Department of State to develop a high-level computerized message system to provide fast and secure communications among U.S. government installations throughout Europe. PSI, which is headquartered in Los Angeles, will build a new automated factory in Ciudad Juárez, Mexico, to assemble the electronic components for the new system.

THREE Ps (CONTINUED)

You decide to write to PSI to see whether it might have an opening for someone with your qualifications. You will, of course, include a copy of your résumé with your letter. (See Model 26 on page 291 for the résumé.) Send your letter to Ms. Phyllis Morrison, Assistant Director of Human Resources, Precision Systems, Inc., P.O. Box 18734, Los Angeles, CA 90018.

Process

1. Will this letter be a solicited or an unsolicited (prospecting) letter?

    Unsolicited—I don't know whether PSI has an opening.

2. Write an opening paragraph for your letter that gets attention and that relates your skills to PSI's needs. Make sure the purpose of your letter is made clear in your opening paragraph.

    PSI's recently accepted proposal to the State Department estimated that you would be adding as many as 3,000 new staff members for the Ciudad Juárez project. With this dramatic increase in personnel, do you have an opening in your human resources department for a college graduate with a major in labor relations and a minor in psychology?

3. Compare your education with PSI's likely requirements. What will help you stand out from the competition?

    *   It's somewhat unusual for a labor relations major to have a psychology minor.
    *   My course work in my major and minor were pretty standard, so there's no need to list individual courses.

4. Compare your work experiences with PSI's likely requirements. What qualifications from your résumé should you highlight in your letter?

    *   The interpersonal and human relations skills developed as a teller will be an important asset in labor management.
    *   Written and oral communications skills developed through work and extracurricular activities will enable me to communicate effectively with a widely dispersed work force.

5. What other qualifications should you mention?

    My degree in labor relations, combined with my union membership, will help me look at each issue from the perspective of both management and labor.

6. Write the sentence in which you request the interview.

    I would welcome the opportunity to come to Los Angeles to discuss with you the role I might play in helping PSI manage its human resources in an efficient and humane manner.

Product

15 Turner Hall
Boston University
Boston, MA 02215
February 7, 20—

Ms. Phyllis Morrison
Assistant Human Resources Director
Precision Systems, Inc.
P.O. Box 18734
Los Angeles, CA 90018

Dear Ms. Morrison

PSI's recent proposal to the State Department estimated that you would be adding up to 3,000 new positions for the Ciudad Juárez project. With this increase in personnel, will you have an opening in your human resources department for a recent college graduate with a major in labor relations and a minor in psychology?

My combination of course work in business and liberal arts will enable me to approach each issue from both a management and a behavioral point of view. Further, my degree in labor relations along with my experience as a union member will help me consider each issue from the perspective of both management and labor.

During my term as webmaster for a student association, the Scholastic Internet Association recognized our site for its "original, balanced, and refreshingly candid writing style and format." On the job, dealing successfully with customers' overdrawn accounts, bank computer errors, and delayed-deposit recording has taught me the value of active listening and has provided me experience in explaining and justifying the company's position. As detailed on the enclosed résumé, these communication and human relations skills will help me to interact and communicate effectively with PSI employees at all levels and at widely dispersed locations.

I would welcome the opportunity to come to Los Angeles at your convenience to discuss with you the role I might play in helping PSI manage its human resources in an efficient and humane manner. I will call your office on February 21, or you may call me at any time after 2 p.m. daily at 617-555-9833.

Sincerely

Raymond J. Arnold

Raymond J. Arnold

Enclosure

PORTFOLIO PROJECT 7

Online Study Center
Prepare for Class
Portfolio Stationery

Résumé and Cover Letter

Problem

You are finally in your last term of college before graduating and are searching for the perfect full-time post-college job. Using the information gleaned from this chapter and the end-of-chapter exercises, from your campus career center, and from other sources:

1. Prepare a factual résumé in traditional format.

2. Go online to locate an advertised position in which you might be interested. Online suggestions include the following websites:

   America's Job Bank (**http://www.ajb.dni.us**)

   CareerBuilder (**http://www.careerbuilder.com**)

   Monster.com (**http://www.monster.com**)

   Print out the job description for which (for this assignment) you're going to apply.

3. Compose and format an application letter for this position.

Process

Compose a few paragraphs describing how you solved this problem. In narrative form, provide information such as the following:

1. What factors entered into your description of your job objective?

2. How did you decide whether to place your education or job experience first?

3. How did you determine which optional information to include (and which to exclude)?

4. Did you use a chronological or a functional arrangement for your job experience? Why?

5. How did you decide which of your qualifications to stress in your application letter?

Product

Compose your résumé and application letter.

LEARNING OBJECTIVE REVIEW

 Perform a self-analysis and research possible employers.

- Think about your life, interests, strengths, and experiences to help determine what type of career might be most satisfying to you.

- Search for information on different careers through electronic sources, a college career service office, professional associations, and periodicals.

- Evaluate the projections on job trends by the U.S. Department of Labor to determine those with the most opportunities.

- Using SIC codes, learn about different companies within industries and visit their homepages.

- Network with friends, family, colleagues, and others to learn about job opportunities.

 Compose and format a résumé.

- A résumé is a brief record of your personal history and qualifications designed to get you an interview.

- The best résumés are one page long and contain all relevant information.

- Choose a simple, clear résumé format that provides all necessary information and is 100 percent error-free.

- Include information that will help the employer get in touch with you as well as your job objective; educational background; jobs held; and any special abilities, skills, or honors.

- Include a statement that references will be provided upon request.

- An electronic résumé is used by some companies to screen job applicants.

- Remember to include key words that signify specific job skills and experiences.

3 *Compose a job-application letter.*

- An application letter accompanies a résumé and communicates briefly your qualifications.
    - In the opening, state how you heard about the job.
    - In the body, highlight your strongest qualifications and show how they can benefit the employer.
    - In the closing, ask for an opportunity to discuss your qualifications with the employer.

EXERCISES

1. Self-Assessment (12.1)

As a first step in your job campaign, answer the 12 questions given on pages 280–281. Type each question and then your answer. Although the content of the answer is certainly more important than mechanics and format, use this exercise as a measure of your basic writing skills as well. Take care to use complete sentences, correct grammar, and a competent writing style.

2. Who Am I? (12.2)

Assume that you are beginning your last term of college before graduating. Using factual data from your own education, work experience, and so on (include any data that you expect to be true at the time of your graduation), answer the following questions (you will use this information to prepare a traditional résumé for your job portfolio):

a. How will you word your name at the top of your résumé—for example, with or without any initials? (Remember *not* to include a personal title before your name.)

b. What is your mailing address? If you will be changing addresses during the job search, include both addresses, along with the effective dates of each.

c. What is your daytime phone number? When can you typically be reached at this number? What is your e-mail address?

d. For what type of position are you searching? Prepare an effective one-sentence job objective—one that is neither too general nor too specific.

e. What is the title of your degree? The name of your college? The location of the college? Your major and minor? Your expected date of graduation (month and year)?

f. What is your grade-point average overall and in your major? Is either one high enough to be considered a personal selling point?

g. Have you received any academic honors throughout your collegiate years, such as scholarships or inclusion on the dean's list? If so, list them.

h. Did you take any elective courses (courses that most applicants for this position probably did *not*

take) that might be especially helpful in this position? If so, list them.

i. List in reverse chronological order (most recent job first) the following information for each job you've held during your college years: job title, organizational name, location (city and state), inclusive dates of employment (month and year), and full- or part-time status. Describe your specific duties in each position, stressing those duties that helped prepare you for your job objective. Use short phrases, possibly beginning each duty or responsibility with one of the action verbs on page 288 and showing, where possible, specific evidence of the results you achieved.

j. Will your education or your work experience be more likely to impress the recruiter?

k. What additional information, such as special skills, professional affiliations, offices held, or willingness to relocate or travel, might you include?

l. Are your reference letters on file at your school's placement office? If so, provide the office name, address, and phone number. (If not, include a statement such as "References available on request" at the bottom of your résumé.)

3. Your Electronic Résumé (12.2)

After you have prepared your résumé in traditional format for your job portfolio at the end of this chapter, reformat your résumé for accurate scanning into a computer.

4. Application Letter Project (12.3)

This project consists of writing both a solicited and an unsolicited application letter. Prepare each letter in an appropriate format and on appropriate paper. Include a copy of your résumé with each letter. Submit each letter to your instructor folded and inserted into a correctly addressed envelope (don't forget to sign your letter).

a. Identify a large prospective employer—one that has *not* advertised for an opening in your field. Write an unsolicited application letter.

b. For various reasons, you might not secure a position directly related to your college major. In such a situation, it is especially important to be able to show how your qualifications (no matter what they are) match the needs of the employer. Using your own background, apply for the following position, which was advertised in last Sunday's *New York Tribune:*

Manager-Trainee Position. Philip Morris is looking for recent college graduates to enter

its management-trainee program in preparation for an exciting career in one of the diversified companies that make up Philip Morris. Excellent beginning salary and benefits, good working conditions, and a company that cares about you. (Reply to Box 385-G in care of this newspaper.)

Additional exercises are available at the Online Study Center website: **college.hmco.com/pic/oberSASfund**.

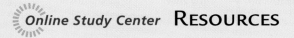 **RESOURCES**

Prepare for Class, Improve Your Grade, and ACE the Test. Student Achievement Series resources include:

ACE Practice Tests	Ask Ober	Audio Chapter Reviews and Quizzes
Chapter Outlines	Communication Objectives	Crossword Puzzles
Flashcards	Glossaries	Handouts
LAB Tests	Portfolio Project Stationery	Sample Reports

To access these learning and study tools, go to **college.hmco.com/pic/oberSASfund**.

13 Employment Interviewing and Follow-Up

Monster.com is one of the largest online recruiting job sites in the world. Its founder, Jeff Taylor, has been in the business long enough to know that your résumé may get you a phone call, but it is the interview that really wins or loses the job. His website offers simple advice on preparing questions, researching the company and the position, and following up after an interview.

1 ▸ *Prepare for a job interview.*

2 ▸ *Conduct yourself appropriately during a job interview.*

3 ▸ *Complete the communication tasks needed after the interview.*

Chapter Outline

Online Study Center
Prepare for Class
Chapter Outline

4 ▶ *Practice business etiquette in the workplace.*

A Monster of an Interview

Jeff Taylor may be chief monster, but he still takes time to interview applicants for certain jobs. Taylor launched The Monster Board in 1994 as the Web's first online recruiting site. Today the company, renamed Monster.com, has more than 1,400 employees in 19 countries and a database of more than 30 million résumés. The site (at http://www.monster.com) features hundreds of thousands of job postings plus expert advice on career management.

During an employment interview, Taylor mentions specifics from the candidate's résumé to "establish that I'm taking an interest and to offer clues that will help the candidate ad lib around particular subjects."

Candidates for Monster jobs are expected to come prepared with questions of their own. "I like to see that the candidate has done a little research about the position, about our company, or about me," Taylor says. "One of the worst things you can do at the end of a rigorous interview is to have no questions to ask."

on the job

JEFF TAYLOR
Founder and
Chief Monster,
Monster.com
(Maynard,
Massachusetts)

Finally, Taylor stresses the importance of following up after the interview. "Some sort of correspondence is appropriate, whether it's handwritten or typed, mailed or e-mailed," he says. ■

PREPARING FOR A JOB INTERVIEW

 Prepare for a job interview.

Ninety-five percent of all employers require one or more employment interviews before extending a job offer, resulting in as many as 150 million employment interviews conducted annually.[1] The employer's purpose in these interviews is to verify information on the résumé, explore any issues raised by the résumé, and get some indication of the probable chemistry between the applicant and the organization. (It is estimated that 90 percent of all job failures result from personality clashes or conflicts—not incompetence.[2]) The job applicant can use the interview to glean important information about the organization and to decide whether the culture of the organization meshes with his or her personality.

Consider the employment interview to be a sales presentation. Just as any good sales representative would never walk into a potential customer's office without having a thorough knowledge of the product, neither should you. You are both the product and the product promoter, so do your homework—both on yourself and on the potential customer.

Researching the Organization

As a result of having developed your résumé and written your application letters, you have probably done enough general homework on yourself. You are likely to have a reasonably accurate picture of who you are and what you want out of your career. Now is the time to zero in on the organization at which you will be interviewing.

It is no exaggeration to say that you should learn everything you possibly can about the organization. Research the specific organization in depth. Search the current business periodical indexes and go online to learn what has been happening recently with the company. Many libraries maintain copies of the annual reports from large companies. Study these or other sources for current product information, profitability, plans for the future, and the like. Learn about the company's products and services, its history, the names of its officers, what the business press has to say about the organization, its recent stock activity, its financial health, its corporate structure, and the like, including the workplace environment.

Relate what you discover about the individual company to what you've learned about competing companies and about the industry in general. By trying to fit what you've learned into the broader perspective of the industry, you will be able to discuss matters more intelligently during your interview instead of just having a bunch of jumbled facts at your disposal.

If you're interviewing at a governmental agency, determine its role, recent funding levels, recent activities, spending legislation affecting the agency, and the extent to which being on the "right" side (that is, the official side) of a political question matters. If you're interviewing for a teaching position at an educational institution, determine the range of course offerings, types of students, conditions of the facilities and equipment, professionalism of the staff, and funding levels. In short, every tidbit of information you can gather about your prospective employer will help you make the most appropriate career decision. You will use this information as a resource to help you understand and discuss topics with some familiarity during the interview.

In short, bring up such information only if it flows naturally into the conversation. Even if you're never able to discuss some of the information you've gathered, the knowledge itself will still provide perspective in helping you to make a reasonable decision if a job offer is extended.

Practicing Interview Questions

Following is a sample of typical questions that are often asked during an employment interview:

- Tell me about yourself.

- How would you describe yourself?

- Tell me something about yourself that I won't find on your résumé.

- What do you take real pride in?

- Why would you like to work for our organization?

- Why should we hire you?

- What are your long-range career objectives?

- What types of work do you enjoy doing most? Which do you enjoy least?

- What accomplishment has given you the greatest satisfaction?

- What would you like to change in your past?

- What courses did you like best and least in college?

- Specifically, how does your education or experience relate to this job?

Questions such as these provide the interviewer with important clues about the applicant's qualifications, personality, poise, and communication skills. The interviewer is interested not only in the content of your responses but also in *how* you react to the questions themselves and *how* you communicate your thoughts and ideas.

Sometimes, however, interviewers may pose more difficult questions—ones that seemingly have no "right" answer. Examples of such questions are "What do you consider your major weakness?" or "What aspect of your present job do you like least?" Sometimes they even try to create a stressful situation by asking pointed questions, interrupting, or feigning disbelief in an attempt to gauge your behavior under stress.

The strategy to use in such a circumstance is to keep the desired job firmly in mind and to formulate each answer—no matter what the question—so it highlights your ability to perform the desired job competently. You don't have to accept each question as asked. You can ask the interviewer to be more specific or to rephrase the question. Doing so not only will provide guidance for answering the question but will give you a few additional moments to prepare your response.

DILBERT

Dilbert: © Scott Adams / Dist. by United Feature Syndicate, Inc.

Preparing Your Own Questions

During the course of the interview, many of the questions you may have about the organization or the job will probably be answered. However, an interview is a two-way conversation, so it is legitimate for you to pose relevant questions at appropriate moments, and you should prepare those questions beforehand.

Questions such as the following will provide useful information on which to base a decision if a job is offered:

▌ How would you describe a typical day on the job?

▌ How is an employee evaluated and promoted?

▌ What types of training are available?

▌ What are your expectations of new employees?

▌ What are the organization's plans for the future?

▌ To whom would I report? Would anyone report to me?

▌ What are the advancement opportunities for this position?

Each of these questions not only secures needed information to help you make a decision but also sends a positive nonverbal message to the interviewer that you are interested in this position as a long-term commitment.

Avoid asking about salary and fringe benefits during the initial interview. There will be plenty of time for such questions later, after you've convinced the organization that you're the person it wants. In terms of planning, you should know ahead of time the market value of the position for which you're applying. Check the classified ads, reports collected by your college career service, and library and Internet sources to learn what a reasonable salary figure for your position would be.

Dressing for Success

The importance of making a good first impression during the interview can hardly be overstated. One study has shown that 75 percent of the interviewees who made a good impression during the first five minutes of the interview received a job offer, whereas only 10 percent of the interviewees who made a bad impression during the first five minutes received a job offer.[3]

The most effective strategy for making a good impression is to pay careful attention to your dress, grooming, and posture. Dress in a manner that flatters your appearance while conforming to the office norm. You want the interviewer to remember what you had to say and not what you wore. Although different positions, companies, industries, and parts of the country and world have different norms, in general choose well-tailored, clean, conservative clothing for the interview.

CONDUCTING YOURSELF DURING THE INTERVIEW

 Conduct yourself appropriately during a job interview.

Observe the organizational environment very carefully and treat everyone you meet, including the receptionist and the interviewer's assistant or secretary, with scrupulous courtesy. Maintain an air of formality. When shown into the interview room, greet the interviewer by name, with a firm handshake, direct eye contact, and a smile.

Show interest in everything the interviewer is saying; don't concentrate so hard on formulating your response that you miss the last part of any question. Answer each question in a positive, confident, forthright manner. Recognize that more than yes-or-no answers are expected.

Control nervousness during the interview the same way you control it when making an oral presentation; that is, practice until you're confident you can face whatever the interviewer throws your way. The career centers at many colleges conduct mock interviews to prepare prospective interviewees. If yours does not, ask a professor or even another student to interview you. Practice answering lists of common questions.

Throughout the interview, your attitude should be one of confidence and courtesy. Assume a role that is appropriate for you. Follow the interviewer's lead, letting him or her determine which questions to ask, when to move to a new area of discussion, and when to end the interview.

Answer each question put to you as honestly as you can. Keep your mind on the desired job and how you can show that you are qualified for that job. Don't try to oversell yourself, or you may end up in a job for which you're unprepared. However, if the interviewer doesn't address an area in which you believe you have strong qualifications, be ready to volunteer such information at the appropriate time, working it into your answer to one of the interviewer's questions.

If asked about your salary expectations, try to avoid giving a salary figure, indicating that you would expect to be paid in line with other employees at your level of expertise and experience. If pressed, however, be prepared to reveal your salary expectations, preferably using a broad range.

When discussing salary, talk in terms of what you think the position and responsibilities are worth rather than what you think *you* are worth. If salary is not discussed, be patient. Few people have ever been offered a job in an industry without first being told what they would be paid.

It is also likely that you will be interviewed more than once—having either multiple interviews the same day or, if you survive the initial interview, a more intense set of interviews to be scheduled for a later date. The different interviewers will typically get together later to discuss their reactions to you and your responses.

CONCEPT CHECK 13.1

Using a government source (such as the *Occupational Employment Statistics* at http://stats.bls.gov/oes), determine the median annual income for each of the following occupations:

a. Administrative assistant/executive secretary

b. Computer programmer

c. Medical assistant

d. Paralegal

e. Your occupational choice

When the interview ends, if you've not been told, you have a right to ask the interviewer when you might expect to hear from him or her. You will likely be evaluated on these four criteria:

▌ *Education and experience:* Your accomplishments as they relate to the job requirements, evidence of growth, breadth and depth of your experiences, leadership qualities, and evidence of your willingness to assume responsibility.

▌ *Mental qualities:* Intelligence, alertness, judgment, logic, perception, creativity, organization, and depth.

▌ *Manner and personal traits:* Social poise, sense of humor, mannerisms, warmth, confidence, courtesy, assertiveness, listening ability, manner of oral expression, emotional balance, enthusiasm, initiative, energy, ambition, maturity, stability, and interests.

▌ *Appearance:* Grooming, dress, posture, cleanliness, and apparent health.

COMMUNICATING AFTER THE INTERVIEW

 3 ► *Complete the communication tasks needed after the interview.*

Immediately after the interview, conduct a self-appraisal of your performance. Try to recall each question that was asked and evaluate your response. If you're not satisfied with one of your responses, take the time to formulate a more effective answer. Chances are that you will be asked a similar question in the future.

Also reevaluate your résumé. Were any questions asked during the interview that indicated some confusion about your qualifications? Does some section need to be revised or some information added or deleted?

In addition, determine whether you can improve your application letter on the basis of your interview experience. Were the qualifications you discussed in your letter the ones that seemed to impress the interviewers the most? Were these qualifications discussed in terms of how they would benefit the organization? Did you provide specific evidence to support your claims?

You should also take the time to send the interviewer (or interviewers) a short thank-you note or e-mail message as a gesture of courtesy and to reaffirm your interest in the job. The interviewer, who probably devoted quite a bit of time to you before, during, and after the interview session, deserves to have his or her efforts on your behalf acknowledged.

Recognize, however, that your thank-you note may or may not have an effect on the hiring decision. Most decisions to offer the candidate a job or to invite him or her back for another round of interviewing are made the day of the interview, often during the interview itself. Thus, your thank-you note may arrive after the decision, good or bad, has been made.

The real purpose of a thank-you note is to express genuine appreciation for some courtesy extended to you.

Your thank-you note should be short and may be either typed or handwritten. Consider it a routine message that should be written in a direct organizational pattern. Begin by expressing appreciation for the interview; then achieve credibility by mentioning some specific incident or insight gained from the interview. Close on a hopeful, forward-looking note. The thank-you note in Model 30 on page 319 corresponds to the application letter presented in Model 29 on page 301.

CONCEPT CHECK 13.2

Why should you write a thank-you note after the interview? And why should you *not* write a thank-you note?

MODEL 30

Interview
Follow-Up Letter

Addresses the person in the salutation as he or she was addressed during the interview.

Begins directly, with a sincere expression of appreciation.

Mentions a specific incident that occurred and relates it to the writer's background.

Closes on a confident, forward-looking note.

April 15, 20—

① Mr. David Norman, Partner
Ross, Russell & Weston
452 Fifth Avenue
New York, NY 10018

② Dear Mr. Norman:

Thank you for the opportunity to interview for the position of EDP specialist yesterday. I very much enjoyed meeting you and Arlene Worthington and learning more about the position and about Ross, Russell & Weston.

③ I especially appreciated the opportunity to observe the long-range planning meeting yesterday afternoon and to learn of your firm's plans for increasing your consulting practice with nonprofit agencies. My experience working in city government leads me to believe that nonprofit agencies can benefit greatly from your expertise.

④ Again, thank you for taking the time to visit with me yesterday. I look forward to hearing from you.

Sincerely,

Aurelia Gomez

Aurelia Gomez
225 West 70 Street
New York, NY 10023
Phone: 212-555-3821
Email: agomez@nyu.edu

Grammar and Mechanics Notes

1. Use the ampersand (&) in a firm name only if it is used by the firm itself.
2. Use a colon (not a comma) even if the salutation uses the reader's first name.
3. *nonprofit:* Write most words beginning with *non* solid—without a hyphen.
4. *Again,:* Use a comma after an introductory expression.

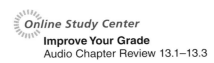

Online Study Center
Improve Your Grade
Audio Chapter Review 13.1–13.3

If you have not heard from the interviewer by the deadline date he or she gave you for making a decision, telephone or e-mail the interviewer for a status report. If no decision has been made, your inquiry will keep your name and your interest in the position in the interviewer's mind. If someone else has been selected, you need to know so that you can continue your job search. Checklist 17 on page 324 summarizes the steps in the interview process.

TEST PREPPER 13.1–13.3   ANSWERS CAN BE FOUND ON P. 412

True or False?

_____ 1. You should consider the interviewer's desk as off-limits during an interview.

_____ 2. Most successful job candidates are interviewed only once.

_____ 3. You should avoid asking about salary and fringe benefits during the initial interview.

_____ 4. Most applicants who make a good impression during the first five minutes of the interview receive a job offer.

_____ 5. The purpose of a thank-you note following the interview is to reiterate your interest in and qualifications for the position.

Critical Thinking

6. Assume during your job interview that you're asked, "What do you like most or least about your present job?" How might you answer?

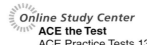

Online Study Center
ACE the Test
ACE Practice Tests 13.1–13.3

Online Study Center
Improve Your Grade
Audio Chapter Quiz 13.1–13.3
PowerPoint Review 13.1–13.3

BUSINESS ETIQUETTE

4 ▸ *Practice business etiquette in the workplace.*

business etiquette   The practice of polite and appropriate behavior in a business setting.

Business etiquette is the practice of polite and appropriate behavior in a business setting. It dictates what behaviors are proper and under what circumstances; thus, business etiquette is really concerned with interaction between people—not meaningless ritual.

Each organization has its own rules about what is and is not considered fitting in terms of dress, ways of addressing superiors, importance of punctuality, and the like. In addition, every country and every culture has its own rules. Generally, these rules are not written down but must be learned informally or through observation. Executives who follow correct business etiquette are more confident and appear more in charge; the higher you advance in your career, the more important such behavior will become.

Meeting and Greeting

The important point to remember about making introductions is simply to *make them.* The format for an introduction might be like this: "Helen, I'd like you to meet Carl Byrum. Carl just began working here as a junior account manager. Carl, this is Helen Smith, our vice president." Or in a social situation, you might just say, "Rosa, this is Gene Stauffer. Gene, Rosa Bennett." The appropriate response to an introduction is "How do you do, Gene?" Regardless of the gender of the two people being introduced, either may initiate the handshake—a gesture of welcome.

To help remember the name of someone you've met, make a point of using his or her name when shaking hands. And using the person's name again at least once during the conversation will help fix that name in your mind. If you cannot remember someone's name, when the person approaches you, simply extend your hand and say your name. The other person will typically respond by shaking your hand and also giving his or her name.

Whenever you greet an acquaintance whom you've met only once some time ago, introduce yourself and immediately follow it with some information to help the other person remember, unless he or she immediately recognizes you—for example, "Hello, Mr. Wise, I'm Eileen Wagoner. We met at the Grahams' party last month."

Today, most American businesspeople have business cards, although the protocol for exchanging them isn't as strict here as it is in some other countries. In business settings, you should present your card at the end of the encounter—as a way of establishing that you're interested in continuing the relationship. Never present your card during a meal (wait until it is over), and never offer your card at any time during a social function.

Dining

The restaurant you select for a business meal reflects on you and your organization. Choose one where the food is of top quality and the service is dependable. In general, the more important your guest, the more exclusive the restaurant. If a maitre d' (headwaiter) seats you and your guest, your guest should precede you to the table. If you're seating yourselves, take the lead in locating an appropriate table. Give your guest the preferred seat, facing the window with an attractive view or facing the dining room if you're seated next to the wall.

Here are some additional tips to follow for a successful and enjoyable business meal:

▌ The guests wait until the host unfolds the napkin and places it in the lap before doing the same. Do not begin eating until the host takes the first bite of food.

▌ If you're the host, to signal the waiter that you're ready to order, close your menu and lay it on the table. To get the server's attention, say, "Excuse me" when he or she is nearby, or catch the server's eye and quietly signal for him or her to come to the table, or ask a nearby server to ask yours to come to your table. The host's order is generally taken last.

▌ If you leave the table during the meal, leave your napkin on your chair. At the end of the meal, place the napkin, unfolded, on the table.

▌ When using silverware, start from the outside. Place your glass to the right of your place setting. When passing food or condiments, pass to the right, offering items to someone else before you serve yourself.

▌ Don't put your elbows on the table while eating, although you may do so between courses.

▌ Place the knife across the top edge of the plate, with the cutting edge toward you, when it is not being used. To signal the waiter that you are through with your plate, place your knife and fork diagonally across the middle of the plate.

▌ Spoon soup away from you. Avoid salting food before tasting it; if asked to pass the salt or pepper, pass both together.

The person who issues the invitation is expected to pay the bill. In most parts of the country, the usual tip for standard service is 15 to 20 percent of the food and bar bill and 10 percent of the cost of the wine. An appropriate tip for the cloakroom attendant is $.50 to $.75 per coat, or $1 in an expensive restaurant. If you use valet parking, tip the attendant $1 to $2 after your car is brought to the door.

Send a thank-you note immediately after the meal. Be sure to write more than a token note, mentioning something special about the décor, the food, the service, the company of the people with whom you dined, or your satisfaction with the business discussed.

Giving Gifts

Giving gifts to suppliers, customers, or workers within one's own organization is typical at many firms, especially in December during the holiday period. Although such gifts are often deeply appreciated, you must be sensitive in terms of whom you give a gift to and the type of gift you select. Most people would consider a gift appropriate if it meets these four criteria:

- *It is an impersonal gift.* Gifts that can be used in the office or in connection with one's work are nearly always appropriate.

- *It is presented as a thank-you for past favors.* Gifts should be used to thank someone for past favors, business, or performance—*not* to create obligations for the future. A gift to a prospective customer who has never ordered from you before might be interpreted as a bribe.

- *It is given to everyone in similar circumstances.* Singling out one person for a gift and ignoring others in similar positions would not only embarrass the one selected but also create bad feelings among those who were ignored.

- *It is not extravagant.* A very expensive gift might make the recipient uneasy, create a sense of obligation, and call into question your motives for giving.

Although it is often the custom for a superior to give a subordinate a gift, especially one's assistant, it is less usual for the subordinate to give a personal gift to a superior. More likely, coworkers will contribute to a joint gift for the boss, again selecting one that is neither too expensive nor too personal. As always, follow local customs when giving gifts to international colleagues.

Around the Office

Many situations occur every day in the typical office that call for common courtesy. The basis for appropriate behavior is always the golden rule: "Treat others as you yourself would like to be treated."

Cubicle Courtesy

An estimated 40 million people in today's work force spend their work hours in a cubicle.[4] Because cubicles provide so little privacy, cubicle courtesy is especially important. Always knock or ask permission before entering someone's cubicle, and never wander into someone's unoccupied cubicle without permission. Never shout a comment to someone in the next cubicle. If it's too hard to walk over, call instead. Do not leave valuables in your cubicle unattended. Avoid talking on the phone or to visitors too loudly, and avoid strong perfumes or colognes. Finally, honor occupants' privacy by not staring at their computer screens or listening to their conversations.

Drinking Coffee

If there is a container provided to pay for the coffee, do so every time you take a cup; don't force others to treat you to a cup of coffee. Also, take your turn making the coffee and cleaning the pot if that is a task performed by the group. Although in most offices it is acceptable to drink coffee or some other beverage while working, some offices have an unwritten rule against snacking at one's desk. Regardless, never eat while talking to someone in person or on the telephone.

Smoking

Many offices prohibit smoking anywhere on the premises. If you smoke, follow the rules strictly. Smoking in public anywhere is increasingly considered bad manners, not to mention a health hazard.

Using the Copier or Fax Machine

If you're using the copier or fax machine for a large job, and someone approaches with a small job, let that person go ahead of you. Also, be sure to refill the paper holder after completing a job, and reset the copier machine counter after using it. The next user, intending to make one copy, will not appreciate having to wait for— and pay for—100 copies instead, simply because you failed to reset the counter.

Online Study Center
Improve Your Grade
Audio Chapter Review 13.4
Handouts

TEST PREPPER 13.4   ANSWERS CAN BE FOUND ON P. 412

True or False?

_____ 1. When introducing someone, you should address the introduction to the higher-ranking person.

_____ 2. Either person being introduced may initiate a handshake.

Vocabulary

Define the following term in your own words:

3. Business etiquette

Critical Thinking

4. Would it be appropriate to give your instructor a gift at the end of the term? Why or why not?

Online Study Center
ACE the Test
ACE Practice Tests 13.4

Online Study Center
Improve Your Grade
Audio Chapter Quiz 13.4
PowerPoint Review 13.4

CHECKLIST 17

Employment Interviews

Preparing for an Employment Interview

✓ Before going on an employment interview, learn everything you can about the organization.

✓ Practice answering common interview questions and prepare questions of your own to ask.

✓ Select appropriate clothing to wear.

✓ Control your nervousness by being well prepared, well equipped, and on time.

Conducting Yourself During the Interview

✓ Throughout the interview, be aware of the nonverbal signals you are communicating through your body language.

✓ Answer each question completely and accurately, always trying to relate your qualifications to the specific needs of the desired job.

✓ Whether you are interviewed by one person or a group of people, you will be evaluated on your education and experience, mental qualities, manner and personal traits, and general appearance.

Communicating After the Interview

✓ Immediately following the interview, critique your performance and also send a thank-you note or e-mail message to the interviewer.

THREE Ps
PROBLEM, PROCESS, PRODUCT

A Job-Rejection Letter

Problem

You are Aurelia Gomez, whose résumé is shown in Model 25 on page 290. As a result of your application letter to David Norman, partner at Ross, Russell & Weston (see Model 29 on page 301), you participated in two job interviews at the accounting firm and just received the following letter:

> Dear Aurelia:
>
> I am pleased to offer you the position of EDP specialist with our firm, effective June 1, at an annual salary of $42,400. Your duties are outlined in the enclosed job description.
>
> This offer is conditional upon your passing a comprehensive medical examination (see enclosed). In addition, your probationary period, during which time you may be released with two weeks' notice, will extend until you receive a passing score on all parts of the New York State CPA examination.
>
> I look forward to having you join our firm, Aurelia, and would appreciate receiving a written acceptance of this offer by May 30.
>
> Sincerely,

Your excitement at receiving this letter is tempered by the fact that last week you orally accepted an offer of $37,200 from Modlin and Associates, another accounting firm, and their confirming letter arrived yesterday. Although you've not yet answered Modlin's letter, you planned to do so this weekend. You had also planned to write Ross, Russell & Weston this weekend, asking them to withdraw your name from further consideration.

Process

1. Which job offer is more appealing to you?

   In addition to their offering a larger salary, another factor I like about Ross, Russell & Weston is that they are more active in city politics than Modlin and Associates. If their offer had arrived first, I would definitely have taken it.

2. Because you haven't responded in writing to the Modlin and Associates offer, are you still free to accept the Ross, Russell & Weston offer?

   No, I definitely accepted the Modlin offer over the phone. In addition to the ethical dimension, public accounting firms are a very "clubby" group. Partners in different firms tend to have frequent contacts with one another, and it is likely that my action would become known to both firms.

3. Should your rejection letter be written in the direct or indirect organizational pattern?

   Indirect. Presumably, they will consider my rejection of their job offer as bad news because they will have to reopen their search process.

4. Can you leave open the possibility of future employment with Ross, Russell?

   Considering the fact that one in four entry-level employees fails to make it through the first year, there is always that possibility. However, any direct reference to future employment there would be inappropriate.

5. Should you express regret that you cannot accept their offer?

   No. It might invite additional job negotiations from Ross, Russell, which would not be in my best interests. I accepted the Modlin offer because I thought it would be a good career move. Despite the new offer, I still feel I will be happy and productive at Modlin.

THREE PS (CONTINUED)

Product

April 20, 20—

Mr. David Norman, Partner
Ross, Russell & Weston
452 Fifth Avenue
New York, NY 10018

Dear Mr. Norman:

The opportunity to join a progressive accounting firm in New York City, especially one that is active in the political life of our city, is certainly attractive.

I am sure, therefore, that you can appreciate the mixed feelings with which I inform you that I accepted another job offer last week. Your letter arrived before I had a chance to inform you of my decision.

I thank you sincerely for the opportunity I had to learn about your firm, its employees, and its management philosophy. I found the entire process very educational and rewarding, and I look forward to continuing to get to know you and your firm better as my career in public accounting progresses.

Sincerely,

Aurelia Gomez

Aurelia Gomez
225 West 70th Street
New York, NY 10023

PORTFOLIO PROJECT 8

Videotape of Practice Interview

Problem

Assume that, based on your résumé and job-application letter (see Portfolio Project 7 on page 308), you've been asked to come in for an initial interview. In preparation for a job interview, learn as much about your prospective employer as you can. Then ask someone to tape a 15-minute practice job interview, with your instructor or a career-center representative playing the role of the prospective employer.

Process

Compose a few paragraphs describing how you solved this problem. In narrative form, provide information such as the following:
1. How did you prepare for your practice interview?
2. How did you decide how to dress for your interview?

Product

Make a videotape of your practice interview.

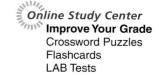

Online Study Center
Improve Your Grade
Crossword Puzzles
Flashcards
LAB Tests

LEARNING OBJECTIVE REVIEW

 Prepare for a job interview.

- Before your interview, use electronic and other sources to learn as much as you can about the company: products, services, history, officers, financial picture, corporate structure.
- Learn about competing companies.
- Prepare and practice responses to commonly asked interview questions.
- Be ready to ask some questions of the interviewer.
- Make a good impression by dressing in a way that conforms to the office norm.

2 *Conduct yourself appropriately during a job interview.*

- Be confident and courteous.
- Overcome nervousness by being prepared.
- Answer questions honestly.
- Avoid direct questions regarding salary, or speak about salary in relation to the position and only discuss salary ranges.
- Remember you'll be judged on your education and experience, mental qualities, manner, and personal traits as well as your appearance.

Complete the communication tasks needed after the interview.

- Immediately after the interview:
  - Conduct a self-appraisal of your performance.
  - Reevaluate your résumé.
  - Reevaluate your application letter on the basis of your interview experience.

- Write a follow-up letter within two days of the interview thanking the interviewer for his or her time.

 Practice business etiquette in the workplace.

- Learn what is considered appropriate behavior in the organization.
- Learn how to make introductions.

- When planning a business dinner, select a restaurant where the food is of top quality and the service is dependable.

- A business gift is appropriate if it meets four criteria:
  - It is an impersonal gift.
  - It is presented as a thank-you for past favors.
  - It is given to everyone in similar circumstances.
  - It is not extravagant.

- Observe common courtesies in the office:
  - Always knock, don't shout across cubicle walls, avoid talking too loudly on the phone or to visitors, and do not stare at a coworker's computer screen.
  - Pay close attention to written and unwritten rules regarding coffee drinking, eating at one's desk, smoking, and using the copier or fax machine.

EXERCISES

1. Researching the Organization (▶ 13.1)

Assume you're interested in a job with Monster.com (see pages 313–314). Go online to the company's home page (http://www.monster.com) as well as to other sources to find answers to the following questions. Write a short memo to your instructor containing your findings.

a. What industry is Monster.com in? What does the company do? What types of customers does it serve? Where are its offices located?

b. How do your skills and personal interests match with Monster.com's industry, operations, and locations?

c. Browse through Monster.com's online job listings. What types of positions does the company recruit for? Are your education and work experience appropriate for the positions that sound interesting? What other qualifications do you need to apply for the jobs that interest you?

2. Preparing for the Interview (▶ 13.1)

Page 315 lists some commonly asked interview questions. Prepare a written answer for each question based on your own qualifications and experience. Type each question and then your answer.

3. Work-Team Communication—Mock Interviews (▶ 13.2)

(This project uses information collected as part of Exercise 4 on pages 310–311 of Chapter 12.) Divide into groups of six students. Draw straws to determine which three members will be interviewers and which three will be job applicants. Both groups now have homework to do. The interviewers must get together to plan their interview strategy (10 to 12 minutes for each candidate); the applicants, working individually, must prepare for this interview; and both groups must learn more about Philip Morris.

The interviews will be conducted in front of the entire class, with each participant dressed appropriately. On the designated day, the three interviewers, as a group, will interview each of the three job applicants in turn (while the other two are out of the room). Given the short length of each interview, the applicant should refrain from asking any questions of his or her own, except to clarify the meaning of an interviewer's question.

After each round of interviews, the class as a whole will vote for the most effective interviewer and interviewee.

4. Interview Evaluation (▶ 13.2)

You are employed by EverGreen, Inc., a plant nursery in Plano, Texas. You and two other people in the human resources department have been asked to prepare an interview evaluation rating form to be used after interviewing each job applicant. Based on what you have learned regarding interviewing skills, develop a form that could be used to rate applicants' interviewing skills.

5. Thank-You Letters—Pedaling Toward Employment (▶ 13.3)

As your friends interview for jobs with investment banking firms and corporate giants, you decide on a different career path: retailing. You recently bought a Trek mountain bike at Zane's Cycles, a high-volume bicycle retailer located near New Haven, Connecticut. You were impressed by the store's huge selection, knowledgeable salespeople, and customer service culture. Zane's also operates a highly successful business selling bikes to businesses that give the bicycles away as rewards for sales performance and other achievements. This operation suggests that other opportunities exist beyond the retail side of the business. Another reason Zane's seems so appealing is that the founder, Chris Zane, lets his staff run the day-to-day operation—which means that managers have the responsibility and authority to do their jobs as they see fit.

You sent an unsolicited job-application letter and résumé to the store's human resources director, asking about a management trainee position. After going through an initial interview with two human resources experts, you're called back for a second interview. This time, you meet directly with Chris Zane to hear his vision for the store and his expectations for new managers. As soon as you get home, you turn on your computer to write a brief but professional thank-you note. What should you say in this note? Should you send a printed letter or an email message? Should you communicate with the human resources director at this time, even though you didn't see him during your second interview? Using your knowledge of employment communication, draft this thank-you note (making up appropriate details if needed).

6. Pleased to Meet You (▶ 13.4)

Assume the role of Marc Kaplan, vice president of marketing. You are expecting Ms. Sonia Muñoz, an important client, who will be accompanied by Mr. Gunnar Burns, her personal assistant. You've met them both once before. During the course of the day, make the following introductions:

a. Sonia Muñoz and Amy Stetsky, the president's administrative assistant.
b. Amy Stetsky and Gunnar Burns.
c. Gunnar Burns and Diana Coleman, vice president of administration.
d. Gunnar Burns and Dave Kaplan, president.

Additional exercises are available at the Online Study Center website: **college.hmco.com/pic/oberSASfund**.

Online Study Center **RESOURCES**

Prepare for Class, Improve Your Grade, and ACE the Test. Student Achievement Series resources include:

ACE Practice Tests	Ask Ober	Audio Chapter Reviews and Quizzes
Chapter Outlines	Communication Objectives	Crossword Puzzles
Flashcards	Glossaries	Handouts
LAB Tests	Portfolio Project Stationery	Sample Reports

To access these learning and study tools, go to **college.hmco.com/pic/oberSASfund**.

Language Arts Basics

A Business Sentence Structure

▶ PARTS OF SPEECH

Of the hundreds of thousands of words in an unabridged dictionary, each can be classified as one of just eight parts of speech: noun, pronoun, verb, adjective, adverb, preposition, conjunction, or interjection. These eight parts of speech are illustrated in the following sentence:

	Pronoun		Preposition		Conjunction	
Interjection		Adverb	Verb	Adjective	Noun	Noun

Oh, I eagerly waited for new computers and printers.

Many words can act as different parts of speech, however, depending on how they are used in a sentence. As you learned long ago, a *sentence* is a group of words that contains a subject and verb (predicate) and that expresses a complete thought.

Consider, for example, the different parts of speech represented by the word *following*:

We agree to do the following. *(Noun)*

I was only following your example. *(Verb)*

We met the following day. *(Adjective)*

Following his remarks, he sat down. *(Preposition)*

Not all words serve more than one function, but many do. This module offers a brief introduction to the eight parts of speech. They will be explored in more detail in later modules. Although you are undoubtedly already familiar with the definitions of most of these terms, each is defined in this module in case you need a refresher.

Nouns

A *noun* is a word that names something, such as a person, place, thing, or idea:

Person: employee, Ms. Campbell
Place: office, Chicago
Thing: animal, computer
Idea: concentration, impatience, week, typing

The words in italics in the following sentences are nouns.

Samuel promoted his *idea* to the *vice president* on *Wednesday.*

Word processing is just one of the *skills* you'll need as a *temp.*

How much does one *quart* of *water* weigh on our bathroom *scale*?

The animal *doctor* treated that *animal* well in *Houston*.

If you were asked to give an example of a noun, you would probably think of a *concrete noun*, a physical object that you can see, hear, feel, taste, or smell. An *abstract noun*, on the other hand, names a quality or concept rather than something physical. Here are examples of each:

Concrete Noun	Abstract Noun
book	success
stapler	patience
computer	skills
dictionary	loyalty

A *common noun*, as its name suggests, is the name of a *general* person, place, thing, or idea. If you want to give the name of a *specific* person, place, thing, or idea, you would use a *proper noun*. Proper nouns are always capitalized. Examples of common nouns and proper nouns are listed below:

Common Noun	Proper Noun
man	Lon Adams
city	Los Angeles
car	Corvette
religion	Judaism

A *singular noun* names one person, place, thing, or idea. A *plural noun* names more than one. Examples are listed below:

Singular Noun	Plural Noun
Armstrong	Armstrongs
watch	watches
computer	computers
victory	victories

Pronouns

A *pronoun* is a word used in place of a noun. Consider the following sentence:

> *Anna* went into *Anna's* kitchen and made *Anna's* favorite dessert because *Anna* was going to a party with *Anna's* friends.

The noun *Anna* is used five times in this awkward sentence. A smoother, less monotonous version of the sentence substitutes pronouns for all but the first *Anna*:

> Anna went into *her* kitchen and made *her* favorite dessert because *she* was going to a party with *her* friends.

The words in italics in the following sentences are pronouns. The nouns to which they refer are underlined:

> Edmundo thought *he* might get the promotion.

> *None* of the speakers were interesting.

> Ms. Kimura forgot to bring *her* slides.

> *Those* were the poorest nations.

Verbs

A *verb* is a word (or group of words) that expresses action or a state of being. The first kind of verb is called an *action verb*; the second kind is known as a *linking verb*. Without a verb, you have no sentence because the verb makes a statement about the subject. Most verbs express action of some sort—either physical or mental—as indicated by the verbs in italics in the following sentences:

> Ignacio *planted* his garden while Ann *pulled* weeds.
>
> I *solved* my problems as I *baked* bread.
>
> Ms. Tamura *decided* she should *call* a meeting.

A small (but important) group of verbs do not express action. Instead, they simply link the subject with words that describe it. The most common linking verbs are forms of the verb *to be,* such as *is, am, are, was, were,* and *will.* Other forms of linking verbs involve the senses, such as *feels, looks, smells, sounds,* and *tastes.* The following words in italics are linking verbs (note that verbs can comprise one or more words):

> Edna *was* angry because Xun *sounded* impatient.
>
> If Tina *is having* a party, I *should have been* invited.
>
> Ms. Tanaka *had* already *seen* the report.

Adjectives

You can make sentences with only nouns or pronouns and verbs (such as "Dogs bark" or "I agree"), but most of the time you'll need to add other parts of speech to make the meaning of the sentence clearer or more complete. An *adjective* is a word that modifies a noun or pronoun. Adjectives answer questions about the nouns or pronouns they describe, such as How many? What kind? Which one? As shown by the words in italics in the following sentences, adjectives may come before or after the nouns or pronouns they modify:

> *Seventeen* applicants took the *typing* test.
>
> The interview was *short,* but *comprehensive.*
>
> She took the *last* plane and landed at a *small Mexican* airport.

Adverbs

An *adverb* is a word that modifies a verb, an adjective, or another adverb. Adverbs often answer the following questions: When? Where? How? or To what extent? The words in italics in the following sentences are adverbs:

> Please perform the procedure *now. (When?)*
>
> Put the papers *here. (Where?)*
>
> Donald performed *brilliantly. (How?)*
>
> I have *almost* finished. *(To what extent?)*
>
> The *exceedingly* expensive car was *very carefully* protected. *(To what extent?)*

In the last sentence, the adverb *exceedingly* modifies the adjective *expensive* (how expensive?) and the adverb *very* modifies the adverb *carefully* (how carefully?). Many (but by no means all) adverbs end in *-ly,* for example, *loudly, quickly, really,* and *carefully.* Of course, not all words that end in *-ly* are adverbs; for example, *friendly, stately,* and *ugly* are all adjectives.

Prepositions

A *preposition* is a word (such as *to, for, from, of,* and *with*) that shows the relationship between a noun or pronoun and some other word in the sentence. The noun or pronoun that follows the preposition is called the *object* of the preposition, and the entire group of words is called a *prepositional phrase*. In the following sentences, the preposition is shown in italics; the entire prepositional phrase is underlined:

> The ceremony occurred *on* the covered bridge.
> The ceremony occurred *under* the covered bridge.
> Marsha talked *with* Mr. Hines.
> Marsha talked *about* Mr. Hines.

Conjunctions

A *conjunction* is a word (such as *and, or,* or *but*) that joins words or groups of words. For example, in the sentence "Jonathan and Vincent are brokers," the conjunction *and* connects the two nouns *Jonathan* and *Vincent*. In the following sentences, the conjunction is shown in italics; the words it joins (conjunction → conjoins) are underlined:

> Conceptin *or* Nancy will attend the conference. *(Joins two nouns)*
> Pancho spoke quietly *and* deliberately. *(Joins two adverbs)*
> Ms. Duncan tripped *but* caught her balance. *(Joins two verbs)*

Interjections

An *interjection* is a word that expresses strong emotions. Interjections are used more often in oral communication than in written communication. If an interjection stands alone, it is followed by an exclamation point. If it is part of the sentence, it is followed by a comma. You should not be surprised that some words can serve as interjections in some sentences and as other parts of speech in other sentences. In the following sentences, the interjection is shown in italics:

> *Good!* I'm glad to learn that the new employee is competent.
> *Oh!* I didn't mean to startle you.
> *Oh,* I wouldn't say that.
> *Gosh,* that was an exhausting exercise. *Whew!*

▶ PARTS OF A SENTENCE

A sentence must, first of all, make sense by itself; that is, it must contain a complete thought. In addition, there are other required and optional parts of a sentence.

Subjects and Predicates

Every sentence must contain a subject and a predicate. The *subject* of a sentence is the word or group of words that does something, has something done to it, or is identified or described. The *predicate* is the word or group of words that tells what the subject does, what is done to it, or how it is identified or described. In other words, the predicate makes a statement about the subject.

Subject	Predicate
Mr. Sánchez and I *(Did something)*	typed the report. *(Tells what the subject did)*
The report *(Had something done to it)*	was typed by Mr. Sánchez and me. *(Tells what was done to the subject)*
Wanda *(Is identified)*	was the instigator. *(Identifies the subject)*
The report *(Is described)*	was quite long. *(Describes the subject)*

All of the words that function together as the subject are called the *complete subject*. The noun or pronoun that serves as the essential element of the subject is called the *simple subject*. Similarly, all of the words that function together as the predicate are called the *complete predicate*. The verb that serves as the essential element of the predicate is called the *simple predicate*.

Complete subject

The accounting department's slow and unreliable copier needed replacing.

Simple subject

Complete predicate

Our network was down last week for three days.

Simple predicate

Most sentences contain a single subject and a single predicate. When two or more nouns or pronouns are linked together, they form a *compound* subject. Similarly, when two or more verbs are linked together, they form a *compound* predicate.

Compound subject

Friends and coworkers ‖ applauded.

Single predicate

Single subject

Coworkers ‖ stood and applauded.

Compound predicate

Occasionally, the subject of the sentence is implied rather than stated directly. For example, if your superior tells you "File the report," it is understood that she is telling *you* to file the report. In this case, the subject is the unstated (but understood) *you*.

Optional Sentence Elements

The expression "Phones rang" is a complete sentence. Most sentences in business writing, of course, have more parts than a one-word subject and predicate. This section discusses some additional elements of a sentence.

Phrases   A *phrase* is a group of related words that do not have *both* a subject and a predicate. As shown below, phrases can be used as nouns, verbs, adjectives, or adverbs. Each phrase is shown in italics:

Between Thanksgiving and Christmas is our busiest season. *(Noun phrase)*

Henderson *will be attending* the national conference. *(Verb phrase)*

Lab tests *of many kinds* were then ordered. *(Adjectival phrase)*

We will finish the tests *before lunch. (Adverbial phrase)*

Clauses   A *clause* is a group of related words that contain *both* a subject and a predicate. (A phrase may contain either a subject *or* a predicate—but not both.)

Phrase: After the break, we'll continue. *(Lacks a subject and predicate)*

Clause: After we take a break, we'll continue.

Phrase: Reading the computer program was difficult. *(Contains a subject but no predicate)*

Clause: When I was reading the computer program, I discovered the error.

Phrase: By 2005 Jonathan Stein *will have been working for 30 years. (Contains a predicate but no subject)*

Clause: By 2005 *Jonathan Stein will have been working for 30 years.*

An *independent* (or *main*) *clause* can stand alone as a complete sentence. Every sentence has at least one independent clause. A *dependent* (or *subordinate*) *clause* does not express a complete thought but is used along with an independent clause to express a related idea. In the following sentences, the independent clauses are underlined and the dependent clauses are italicized:

I quit.

Ms. Méndez entered the sales data into the new accounting system.

Although Sandra tried diligently, she was not able to eliminate the virus.

Sandra tried diligently *but was not able to eliminate the virus.*

Cindy, *who was hired last week,* was a Rhodes scholar.

Objects   Recall that a verb is a word that expresses action (an *action verb*) or a state of being (a *linking verb*). Some action verbs require an object to complete the action. For example, you wouldn't say, "The company built," and leave it at that. The listener or reader would say, "Yes, go on. The company built what?"

A *direct object* is a noun or pronoun that receives the action of the verb. It always appears *after* the verb, as illustrated by the italicized words below (the verbs are underlined):

The company built a *warehouse.*

Gene took *notes* at the meeting.

Mr. Menéndez received *the Medal of Honor* for his service in Vietnam.

Ernest thanked *me* for my participation.

To test for the presence of a direct object, repeat the subject and verb and ask "whom?" or "what?" For example, in the first sentence, "The company built *what?*" or in the last sentence, "Ernest thanked *whom?*" Thus, *warehouse* and *me* are direct objects of the two sentences. Not all action verbs, of course, require an object, as illustrated below:

Think before you speak.

Janet ate while I wrote.

Who cares?

The eager audience shouted and clapped after the new CEO spoke about the revised retirement plan.

An *indirect object* tells to whom or for whom the action in the verb was done. Although a sentence can have a direct object without having an indirect object, the opposite is *not* true. A sentence *must* contain a direct object for it to contain an indirect object. The indirect object (a noun or pronoun) always comes *before* the direct object, as illustrated by the italicized indirect objects shown below (the direct objects are underlined):

I'll bring *Annette* the <u>notes</u>.

My boss promised *me* a <u>raise</u>.

Justine's gives its regular *customers* <u>a discount</u>.

The doctor gave the *patient* <u>a new regimen to follow</u>.

If the first sentence had read "I'll bring the notes *to Annette*," the sentence would not contain an indirect object. Remember that an indirect object always comes *before* the direct object.

Complements   Instead of expressing action, linking verbs simply link the subject with words that identify or describe it. The word or words in the predicate that complete the sense of the verb are called the *complement*. (Note the spelling of *complement*: A complement *completes* the sense of the verb.) It may be a noun, a pronoun, or an adjective. The complement is shown in italics in the following examples:

Ling is our new *programmer*. (The noun "programmer" refers to "Ling.")

The person to contact is *she*. (The pronoun "she" refers to "person.")

His harsh assessment was *accurate*. (The adjective "accurate" modifies "assessment.")

▶ COMPLEXITY OF SENTENCES

Sentences are made up of words, phrases, and clauses. Although simple information can be communicated in a short, simple sentence, often the situation calls for more complex sentences. The competent communicator uses variety in sentence complexity to achieve his or her communication goal.

Simple Sentences

A *simple sentence* contains one independent clause and *no* dependent clauses. Although they are generally short, simple sentences can sometimes be long, especially if they contain a compound subject or compound predicate. The sentence is still a simple sentence if it contains only one subject and one predicate (whether simple or compound). All of the following are simple sentences:

Ms. Banks volunteered.

The spreadsheets and database reports were finally completed and proofread.

The president and two of her vice presidents asked both the sales and marketing departments for their reactions to the addition of generic brands to our product mix in the European and Asian markets.

Compound Sentences

A *compound sentence* contains two or more independent clauses and *no* dependent clauses.

> Kenneth typed and I proofread.
>
> Ms. Bennett filed the papers at the courthouse; afterward, she grabbed some lunch.
>
> The on-the-scene officer called for backup, the emergency squad arrived eight minutes later, and the robber was apprehended and taken into custody.

Complex Sentences

A *complex sentence* contains one independent clause and one or more dependent clauses.

> After I left the room, the vote was taken.
>
> The vote was taken after I left the room.
>
> On April 13, Bonnie, who had no experience, received the job offer that she had applied for and hoped to get.

Compound-Complex Sentences

A *compound-complex sentence* contains two or more independent clauses *and* one or more dependent clauses.

> I wanted to write the report myself, but I soon realized that I needed the advice of our legal department. *(Two independent clauses and one dependent clause)*
>
> If I can, I'll do it; if I cannot, I'll ask Dennis to do it. *(Two independent clauses and two dependent clauses)*

▶ SENTENCE ERRORS

A *sentence fragment* is part of a sentence that is written and punctuated as if it were a complete sentence. However, it lacks one crucial element—it does not make sense by itself. As shown below, it is easy to revise fragments into complete sentences:

> **NOT:** Lack of proofreading skills, one of the most common weaknesses in office workers.
> **BUT:** Lack of proofreading skills is one of the most common weaknesses in office workers.
>
> **NOT:** The attorneys, all busy with their clients.
> **BUT:** The attorneys were all busy with their clients.
>
> **NOT:** After all the lab tests came back negative and the patient was relieved.
> **BUT:** After all the lab tests came back negative, the patient was relieved.

A *run-on sentence* is two or more independent clauses (1) that run together without any punctuation between them or with only a comma between them (the latter error is called a *comma splice*) or (2) that would be more effectively stated as separate sentences. Revise run-on sentences by turning them into separate sentences, inserting a semicolon between them (instead of a comma or no punctuation), inserting a comma and a coordinating conjunction (such as *and*, *or*, or *but*), or changing one of the independent clauses into a dependent clause.

NOT: Please sign the contract quickly, Mr. Muñoz is waiting for it.

BUT: Please sign the contract quickly. Mr. Muñoz is waiting for it. *(Making into separate sentences)*

OR: Please sign the contract quickly; Mr. Muñoz is waiting for it. *(Inserting a semicolon)*

OR: Please sign the contract quickly because Mr. Muñoz is waiting for it. *(Creating a dependent clause)*

NOT: Hans is a fast worker he is not very accurate.

BUT: Hans is a fast worker, but he is not very accurate. *(Inserting a comma and a coordinating conjunction)*

NOT: I really want this job and if you hire me I promise I'll work hard for you and increase your customer base and also I'll redesign your company's marketing representative orientation program to make it more efficient and more effective.

BUT: I really want this job. If you hire me, I promise I'll work hard for you and increase your customer base. Also, I'll redesign your company's marketing representative orientation program to make it more efficient and more effective. *(Making into separate sentences)*

EXERCISES

Parts of Speech

1. List the eight parts of speech:

2. For each word in the following sentence, identify its part of speech directly above or below:

   Whew! Johnny and I quickly asked for more time.

3. List three words that can be used as more than one part of speech; identify the relevant parts of speech.

4. a. Circle all of the nouns in the following sentence.

   Dan, accompanied by the Rochester Orchestra, performed his songs on the first anniversary of his greatest success.

   b. Write the nouns you circled in the appropriate categories below (some nouns will be used more than once).

   Abstract:

   Common:

   Concrete:

   Proper:

   Singular:

   Plural:

5. Write an appropriate pronoun above each italicized expression in the following paragraph to substitute for the noun.

   Give Tony *Tony's* disk to help *Tony and Manual* finish *Tony and Manual's* report. *Tony and Manual* will then give *the report* to Mr. Ellis.

6. Circle all of the verbs in the following sentences. Above each verb, indicate whether it is an action verb *(A)* or a linking verb *(L)*.

   Leo and Bao watched me while I moved the furniture. They were curious because they felt strange in their new offices. When will they get comfortable?

7. Indicate whether an adjective or an adverb answers each of the following questions.

   How many?

   How?

   To what extent?

   What kind?

   When?

   Where?

   Which one?

8. In the following sentence, circle all conjunctions and underline all prepositions.

   Under the circumstances, Ms. Svoboda and Mr. Woods gave a lesson or two to Teodora about getting along well with others, but he didn't seem to understand.

9. Compose a sentence that contains an interjection that you might properly include in a business letter.

10. Compose a sentence that contains all parts of speech and label each word according to its part of speech.

Parts of a Sentence

11. Circle the subject in each of the following sentences (be sure not to circle a prepositional phrase).

    a. For that reason, Ms. Cook decided to accept the new job.
    b. Your complaint will be thoroughly investigated by the detectives.
    c. There are three computers left to be assembled.
    d. Four of the employees tested positive.
    e. Why was the job not finished on time?
    f. The prize was donated by Paola.
    g. Across the hall is our new photocopying center.
    h. In Leon's view, the real cause was a lack of coordination.
    i. Three computers are left to be assembled.
    j. Four employees tested positive.
    k. Paola donated the prize.

12. Circle all verbs in the following sentences.

    a. In October, Quon will have been working here for twenty years.

    b. Will she have the support she needs?

    c. I could not possibly have guessed the real reason for the delay.

    d. That response was open to much interpretation.

    e. He seemed hesitant at first but soon lost his shyness.

13. Over each italicized expression, indicate whether the expression is a phrase *(P)* or a clause *(C)*.

    a. *Because a phrase does not contain both a subject and a verb*, it can never serve *as a complete sentence*.

    b. I enjoyed *planning the event*, but I *will be taking* a few days off.

    c. I moved my desk *against the wall* so that *I would have more room*.

    d. *To type accurately* is just as important as *to type rapidly*.

    e. We must finish *all of the puzzle* today *because I leave for home tomorrow*.

14. In the following sentences, write *DO* above each direct object, *IO* above each indirect object, and *C* above each complement.

    a. I was so angry I had to bite my tongue.

    b. Leonard practiced while I rested in bed.

    c. The company offered Nina early retirement.

    d. The company offered early retirement to Nina.

    e. The doctor ordered bed rest for Rhonda because of her chronic fatigue.

    f. The manager was so generous he gave me a quick raise.

Complexity of Sentences

15. In the space provided, indicate the complexity of each sentence by writing *S* for simple, *CP* for compound, *CX* for complex, or *CC* for compound-complex. Underline each dependent clause in the sentences.

    a. _____ After a delicious dinner, we went to a first-rate movie.

    b. _____ Before we left, Haruko wanted a brief rehearsal.

    c. _____ Both Mr. Cooper and Ms. Dvorak quit their jobs, applied for unemployment benefits, and began outplacement counseling.

    d. _____ Wendy first thought that she could handle the job herself but then found out that she needed extra help.

    e. _____ Haruko wanted a brief rehearsal before we left.

    f. _____ Florence quit.

    g. _____ George began the audit quickly enough; however, he soon found unexpected problems.

    h. _____ Kaori talked while I listened.

    i. _____ The chef planned the menu, the host made out the guest list, and the musician chose the songs for the entertainment.

    j. _____ The package that was sitting unopened on the conference table was not the one that I had been expecting.

    k. _____ The package, which was sitting unopened on the conference table, was not the one that I had been expecting.

    l. _____ While waiting for the verdict to be read, the attorney planned her appeal and the defendant watched the jury.

    m. _____ Why are both the delivery van and the panel truck in the repair shop at the same time?

16. Compose a sentence of each of the following types, inserting the correct punctuation at the end.

    a. Simple:

    b. Compound:

    c. Complex:

    d. Compound-complex:

Sentence Errors

17. Some of the following expressions are sentence fragments, while others are run-on sentences. Put a *C* next to the correct sentences. Revise the others to make them correct.

    a. _____ Gloria modeled the new uniform, everyone applauded.

    b. _____ Although I'm very good at figuring out these puzzles.

    c. _____ As we entered the elevators to join our colleagues in the third-floor conference room where the meeting had already begun.

    d. _____ Because computers had always fascinated him so much and he was good at working with his hands.

    e. _____ He has patented five inventions.

    f. _____ Ms. Rios explained how to operate the new equipment the demonstration lasted nearly three hours.

    g. _____ Shoshana usually finishes in an hour this time she took longer.

    h. _____ Since the company purchased a new color printer for the sales department, everyone wants one.

    i. _____ Ten minutes after the bank closed for the day.

    j. _____ The company purchased a new color printer for the sales department, now everyone wants one.

    k. _____ The five inventions that he has patented.

    l. _____ Those loose wires are dangerous be careful.

    m. _____ To work as safely as possible.

    n. _____ Try to work as safely as possible.

B Business-Style Punctuation

▶ WHY PUNCTUATION?

Punctuation serves as a roadmap to help guide the reader through the twists and turns of your message—pointing out what is important (italics), subordinate (commas), copied from another source (quotation marks), explained further (colon), considered as a unit (hyphens), and the like. Sometimes correct punctuation is absolutely essential for comprehension. Consider, for example, the different meanings of the following sentences, depending on the placement of the comma:

> Our new model comes in red, green and brown, and white.
> Our new model comes in red, green, and brown and white.

> While he was walking his dog, Benjamin Franklin got lost.
> While he was walking his dog Benjamin, Franklin got lost.

> The award went to Maritza, and Carl and Uang protested.
> The award went to Maritza and Carl, and Uang protested.

> We must still play Michigan, which tied Ohio State, and Minnesota.
> We must still play Michigan, which tied Ohio State and Minnesota.

You already know much about punctuation. For example, you already know to end a statement with a period and a question with a question mark. In this module, you will learn the most common uses of punctuation in narrative business writing. You should learn these punctuation rules thoroughly because you will use them frequently.

▶ COMMAS

We start our discussion of punctuation with the comma—the most commonly used mark of punctuation. The punctuation rules presented in this module do not cover every possible situation. Comprehensive style manuals, for example, routinely give more than 100 rules for using the comma rather than just the 10 rules presented here (the use of commas with numbers is covered in Module E). These 10 rules cover the most common uses of the comma.

Commas Used *Between* Expressions

Three types of expressions (that is, words or groups of words) typically require commas between them: independent clauses, adjacent adjectives, and items in a series.

Rule 1. Independent Clauses   Use a comma between two independent clauses joined by a coordinate conjunction.

> Norma discussed last month's performance, and Rosa presented the sales projections.

> The meeting was running late, but Ernesto was in no hurry to adjourn.

The major coordinate conjunctions are *and, but, or,* and *nor.* Recall from Module A that an independent clause is a subject-predicate combination that can stand alone as a complete sentence.

Do not confuse two independent clauses joined by a coordinate conjunction and a comma with a compound predicate, whose verbs are *not* separated by a comma. *Hint:* Cover up the conjunction with your pencil. If what's on both sides of your pencil could stand alone as complete sentences, a comma is needed.

> NO COMMA: Carla had read the report but had not discussed it with her colleagues. (*"Had not discussed it with her colleagues" is not an independent clause; it lacks a subject.*)

> COMMA: Carla had read the report, but she had not discussed it with her colleagues.

Exception: If the sentence containing two independent clauses is quite short (say, ten words or fewer) and no confusion results, omit the comma before the conjunctions *and* or *or* (but not before the conjunction *but*).

> I typed_and she proofread.

> BUT: I typed, but she proofread.

> The firm hadn't paid_and John was angry.

Rule 2. Adjacent Adjectives   Use a comma between two adjacent adjectives that modify the same noun.

> He was an aggressive, unpleasant manager.

> BUT: He was an aggressive_and unpleasant manager. (*The two adjectives are not adjacent; they are separated by the conjunction "and."*)

Do not use a comma if the first adjective modifies the combined idea of the second adjective plus the noun. *Hint*: Mentally insert the word "and" between the two consecutive adjectives. If it does not make sense, do not use a comma.

> Please order a new bulletin_board for the executive_conference room.

> BUT: Please order a new, larger bulletin_board for the executive conference room.

In the first sentence, *new* modifies *bulletin board*; you would not say "new and bulletin board." Similarly, *executive* modifies *conference room*; you would not say "executive and conference room." In the second sentence, you could say "new and larger bulletin board"; hence, we use the comma.

Rule 3. Items in a Series   Use a comma between each item in a series of three or more. (*Do not use a comma after the last item in the series.*)

> The committee may meet on Wednesday, Thursday, or Friday_of next week.

> Carlota wrote the questionnaire, Vernon distributed the forms, and Louis tabulated the results_for our survey on employee satisfaction.

> Planning the agenda, preparing the handouts, and appointing a secretary_are the three jobs left to complete.

Some style manuals indicate that the last comma before the conjunction is optional. However, to avoid ambiguity in business writing, insert this comma.

> NOT: We were served salads, macaroni and cheese and crackers.
>
> BUT: We were served salads, macaroni and cheese, and crackers.
>
> OR: We were served salads, macaroni, and cheese and crackers.

Commas Used *After* Expressions

An introductory expression is a word, phrase, or clause that comes before the subject and verb of the independent clause. Introductory expressions typically require commas after them.

Rule 4. Introductory Expressions   Use a comma after an introductory expression. (When the same expression occurs at the end of the sentence, no comma is used.)

> No, the status report is not ready. *(Introductory word)*
>
> Of course, you are not required to sign the petition. *(Introductory phrase)*
>
> As a matter of fact, Carmela was instrumental in successfully defending the countersuit. *(Introductory clause)*
>
> To do that, you will need the cooperation of the accounting department. *(Introductory clause)*
>
> When the status report is ready, I shall call you. *(Introductory clause)*
>
> BUT: I shall call you when the status report is ready.
>
> I'm happy to do that, but if you're not willing to do so, we will need to try something else. *("If you're not willing to do so" is an introductory clause for the second independent clause.)*

Do not use a comma between the subject and verb—no matter how long or complex the subject is.

> To finish that boring and time-consuming task in time for the monthly sales meeting_was a major challenge.
>
> The effort to bring all of our products into compliance with ISO standards and to be eligible for sales in European Union countries_required a full year of detailed planning.

Commas Used *Before* and *After* Expressions

Numerous types of expressions typically require commas before *and* after them. Of course, if one of these expressions comes at the beginning of a sentence, use a comma only after the expression; if it comes at the end of a sentence, use a comma only before.

Rule 5. Nonrestrictive Expressions   Use commas before and after a nonrestrictive expression. A *restrictive expression* is one that limits (restricts) the meaning of the noun or pronoun that it follows and is, therefore, essential to complete the basic meaning of the sentence. A *nonrestrictive expression,* in contrast, may be omitted without changing the basic meaning of the sentence.

> RESTRICTIVE: Anyone with extensive experience should apply for the position. *("With some experience" restricts which "anyone" should apply.)*

NONRESTRICTIVE:	Bernardo Álvarez, a clerk with extensive experience, should apply for the position. *(Because Bernardo Álvarez can be only one person, the phrase "a clerk with extensive experience" does not serve to further restrict the noun and is, therefore, not essential to the meaning of the sentence.)*
RESTRICTIVE:	Only the papers left on the conference table are missing. *(Identifies which papers are missing)*
NONRESTRICTIVE:	Lever Brothers, one of our best customers, is expanding in Europe. *("One of our best customers" could be omitted without changing the basic meaning of the sentence.)*
RESTRICTIVE:	Ms. Turner, using a great deal of tact, disagreed with her.
NONRESTRICTIVE:	The manager using a great deal of tact was Ms. Turner.

Whenever an identifying expression follows a proper noun, it is typically nonrestrictive because the proper noun already restricts the noun to one person, place, or thing. Thus, such expressions require commas before and after.

An *appositive* is a noun that identifies another noun or pronoun that comes immediately before it. If the appositive is nonrestrictive, insert commas before and after the appositive.

RESTRICTIVE:	The word *plagiarism* strikes fear into the hearts of many. *("Plagiarism" is an appositive that identifies which word; therefore, it is restrictive.)*
NONRESTRICTIVE:	Ms. Burns, president of the corporation, is planning to resign. *("President of the corporation" is an appositive that provides additional but nonessential information about Ms. Burns.)*

Rule 6. Interrupting Expressions   Use commas before and after an interrupting expression. An interrupting expression breaks the normal flow of a sentence. Common examples of interrupting expressions are *in addition, as a result, therefore, in summary, on the other hand, however, unfortunately,* and *as a matter of fact.*

> You may, of course, cancel your subscription at any time.
>
> One suggestion, for example, was to undertake a leveraged buyout.
>
> I believe it was Carmen, not Jiro, who raised the question.
>
> It is still not too late to make the change, is it?
>
> Mr. Kennedy's present salary, you must admit, is not in line with salaries of other network managers.
>
> BUT: You must admit_Mr. Kennedy's present salary is not in line with salaries of other network managers.

If the expression does not interrupt the normal flow of the sentence, do not use a comma.

> There is no doubt that you are qualified for the position.
>
> BUT: There is, no doubt, a good explanation for his actions.

Be sure to insert the commas in the correct position when punctuating interrupting expressions. Make sure the sentence makes sense when you mentally omit the expression between the two commas.

Online Study Center   college.hmco.com/pic/oberSASfund

NOT: That is the most convenient, but not the cheapest ticket, to purchase. *("That is the most convenient to purchase" doesn't make sense; the noun is missing.)*

BUT: That is the most convenient, but not the cheapest, ticket to purchase.

NOT: Ms. Cerny has a great fondness for, as well as much expertise, in web-page development. *(You would not say, "Ms. Cerny has a great fondness for in webpage development.")*

BUT: Ms. Cerny has a great fondness for, as well as much expertise in, web-page development.

Rule 7. Date   Use commas before and after the year when it follows the month and day. Do not use a comma after a partial date or when the date is formatted in day-month-year order. If the name of the day precedes the date, also use a comma *after* the name of the day.

The note is due on May 31, 2007, at 5 p.m.

BUT: The note is due on May 31 at 5 p.m.

BUT: The note is due in May 2007.

BUT: The note is due on 31 May 2007 at 5 p.m.

Let's plan to meet on Wednesday, December 15, 2007, for our year-end review.

Rule 8. Place   Use commas before and after a state or country that follows a city and between elements of an address in narrative writing.

The sales conference will be held in Phoenix, Arizona, in May.

Our business agent is located in Brussels, Belgium, in the P.O.M. Building.

You may contact her at 500 Beaufort Drive, LaCrosse, VA 23950. *(Note that no comma appears between the state abbreviation and the zip code.)*

Rule 9. Direct Address   Use commas before and after a name used in direct address. A name is used in direct address when the writer speaks directly to (that is, directly addresses) another person.

Thank you, Carol, for bringing the matter to our attention.

Ladies and gentlemen, we appreciate your attending our session today.

Rule 10. Direct Quotation   Use commas before and after a direct quotation in a sentence.

The president said, "You have nothing to fear," and then changed the subject.

"I assure you," the human resources director said, "that no positions will be terminated."

If the quotation is a question, use a question mark instead of a comma.

"How many have applied?" she asked.

▶ SEMICOLONS

Semicolons show where elements in a sentence are separated. The separation is stronger than that implied by a comma but not as strong as that implied by a period. When typing, leave one space after a semicolon and begin the following word with a lowercase letter.

Rule 11. Independent Clauses with Commas If a misreading might otherwise occur, use a semicolon (instead of a comma) to separate independent clauses that contain internal commas. Make sure that the semicolon is inserted *between* the independent clauses—not *within* one of the clauses.

CONFUSING: I ordered juice, toast, and bacon, and eggs, toast, and sausage were sent instead.

CLEAR: I ordered juice, toast, and bacon; eggs, toast, and sausage were sent instead.

CONFUSING: I attended the meetings on October 29, 30, and 31, and on November 2 I returned home.

CLEAR: I attended the meetings on October 29, 30, and 31; and on November 2, I returned home.

BUT: Although high-quality paper was used, the photocopy machine still jammed, and neither of us knew how to repair it. (*No misreading is likely to occur.*)

Rule 12. Independent Clauses Without a Conjunction Use a semicolon between independent clauses that are not connected by a coordinate conjunction (such as *and, but, or,* or *nor*). You have already learned to use a comma before coordinate conjunctions when they connect independent clauses. This rule applies to independent clauses *not* connected by a conjunction.

The president was eager to proceed with the plans; the board still had some reservations.

BUT: The president was eager to proceed with the plans, but the board still had some reservations. (*Use a comma instead of a semicolon if the clauses are joined by a coordinate conjunction.*)

I slept through my alarm; consequently, I was late for the meeting.

Bannon Corporation exceeded its sales goal this quarter; furthermore, it rang up its highest net profit ever.

BUT: Bannon Corporation exceeded its sales goal this quarter, and, furthermore, it rang up its highest net profit ever. (*Use a comma instead of a semicolon if the clauses are joined by a coordinate conjunction.*)

Rule 13. Series with Internal Commas Use a semicolon after each item in a series if any of the items already contain a comma. Normally, we separate items in a series with commas. If any of those items already contain a comma, however, we need a stronger mark (semicolon) between the items.

The human resources department will be interviewing in Dallas, Texas; Stillwater, Oklahoma; and Little Rock, Arkansas, for the new position.

Among the guests were Jerome Carpenter, our attorney; his wife Veronica; and Carolyn Hart-Wilder, our new controller.

Make sure the semicolon is inserted between (not within) the items in the series. Even if only one of the items contains an internal comma, separate all of them with semicolons.

NOT: That emergency procedure was assigned to Aaron, Hiroshi, who had just arrived from Osaka, and Lorraine.

BUT: That emergency procedure was assigned to Aaron; Hiroshi, who had just arrived from Osaka; and Lorraine.

If commas do not occur within the series but do occur elsewhere in a sentence, use commas to separate the items within the series.

> If it is convenient for you, you may schedule the appointment on Tuesday, Wednesday, or Thursday of next week. *(Not: "Tuesday; Wednesday; or Thursday")*

► COLONS

Another title for this section could be "Announcing the Colon" because that is exactly what the colon does. It announces a list, rule, explanation, and the like. When typing, leave one space after a colon; do not begin the following word with a capital letter.

Rule 14. Explanatory Material Use a colon to introduce explanatory material that is preceded by an independent clause. Expressions commonly used to introduce explanatory material are *the following, as follows, this,* and *these.*

> His directions were as follows: turn right and proceed to the third house on the left.
>
> I now have openings on the following dates: January 18, 19, and 20.
>
> Just remember this: you may need a reference from her in the future.
>
> The fall trade show offers the following advantages: inexpensive show space, abundant traffic, and free press publicity.
>
> The new contract contains a number of improvements: one more personal day off, flexible work schedules, and cafeteria-type benefits.
>
> There is only one word to describe Leroy's behavior: boorish. *(Use a colon even if what follows is a single word.)*

Make sure the clause preceding the explanatory material can stand alone as a complete sentence. Do not place a colon after a verb or a preposition that introduces a listing.

> NOT: I now have openings on: January 18, 19, and 20.
> BUT: I now have openings on January 18, 19, and 20.
>
> NOT: My responsibilities were: opening the mail, sorting it, and delivering it to each department.
> BUT: My responsibilities were opening the mail, sorting it, and delivering it to each department.

Do use a colon, however, if the items following a verb or preposition are listed on separate lines.

> The members include:
> 1. Roger Axelrod
> 2. Wanda Hunicutt
> 3. Woody Slades

> The menu consists of:
> Caesar salad
> Roast duckling
> Vegetable medley
> Key lime pie

► QUOTATION MARKS

Quotation marks are used for direct quotations, for expressions needing special attention, and for titles of certain publications. Commas and periods always go inside the closing quotation mark; colons and semicolons always go outside. Question marks and exclamation points go inside if they apply only to the quoted matter; they go outside if they apply to the entire sentence.

Rule 15. Direct Quotation   Use quotation marks before and after a direct quotation—that is, the *exact* words of a person.

> "When we return on Thursday," Akira said, "we need to meet with you." *(Note the placement of commas and periods inside quotation marks.)*
>
> BUT: Akira said that when we return on Thursday, we need to meet with you. *(No quotation marks are needed in an indirect quotation.)*

> Did Marvin say, "He will represent us"?
>
> Marvin asked, "Will he represent us?"

Note in the last two sentences above, when the quoted matter is itself a question, the question mark comes *before* the closing quotation mark; when the entire sentence is a question, the question mark comes *after* the closing quotation mark. (The same is true for exclamation points.) Note also that one terminal mark of punctuation is sufficient. For example, in the last sentence above, a period does not follow the closing quotation mark—even though the entire sentence is a statement.

Rule 16. Special Attention   Use quotation marks around an expression that needs special attention.

> Net income after taxes is known as "the bottom line"; that's what's important around here. *(Semicolons and colons go outside the closing quotation mark.)*
>
> The job title changed from "chairperson" to "chief executive officer." *(Periods and commas go inside the closing quotation marks.)*
>
> All items marked "hazardous" must be disposed of according to federal guidelines.
>
> Please bring me the file folder labeled "Hudson Project."

Rule 17. Title   Use quotation marks around the title of a newspaper or magazine article, chapter in a book, report, conference, and similar items.

> Read the article entitled "Wall Street Recovery."
>
> Chapter 4, "Market Segmentation," of *Industrial Marketing* is of special interest.
>
> The theme of this year's sales conference is "Quality Sells."
>
> The report "Common Carriers" shows the extent of the transportation problems.

Note: The titles of *complete* published works are shown in italics (see Rule 20 below). The titles of *parts* of published works and most other titles are enclosed in quotation marks.

▶ ITALICS

Before the advent of word processing software, underlining was used to emphasize words or indicate certain titles. Today, the use of italics is preferred for these functions.

Rule 18. Word Used as a Word   Italicize a word used as a word. Such expressions are used as nouns in the sentence and are often introduced by the expression *the word* or *the term*.

> The word *angry* doesn't begin to explain the intensity of my reaction.
>
> Are you aware of the real meaning of *edify*?
>
> Should you capitalize the preposition *with* in the title of a book?

Rule 19. Emphasis   Italicize a word or phrase for special emphasis. (To ensure that such italicized expressions do, in fact, receive special emphasis, employ this use of italics sparingly.)

> For the hundredth time, I will *not* agree to chair that task force.

Rule 20. Title   Italicize the title of a book, magazine, newspaper, and other *complete* published works.

> Irene's book, *All That Glitters*, was reviewed in *The New York Times* and in the *Atlantic Monthly*.
>
> The cover story in last week's *Time* magazine was "Is the Economic Expansion Over?"

 ## HYPHENS

Use hyphens to form some compound adjectives and numbers and to divide words at the ends of lines. When typing, do not leave a space before or after a regular hyphen. Likewise, do not use a hyphen with a space before and after to substitute for a dash.

Rule 21. Compound Adjectives   Hyphenate a compound adjective that comes *before* a noun (unless the adjective is a proper noun or unless the first word is an adverb ending in -*ly*).

> We hired a first-class management team.
>
> BUT: Our new management team is first class.

> The long-term outlook for our investments is excellent.
>
> BUT: We intend to hold our investments for the long term.
>
> BUT: The General Motors warranty received high ratings.
>
> BUT: Beryl presented a poorly conceived proposal.

Note: Don't confuse compound adjectives (which are generally temporary combinations) with compound nouns (which are generally well-established concepts). Compound nouns (such as *Social Security, life insurance, word processing,* and *high school*) are not hyphenated when used as adjectives that come before a noun.

> income tax form   real estate agent
>
> public relations firm   data processing center

Rule 22. Numbers   Hyphenate fractions and compound numbers 21 through 99 when they are spelled out.

> Nearly three-fourths of our new applicants were unqualified.
>
> Seventy-two orders were processed incorrectly last week.

► APOSTROPHES

Apostrophes are used to show that letters have been omitted (as in contractions) and to show possession. When typing, do not space before or after an apostrophe (unless a space after is needed before another word).

Remember this helpful hint: Whenever a noun ending in -*s* is followed by another noun, the first noun is probably a possessive, requiring an apostrophe. However, if the first noun *describes* rather than establishes ownership, no apostrophe is used.

Wayne's department *(Shows ownership; therefore, an apostrophe)*

the sales department *(Describes; therefore, no apostrophe)*

Rule 23. Singular Nouns   To form the possessive of a singular noun, add an apostrophe plus *s*.

my accountant's fee	a child's toy
the company's stock	Ellen's choice
Alzheimer's disease	Mr. and Mrs. Dye's home
a year's time	the boss's contract
Ms. Morris's office	Liz's promotion
Gil Hodges's record	Carl Bissett, Jr.'s birthday

Rule 24. Plural Nouns Ending in -s   To form the possessive of a plural noun that ends in -*s* (that is, most plural nouns), add an apostrophe only.

our accountants' fees	both companies' stock
the Dyes' home	two years' time

Rule 25. Plural Nouns Not Ending in -s   To form the possessive of a plural noun that does not end in -*s*, add an apostrophe plus *s* (just as you would for singular nouns).

the children's hour	the men's room
the alumni's contribution	the mice's diet

Hint: To avoid confusion in forming the possessive of plural nouns, first form the plural; then apply the appropriate rule to the plural form.

Singular	*Plural*	*Plural Possessive*
employee	employees	employees' bonuses
hero	heroes	heroes' welcome
Mr. and Mrs. Lake	the Lakes	the Lakes' home
lady	ladies	ladies' clothing

Rule 26. Indefinite Pronouns   To form the possessive of an indefinite pronoun, add an apostrophe plus *s*. Do not use an apostrophe to form the possessive of a personal pronoun. Examples of indefinite possessive pronouns are *anybody's, everyone's, no one's, nobody's, one's,* and *somebody's.* Examples of personal possessive pronouns are *hers, his, its, ours, theirs,* and *yours.*

It is someone's responsibility.

BUT: The responsibility is theirs.

I will review everybody's figures.

BUT: The bank will review its figures.

Note: Do not confuse the possessive pronouns *its, theirs,* and *whose* with the contractions *it's, there's,* and *who's.*

It's time to put litter in *its* place.

There's no reason to take *theirs.*

Who's determining *whose* jobs will be eliminated?

Rule 27. Gerunds Use the possessive form for a noun or pronoun that comes before a gerund. (A gerund is the *-ing* form of a verb used as a noun.)

Garth questioned *Karen's* leaving so soon.

Stockholders' raising so many questions delayed the adjournment.

Mr. Matsumoto knew Karl and objected to *his* going to the meeting.

 ## SUMMARY

Here are the punctuation rules we have learned in this module. Would you be able to apply all of them correctly in your on-the-job writing?

Commas

1. Use a comma between two independent clauses joined by a coordinate conjunction.
2. Use a comma between two adjacent adjectives that modify the same noun.
3. Use a comma between each item in a series of three or more.
4. Use a comma after an introductory expression.
5. Use commas before and after a nonrestrictive expression.
6. Use commas before and after an interrupting expression.
7. Use commas before and after the year when it follows the month and day.
8. Use commas before and after a state or country that follows a city and between elements of an address in narrative writing.
9. Use commas before and after a name used in direct address.
10. Use commas before and after a direct quotation in a sentence.

Semicolons

11. If a misreading might otherwise occur, use a semicolon to separate independent clauses that contain internal commas.
12. Use a semicolon between two independent clauses that are not connected by a coordinate conjunction.
13. Use a semicolon after each item in a series if any of the items already contain a comma.

Colons

14. Use a colon to introduce explanatory material that is preceded by an independent clause.

Quotation Marks

15. Use quotation marks around a direct quotation.
16. Use quotation marks around an expression that needs special attention.

17. Use quotation marks around the title of a newspaper or magazine article, chapter in a book, report, conference, and similar items.

Italics

18. Italicize a word used as a word.
19. Italicize a word or phrase for special emphasis.
20. Italicize the title of a book, magazine, newspaper, and other *complete* published works.

Hyphens

21. Hyphenate a compound adjective that comes *before* a noun (unless the adjective is a proper noun or unless the first word is an adverb ending in -ly).
22. Hyphenate fractions and compound numbers 21 through 99 when they are spelled out.

Apostrophes

23. To form the possessive of a singular noun, add an apostrophe plus *s*.
24. To form the possessive of a plural noun that ends in -*s*, add an apostrophe only.
25. To form the possessive of a plural noun that does not end in -*s*, add an apostrophe plus *s*.
26. To form the possessive of an indefinite pronoun, add an apostrophe plus *s*.
27. Use the possessive form for a noun or pronoun that comes before a gerund.

EXERCISES

Commas

1. Insert any needed commas in the following sentences.

   a. Aldo had the time for as well as much interest in serving as program chair.
   b. Any network administrator who speaks Spanish may attend the international conference.
   c. Drivers start your engines.
   d. Emerson Company plans to close 30 plants and move much of its production to Mexico.
   e. Huo was first in line but even so she did not get into the arena until noon.
   f. If you will do the research analyze the data and draft the report I'll edit proofread and format it.
   g. In the beginning we did not charge for this extra service.
   h. Ireland Scotland and Wales are on her agenda.
   i. Loretta's recipe which received the most votes won the bake-off.
   j. Lori's new address is 1323 Charleston Avenue Portsmouth VA 23701.
   k. Margarita is scheduled to visit Ireland Scotland and Wales.
   l. Mr. Len signed the revision to the contract in Seattle in April 2005.
   m. Our president April Parker will address the conference.
   n. Please sign the revision to the contract in Bonn Germany on 3 April 2005.
   o. President April Parker will address the conference.

Online Study Center college.hmco.com/pic/oberSASfund

2. Insert any needed punctuation in the following sentences.

   a. Running the marathon on that snowy day while still nursing a cold and suffering from an upset stomach was a real challenge.

   b. Selling in Asia is a complex time consuming task.

   c. That was a startling development wouldn't you say?

   d. The drive was exhausting but Jeremy enjoyed the scenery.

   e. Our new network administrator who speaks Spanish will attend the international conference.

   f. The new desktop computer replaces a four-year-old model.

   g. "The new policy will start on May 1" Ms. Yang replied "and will continue for the remainder of the year."

   h. The recipe that received the most votes won the contest.

   i. The revision to the contract was signed on April 3 2005 in Seattle Washington.

   j. The weather cooperated and we finished painting early.

   k. This problem by the way was at least partially caused by the new tax laws.

   l. We did not charge for this extra service in the beginning.

   m. Welcome Class of 2011 to our orientation assembly; we hope you enjoy your stay here.

   n. "Who will be transferred" Maria asked.

   o. Yin was nevertheless still willing to cooperate.

Semicolons and Colons

3. Insert any needed punctuation in the following sentences.

   a. Adriana reviewed the operations in South Carolina Tennessee and North Carolina and Virginia reviewed the operations in Pennsylvania.

   b. Dario visited the Hertford Ahoskie and Windsor plants and Marilyn visited the Williamston and Greenville plants.

   c. Here is what you will need 3 yards of fabric a staple gun and plenty of patience.

   d. The dates under consideration are November 3 2007 November 27 2007 and January 13 2008.

   e. The expectation was for a small profit by the end of the first year the reality was that we didn't make a profit for three years.

   f. The point to remember is this all expenses must be accompanied by receipts.

   g. We expected a small profit at the end of the first year but the reality was that we didn't make a profit for three years.

   h. You will need 3 yards of fabric a staple gun and plenty of patience.

   i. Your presentation was not just acceptable it was fantastic.

Quotation Marks, Italics, and Hyphens

4. Insert any needed punctuation in the following sentences. Underline an expression that should be shown in italics. [*Note:* Sentences (a) to (c) contain direct quotations.]

   a. A lot of the criticism is misguided Bill Ford said I don't know what tougher steps I could have taken

   b. Did Karina say I was unprepared for the fallout

   c. Karina said Were you prepared for the fallout

d. All visitors must sign the register before being granted access into the building. *(Emphasize the third word in this sentence.)*

e. President Reagan was known as the Great Communicator

f. That rarely used parliamentary procedure caused a time consuming delay

g. The article entitled Nice Guy, Knows Karate appeared in the April issue of Forbes magazine

h. The Best Western hotel chain recently remodeled two thirds of its properties

i. The word facetious contains all five vowels in order

j. The word processing center is a well run operation

Apostrophes

5. Insert any needed apostrophes in the following sentences.

a. After five minutes rest from painting my offices, they will paint yours.

b. Doris Cermaks updating of the lobbies furnishings was hugely successful.

c. Mens wallets and womens handbags are featured in this weeks sale.

d. The Browns auwtomobile is two weeks newer than the Wilsons.

e. The inns guests complained about the geeses honking.

f. The mayors voted to require three years experience for the new position.

g. Those peoples reports were prepared on the secretaries computers.

Punctuation

6. Insert any needed punctuation in the following letter.

In accordance with the law I have enclosed twenty five copies of the Annual Report to Shareholders for the fiscal year ended December 31 2006. This report is being sent today by first class mail to shareholders of the above company and we are providing copies to the business press as well.

I am advised by the corporations accountants that the financial statements appearing in this annual report do not reflect a change from the preceding years report in any accounting principles or practices or in the method of applying any such principles or practices.

7. Insert any needed punctuation in the following memo.

In my opinion the Smith and Miller Company would be able to collect against our company for late delivery of its order for 45 desk lamps.

The terms of our agreement specified delivery to its client the Pine Cliff Inn on or before January 31. Delivery was made within eight days. Although the opening date of the inn had been changed to February 11 the customers refusal to accept the shipment had far reaching implications. The fact that the opening date of the Pine Cliff Inn was changed is not grounds for a collection suit against Smith and Miller.

I think it would be worthwhile for you to go ahead with plans to secure acceptance of the order if you can reach a reasonable settlement. We may be forced to take a small loss on the transaction it would be quite difficult for us to sell these specially constructed lamps to our regular customers.

C Verbs and Subject-Verb Agreement

▶ VERB FUNCTIONS

As we learned in Module A, a verb expresses either physical or mental action (known, logically enough, as an *action verb*) or a state of being (known as a *linking verb*).

Action Verbs

Action verbs may be either active or passive and either transitive or intransitive. A *transitive verb* requires a direct object to complete its meaning; that is, a transitive verb requires something (a noun or pronoun) to receive the action of the verb.

> Gail *typed* the medical report. *("Medical report" receives the action of the transitive verb "typed.")*

> The board of directors gave the president a pay raise. *("Pay raise" receives the action of the transitive verb "gave." Note that "president" is an indirect object.)*

An *intransitive verb*, on the other hand, does not require an object. Thus, nothing receives the action of the verb. Although other words may follow the verb, they are used as complements or modifiers—not as objects.

> I *smiled.*

> I *smiled* weakly. *("Weakly" is an adverb modifying the intransitive verb "smiled"; it does not receive the action of the verb.)*

> Greer *walked* into a room full of inquisitive reporters.

Some verbs are always transitive; other verbs are always intransitive. As is true for the parts of speech, however, whether a verb is transitive or intransitive often depends on how it is used in the sentence, as illustrated below:

> TRANSITIVE: The doctor *increased* my dosage of Celebrex.
> INTRANSITIVE: Interest rates *increased* rapidly.

> TRANSITIVE: Lena *grew* flowers on her patio.
> INTRANSITIVE: Lena *grew* increasingly anxious.

Why is it important to know the difference between transitive and intransitive verbs? First, you must understand the difference between transitive and intransitive verbs so you do not confuse frequently misused irregular verbs (such as *lie–lay, sit–set,* and *rise–raise*).

Second, when looking up a verb in the dictionary, you must know whether it is transitive or intransitive to be able to use the new word correctly. Note, for example, the definitions of *swoon* found in the fourth edition of the *American Heritage College Dictionary:*

swoon (swoon) *intr. v.* **swooned, swoon·ing, swoons. 1.** To faint. **2.** To be over-powered by ecstatic joy. —n. **1.** a fainting spell; syncope. **2.** a state of ecstasy or rapture.

Note that the verb *swoon* is always intransitive (*intr. v.*) and thus may not be followed by an object. Therefore, to say, "the witness swooned" or "the witnesses swooned at the sight of the defendant" would be correct, but to say, "the witness swooned the defendant" would be incorrect.

Linking Verbs

Recall from Module A that a small (but important) group of verbs do not express action but instead simply link the subject with words in the predicate. The most common linking verbs are forms of the verb *to be* and verbs involving the senses. Below is a list of the most common linking verbs. Keep in mind that some of these verbs may also function as action verbs, depending on their use in the sentence.

am	been	look	taste
appear	being	seem	was
are	feel	smell	were
be	is	sound	

Linking verbs do not have a voice (that is, they are neither active nor passive). Because they are always intransitive, they cannot take an object. Instead, they may be followed by a complement (either a noun or a pronoun that renames the subject) or by an adjective that describes the subject. The linking verbs in the following sentences are italicized:

> Catherine Nickersen *is* our new advertising director. *("Our new advertising director" is a noun that renames the subject "Catherine Nickersen.")*

> Today's weather *has been* cool. *("Cool" is an adjective that describes the subject "weather.")*

> Those new cookies *taste* great. *("Great" is an adjective that describes the subject "cookies." Note, however, that in the sentence, "Did John taste the new cookies?" the verb "taste" is a transitive verb, with "cookies" serving as the direct object.)*

If you have trouble deciding whether a verb is a linking verb or a transitive verb, try substituting an equals sign (=) for the verb. If it makes sense, the verb is linking. Applying this hint to the sentences above, we would have:

> Catherine Nickersen = our new advertising director. *(Makes sense, so the verb "is" is a linking verb)*

> Today's weather = cool. *(Makes sense, so the verb "has been" is a linking verb)*

> Those new cookies = great. *(Makes sense, so the verb "taste" is a linking verb)*

> John = the new cookies. *(Does not make sense, so the verb "taste" in this sentence is a transitive verb)*

Helping Verbs

A *helping verb* is used before the main verb to build a verb phrase and thus make the main verb more precise. For example, in the sentence "The pie has been eaten," the main verb is *eaten* and the helping verbs are *has been*. The helping verb *has been* makes the time of the action more precise (as compared to, for example, "The pie *will be* eaten"). The most common helping verbs are the following:

am	can	had	might	were
are	could	has	must	will
be	did	have	shall	would
been	do	is	should	
being	does	may	was	

▶ PRINCIPAL PARTS OF VERBS

The four parts of a verb, on which all verb tenses are formed, are the present, past, past participle, and present participle. They are formed differently, depending on whether the verb is regular or irregular.

Regular Verbs

A *regular verb* forms the past tense and past participle by adding *d* or *ed* to the present tense. The present participle of all verbs (regular or irregular) is formed by adding *ing* to the present tense. Most verbs are regular.

Present	*Past*	*Past Participle*	*Present Participle*
follow	followed	(has) followed	(is) following
occur	occurred	(has) occurred	(is) occurring

Note that the identifying terms *present* and *past* above each comprise one word, and all verbs in the present and past tenses comprise one word. The identifying terms *past participle* and *present participle* each comprise more than one word, and all past participle and present participle verbs comprise more than one word. The helping verbs for the past participle are *have, has,* or *had.* The helping verbs for the present participle are *is, am, are, was, were, be,* or *been.*

To choose the correct present-tense verb, say to yourself, "Today, I _____" and then fill in the blank. To choose the correct past-tense verb, say, "Yesterday, I _____." To choose the correct past participle, say, "I have _____" and to choose the correct present participle, say, "I am _____." For example:

> Today, I *try. (Present)*
>
> Yesterday, I *tried. (Past)*
>
> I have *tried. (Past participle)*
>
> I am *trying. (Present participle)*

This simple memory device works for both regular and irregular verbs.

Irregular Verbs

Most people (whether native English speakers or English-as-second-language [ESL] speakers) have little difficulty using regular verbs correctly. Fortunately, most verbs are regular. Several verbs (called *irregular verbs*), however, do not form the past tense and past participle by adding *d* or *ed.* Because irregular verbs do not form their past tense and past participles in any consistent fashion, you will simply need to learn the different forms of these verbs. Do not confuse the past participle with the past tense of irregular verbs.

> **NOT:** Her blouse *shrunk* when she washed it.
>
> **BUT:** Her blouse *shrank* when she washed it.

NOT: Mr. Vasilev *begun* to read aloud his statement.

BUT: Mr. Vasilev *began* to read aloud his statement.

Similarly, do not confuse the past tense with the past participle.

NOT: Jessica had already *broke* the rules by arriving late.

BUT: Jessica had already *broken* the rules by arriving late.

NOT: I have *sank* that putt numerous times.

BUT: I have *sunk* that putt numerous times.

Three pairs of irregular verbs deserve special consideration because of their frequent misuse. Here are their principal parts:

Present	Past	Past Participle	Present Participle
lay (to place)	laid	laid	laying
lie (to recline)	lay	lain	lying
raise (to lift)	raised	raised	raising
rise (to ascend)	rose	risen	rising
set (to place)	set	set	setting
sit (to rest)	sat	sat	sitting

The first verb in each group *(lay, raise, set)* is transitive, meaning that it will always require a direct object. The second verb in each group *(lie, rise, sit)* is intransitive and is not followed by a direct object. Here is a memory aid: The three intransitive verbs all contain the letter *i*; associate that *i* with *intransitive*.

The direct objects in the following sentences are italicized.

Please lay your *books* on the table and lie down to relax.

Raise your *hand* and rise when you take the oath of office.

I will set the *report* on the table and then sit for a while.

She laid her *books* on the table and lay down to relax.

He raised his *hand* and rose when he took the oath of office.

I set the *report* on the table and then sat for a while.

She had laid her *books* on the table and was lying down to relax when the doorbell rang.

He had raised his *hand* and was rising when the judged walked in.

I had set the *report* on the table and was now sitting in the audience.

▶ SUBJECT AND VERB AGREEMENT

The basic rule of subject-verb agreement is this: Use a singular verb with a singular subject and a plural verb with a plural subject. (Your subject and verb will then *agree*.) To make the subject and verb agree, you must, of course, first be able to identify the subject and verb. In many sentences, doing so is easy:

Sarah needs the contract for the new lease.

The *accountants* want to verify the financial terms of the lease.

In the first sentence, *Sarah* is the subject; *needs* is the verb. Both are singular; that is, they agree. In the second sentence, *accountants* is the subject; *want* is the verb. Both are plural, meaning that they also agree. Note that most nouns become plural by adding *s*; however, most verbs become plural by omitting *s*. Thus, one *s* in the subject-verb combination is usually *just right*: "Sarah need<u>s</u>" or "accountant<u>s</u> want."

Compound Subjects

When two subjects are joined by *and*, the subject is plural and requires a plural verb.

> Ms. Qasim *and* Ms. Olson <u>make</u> this presentation every quarter.
> The driver of the bus *and* two passengers <u>were</u> injured in the accident.
> The paralegal *and* his supervisor <u>are</u> proofreading the deposition.

Note: To focus attention on subject-verb agreement, only the part of the verb that changes is underlined in these examples. For example, in the last example, the complete verb is *are proofreading*. Because *proofreading* remains the same whether the verb is singular or plural, however, only *are* is underlined.

Here is one exception to our rule (Aren't there exceptions to all rules?): If the two subjects connected by *and* are preceded by the word *each* or *every*, the subject is singular and requires a singular verb.

> *Each* lease and purchase agreement <u>is</u> reviewed for tax purposes.
> *Every* man, woman, and child <u>is</u> eligible for medical coverage.
> **BUT:** The *man, woman, and child* <u>are</u> eligible for medical coverage.

When two subjects are joined by *or, either/or, nor, neither/nor,* or *not only/but also,* the verb must agree with the subject closer to it. In other words, it doesn't matter whether the other subject (the one farther from the verb) is singular or plural.

> Monday or *Tuesday* <u>is</u> a good day for the conference.
> Mondays or *Tuesdays* <u>are</u> good days for the conference.
> The managers or their *assistant* <u>is</u> required to attend.
> Not only the computer but also the *printers* <u>are</u> to be upgraded.
> Not only the computer but also the *printer* <u>is</u> to be upgraded.
> Not only the computers but also the *printer* <u>is</u> to be upgraded.

Indefinite Pronouns as Subjects

An *indefinite pronoun* is a word that stands for a noun but that does not refer to a *specific* noun. Examples are *all, somebody, one, several,* and *everything*. When used as subjects or as adjectives that modify subjects, some indefinite pronouns are always singular, some are always plural, and some may be either singular or plural, depending on how they are used in the sentence.

The following indefinite pronouns are always singular and require a singular verb:

another	either	much	one
each	every	neither	

Plus: all pronouns ending with *body, one,* or *thing.*

> *Each* <u>is</u> required to notify the agency within two days. *("Each" is the subject.)*

Each company <u>is</u> required to notify the lease agency within two days.
("Each" modifies the subject "company.")

Much <u>remains</u> to be done.

Everybody <u>has</u> to contribute to the effort.

Neither <u>is</u> correct.

Neither of the offices <u>was</u> large enough for our purposes.

Note in the last two sentences above that when *neither* appears by itself as the subject, it is always singular; but when it appears in a *neither/nor* combination, it may be singular or plural, depending on the noun closer to the verb. The same is true, of course, for *either* and *either/or*.

The following indefinite pronouns are always plural and require a plural verb:

both   few   many   others   several

Many <u>are</u> called but *few* <u>are</u> chosen.

A *few* <u>were</u> chosen.

The *others* <u>are</u> awaiting our decision.

Several files <u>are</u> missing.

Several of the files <u>are</u> missing.

The following indefinite pronouns may be singular or plural, depending on the noun they refer to:

all   none   any   some   more   most

All of the *report* <u>has</u> to be retyped. *(All of one thing)*

All of the *reports* <u>have</u> to be retyped. *(All of several things)*

Some *effort* <u>was</u> spent on reading her handwriting. *(Some of one thing)*

Some *grievances* <u>were</u> referred to the arbitrator. *(Some of several things)*

Measurements

Expressions of time, money, and quantity generally refer to *total amounts* and are singular. Only when emphasizing the *individual units* of time, money, and quantity would you use a plural verb.

Three weeks was too long to spend on this project. *(Refers to a total amount)*

For me, *$15* was a high price to pay for admission. *(Refers to a total amount)*

BUT: *Two full days* were required to update the financial information. *(Emphasizes the individual units)*

Fractions and portions may be singular or plural, depending on the noun they refer to.

Half of the *time* was spent in updating the financial information.

Three-fourths of the *reports* are still in need of updating.

A minimum of *effort* is needed for the project.

A large percentage of the *voters* were uninformed on the issue.

The expression *the number* refers to one thing and is singular; the expression *a number* refers to more than one thing and is plural.

The number of complaints has decreased dramatically.

A number of these complaints have involved the packaging of the napkins.

Special Types of Subjects

Proper nouns (such as company names, names of products, and titles of publications), collective nouns, and clauses beginning with *who, which,* or *that* require special consideration when determining subject-verb agreement.

Company Names, Products, and Publication Titles   Company and product names and publication titles are considered singular, even though they may look like they are plural in form. It helps to remember that in each case, we're talking about just one thing.

> *Standard & Poor's* is a financial information company. *(One company)*
>
> *Shake 'n Bake* is what I will prepare for dinner tonight. *(One product)*
>
> *Consumer Reports* is on my required reading list each month. *(One magazine)*
>
> *The Agony and the Ecstasy* is my all-time favorite novel. *(One book)*

Collective Nouns   A *collective noun* is a word that is singular in form (such as *committee, company, department, group,* and *team*) but that represents a group of people or things. In general, consider collective nouns as singular.

> The *committee* is finishing up its assignments this afternoon.
>
> Our *board of directors* meets on the first Friday of each quarter.

Who, Which, and That Clauses   Verbs that follow *who, which,* or *that* clauses must agree with the word these pronouns refer to. Most of the time, this word comes immediately before the pronoun. *Hint:* For purposes of determining which verb to use after these pronouns, mentally delete the pronoun.

> *Hester,* who <u>is</u> one of our best employees, won the "I Care" award last month.
> *(Hester <u>is</u> one of our best employees.)*
>
> *Hoshiko and Lester,* who <u>are</u> also excellent employees, were the runners-up.
> *(Hoshiko and Lester <u>are</u> also excellent employees.)*
>
> The new *desk,* which <u>belongs</u> to Mr. Davenport, is in the hall.
> *(The desk <u>belongs</u> to Mr. Davenport.)*

EXERCISES

Verb Functions

1. **Action Verbs**   Complete the following sentences and then indicate whether the verb is transitive or intransitive (T *or* I).

Transitive or Intransitive

a. Ruth threw _____   _____

b. Jesús will speak _____   _____

c. Today is _____   _____

d. This past week has been _____   _____

e. Rita has taken_____   _____

f. Your plan sounds_____   _____

g. Beth read_____   _____

h. I gave _____   _____

2. **Linking and Helping Verbs**   Underline each linking verb once and each helping verb twice in the following sentences.

a. Catherine will be able to pay for the refreshments from petty cash.

b. I am at a loss for words.

c. I am going to pursue that lead tomorrow.

d. Ms. Ortega could not have been thinking when she made that remark.

e. That seems like a tremendous amount of work.

f. We can still get there on time if we hurry.

Principal Parts of Verbs

3. Circle the correct verb in parentheses in the following sentences.

a. Don't just (sit, set) there; do something.

b. Dr. Hashimoto has (wore, worn) out his welcome with us.

c. He (sat, set) down at the head chair.

d. He (sat, set) down his books and began playing the piano.

e. I felt like I had (ate, eaten) enough for three people.

f. I have already (broke, broken) in my new baseball glove.

g. I'm glad you have (chose, chosen) to continue your education here.

h. Just (lay, lie) down until the nausea subsides.

i. Kathryn (began, begun) work on the inventory project immediately.

j. They had (lay, laid, lain) the folders on the file cabinet.

k. We (saw, seen) the intersection where the accident occurred.

l. We (see, seen) several opportunities to cut costs.

Subject and Verb Agreement

4. **Basic Rule of Agreement**   Circle the correct verb in parentheses in the following sentences.

   a. One of the companies (need, needs) an effective turnaround strategy.

   b. I (has, have) seriously considered the consequences of this action.

   c. They (was, were) not aware that the federal regulations had changed.

   d. You both (has, have) been selected to work on the project.

   e. Taxes (are, is) the most important issue.

   f. On the shelf behind all those plants (are, is) the backup file.

   g. The box of ribbons and cartridges (was, were) stored in Warehouse 3.

5. **Subjects**   Circle the correct verb in parentheses in the following sentences.

   a. Both September and October (are, is) good months for the trial run.

   b. Each hamburger and hot dog (require, requires) a different type of wrapper.

   c. Either the Chamber of Commerce or the Federal Reserve (are, is) predicting a low rate of inflation next quarter.

   d. Every Monday, Wednesday, and Friday (are, is) considered a file-backup day.

   e. Expenses or salaries (has, have) to be adjusted.

   f. James and Arvetta (has, have) to prepare the quarterly FICA statements.

   g. Neither personal checks nor money orders (are, is) acceptable for payment.

   h. Not only the marketing division but also the manufacturing division (has, have) to come into compliance.

   i. The two tables and one wide chair (need, needs) to be moved to the conference room.

6. **Indefinite Pronouns**   Circle the correct verb in parentheses in the following sentences.

   a. All of the agenda items (was, were) covered during the meeting.

   b. All of the cake (was, were) eaten before the meeting ended.

   c. Any one of the computer manuals (are, is) sure to contain the solution.

   d. Both employees (want, wants) to apply for the position.

   e. Each (has, have) to be considered on its own merits.

   f. Each grievance (has, have) to be addressed in our response.

   g. Either of the two alternatives (satisfies, satisfy) the diversity objective.

   h. Many of the new employees in the accounting area (need, needs) to be tested.

   i. More than one customer (has, have) complimented us on the design of our logo.

   j. Most of the problem (was, were) due to poor communication.

   k. Much (has, have) been accomplished in the past few weeks.

   l. Neither of the alternatives (are, is) acceptable.

   m. Neither one of the secretaries (take, takes) shorthand.

   n. Several new vendors (was, were) considered for the contract.

   o. Some of the assemblers (has, have) already met their quotas.

   p. Something (seem, seems) suspicious about the low bid.

   q. Two temporaries reported yesterday; another (are, is) due to report tomorrow.

7. **Measurements**   Circle the correct verb in parentheses in the following sentences.

   a. A majority of the committee members (agree, agrees) with our proposal.
   b. A number of trials (was, were) necessary before we got it right.
   c. A small percentage of the budget (was, were) spent on entertainment.
   d. I thought that $100 (was, were) too much to spend on a going-away gift.
   e. Nearly two-thirds of the workers (are, is) also covered by their spouses' insurance.
   f. That $5,000 (was, were) spent within two weeks.
   g. The five corner lots (are, is) to be auctioned at noon.
   h. The number of team members (depend, depends) on the complexity of the task.
   i. Three-fourths of the document (refer, refers) to OSHA requirements.

8. **Special Types of Subjects**   Circle the correct verb in parentheses in the following sentences.

   a. *Bob and Tom* (are, is) my favorite radio talk show.
   b. Brooks Brothers (are, is) having a sale on men's lightweight suits.
   c. Microsoft (has, have) been sued by the federal government as well as several states.
   d. Our department (are, is) extremely angry about the change in coverage.
   e. *Pride and Prejudice* (was, were) an alternate selection for the company-sponsored play.
   f. The AlphaSmart is a basic word processing device that (cost, costs) only $250.
   g. The evaluators, who (was, were) present for the demonstration, are still deliberating.
   h. The ISO 9000 team (are, is) scheduled to report next month.
   i. The pieces of evidence, which (are, is) still in custody, are not challenged by our counsel.
   j. The team players (are, is) scheduled to have a dress rehearsal Friday evening.

D Using Pronouns, Adjectives, and Adverbs

▶ PRONOUNS

As noted earlier, pronouns are little words that can cause big problems—until, that is, you study this module. Although many thousands of nouns (*millions*, if you include proper nouns) exist, the English language includes fewer than 100 pronouns. The most common pronouns are listed below:

all	few	nobody	someone	which
another	he	none	something	whichever
any	her	no one	that	who
anybody	hers	nothing	their	whoever
anyone	him	one	theirs	whom
anything	his	one another	them	whomever
both	I	ones	these	whose
each	it	other	they	whosoever
each one	its	our	this	you
each other	many	ours	those	your
either	me	several	us	yours
everybody	mine	she	we	
everyone	my	some	what	
everything	neither	somebody	whatever	

Because pronouns take the place of nouns, your first job is to ensure that the noun the pronoun replaces is clear. Consider, for example, the following sentence:

> Robin explained the proposal to Joy, but *she* was not happy with it.

Who was not happy with the proposal—Robin or Joy? It is not clear from the sentence. This error of writing is called a *vague pronoun reference*. In such a situation, you have no choice but to rename the noun instead of using a pronoun.

> Robin explained the proposal to Joy, but *Robin* was not happy with it.
>
> OR: Robin explained the proposal to Joy, but *Joy* was not happy with it.

The Case of Personal Pronouns

Personal pronouns include the pronouns *I, you, he, she, it,* and *they* and their related forms (such as *my, mine, your, yours, her,* and *us*). The *case* of a personal pronoun indicates how it is used in the sentence (either *nominative, objective,* or *possessive,* which we will explain shortly).

Nominative Case The nominative-case pronouns are *I, we, you, he, she, it,* and *they.* In Table D.1, *person* is the characteristic of a pronoun that indicates whether a person is speaking (first person), being spoken to (second person), or being spoken

TABLE D.1

Nominative Case

	Singular	Plural
First person	I	we
Second person	you	you
Third person:		
Masculine gender	he	they
Feminine gender	she	they
Neuter gender	it	they

about (third person). *Gender* refers to the sex of a pronoun—that is, masculine (*he*), feminine (*she*), or neuter (*it*). A pronoun that can refer to either a male or female (such as *child* or *employee*) is considered to be of *common* gender.

Study Table D.1 to avoid errors in using personal pronouns in the nominative case. Work through this table by inserting each listed pronoun into the sentence "_____ smelled like a rose."

Whenever a pronoun is used as the subject of a verb, it must be in the nominative case.

> *She* manually counted the votes from the first and second precincts. *("She" is the subject of the sentence.)*

> Arthur agreed, but *he* failed to give convincing reasons. *("He" is the subject of the second independent clause.)*

> Cathy wanted to know whether *I* had finished my assignments. *("I" is the subject of the dependent clause.)*

Nominative pronouns are also used as subject complements. Thus, when a pronoun follows a linking verb (such as *am, are, was, were, is,* or *has been*) and renames the subject, it must be in the nominative case.

> It could have been *he* who inadvertently gave away the secret. *(It = he)*

> This is *she. (This = she)*

> If Earl were *he,* he would have acted differently. *(Earl = he)*

> The nominee was expected to be *she. (Nominee = she)*

When a telephone caller asks for you by name, how do you respond? Do you say, "This is him" or "This is her"? Such a response might be tolerated in informal oral communication because it sounds so natural, but it would not be acceptable in writing. Grammatically, of course, you should respond, "This is *he*" or "This is *she.*" However, to avoid sounding pompous, you might opt for the more graceful "This is Johnny" or "This is Jenny."

Objective Case   The objective-case pronouns are *me, us, you, him, her, it,* and *them.* Logically enough, objective-case pronouns serve as *object*—direct objects, indirect objects, or objects of prepositions. Study Table D.2 to avoid errors in using personal pronouns in the objective case. Work through the table by inserting each listed pronoun into the sentence "She thanked _____."

TABLE D.2

Objective Case

	Singular	Plural
First person	me	us
Second person	you	you
Third person:		
Masculine gender	him	them
Feminine gender	her	them
Neuter gender	it	them

▌ **Direct Object**   A pronoun serves as a direct object when it receives the action of the verb.

> Katie asked *me* for help on the project.
>
> The training director asked *them* to complete the exercise.

▌ **Indirect Object**   A pronoun serves as an indirect object when it tells to whom or for whom the action of the verb was done.

> Please give *her* your response by tomorrow afternoon.
>
> Did Fatima hand *him* the papers he needed?

▌ **Object of a Preposition**   The pronoun following the preposition is its object.

> Ms. Batista worked with *me* to complete the examination on time. *("With me" is the prepositional phrase.)*
>
> The monthly revision was handled by *him*. *("By him" is the prepositional phrase.)*

Possessive Case   Possessive-case pronouns show ownership. Most (but not all) personal pronouns have two possessive forms. Work through Table D.3 by inserting the listed pronoun into either the sentence "This is _____ report" or the sentence "This report is _____."

Use *my, our, your, his, her, its,* or *their* when the pronoun comes *before* the noun it modifies. Use *mine, ours, yours, his, hers, its,* or *theirs* when the pronoun comes *after* the noun it modifies.

> This is *my* report.   This report is *mine*.
>
> Mr. Ortiz was *her* colleague.   Mr. Ortiz was a colleague of *hers*.
>
> It is *their* decision.   The decision is *theirs*.

Do not confuse possessive pronouns ending in *s* with contractions. Possessive personal pronouns *never* contain an apostrophe; contractions *always* do.

▌ ***its/it's:*** *Its* is a possessive pronoun; *it's* is a contraction for "it is" or "it has."

> *It's* time to let the department increase *its* budget.

▌ ***their/they're:*** *Their* is a possessive pronoun; *they're* is a contraction for "they are."

> *They're* too busy with *their* work to attend the conference.

TABLE D.3

Possessive Case

	Singular	Plural
First person	my/mine	our/ours
Second person	your/yours	your/yours
Third person:		
Masculine gender	his	their/theirs
Feminine gender	her/hers	their/theirs
Neuter gender	its	their/theirs

▮ ***theirs/there's:*** *Theirs* is a possessive pronoun; *there's* is a contraction for "there is."

> We finished our meal, but *there's* no time for them to finish *theirs.*

▮ ***whose/who's:*** *Whose* is a possessive pronoun; *who's* is a contraction for "who is" or "who has."

> *Who's* going to let us know *whose* turn it is to make coffee?

▮ ***your/you're:*** *Your* is a possessive pronoun; *You're* is a contraction for "you are."

> *You're* going to present *your* report first.

To test for the correct form (possessive pronoun or contraction), mentally substitute the full term for the contraction. If the substitution does not make sense, use the possessive form. For instance, if we make substitutions in the first example above:

> *It is* time to let the department increase *it is* budget.

"It is time" makes sense, so the contraction (with the apostrophe) is correct. "It is budget" does not make sense, so the possessive pronoun (without the apostrophe) is correct.

A *gerund* is the *-ing* form of a verb used as a noun. Use the possessive case for a pronoun that modifies a gerund.

> Antonia questioned *my leaving* so soon. *(Not "me leaving")*
>
> *Their raising* so many questions delayed the adjournment. *(Not "them raising" or "they raising")*
>
> Art objected to *his going* to the meeting. *(Not "him going")*

Remember that gerunds are nouns. If you have trouble with pronouns that modify a gerund, simply substitute another noun for the gerund. For example, revising the sentences above makes clear that the possessive pronoun is the correct form.

> Antonia questioned *my* decision to leave so soon.
>
> *Their* questions delayed the adjournment.
>
> Art objected to *his* presence at the meeting.

Problems in Determining Pronoun Case

Discussed in the following subsections are situations that sometimes cause problems in determining the correct case of pronouns.

Compound Subjects and Objects   Pay special attention to the correct use of pronouns in compound subjects and objects. No one (we hope) would say, "Me is having fun." However, you occasionally hear people say, "Mitzi and me are having fun." To avoid problems like this one, mentally omit the first noun. You can then generally "hear" the correct form of the pronoun.

> NOT: Betty and *me* were having fun.
>
> BUT: Betty and *I* were having fun. *(I was having fun.)*

> NOT: Are L. J. and *them* finished with their audit?
>
> BUT: Are L. J. and *they* finished with their audit? *(Are they finished?)*

> NOT: Mr. Matthews asked Ms. Little and *I* for help.
>
> BUT: Mr. Mathews asked Ms. Little and *me* for help. *(Mr. Matthews asked me for help.)*

> NOT: To Betty and *I*, the solution was obvious.
>
> BUT: To Betty and *me*, the solution was obvious. *(To me, the solution was obvious.)*

Be especially careful with compound objects preceded by *between*. Because *between* is a preposition, the pronoun must be in the objective case.

> NOT: Between Arturo and *I*, we could answer all of the questions.
>
> BUT: Between Arturo and *me*, we could answer all of the questions.

Appositives   When a pronoun is used with an appositive, mentally omit the noun to determine the correct case of the pronoun.

> *We* employees need to speak with one voice. *(We need to speak with one voice.)*
>
> The union wants *us* employees to speak with one voice. *(The union wants us to speak with one voice.)*

Comparisons   When a pronoun follows *than* or *as* in a statement of comparison, sometimes you need to mentally supply any missing words to select the correct form of pronoun.

> NOT: Mr. Liu works harder than *me*.
>
> BUT: Mr. Liu works harder than *I*. *(Mr. Liu works harder than I "do.")*

> NOT: Eduardo is not as creative as *her*.
>
> BUT: Eduardo is not as creative as *she*. *(Eduardo is not as creative as she "is.")*

> NOT: Uncertainty worries the new employees more than *I*.
>
> BUT: Uncertainty worries the new employees more than *me*. *(Uncertainty worries the new employees more than it worries "me.")*

Self Pronouns   The *-self* pronouns are shown in Table D.4. Pronouns ending in *-self* either emphasize the noun or pronoun already expressed or reflect the action to the subject.

TABLE D.4

Self Pronouns

	Singular	Plural
First person	myself	ourselves
Second person	yourself	yourselves
Third person:		
Masculine gender	himself	themselves
Feminine gender	herself	themselves
Neuter gender	itself	themselves

I will tell her *myself. (Emphasizes the pronoun "I")*

Armando *himself* was confused by her statement. *(Emphasizes the noun "Armando")*

Ms. Zhu disappointed *herself* by her inaction to challenge the decision. *(Reflects the action to "Ms. Zhu")*

Never use the words *hisself, ourself, themself,* or *theirselves.* Also, do not use a *-self* pronoun unless the noun or pronoun to which it refers appears in the same sentence.

NOT:　Bruce did the work *hisself.*
BUT:　Bruce did the work *himself.*

NOT:　The award went to Douglas and *myself.*
BUT:　The award went to Douglas and *me.*

Who/Whom　*Who* (or *whoever*) is the nominative form and *whom* (or *whomever*) is the objective form. Here's a hint: if *he* or *she* can be substituted, *who* is the correct choice; if *him* or *her* can be substituted, *whom* is the correct choice *(who = he; whom = him).*

Who is chairing the meeting? *(He is chairing the meeting.)*

Mr. Aguirre wanted to know *who* was responsible. *(He was responsible.)*

To *whom* shall we mail the specifications? *(Mail them to him.)*

Louise is the type of person *who* can be depended upon. *(She can be depended upon.)*

Louise is the type of person *whom* we can depend upon. *(We can depend upon her.)*

▶ ADJECTIVE OR ADVERB?

Recall from Module A that adjectives modify nouns or pronouns and adverbs modify verbs, adjectives, or other adverbs. Modifiers are present in most sentences. Even as short a sentence as "Sit down" contains a modifier.

I tend to be *quiet* when I'm around *assertive* people.

Maurice spoke *very excitedly* about the option that was *less* popular.

Online Study Center college.hmco.com/pic/oberSASfund

In the first sentence, *quiet* is an adjective modifying the pronoun *I*, and *assertive* is an adjective modifying the noun *people*. In the second sentence, *excitedly* is an adverb modifying the verb *spoke*, *very* is an adverb modifying the adverb *excitedly*, and *less* is an adverb modifying the adjective *popular*.

Which of the following two sentences is correct?

The operation runs *smoother* now than it did before.

The operation runs *more smoothly* now than it did before.

To benefit from the instruction that follows, you must, first of all, know the difference between adjectives and adverbs. Because they both modify other words, writers sometimes confuse one with the other. To avoid problems, always identify the word that the adjective or adverb is modifying. If that word is a noun or pronoun, the modifier is an adjective. If it is a verb, an adjective, or another adverb, the modifier is an adverb.

A modifier that follows an action verb is an adverb. A modifier that follows a linking verb is an adjective—not an adverb. Remember that adjectives tend to answer the questions *What kind? How many?* or *Which one?* Adverbs tend to answer the questions *When? How? Where?* or *To what extent?*

The surface of the refinished counter is *smooth*. *("Was" is a linking verb, which requires an adjective.)*

The entire operation ran *smoothly*. *(Not "smooth" because "ran" is an action verb, which requires an adverb)*

The surface of the refinished counter felt *smoother* than the one it replaced. *(Not "more smoothly," because "felt" is a linking verb, which requires an adjective)*

The entire operation runs *more smoothly* now than it did before we installed the new system. *(Not "smoother," which is an adjective)*

Our new variety of yogurt tastes *sweet*. *(Not "sweetly" because "tastes" is a linking verb, which requires an adjective)*

NOT: Giuseppe was *sure* glad that the meeting ended on time. *("Sure" is an adjective and thus cannot modify another adjective.)*

BUT: Giuseppe was *surely* glad that the meeting ended on time. *(The adverb "surely" modifies the adjective "glad.")*

Some words (such as *fast, long, hard, early,* and *better*) can serve as either adjectives or adverbs, depending on how they are used in the sentence.

I read the *first* [adjective telling what kind] draft *first* [adverb telling when], before reading the revisions.

I am *better* [adverb telling to what extent] at math than most people, but it still took me the *better* [adjective telling how much] part of the day to complete the assignment.

Most adverbs end in *-ly*. Most adjectives do not.

Noun	Adjective	Adverb
intention	intentional	intentionally
interest	more interested	interestingly
theory	theoretical	theoretically
truth	truthful	truthfully

However, some adverbs do *not* end in *-ly*, and, to confuse the situation even more, some adjectives *do* end in *-ly*. Shown below are some common examples:

Adverbs Not Ending in -ly		*Adjectives Ending in -ly*	
almost	quite	earthly	lonely
around	soon	fatherly	lovely
down	then	friendly	neighborly
here	very	homely	orderly
now	when	lively	worldly
often			

In the first sentence below, even though they do not end in *-ly*, the words *around, down,* and *here* serve as adverbs because they answer the question *Where? Then* is also an adverb because it answers the question *When?*

> He drove *around* the circle and *then down* the block before he got *here.*
>
> The *lively* discussion of alternatives resulted in a *friendly* debate.
>
> Mr. Alvarado spoke in a *fatherly* manner when addressing the *lonely* teenager.

In the last two sentences, even though they end in *-ly*, the words *lively, friendly, fatherly,* and *lonely* serve as adjectives because they modify nouns and answer the question *What kind?*

► COMPARISON OF ADJECTIVES AND ADVERBS

When we talk about *comparison* of adjectives and adverbs, we simply mean the manner by which an adjective or adverb expresses a greater or lesser degree of the same quality. The three degrees (or *forms*) of an adjective or adverb are *positive, comparative,* and *superlative.*

Regular Comparisons

The positive degree is the basic adjective or adverb; it doesn't compare one with another. Use the comparative degree *(-er, more,* or *less)* to refer to two persons, places, or things and the superlative degree *(-est, most,* or *least)* to refer to more than two.

> I talked *fast. (Positive degree of the adverb "fast")*
>
> I talked *faster* than Rivero. *(Comparative degree of the adverb "fast")*
>
> I talked the *fastest* of the three speakers. *(Superlative degree of the adverb "fast")*
>
> Ms. Rivas is *competent. (Positive degree of the adjective "competent")*
>
> Ms. Rivas is *more competent* than Rachael. *(Comparative degree of the adjective "competent")*
>
> Ms. Rivas is the *most competent* of the five court reporters. *(Superlative degree of the adjective "competent")*

For one-syllable adjectives and adverbs, use *-er* or *-est* to form the comparative and superlative degrees, as in *fast, faster,* and *fastest.* For three- (or more) syllable adjectives and adverbs, use *more/less* or *most/least,* as in *competent, less competent,* and *least competent.*

But how do we form the comparative and superlative forms of two-syllable adjectives and adverbs? The safe answer (as with so many questions about

Dictionary Entries for *Funny* and *Recent*

fun·ny (fŭn′ē) *adj.* **-ni·er, -ni·est. 1. a.** Causing laughter or amusement. **b.** Intended or designed to amuse. **2.** Strangely or suspiciously odd; curious. **3.** Tricky or deceitful. –*n., pl.* **-nies.** *Informal.* **1.** A joke; a witticism. **2. funnies. a.** Comic strips. **b.** The section of a newspaper containing comic strips. [<FUN.] –**fun′ni·ly** *adv.* –**fun′ni·ness** *n.*

re·cent (rē′sənt) *adj.* **1.** Of, belonging to, or occurring at a time immediately before the present. **2.** Modern; new. **3. Recent.** *Geol.* Of, belonging to, or being the Holocene Epoch. See table at **geologic time.** [ME, new, fresh <Lat. *recēns, recent-,* See ken-*.] –**re′cen·cy, re′cent·ness** *n.* –**re′·cent·ly** *adv.*

business English) is, "Look it up." For example, if you look up *funny* and *recent* in the *American Heritage College Dictionary*, you will find the entries shown in Figure D.1. If an adjective or adverb can be compared by adding *-er* or *-est* to the positive form, those forms will be shown immediately after the part of speech of the root word (see the entry for *funny* in Figure D.1). If these forms are not shown, compare these words by inserting *more/less* or *most/least* (see the entry for *recent* in Figure D.1). Most of the time, however, your ear will tell you which is correct. For example, you can probably "hear" that *most fun* does not sound as natural as *funniest* and that *recenter* does not sound as natural as *more recent*.

His *more recent* routines are *funnier* than his earlier ones.

The important point is to use one or the other forms of comparison—not both. Do not combine two comparatives or two superlatives.

NOT: Quitting college was the *most stupidest* thing I ever did.

BUT: Quitting college was the *stupidest* thing I ever did.

NOT: Ms. Rivera was *more friendlier* to me after the contest ended.

BUT: Ms. Rivera was *more friendly* to me after the contest ended.

Irregular Comparisons

A few adjectives and adverbs have irregular comparisons.

Positive	*Comparative*	*Superlative*
bad/ill	worse	worst
far	farther/further	farthest/furthest
good/well	better	best
little	littler/less	littlest/least
many/much	more	most

Absolute Modifiers

Some adjectives and adverbs are *absolute*; that is, either you have the quality or you don't. These modifiers state the ultimate or perfect degree of something and thus cannot be compared. For example, you cannot be *deader* than someone who is merely *dead*. Here are some common absolute modifiers that cannot be compared: *square, round, complete, unique, perfect, dead, unanimous, true,* and *infinite*.

> **NOT:** Vivian is a *very unique* individual.
> **BUT:** Vivian is a *unique* individual.

> **NOT:** The final vote was *quite unanimous*.
> **BUT:** The final vote was *unanimous*.

These same words can, however, be *qualified,* as in "The accident victim was *nearly dead* when the ambulance arrived" or "The highway reconstruction is *almost complete*."

Comparisons Within a Group

When comparing a person or thing to a group, use the phrase *other* or *else* to make clear that the person or thing you're comparing is a member of the group.

> **NOT:** Javier is a faster typist than any typist in our department. *(Implies that Javier is not in our department)*
> **BUT:** Javier is a faster typist than any *other* typist in our department.

> **NOT:** Alvin is more sensitive to the political situation than anyone on the staff. *(Implies that Alvin is not on the staff)*
> **BUT:** Alvin is more sensitive to the political situation than anyone *else* on the staff.

EXERCISES

The Case of Personal Pronouns

1. Circle the correct word in parentheses in the following sentences.

   a. All members of the department gave (their, theirs, there, they're) views on the new proposal.

   b. Although Howard had taken his qualifying test, Lawrence and Máximo had not taken (theirs, their's, theres, there's).

   c. Anwar tried but (he, him) was unable to unlock the safe.

   d. Did (her, she) work overtime to complete the project?

   e. Did you offer (he, him) the job of chief legal assistant yet?

   f. Edward asked if (I, me) would help him repaint the office.

   g. For (her, she), it was a simple job to rewire the computer.

   h. I want to know (whos, who's, whose) Ms. Howell supposed to see once she gets there.

   i. I was annoyed by (he, him, his) continuing to make so many demands.

   j. I was told (theirs, their's, theres, there's) no time to apply a second coat of paint.

   k. It might have been Damon and (he, him) who gave the original order.

   l. It will soon be (you're, your) turn to speak to the new employees.

2. Circle the correct word in parentheses in the following sentences.

   a. Ms. Vásquez instructed (I, me) on the new procedures.
   b. My task was simplified immensely by (their, there, they're, they) offering to help.
   c. Please give Arlene and (I, me) directions to the branch office.
   d. The director asked (them, they) to wait outside until called.
   e. The dog was crying because (its, it's) collar was too tight.
   f. The final judgment regarding the matter is (their, theirs, there, they're) to make.
   g. The manager thinks (its, it's) a shame that the deadline passed unnoticed.
   h. The network administrators shouldn't quit when (their, there, they're) so close to finding a solution.
   i. The new energy czar is expected to be (he, him).
   j. The observer asked, "(You're, Your) sure you know what you're doing?"
   k. The press asked (whos, who's, whose) idea it was in the first place.
   l. The stranger gruffly answered, "This is (he, him) speaking."
   m. They quickly gave (their, there, they're) approval for the increased expenditures for the investigation.
   n. They were bluntly told that it really was no one's business but (her's, hers).

Problems in Determining Pronoun Case

3. Circle the correct word in parentheses in the following sentences.

   a. (Who, Whom) do you know on the staff of the review committee?
   b. Because of the strike, they had to do the work (themself, themselves).
   c. Between Joyce and (he, him), they were able to piece together what had actually happened.
   d. Clyde finished his design project faster than (I, me).
   e. For Mr. Bryant and (her, she), the decision meant rescheduling their planned vacations.
   f. Have Mr. Hawkins and (them, they) read the x-rays and made a decision?
   g. I think (whoever, whomever) is responsible should fix the problem.
   h. It is generally the clerical workers (who, whom) favor the flexible shifts the most.
   i. It was Ms. Hayes (who, whom) made the original offer.
   j. Management wanted (us, we) clerks to use the same style manual.
   k. Mr. Dixon asked Amy and (I, me) to lock up the office when we left.
   l. Mr. Myer mailed off the package (himself, hisself).
   m. Mr. Snyder is not as happy about the matter as (her, she).
   n. Ms. Powell and (I, me) are having trouble grasping the concept.
   o. Should (us, we) court reporters ask for a raise in transcription fees?
   p. Tell me (who, whom) you will ask to draw up the documents.
   q. The job of cleaning up afterwards went to (me, myself).

Adjective or Adverb?

4. Circle the correct adjective or adverb in parentheses in the following sentences.

   a. Although lunch smelled (delicious, deliciously), I decided not to eat until later.
   b. I am (sure, surely) glad that you decided to join our company.
   c. I am convinced that the mistake was not (intentional, intentionally).
   d. I feel (bad, badly) that you were inconvenienced.

e. Please try to finish the job (quick, quickly).

f. Raymond feels (good, well) when he argues a case successfully.

g. The doctor's (father, fatherly) manner soothed the patient.

h. The lemon pie tasted (bitter, bitterly).

i. The new president tends to dress very (conservative, conservatively).

j. When repairs became so (frequent, frequently), we traded in the copier for a newer model.

Comparison of Adjectives and Adverbs

5. Circle the correct alternative in parentheses in the following sentences.

a. Because she is (decenter, more decent) than her opponent, Hazel refused to retaliate.

b. Crystal is a more efficient technician than (anyone, anyone else) in her department.

c. Miyoko received (a perfect, the most perfect) score on the entrance exam.

d. Mr. Payne was the (carefulest, most careful) proofreader I've ever worked with.

e. Ms. Lawson is the (more, most) impatient of the two clients waiting to see you.

f. My kitten was the (littlest, most little) of the entire litter.

g. Of the three choices, the one involving doing nothing is the (baddest, worse, worst).

h. Suzanne is (happier, happy, more happier, more happy) now than she was five days ago.

i. The session on benefits was (more short, shorter) than the one on safe work practices.

j. This stew tastes (badder, worse, worst) now that you've added salt to it.

E Mechanics in Business Writing

▶ CAPITALIZATION

Did you know that English is the only language to capitalize the first-person singular pronoun *I*? Why? There is no logical reason—only custom. As we shall see, the function of capitalization is usually to emphasize words and make them stand out. Some of the rules that follow will already be familiar to you; others may not be. Some of the rules are absolutes—you *always* capitalize that type of expression. Others require more careful judgment or knowledge of the writer's intention. In any event, it would be a capital idea for you to learn these rules.

First Words

We have already mentioned that in English, you should capitalize the first-person pronoun *I*. In addition, capitalize the first word of:

▌ A sentence or partial sentence. (*Exception:* Do not capitalize the first word of a sentence following a colon.)

> Capitalize the first word of a sentence. Even a partial sentence. Why?
> Because standard usage requires it!
> One more job remains: we need to replace the furnace filter.

▌ A quoted sentence.

> Francis replied, "She would rather be right than rich."
> **BUT:** Francis replied that Ilsa would rather "be right than rich."

▌ Each item in a list or outline.

> Please bring to the meeting:
>   1. Your agenda.
>   2. The draft budget.
>   3. A list of questions or concerns you have.

People

Capitalize the name of a particular person, race, nationality, language, and religion. Also capitalize nicknames or other designations for people. Be sure to treat a person's name exactly as he or she prefers—in terms of spelling, capitalization, punctuation, and spacing.

John F. Kennedy, Jr.	African American
F. W. Woolworth	Italian
Madonna	Sioux

F. Scott Fitzgerald	Catholic
Elizabeth II	Amish
the Great Emancipator	William the Conqueror

Titles With Names

Capitalize personal and official titles when they precede personal names. Do not capitalize titles when they follow or replace a person's name or when they are followed by an appositive.

Ms. Ida Ryan	Vice President Anthony
Professor J. Randall Scott	Colonel Wright
J. Randall Scott, professor of law	Dr. Lian Yuan
Senator Ashley	Mayors York and Lindsey
my professor, J. Randall Scott,	the professor

Capitalize a title used in direct address (but not terms such as *sir*, *madam*, and *miss*).

I want to know, Doctor, if there are other options available.

Please answer the question, sir, if you can.

Do not capitalize *ex-*, *-elect*, *late*, or *former* when used with official titles.

Governor-elect Johnson	ex-President Clinton

Capitalize family titles when they stand alone or are followed by a personal name. Do not capitalize them when they are preceded by possessive pronouns.

Let me ask Dad and Uncle Chad for their help.

Let me ask my dad and my uncle, Chad Vaughan, for their help.

Places

Capitalize the official names of places: continents, countries, states, cities, streets, regions, rivers, oceans, mountains, parks, squares, monuments, statues, buildings, houses of worship, colleges, and the like. Also capitalize names that substitute for these places and adjectives derived from these place names.

Asia	Canada
Florida, the Sunshine State	Smithsonian Institution
Great Lakes	Rocky Mountains
Statue of Liberty	Sears Tower
University of Phoenix	Japanese cherry tree
German-made automobile	North Carolinian

Capitalize a common noun (and its plural form) if it is part of the official name. Do not capitalize a common noun that is not part of the official name or that serves as a short form for the official name. Capitalize *the* (or its foreign-language equivalent) only if it is part of the official name. Do not capitalize *state* unless it follows the official name of the state.

Stapleton Airport	the airport in Denver
Kansas City	the city of Charlotte
Fifth Avenue	the avenue

the Federal Bureau of Investigation	the federal government
Georgia State University	the state of Georgia
Hamilton County	the county of Hamilton
the Atlantic Ocean	the Atlantic and Pacific Oceans
St. Patrick's Cathedral	the cathedral in New York City
the United States of America	The Hague
New York State	the state of New York

Capitalize a compass point that designates a definite region or that is part of an official name. Do not capitalize compass points used as directions.

Margot lives in the South.

Our display window faces west.

Northern State University is in northern South Dakota.

Organization and Brand Names

Capitalize the names of companies, organizations, associations, clubs, teams, and the like. In general, do not capitalize articles *(the, a, an)*, conjunctions, or prepositions containing three or fewer letters. However, treat the organization's name exactly as the organization prefers—in terms of spelling, capitalization, punctuation, and spacing. Do not capitalize shortened forms of the name.

United Airlines	Delta Air Lines
Disney World	Disneyland
the Elks	the Republican Party
the Centers for Disease Control	**BUT:** the centers
BankAmerica Corp.	**BUT:** the corporation
the U.S. Army	**BUT:** the army

Capitalize brand names exactly as the owner of the brand name does, but do not capitalize a generic name that follows.

IBM computer	Kleenex tissues
Air Jordan sneakers	Lincoln sedan

Capitalize the name of a department or division within an organization if it is preceded by the word *the* and is the official name of the department or division. In all other circumstances, use lowercase letters.

the Department of Administrative Services
> **BUT:**   our administrative services department

the Finance Committee of your firm
> **BUT:**   your finance committee

the Board of Directors of Honeywell, Inc.
> **BUT:**   our board of directors

Publications and Creative Works

Capitalize the important words in titles of books, magazines, newspapers, television programs, speeches, and other important literary or creative works. Also capitalize the first and last words, the first word after a colon or dash, and all other words except articles, conjunctions, and prepositions containing three or fewer letters.

the article "A Word to the Wise"

Pricing Strategies: The Link With Reality

Archie Bunker from *All in the Family*

Miscellaneous

Nouns Followed by a Number   Capitalize a noun followed by a number or letter (except for page, size, line, and paragraph numbers).

Table 3	page 79
Flight 107	size 12D
Route 95	line 13

Days, Months, and Holidays   Capitalize the names of days, months, and holidays, but do not capitalize the names of seasons.

St. Patrick's Day occurred in the spring on Friday, March 17.

Academic Courses and Degrees   Capitalize the names of specific course titles; do not capitalize the names of general areas of study. Capitalize the name of a degree (whether written in full or abbreviated) when it follows a person's name.

I took Management 301, accounting, and business English last term.

She received a master's degree in international business.

Margot Spencer, Ph.D. *(Or "Margot Spencer, Doctor of Philosophy")*

▶ NUMBER EXPRESSION

Business writing would not be business writing without numbers. Think how often you find dates, amounts of money, identification numbers, sizes, and the like, in letters, e-mail, memos, and business reports. Because figures are easier (and faster) to comprehend than words, we use them for most business numbers. Nevertheless, figures interrupt the flow of the sentence more than words do (after all, the rest of the sentence is also composed of words), so words are typically used for small and isolated references to numbers.

Authorities do not always agree on a single style for expressing numbers—whether to spell out a number in words or to write it in figures. The following guidelines apply to typical business writing.

General Rules

General Business Writing   Spell out the numbers zero through ten and use figures for 11 and higher. Separate thousands by commas.

the first three pages	ten complaints
18 photocopies	5,376 stockholders

At the Beginning of a Sentence   Spell out a number that begins a sentence. If the number requires more than two words when spelled out, reword the sentence instead.

> Eight temporary employees lost their jobs.
>
> Fifteen people attended the seminar.
>
> One hundred homes were damaged in the flood.

Adjacent Numbers   When adjacent numbers are expressed both in figures or both-in words, separate them with a comma. If one of the adjacent numbers is a compound modifier, express the number with fewer letters in words and the other number in figures.

> In *2004, 18* people showed up to testify. *(Both numbers are in figures.)*
>
> At *nine, three* people showed up to testify. *(Both numbers are in words.)*
>
> I examined *8 two*-room office suites and *two 8*-room suites. *("Eight" contains more letters than "two.")*
>
> Grace printed *500 four*-page flyers and *four 500*-page catalogs.

Related Numbers   Within the same sentence, express related numbers in the same way. If both numbers are ten or lower, use words. If *either* is greater than ten, use figures (unless the number begins a sentence). If the numbers in the same sentence are not related, follow the general rules for number expression.

> Either *nine or ten* of the test results were positive. *(Both related numbers are ten or lower.)*
>
> Only *6 men and 13 women* chose that life insurance option. *(One of the related numbers is greater than ten.)*
>
> *Fifteen to twenty* people attended the seminar. *(The first related number begins a sentence.)*
>
>   **BUT:** I administered *two* of the hemoglobin tests to the *47* patients. *(The numbers are not related.)*

Indefinite Numbers   Spell out indefinite numbers.

> a few hundred complaints   thousands of dollars
>
> tens of thousands of people   more than a million acres

Ordinal Numbers   With the exception of numbered street names and certain dates (discussed later), spell out ordinal numbers (such as *first, second, thirtieth*) that can be expressed in one or two words.

> the twenty-second century   her fifty-third birthday
>
> thirty-second-floor apartment   our one hundredth anniversary
>
> our one millionth visitor   **BUT:**   our 117th anniversary

Fractions, Decimals, and Percentages

Fractions   Spell out and hyphenate a fraction that stands alone, unless it requires more than two words or is used in a calculation. Use figures for a mixed number (a whole number plus a fraction).

a two-thirds majority	one-fourth of the population
nine-tenths of the vote	one-third smaller than before
multiply by 3/5	13/42 of the time *(Not "13/42nds")*
interest rate of 7 5/8	adding 1½ cups of sugar

When constructing fractions that do not appear on the keyboard (see *7 5/8* above), use a diagonal and leave a space (not a hyphen) between the whole number and the fraction. Do not leave a space between a whole number and a *formatted* fraction (such as *1½* above).

Decimals   Write decimals in figures. If a whole number does not precede the decimal, insert a zero before the decimal point (to avoid misreading).

   4.21   98.6   0.16   14,876.38

Percentages   Write percentages in figures and spell out the word *percent*. (Use the % symbol only in tables, business forms, technical writing, or other situations in which space is at a premium or percentages occur frequently.)

   8 percent   15.5 percent   7½ percent   0.5 percent

Dates

Use figures for dates. When the day follows the month, use cardinal figures (such as *1, 2,* and *30*). When the day precedes the month or stands alone, use ordinal figures (such as *1st, 2nd,* and *30th*).

January 25	March 1, 2004
the 8th of August	going to trial on the 23rd

Use a comma before and after the year in a complete date unless some other punctuation mark is needed after the year. Do not use a comma with incomplete dates.

> We had to sign the contract before April 15, 2004, and wanted to sign on April 10, 2004; we actually signed on April 11, 2004 (because of the rolling electrical blackout on April 10).

> The April 11, 2004, signing was attended by 35 members from management and labor.

> We notarized the signatures on April 11 for legal reasons.

> We notarized the signatures in April 2004 for legal reasons.

Money

Use figures for definite amounts of money and words for indefinite amounts of money.

$5	$18.53	Nearly $50,000
$500 worth	a $10 bill	a $67,500-a-year opening

BUT: a few thousand dollars   millions of dollars   nearly a hundred dollars

Do not add a decimal point and zeros to a whole-dollar amount that occurs by itself or with other whole-dollar amounts. Do add a decimal point and zeros if the whole-dollar amount appears in the same context as a fractional-dollar amount.

My check for $78 is enclosed.

The amount of your order is $32.50, plus $3.00 shipping and handling, for a total of $35.50.

Express round large amounts of money (a million dollars or more) partly in words.

$57 million	$6.7 billion
$5 1/2 million	a $5 million-plus mansion

In general, use figures and the word *cents* for amounts less than a dollar. Use the dollar sign only if related amounts of money require it.

Phaedra paid me the *5 cents* I was owed. *(Not "five cents" or "$.05" or "5¢")*

The price was *$2.97* plus *$.12* tax, for a total of *$3.09.*

Measurements

Express measurements that serve as significant statistics in figures. Within sentences, spell out the unit of measurement.

You must be less than *6 feet* tall to apply for that position.

The express package weighed *2 pounds 8 ounces.* *(No comma between elements of a measurement because it is thought of as a single unit)*

The first lab test required *5 hours 30 minutes* to complete.

Our sedan got *32 miles per gallon* on the *375-mile* trip.

A *9-foot-6-inch* rug was placed in the room that was *12 by 14 feet.*

Follow the rules for general number expression for an isolated, nontechnical reference to a measurement within a sentence.

I've lost five pounds since June.	I've lost 17 pounds since June.
Olaf drove ten miles farther.	Olaf drove 11 miles farther.

Street Addresses

Write house and building numbers in figures. (*Exception:* For clarity, use words for the number *one.*) Spell out street numbers one through ten and use figures for street numbers greater than ten. Do not abbreviate a compass direction before a street name, and do not insert commas.

9 Loblolly Lane	536 Mission Street
10378 Glendale Road	One Park Avenue
8 East Second Avenue	148-B North 102nd Street

Time

Use figures with *a.m.* or *p.m.* and words with *o'clock.* Do not insert zeros with time on the hour unless a related time in the same sentence requires the expression of minutes.

My flight arrives at *8:05 p.m.*

The meeting is at *three o'clock.*

We're open from *9 a.m.* until *6 p.m.*

We're open from *9:00 a.m.* until *6:30 p.m.*

Follow the rules for general number expression for general references to clock time without *a.m.*, *p.m.*, or *o'clock*. Spell out hours one through ten (and related minutes) and use figures for hours 11 and 12.

> We started at *eight* in the morning and worked until *midnight*.
>
> I arrived at *quarter to eight* and stayed until *half past nine*.
>
> The tea begins at *two-thirty* and ends at *four forty-five*. *(A hyphen is used between hours and minutes unless the minutes themselves are hyphenated.)*
>
> We started at 11 in the morning and worked until 2 in the afternoon. *(Express related numbers in a consistent format.)*

In general, follow the rules for general number expression for time periods other than clock time. Use figures only if the time period represents a significant statistic.

> I worked there for only *six months*; Stacy worked there for only *13 months*.
>
> Almost *five years* ago, I assumed a *30-year* mortgage.

Ages

Write ages in figures when they serve as significant statistics and spell out indefinite ages. Otherwise, follow the general rules for numbers.

> Students must get this vaccination before the age of *8*.
>
> You may retire at age *62½* with at least *20* years of service.
>
> Her dependent is *18* years *7* months old. *(No comma between the years and months)*
>
> Even a *five-year-old* can understand these directions.
>
> Evan is in his early *forties,* and Samantha is in her *mid-thirties*.

Serial Numbers

Express serial numbers in figures. Capitalize the noun preceding the figure (except for *page, size, line,* and *paragraph*). Do not separate thousands with commas.

page 4	Flight 8701	Route 75
size 3	line 48	Table 4

▶ ABBREVIATIONS

An abbreviation is a shortened form of a word or phrase. You should use abbreviations sparingly in narrative writing. Many are appropriate only in technical writing, statistical material, tables, and other situations where space is at a premium.

Consult a dictionary for the correct form for abbreviations, and follow the rule "When in doubt, write it out." If there is any possibility of confusion, spell out the word the first time it is used and follow it with the abbreviation in parentheses. For example, does *CD* stand for "compact disk" or "certificate of deposit" (or even "Civil Defense")? Be consistent in the way you treat abbreviations within a document. For example, is it *C.D.* or *CD*?

Abbreviations Not Used

In narrative writing, do not abbreviate common nouns (such as *acct.*, *assoc.*, *bldg.*, *dept.*, *misc.*, and *pkg.*); measurements; or the names of cities, states (except in addresses), months, and days of the week.

NOT: Please see Thos. in our accounting dept. before Mon., Dec. 13.

BUT: Please see Thomas in our accounting department before Monday, December 13.

NOT: The new security officer is more than 6 ft tall and weighs 250 lbs.

BUT: The new security officer is more than 6 feet tall and weighs 250 pounds.

Abbreviations Always Used

Some abbreviations are always appropriate: *Mr.*, *Ms.*, *Mrs.*, *Dr.*, *a.m.*, *p.m.*, and those that are official parts of company names, such as *Co.*, *Inc.*, or *Ltd.* Follow an individual's preference for using initials or spelling out his or her first or middle names. Well-established acronyms (abbreviations pronounced as words, such as *NATO*—for the North Atlantic Treaty Organization) are also always appropriate. Many times, these acronyms are more familiar to the reader than their spelled-out counterparts.

NOT: Doctor Allumbaugh worked for the National Association of Security Dealers Automated Quotations and volunteered for the United Nations International Children's Emergency Fund at Halloween.

BUT: Dr. Allumbaugh worked for NASDAQ and volunteered for UNICEF at Halloween.

Punctuation and Spacing

Many abbreviations follow the capitalization of the words as if written in full. In most lowercase abbreviations made up of single initials, use a period after each initial but no internal spaces.

a.m.	p.m.	i.e.	e.g.	c.o.d.
Exceptions:		mpg	mph	wpm

In most all-capital abbreviations made up of single initials, do not use periods or internal spaces.

WWW	OSHA	PBS	AMA	ASAP			
CEO	EST	GPA					
Exceptions:		P.O.	U.S.A.	A.A.	B.S.	Ph.D.	B.C.	A.D.

(Do not insert internal spaces in any of these abbreviations.)

Measurements

As discussed and illustrated on pages 385–386, in normal business writing, you should spell out isolated measurements. Abbreviate units of measure only when they occur frequently—for example, in technical and scientific writing, on forms, and in tables. Type them in the following format:

▌ Use lowercase letters without periods.

▮ Leave one space between the number and the abbreviation and between abbreviations.

▮ Use figures for all numbers.

▮ Do not insert a comma between the parts of a single measurement.

▮ Use the same abbreviation for singular and plural forms.

    6 lb 7 oz   5 ft 10 in   10 sq yd   3 gal   34 mpg   50 km

▶ SPELLING

Correct spelling is essential to effective communication. A misspelled word can distract the reader, cause misunderstanding, and send a negative message about the writer's competence. No doubt you already use your computer's spell checker to proofread your spelling. As helpful as these devices are, they do have limitations. For example, most spell checkers will not catch the misuse of *their* for *there*, will not identify an erroneous addition or omission of an -*s* to a word, and can play havoc with proper names. In short, you must still proofread carefully.

Because of the many variations in the spelling of English words, no spelling guidelines are foolproof; there are exceptions to every spelling rule. The five rules-that follow may be safely applied, however, in most business writing situations. Learning them will save you the time of looking up many words in a dictionary.

Doubling a Final Consonant   If the last syllable of a root word is stressed, double the final consonant when adding a suffix.

Last Syllable Stressed		*Last Syllable Not Stressed*	
prefer	preferring	happen	happening
control	controlling	total	totaling
occur	occurrence	differ	differed

One-Syllable Words   If a one-syllable word ends in a consonant preceded by a single vowel, double the final consonant before a suffix starting With a vowel.

Suffix Starting With a Vowel		*Suffix Starting With a Consonant*	
ship	shipper	ship	shipment
drop	dropped	glad	gladness
bag	baggage	bad	badly

Final -e   If a final -*e* is preceded by a consonant, drop the *e* before a suffix starting with a vowel.

Suffix Starting With a Vowel		*Suffix Starting With a Consonant*	
come	coming	hope	hopeful
use	usable	manage	management
sincere	sincerity	sincere	sincerely

Note: Words ending in -*ce* or -*ge* usually retain the *e* before a suffix starting with a vowel: noticeable, advantageous.

Final -y   If a final -*y* is preceded by a consonant, change the *y* to *i* before any suffix except one starting with *i*.

Most Suffixes		*Suffixes Starting With an i*	
company	companies	try	trying
ordinary	ordinarily	forty	fortyish
hurry	hurried	baby	babyish

***ei* and *ie* Words**   Remember the rhyme:

Use *i* before *e*:	believe	yield
Except after *c*:	receive	deceit
Or when sounded as *a*,		
as in *neighbor* and *weigh*:	freight	their

EXERCISES

Capitalization

1. Correct any errors in capitalization in the following sentences.

   a. As you did last Fall, you may park in the visitor's parking lot on Canyon drive in front of the Riverside medical center.

   b. Please report to the admitting department of Riverside hospital, where you will be directed to see Dr. Raymond Shield, chief of staff, who will administer the Exam.

   c. Your Doctor, Guadalupe Suárez, should be returning to her office on Monday; She finishes her Lecture at the Mayo Clinic on Sunday and will be taking flight 307 back to east Orange, New Jersey.

   d. The west Indian ambassador met Ex-president Bush at the LBJ ranch.

   e. Chowan county is not as large as the county of Perquimans; both are located in eastern North Carolina.

   f. I purchased some Starbucks Coffee for the vice president and for each member of the board of directors.

Number Expression

2. Circle the correct alternative(s) in each sentence.

   a. On May 7, (50, fifty) new members were initiated.

   b. Please put (7, seven) (37, thirty-seven)-cent stamps on that package.

   c. Please retype the first (10, ten) pages.

   d. We ordered (100, one hundred) invitations for the reception.

   e. A total of (4, four) men and (12, twelve) women took the test.

   f. A total of (15, fifteen) men took the (3, three)-hour test.

   g. Please make (3, three) (1st, first)-class plane reservations.

   h. The incumbent received nearly a (1,000, thousand) votes more than her challenger.

   i. Last year our profit rose to (4, four) (%, percent) of net sales.

   j. The overtime rate was (1½, 1 1/2, one and one-half) times the normal rate.

   k. We replaced (19/25, 19/25th, nineteen twenty-fifths) of the solution.

   l. I wrote a ($500, five-hundred-dollar) check for the deposit.

   m. The date of April 3, (2004 was chosen; 2004, was chosen).

n. We left on May (18, 18th, eighteenth).

o. We spent ($1,000s, thousands of dollars) to refurbish the studio.

p. By the way, our grandson weighed nearly (9, nine) pounds at birth.

q. Please purchase a credenza that is (4' 8", 4 ft 8 in, 4 feet 8 inches) wide.

r. Their showroom is located at (7, Seven) (E., East) (7th, Seventh) Boulevard.

s. His first appointment is at (9, nine) o'clock.

t. In our city, children can begin school only after they have reached the age of (5, five).

u. Please ensure that the package arrives by (one, 1) p.m. (EST, E.S.T.) tomorrow.

v. The meeting will last from (8, 8:00, eight) until (12:30, twelve thirty, twelve-thirty).

Abbreviations

3. Circle any abbreviations that should not be used in general business writing. Draw a line through any term that would normally be abbreviated, and write the correct form of the abbreviation above it. Correct any abbreviations that are shown in incorrect format. If necessary, use your dictionary.

a. Doctor R. Jason Gage, Jr., sent Angélica Blanco, Esquire, a bill for the amt. she still owed from her visit on Mon.

b. Their address in NYC is 183 W. 53rd St.

c. The Federal Bureau of Investigation set up an appointment on Thurs. at 9 a.m. Eastern Standard Time to talk to me.

d. The NASCAR races in Indy are always held on a Sunday.

e. How many lbs. and ozs. did the FedEx package weigh?

f. The bank's home loan dept. will let you know how much is left in your escrow acct.

g. The Y.M.C.A. is less than 300 ft. from Mister Smith's cement co.

h. I received my BS degree in lib. sci. from the U. of Virginia.

i. I accessed Amazon.com on the W.W.W. to learn whether my package would arrive c.o.d.

j. Please let me know ASAP if the C.E.O. will be able to see Geo. & me about the N.A.S.A. account.

Spelling

4. Correct any misspellings in the following lines.

a. ecstasy	milennium	supercede
b. accidently	minuscule	accomodate
c. iresistible	liaison	harras
d. definitely	ocurence	embarass
e. cemetary	innoculate	sacrilegious
f. confidance	disappoint	defendent
g. occassionally	calendar	merchendise
h. apparant	abreviate	peculiar
i. absence	mayonnaise	commitment
j. acordance	tarrif	phisycian
k. alotted	miniscule	amateurish
l. renumeration	auxiliary	catastrophy
m. changeable	carbueretor	clientele
n. beneficial	milage	techniciality
o. celophane	questionaire	wierd
p. persuasive	unanimiously	caffeine
q. benafactor	subtle	consensus

Style Manual: Formatting Business Documents

▶ FORMATTING CORRESPONDENCE AND MEMOS

The most common features of business letters, memos, and e-mail are discussed in the following sections and are illustrated in Figures 1 and 2.

Letter and Punctuation Styles

The *block style* is the simplest letter style to type because all lines begin at the left margin. In the *modified block style,* the date and closing lines begin at the center point. Offsetting these parts from the left margin enables the reader to locate them quickly.

The *standard punctuation style*—the most common format—uses a colon (never a comma) after the salutation and a comma after the complimentary closing. The *open punctuation style,* on the other hand, uses no punctuation after these two lines.

Stationery and Margins

Most letters are typed on standard-size stationery, 8½ by 11 inches. The first page of a business letter is typed on letterhead stationery, which shows company information printed at the top. Subsequent pages of a business letter and all pages of a personal business letter (a letter written to transact one's personal business) are typed on good-quality plain paper.

Side, top, and bottom margins should be 1 to 1¼ inches (most word processing programs have default margins of 1¼ inches, which works just fine). Vertically center one-page letters and memos. Set a tab at the center point if you're formatting a modified block style letter.

Required Letter Parts

The required letter parts are as discussed in the following subsections.

Date Line

Type the current month (spelled out), day, and year on the first line. Begin either at the center point for modified block style or at the left margin for all other styles.

Inside Address

The inside address gives the name and location of the person to whom you're writing. Include a personal title (such as *Mr., Mrs., Miss,* or *Ms.*). If you use the addressee's job title, type it either on the same line as the name (separated from the name by a comma) or on the following line by itself. In the address, use the two-letter U.S. Postal Service abbreviation, typed in all capitals with no period, and leave one space between the state and the zip code. Type the inside address at the left margin four lines below the date; that is, press Enter four times. For international letters, type the name of the country in all-capital letters on the last line by itself.

Salutation

Use the same name in both the inside address and the salutation. If the letter is addressed to a job position rather than to a person, use a generic but nonsexist greeting, such as "Dear Human Resources Manager." If you typically address the reader in person by first name, use the first name in the salutation (for example, "Dear Lois:"); otherwise, use a personal title and the surname only (for example, "Dear Ms. Lane:"). Leave one blank line before and after the salutation.

Body

Single-space the lines of each paragraph and leave one blank line between paragraphs.

Page 2 Heading

Use your word processor's page-numbering command to insert the page number in the top right margin. Suppress the page number on page 1. You should carry forward to a second page at least two lines of the body of the message.

Complimentary Closing

Begin the complimentary closing at the same horizontal point as the date line, capitalize the first word only, and leave one blank line before and three blank lines after, to allow room for the signature. If a colon follows the salutation, use a comma after the complimentary closing; otherwise, no punctuation follows.

Signature

Some women insert the personal title they prefer (*Ms.*, *Miss*, or *Mrs.*) in parentheses before their signature. Men never include a personal title.

Writer's Identification

The writer's identification (name or job title or both) begins on the fourth line immediately below the complimentary closing. Do not use a personal title. The job title may go either on the same line as the typed name, separated from the name by a comma, or on the following line by itself.

Reference Initials

When used, reference initials (the initials of the typist) are typed at the left margin in lowercase letters without periods, with one blank line before. Do not include reference initials if you type your own letter.

Envelopes

Business envelopes have a printed return address. You may type your name above this address, if you wish. Use plain envelopes for personal business letters; you should type the return address (your home address) at the upper left corner. Envelopes may be typed either in standard upper- and lowercase style or in all-capital letters without any punctuation. On large (No. 10) envelopes, begin typing the mailing address 2 inches from the top edge and 4 inches from the left edge. On small (No. 6¾) envelopes, begin typing the mailing address 2 inches from the top edge and 2½ inches from the left edge. Fold letters as shown in Figure 2.

FIGURE 1

Correspondence Formats

Block style letter

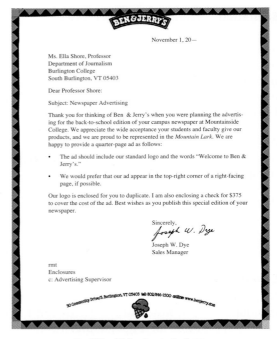

Modified block style letter

Interoffice memorandum

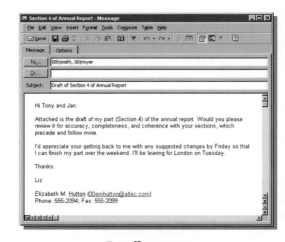

E-mail message

FIGURE 2

Envelopes and Folding Letters

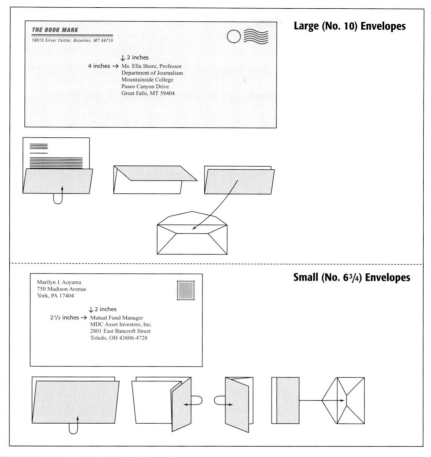

U.S. POSTAL SERVICE ABBREVIATIONS
FOR STATES, TERRITORIES, AND CANADIAN PROVINCES

States and Territories			
Alabama . . . . AL	Kansas . . . . KS	North Dakota . . . . ND	Wyoming. . . . . WY
Alaska . . . . AK	Kentucky. . . . . KY	Ohio . . . . OH	
Arizona . . . . AZ	Louisiana . . . . LA	Oklahoma. . . . . OK	
Arkansas . . . . AR	Maine . . . . ME	Oregon . . . . OR	
California. . . . . CA	Maryland . . . . MD	Pennsylvania . . . . PA	*Canadian Provinces*
Colorado . . . . CO	Massachusetts . . . . MA	Puerto Rico. . . . . PR	Alberta. . . . . AB
Connecticut. . . . . CT	Michigan. . . . . MI	Rhode Island . . . . RI	British Columbia. . . . . . . BC
Delaware. . . . . DE	Minnesota . . . . MN	South Carolina . . . . SC	Labrador . . . . LB
District of Columbia . . . . DC	Mississippi . . . . MS	South Dakota . . . . SD	Manitoba. . . . . MB
Florida. . . . . FL	Missouri . . . . MO	Tennessee. . . . . TN	New Brunswick. . . . . NB
Georgia . . . . GA	Montana. . . . . MT	Texas. . . . . TX	Newfoundland . . . . NF
Guam. . . . . GU	Nebraska . . . . NE	Utah . . . . UT	Northwest Territories . . . . NT
Hawaii . . . . HI	Nevada. . . . . NV	Vermont . . . . VT	Nova Scotia. . . . . NS
Idaho . . . . ID	New Hampshire. . . . . NH	Virginia . . . . VA	Ontario . . . . ON
Illinois IL	New Jersey. . . . . NJ	Virgin Islands VI	Prince Edward Island . . . . PE
Indiana . . . . IN	New Mexico . . . . NM	Washington . . . . WA	Quebec . . . . QC
Iowa. . . . . IA	New York . . . . NY	West Virginia . . . . WV	Saskatchewan . . . . SK
	North Carolina. . . . . NC	Wisconsin. . . . . WI	Yukon Territory. . . . . YT

Optional Letter Parts

Optional letter parts are as discussed in the following subsections.

Subject Line

You should include a subject line in most letters (identified by the words *Subject, Re,* or *In Re* followed by a colon) to identify the topic of the letter. Type it below the salutation, with one blank line before and one after.

Numbered or Bulleted Lists in the Body

Use your word processor's number/bullet feature to insert a numbered list (if the sequence of the items is important) or a bulleted list (when the sequence is not important). If every item takes up only a single line, single-space the items; otherwise, single-space the lines within each item and double-space between items. Either way, leave one blank line before and after the list.

Enclosure Notation

Use an enclosure notation if any additional items are to be included in the envelope. Type "Enclosure" on the line immediately below the reference initials, and as an option, add the description of what is enclosed. (*Note:* For memos, the appropriate term is "Attachment" instead of "Enclosure" if the items are to be physically attached to the memo instead of being enclosed in an envelope.)

Delivery Notation

Type a delivery notation (such as *By Certified Mail, By Fax, By Federal Express*) a single space below the enclosure notation.

Copy Notation

If someone other than the addressee is to receive a copy of the letter, type a copy notation ("c:") immediately below the enclosure notation or reference initials, whichever comes last. Then follow the copy notation with the names of the people who will receive copies.

Postscript

If you add a postscript to a letter, type it as the last item, preceded by one blank line. The heading "PS:" is optional. Postscripts are used most often in sales letters.

▶ FORMATTING REPORTS AND DOCUMENTING SOURCES

If the reader or organization has a preferred format style, use it. Otherwise, follow these generally accepted guidelines for formatting business reports. Make use of your computer's automatic or formatting features to enhance the appearance and readability of your report and to increase the efficiency of the process. A sample report in business style is shown in Figure 3; MLA and APA styles are shown in Figure 4.

Margins

Memo and letter reports use regular correspondence margins as discussed earlier. For reports typed in manuscript (formal report) format, use a 2-inch top margin for the first page of each special part (for example, the table of contents, the executive summary, the first page of the body of the report, and the first page of the reference list). Leave a 1-inch top margin for all other pages and at least a 1-inch bottom margin on all pages. Use 1- to 1¼-inch side margins on all pages.

Spacing

Memo and letter reports are typed single-spaced. Manuscript reports may be either single- or double-spaced. Double spacing is preferred if the reader will likely make many comments on the pages. Note that double spacing leaves one blank line between each line of type; do not confuse double spacing with 1½ spacing, which leaves only *half* a blank line between lines of type.

Regardless of the spacing used for the body of the report, single spacing is typically used for the table of contents, the executive summary, long quotations, tables, and the reference list. Use a ½-inch paragraph indention for double-spaced paragraphs. Do not indent single-spaced paragraphs; instead, double-space between them. Unless directed otherwise, use a 12-point serif font (such as Times New Roman 12).

Report Headings

The number of levels of headings used will vary from report to report. Memo reports may have only first-level subheadings, with no part titles or other headings. Long reports may have as many as four levels of headings. One standard format for the various levels is given here. Recognize, however, that the format presented here is only one of several that might be used. Again, consistency and readability should be your major goals. Regardless of the format used, make sure that the reader can instantly tell which are major headings and which are subordinate headings.

Part Title

Using a slightly larger font size than that used for the body of the report, center a part title (for example, "Contents" or "References") and type it in all capitals and in bold on a new page, leaving a 2-inch top margin. Double-space titles of two or more lines, using an inverted pyramid style (the first line longer). Triple-space after the part title.

First-Level Subheading

Using the same font size as that used in the body of the report, center and bold the first-level subheading in all capitals. Double-space before and after the heading.

Second-Level Subheading

Begin the second-level subheading at the left margin. Use bold type and all capitals, as in first-level headings. Double-space before and after the heading.

FIGURE 3

Sample Report in Business Style

EVALUATION OF THE STAFF BENEFITS PROGRAM

AT MAYO MEMORIAL HOSPITAL

Lyn Santos

I. INTRODUCTION
    A. Purpose and Scope of the Study
    B. Procedures

II. FINDINGS
    A. Knowledge of Benefits
        1. Familiarity with Benefits
        2. Present Methods of Communication
            a. Formal Channels
            b. Informal Channels
        3. Preferred Methods of Communication
    B. Opinions of Present Benefits
        1. Importance of Benefits
        2. Satisfaction with Benefits
    C. Desirability of Additional Benefits

III. SUMMARY, CONCLUSIONS, AND RECOMMENDATIONS
    A. Summary of the Problem and Procedures
    B. Summary of the Findings
    C. Conclusions and Recommendations

APPENDIX
    A. Cover Letter
    B. Questionnaire

Outline

EVALUATION OF THE STAFF BENEFITS PROGRAM

AT MAYO MEMORIAL HOSPITAL

Prepared for

David Riggins
Director of Human Resources
Mayo Memorial Hospital

Prepared by

Lyn Santos
Assistant Director of Human Resources
Mayo Memorial Hospital

December 8, 20—

Title page

MEMO TO: David Riggins, Director of Human Resources

FROM: Lyn Santos, Assistant Director of Human Resources

DATE: December 8, 20—

SUBJECT: Evaluation of the Staff Benefits Program at Mayo Memorial Hospital

Here is the report evaluating our staff benefits program that you requested on October 15.

The report shows that overall the staff is familiar with and values most of the benefits we offer. At the end of the report, I've made several recommendations regarding the possibility of issuing individualized benefits statements annually and determining the usefulness of the automobile insurance benefit, the feasibility of offering compensation for unused sick leave, and the competitiveness of our retirement program.

I enjoyed working on this assignment, Dave, and learned quite a bit from my analysis of the situation that will help me during the upcoming labor negotiations. Please let me know if I can provide further information.

emc
Attachment

Transmittal document

CONTENTS

Table of contents

FIGURE 3

Sample Report in Business Style (continued)

First page

**EVALUATION OF THE STAFF BENEFITS PROGRAM
AT MAYO MEMORIAL HOSPITAL**

Lyn Santos

INTRODUCTION

Employee benefits are a rapidly growing and increasingly important form of employee compensation for both profit and nonprofit organizations. According to a recent U.S. Chamber of Commerce survey, benefits now constitute 37 percent of all payroll cost, averaging $11,857 per year for each full-time employee.[1] Thus, on the basis of cost alone, an organization's employee benefits program must be carefully monitored and evaluated.

Mayo Memorial Hospital employs nearly 2,500 staff personnel, and these employees have not received a cost-of-living increase in two years. As a result, staff salaries may not have kept pace with private industry, and the hospital's employee benefits program may become more important in attracting and retaining good workers. In addition, the contracts of three of the four staff unions expire next year, and the benefits program is typically a major area of bargaining.

PURPOSE AND SCOPE OF THE STUDY

To help ensure that the staff benefits program at Mayo operates as effectively as possible, the director of personnel authorized this report on October 15, 20—. Specifically, this problem was addressed in this study: What are the opinions of staff employees at Mayo Memorial Hospital regarding their employee benefits? To answer this question, the following subproblems were addressed:

1. How knowledgeable are the employees about the benefits program?

2. What are the employees' opinions of the value of the benefits that are presently available to them?

[1]Sarah Berelson et al., *Managing Your Benefit Program*, 13th ed., Novak-Siebold, Chicago, 2002, p. 183.

New-section page

3

FINDINGS

For a benefits program to achieve its goals, employees must be aware of the benefits provided. Thus, the first section that follows discusses the employees' familiarity with their benefits as well as the effectiveness of the hospital's present method of communicating benefits and those methods that employees would prefer. An effective benefits package must also include benefits that are relevant to employee needs. Thus, the employees' opinions of the importance of and their satisfaction with each benefit offered are discussed next. The section concludes with a discussion of those benefits employees would like to see added to the benefits program at Mayo.

KNOWLEDGE OF BENEFITS

One study[3] has shown that employees' satisfaction with benefits is directly correlated with their knowledge of such benefits. Thus, an indication of the staff employees' level of familiarity with their benefits and suggestions for improving communication were solicited.

Familiarity with Benefits. Numerous methods are presently being used to communicate the fringe benefits to employees. According to Lewis Rigby, director of the State Personnel Board, every new state employee views a 30-minute video entitled "In Addition to Your Salary" as part of the new-employee orientation. Also, the major benefits are explained during one-on-one counseling during the first day of the orientation session.

The staff employees were asked to rate their level of familiarity with each benefit. As shown in Table 1, most staff employees believe that most benefits have been adequately communicated to them. At least three-fourths of the employees are familiar with all major benefits except for long-term disability insurance, which is familiar to only a slight majority, and auto insurance, which is familiar to only one-third of the respondents. This low level of knowledge is

[3]Donna Jean Egan and Annette Kantelzoglou (eds.), *Human Resources*, Varsity Books, New Haven, CT, 2005.

Page with audiovisual aids

4

TABLE 1. LEVEL OF FAMILIARITY WITH THE BENEFITS PROGRAM

Employee Benefit	Level of Familiarity			Total
	Familiar	Unfamiliar	Undecided	
Sick leave	94%	4%	2%	100%
Vacation/paid holidays	93%	4%	3%	100%
Hospital/medical insurance	90%	7%	3%	100%
Life insurance	84%	10%	6%	100%
Long-term disability insurance	53%	33%	14%	100%
Retirement	76%	14%	10%	100%
Auto insurance*	34%	58%	8%	100%

*This benefit started six weeks before the survey was taken.

In general, benefit familiarity is not related to length of employment. Most employees are familiar with most benefits regardless of their length of employment. As shown in Figure 1, however, the longer a person has been employed at Mayo, the more likely he or she is to know about the life insurance benefit.

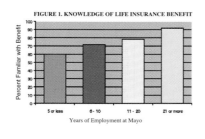

FIGURE 1. KNOWLEDGE OF LIFE INSURANCE BENEFIT

Bibliography

18

BIBLIOGRAPHY

Abbey Petroleum Industries, *2005 Annual Report*, API, Inc., San Francisco, 2006.

Adams, Josiah B., *Compensation Systems*, Brunswick Press, Boston, 2005.

Berelson, Sarah, et al., *Managing Your Benefit Program*, 13th ed., Novak-Siebold, Chicago, 2006.

Directory of Business and Financial Services, Corporate Libraries Assoc., New York, 2005.

Egan, Donna Jean, and Annette Kantelzoglou (eds.); *Human Resources*, Varsity Books, New Haven, CT, 2005.

Ignatio, Enar, "Can Flexible Benefits Promote Your Company?" *Personnel Quarterly*, Vol. 20, September 2004, pp. 804–816.

"Let Employees Determine Their Own Benefits," *Manhattan Times*, January 12, 2006, p. C17, col. 2.

"Market Research," *Encyclopedia of Business*, 2d ed., 2006.

National Institute of Mental Health, *Who Pays the Piper? Ten Years of Passing the Buck*, DHHS Publication No. ADM 82-1195, U.S. Government Printing Office, Washington, 2005.

Preminger, Larry (Executive Producer), *The WKVX-TV Evening News*, Valhalla Broadcasting Co., Los Angeles, August 5, 2004.

Quincy, Dinah J., "Maxwell Announces New Health Benefit," *Maxwell Corp.* November 13, 2004, <http://www.maxcorp.com/NEWS/2004/f93500.html>, accessed on January 14, 2005.

Young, Laurel <lyoung2@express.com>, "Training Doesn't Always Last," June 3, 2004, <http:l/groups.yahoo.com/group/personnel/message/5l>, accessed on April 20, 2003.

FIGURE 4

Sample Report in APA and MLA Styles

Staff Benefit Program 2

Evaluation of the Staff Benefits Program

at Mayo Memorial Hospital

Lyn Santos

Introduction

Employee benefits are a rapidly growing and increasingly important form of employee compensation for both profit and nonprofit organizations. According to a recent U.S. Chamber of Commerce survey, benefits now constitute 37 percent of all payroll cost, costing an average of $11,857 per year for each full-time employee (Adhams & Stevens, 2004, p. 183). Thus, on the basis of cost alone, an organization's employee benefits program must be carefully monitored and evaluated.

Mayo Memorial Hospital employs nearly 2,500 staff personnel, and they have not received a cost-of-living increase in two years. As a result, staff salaries may not have kept pace with private industry, and the hospital's employee benefits program may become more important in attracting and retaining good workers. In addition, the contracts of three of the four staff unions expire next year, and the benefits program is typically a major area of bargaining (Ivarson, 2005, p. 28).

Purpose and Scope of the Study

As has been noted by J. B. Adams (2005), a management consultant, "The success of employee benefits programs depends directly on whether employees need, understand, and appreciate the value of the benefits provided" (p. 220). Thus, to ensure that the benefit program is operating as effectively as possible, David Riggins, director of personnel, authorized this report on October 15, 20—. Specifically, the following problem was addressed in this study: What are the opinions of staff employees at Mayo Memorial Hospital regarding their employee

Report page in APA style

Staff Benefit Program 18

References

Abbey Petroleum Industries. (2006). *2005 annual report*. San Francisco: Author.

Adams, J. B. (2005). *Compensation systems*. Boston: Brunswick Press.

Adhams, R., & Stevens, S. (2000). *Personnel management*. Cambridge, MA: All-State.

Directory of business and financial services. (2005). New York: Corporate Libraries Association.

Ivarson, A., Jr. (2005, September 29). Creating your benefit plan: A primer. *Business Month, 75*, 19–31.

Let employees determine their own benefits. (2006, January 12). *Manhattan Times*, p. C17.

Market research. (2006). In *The encyclopedia of business* (2nd ed., Vol. 2, pp. 436–441). Cleveland, OH: Collins.

National Institute of Mental Health. (2005). *Who pays the piper? Ten years of passing the buck* (DHHS Publication No. ADM 82-1195). Washington, DC: U.S. Government Printing Office.

Preminger, L. (Executive Producer). (2006, August 5). *The WKVX-TV evening news* [Television broadcast]. Los Angeles: Valhalla Broadcasting Co.

Quincy, D. J. (2004, November 13). Maxwell announces new health benefit. New York: Maxwell. Retrieved January 14, 2005, from http://www.maxcorp.com /NEWS/2004/f93500.html

Salary survey of service industries. (n.d.). Retrieved July 8, 2006, from BizInfo database, http://www.bizinfo.com/census.gov/ind.lib/tab-0315.html

Young, L. (2004, June 3). Training doesn't always last. Message posted to http://groups.yahoo.com/group/personnel/message/51

References in APA style

Santos 2

Lyn Santos

Professor Riggins

Management 348

8 December 20—

Evaluation of the Staff Benefits Program

at Mayo Memorial Hospital

Employee benefits are a rapidly growing and increasingly important form of employee compensation for both profit and nonprofit organizations. According to a recent U.S. Chamber of Commerce survey, benefits now constitute 37 percent of all payroll cost, costing an average of $11,857 per year for each full-time employee (Adhams and Stevens 183). Thus, on the basis of cost alone, an organization's employee benefits program must be carefully monitored and evaluated.

Mayo Memorial Hospital employs nearly 2,500 staff personnel, and they have not received a cost-of-living increase in two years. As a result, staff salaries may not have kept pace with private industry, meaning the university's employee benefits program may become more important in attracting and retaining good workers. In addition, the contracts of three of the four staff unions expire next year, and the benefits program is typically a major area of bargaining (Ivarson 28).

As has been noted by Adams, a management consultant, "The success of employee benefits programs depends directly on whether the employees need, understand, and appreciate the value of the benefits provided" (220). Thus, to ensure that the benefit program is operating as effectively as possible, David Riggins, director of personnel, authorized this report on 15 October 20—. Specifically, the following problem was addressed in this study: What are the

Report page in MLA style

Santos 18

Works Cited

Abbey Petroleum Industries. *2005 Annual Report*. San Francisco: Abbey Petroleum Industries, 2006.

Adams, Josiah B. *Compensation Systems*. Boston: Brunswick, 2005.

Adhams, Ramon, and Seymour Stevens. *Personnel Management*. Cambridge: All-State, 2004.

Corporate Libraries Association. *Directory of Business and Financial Services*. New York: Corporate Libraries Association, 2005.

Ivarson, Andrew, Jr. "Creating Your Benefit Plan: A Primer." *Business Month* 29 Sept. 2005: 19–31.

"Let Employees Determine Their Own Benefits." *Manhattan Times* 12 Jan. 2006: C17.

"Market Research." *Encyclopedia of Business*. 2nd ed. Cleveland: Collins, 2006.

National Institute of Mental Health. *Who Pays the Piper? Ten Years of Passing the Buck*. DHHS Publication No. ADM 82-1195. Washington: GPO, 2006.

O'Brian, Douglas. Personal interview. 13 May 2006.

Preminger, Larry (Executive Producer). *The WKVX-TV Evening News*. Los Angeles: Valhalla Broadcasting Co. 5 Aug. 2006.

Quincy, Dinah J. "Maxwell Announces New Health Benefit." *Maxwell Corp. Home Page*. 13 Nov. 2004. 14 Jan. 2005 <http://www.maxcorp.com/news/2004 /f93500.html>.

Waerov, Denis V. E-mail to the author. 18 Aug. 2005.

Works cited page in MLA style

Third-Level Subheading

Double-space before the third-level subheading, indent, and type it in bold. Capitalize the first letter of the first and last words and all other words except articles, prepositions with four or fewer letters, and conjunctions. Leave a period and one space after the subheading; begin typing the text on the same line.

Pagination

Number the preliminary pages, such as the table of contents, with lowercase roman numerals centered on the bottom margin. The title page is counted as page i, but no page number is shown. Page numbers appear on all other preliminary pages, centered at the bottom margin. For example, the executive summary might be page ii and the table of contents might be page iii.

Number all pages, beginning with the first page of the body of the report, with Arabic numerals. The first page of the body is counted as page 1, but no page number is typed (in word processing terminology, the page number is *suppressed*). Beginning with page 2 of the body and continuing through the reference pages, number all pages consecutively at the top right of the page.

CITATION STYLES

Shown on pages 402–405 is a representative list of different types of citations formatted in the three most common citation styles—business style (also appropriate for most academic reports), APA style, and MLA style. Although the list is quite extensive, you may occasionally encounter a type of citation not illustrated here. In that case, simply find a similar type of citation and adapt it to your specific source.

References

Business Style: William A. Sabin, *The Gregg Reference Manual,* 10th ed., McGraw-Hill/Irwin, New York, 2005.

APA Style: *Publication Manual of the American Psychological Association,* 5th ed., Washington, D.C., American Psychological Association, 2001.

MLA Style: Joseph Gibaldi, *MLA Handbook for Writers of Research Papers,* 6th ed. New York, Modern Language Association of America, 2003; "MLA Style," *MLA Home Page,* September 9, 2003, http://www.mla.org (June 14, 2004).

Citation Styles: Within Document

	Business Style[1]
One author—not named in text	In fact, fringe benefits are growing in importance as a part of an overall salary package.[1]
One author—named in text	Adams argues that health insurance is the most important benefit of all.[2]
Multiple authors—not named in text	The personalized benefit statement shown in Figure 3 contains all necessary legal information.[3]
Multiple authors—named in text	According to Berelson, Lazarsfield, and Connell,[4] the personalized benefit statement shown in Figure 3 contains all necessary legal information.
Multiple sources	Numerous research studies[5] have shown that white-collar employees prefer an increase in benefits to an increase in salary.
Author not identified	Another variation that is growing in popularity is the cafeteria-style program.[6]
Direct quotation	According to Ivarson, "There is no such creature as a 'fringe benefit' anymore."[7]

[1] William A. Sabin, *The Gregg Reference Manual,* 9th ed., Westerville, Ohio, Glencoe/McGraw-Hill, 2001.

Citation Styles: End of Report

	Business Style—Bibliography
Annual report	Abbey Petroleum Industries, *2005 Annual Report,* API, Inc., San Francisco, 2006.
Book—one author	Adams, Josiah B., *Compensation Systems,* Brunswick Press, Boston, 2005.
Book—two authors	Adhams, Ramon, and Seymour Stevens, *Personnel Management,* All-State, Cambridge, MA, 2004.
Book—three or more authors	Berelson, Sarah, et al., *Managing Your Benefit Program,* 13th ed., Novak-Siebold, Chicago, 2006.
Book—organization as author	*Directory of Business and Financial Services,* Corporate Libraries Assoc., New York, 2005.

APA Style	MLA Style
In fact, fringe benefits are growing in importance as a part of an overall salary package (Ignatio, 2006).	In fact, fringe benefits are growing in importance as a part of an overall salary package (Ignatio 813).
Adams (2005) argues that health insurance is the most important benefit of all.	Adams argues that health insurance is the most important benefit of all (386–87).
The personalized benefit statement shown in Figure 3 contains all necessary legal information (Berelson, Lazarsfield, & Connell, 2006).	The personalized benefit statement shown in Figure 3 contains all necessary legal information (Berelson, Lazarsfield, and Connell 563).
According to Berelson, Lazarsfield, and Connell (2006, p. 563), the personalized benefit statement shown in Figure 3 contains all necessary legal information.	According to Berelson, Lazarsfield, and Connell, the personalized benefit statement shown in Figure 3 contains all necessary legal information (563).
Numerous research studies have shown that white-collar employees prefer an increase in benefits to an increase in salary (Adhams & Stevens, 2004; Ivarson, 2005; White, 2005).	Numerous research studies have shown that white-collar employees prefer an increase in benefits to an increase in salary (Adhams and Stevens 76; Ivarson 29; White).
Another variation that is growing in popularity is the cafeteria-style program ("Let Employees," 2006).	Another variation that is growing in popularity is the cafeteria-style program ("Let Employees").
According to Ivarson (2005), "There is no such creature as a 'fringe benefit' anymore" (p. 27).	According to Ivarson, "There is no such creature as a 'fringe benefit' anymore" (27).

APA Style–References	MLA Style–Works Cited
Abbey Petroleum Industries. (2006). *2005 annual report.* San Francisco: Author.	Abbey Petroleum Industries. *2005 Annual Report, Abbey Petroleum Industries, 2006.* San Francisco: API, Inc., 2006.
Adams, J. B. (2005). *Compensation systems.* Boston: Brunswick Press.	Adams, Josiah B. *Compensation Systems.* Boston: Brunswick; Press, 2005.
Adhams, R., & Stevens, S. (2004). *Personnel management.* Cambridge, MA: All-State.	Adhams, Ramon, and Seymour Stevens. *Personnel Management.* Cambridge: All-State, 2004.
Berelson, S., Lazarsfield, P. F., & Connell, W., Jr. (2006). *Managing your benefit program* (13th ed.). Chicago: Novak-Siebold.	Berelson, Sarah, Paul Lazarsfield, and Will Connell, Jr. *Managing Your Benefit Program.* 13th ed. Chicago: Novak-Siebold, 2006.
Directory of business and financial services. (2005). New York: Corporate Libraries Association.	Corporate Libraries Association. *Directory of Business and Financial Services.* New York: Corporate Libraries Association, 2005.

Citation Styles: End of Report (continued)

	Business Style–Bibliography
Journal article—paged continuously throughout the year	Ignatio, Enar, "Can Flexible Benefits Promote Your Company?" *Personnel Quarterly,* Vol. 20, September 2006, pp. 804–816.
Magazine article—paged starting anew with each issue	Ivarson, Andrew, Jr., "Creating Your Benefit Plan: A Primer," *Business Month,* September 29, 2005, pp. 19–31.
Newspaper article—unsigned	"Let Employees Determine Their Own Benefits," *Manhattan Times,* January 12, 2006, p. C17, col. 2.
Reference work article	"Market Research," *Encyclopedia of Business,* 2d ed., 2006.
Government document	National Institute of Mental Health, *Who Pays the Piper? Ten Years of Passing the Buck,* DHHS Publication No. ADM 82-1195, U.S. Government Printing Office, Washington, 2005.
Interview	O'Brian, Douglas, Interview by author, May 13, 2006.
Paper presented at a meeting	Patts, Regina. *Tuition Reimbursement,* paper presented at the meeting of the National Mayors' Conference, Trenton, NJ, August 5, 2006.
Television/radio broadcast	Preminger, Larry (Executive Producer), *The WKVX-TV Evening News,* Valhalla Broadcasting Co., Los Angeles, August 5, 2006.
CD-ROM article	Petelin, Rosana, "Wage Administration," *Martindale Interactive Business Encyclopedia* (CD-ROM), Martindale, Inc., Pompton Lakes, NJ, 2005.
World Wide Web page	Quincy, Dinah J., "Maxwell Announces New Health Benefit," *Maxwell Corp.,* November 13, 2004, <http://www.maxcorp.com/NEWS/2004/f93500.html> accessed on January 14, 2005.
Online database article	"Salary Survey of Service Industries," *BizInfo,* n.d., <http://www.bizinfo.com/census.gov/ind.lib/tab-0315.html> accessed on July 8, 2004.
E-mail	Waerov, Denis V., "Reaction to Management's Offer," e-mail message, August 19, 2005.
Electronic discussion message (including Listservs and newsgroups)	Young, Laurel <lyoung2@express.com> "Training Doesn't Always Last," June 3, 2004, <http://groups.yahoo.com/group/personnel/message/51> accessed on April 20, 2005.

APA Style—References	MLA Style—Works Cited
Ignatio, E. (2006). Can flexible benefits promote your company?" *Personnel Quarterly, 20,* 804–816.	Ignatio, Enar. "Can Flexible Benefits Promote Your Company?" *Personnel Quarterly* 20 (2006): 804–16.
Ivarson, A., Jr. (2005, September 29). Creating your benefit plan: A primer. *Business Month, 75,* 19–31.	Ivarson, Andrew, Jr. "Creating Your Benefit Plan: A Primer." *Business Month* 29 Sept. 2005: 19–31.
Let employees determine their own benefits. (2006, January 12). *Manhattan Times,* p. C17.	"Let Employees Determine Their Own Benefits." *Manhattan Times* 12 Jan. 2006: C17.
Market research. (2006). In *The encyclopedia of business* (2nd ed., Vol. 2, pp. 436–441). Cleveland, OH: Collins.	"Market Research." *Encyclopedia of Business,* 2nd ed., Cleveland: Collins, 2006.
National Institute of Mental Health. (2005). *Who pays the piper? Ten years of passing the buck* (DHHS Publication No. ADM 82-1195). Washington, DC: U.S. Government Printing Office.	National Institute of Mental Health. *Who Pays the Piper? Ten Years of Passing the Buck.* DHHS Publication No. ADM 82-1195. Washington: GPO, 2005.
[Not cited in reference list. Cited in text as "D. O'Brian (personal interview, May 13, 2006) suggests that . . ."]	O'Brian, Douglas. Personal interview, 13 May 2006.
Patts, R. (2005, August). *Tuition reimbursement.* Paper presented at the meeting of the National Mayors' Conference, Trenton, NJ.	Patts, Regina. *Tuition Reimbursement.* Paper presented at the meeting of the National Mayors' Conference. Trenton, NJ, 5 Aug. 2005.
Preminger, L. (Executive Producer). (2006, August 5). *The WKVX-TV Evening News* [Television broadcast]. Los Angeles: Valhalla Broadcasting Co.	Preminger, Larry (Executive Producer). *The WKVX-TV Evening News.* Los Angeles: Valhalla Broadcasting Co., 5 Aug. 2006.
Petelin, R. (2005). *Wage administration.* Pompton Lakes, NJ: Martindale, Inc. Retrieved from Martindale database (Martindale Interactive Business Encyclopedia, CD-ROM).	Petelin, Rosana. "Wage Administration," *Martindale Interactive Business Encyclopedia.* CD-ROM. Pompton Lakes, NJ: Martindale, Inc., 2005.
Quincy, D. J. (2004, November 13). Maxwell announces new health benefit. New York: Maxwell. Retrieved January 14, 2005 from http://www.maxcorp.com/NEWS/2004/f93500.html	Quincy, Dinah J. "Maxwell Announces New Health Benefit." *Maxwell Corp. Home Page.* 13 Nov. 2004. 14 Jan. 2005 <http://www.maxcorp.com/NEWS/2004/f93500.html>.
Salary survey of service industries. (n.d.). Retrieved July 8, 2004, from BizInfo database, http://www.bizinfo.com/census.gov/ind.lib/tab-0315.html	"Salary Survey of Service Industries." *BizInfo.* n.d. 8 July 2004 <http://www.bizinfo.com/census.gov/ind.lib/tab-0315.html>.
[Not cited in reference list. Cited in text as "D. V. Waerov (personal communication, August 18, 2003) proposes that . . ."]	Waerov, Denis, V. "Reaction to Management's Offer," E-mail to the author. 19 Aug 2005.
Young, L. (2004, June 3). Training doesn't always last. Message posted to http://groups.yahoo.com/group/personnel/message/51	Young, Laurel. <lyoung2@express.com> "Training Doesn't Always Last." Online posting. 3 June 2004. 20 Apr. 2005 <http://groups.yahoo.com/group/personnel/message/51>.

Business Style Pointers

▌ The major differences between footnote and bibliographic entries are that (a) footnotes use the normal order for author names (e.g., "Raymond Stevens and Seymour Adams"), whereas bibliographies invert the order of the first author (e.g., "Stevens, Raymond, and Seymour Adams"); and (b) page numbers are included in bibliographic entries only when the material being cited is part of a larger work (for example, a journal or newspaper article).

▌ Type the authors' names exactly as they appear in print. For publications by two authors, arrange only the first name in last-name/first-name order. With three or more authors, type only the first name followed by *et al.* (not in italics). Arrange publications by the same author in alphabetical order, according to the publication title.

▌ Include page numbers only when the material being cited is part of a larger work. Do not italicize edition numbers. Be consistent in formatting the ordinal in the raised position (13th) or in the normal position (13th).

▌ Include the two-letter state name (using the U.S. Postal Service abbreviation) only if confusion might otherwise result. Use a shortened form of the publisher's name; e.g., *McGraw-Hill* rather than *McGraw-Hill Book Company,* and use common abbreviations (such as *Assoc.* or *Co.*).

▌ For online citations:

- For e-mail, insert the type of e-mail (e.g., "office communication" or "personal e-mail").
- If the date of an online posting cannot be determined, insert the abbreviation *n.d.* (no date), —not in italics.
- Enclose in parentheses, as the last section of the citation, the date you accessed the site, followed by a period.
- Follow the capitalization, punctuation, and spacing exactly as given in the original online address.
- You may break an online citation *before* (but never after) a dot (.), single slash (/), double slash (//), hyphen (-), underscore (_), "at" symbol (@), or any other mark of punctuation. Do not insert a hyphen within an online address to signify an end-of-line break.

Endnotes

Chapter 1

1. Mark H. McCormack, "Words You Use Tell a Lot About You," *Arizona Republic*, April 13, 2000, p. D4.
2. Watson Wyatt Worldwide, *Linking Communications With Strategy to Achieve Business Goals*, Bethesda, MD, 1999, p. 6.
3. David Shenk, *Data Smog: Surviving the Information Glut*, San Francisco: HarperCollins, 1997.
4. Stephen Karel, "Learning Culture the Hard Way," *Consumer Markets Abroad*, May 1988, pp. 1, 15.
5. Judi Sanders, "Top 20 College Slang Terms," California State Polytechnic University, Pomona Home Page, May 1, 2001, http://www.intraner.csupomona.edu/~jasanders/slang/top20.html (January 17, 2003).

Chapter 2

1. John R. Pierce, "Communication," *Scientific American*, col. 227, September 1972, p. 36.
2. Irving R. Janis, *Victims of Groupthink*, Houghton Mifflin, Boston, 1972.
3. These guidelines are based on principles contained in Peter R. Scholtes, *The Team Handbook: How to Use Teams to Improve Quality*, Madison, WI, Joiner Associates, 1988, pp. 6.23–6.28.
4. *2000 Statistical Abstract of the United States*, Washington, D.C., U.S. Government Printing Office, 2000, Table 16.
5. Sondra Thiederman, "The Diverse Workplace: Strategies for Getting 'Culture Smart,'" *The Secretary*, March 1996, p. 8.
6. *2000 Statistical Abstract of the United States*, Washington, D.C., U.S. Government Printing Office, 2000, Table 16.
7. John C. Maxwell, *There's No Such Thing as "Business" Ethics*, New York, Warner Books, 2003, pp. 5–9.
8. "State Court Cuts Punitive Award in BMW Car Case," *The Wall Street Journal*, May 12, 1997, p. B5.
9. Beth Belton, "U.S. Brings Economy Into Information Age," *USA Today*, March 17, 1999, p. 1B.
10. "Reaching out With E-mail," *PC Week*, May 4, 1998, p. 100.
11. Christina Cavanagh, *Managing Your E-Mail*, Hoboken, NJ, John Wiley, 2003, pp. 23–25.
12. Society for Human Resource Management, "E-Mail Becoming a Workplace Norm," press release, February 8, 1996.
13. Beth Belton, "U.S. Brings Economy Into Information Age," *USA Today*, March 17, 1999, p. 1B.
14. Samantha Miller, *E-mail Etiquette*, New York, Warner Books, 2001, p. 99.
15. Samantha Miller, *E-mail Etiquette*, New York, Warner Books, 2001, pp. 94–96.
16. Jeff Tyson, "How Instant Messaging Works," *Howstuffworks*, n.d., http://www.howstuffworks.com/instant-messaging.htm. Accessed on January 21, 2005.
17. The Hanson Group, a corporate-ethics consultancy in Los Altos, California.
18. This case was adapted from Brenda R. Sims, "Linking Ethics and Language in the Technical Communication Classroom," *Technical Communication Quarterly*, Vol. 2, No. 3, Summer 1993, p. 285.

Chapter 3

1. Peter Drucker, quoted by Bill Moyers in *A World of Ideas*, Garden City, NY: Doubleday, 1990.
2. Albert Mehrabian, "Communicating Without Words," *Psychology Today*, September 1968, pp. 53–55.
3. Edward T. Hall, *The Hidden Dimension*, Garden City, NY: Doubleday, 1966, pp. 107–122.
4. Ralph G. Nichols, "Listening Is a Ten-Part Skill," *Nation's Business*, September 1987, p. 40; "Listen Up!" *American Salesman*, July 1987, p. 29.
5. *Clear Communication*, Vol. 1, No. 2, Fall 1993, p. 2.
6. Federal Communications Commission, *Trends in Telephone Service*, U.S. Government Printing Office, 2003; "International Long Distance Calling," *Consumer and Governmental Affairs Bureau Home Page*, www.fcc.gov/cgb/consumerfacts/hello.html (September 13, 2003); Maggie Jackson, "Turn Off That Cellphone. It's Meeting Time," *New York Times*, Sunday, March 2, 2003, p. BU-12.
7. "Telephone On-Hold Statistics," *National Telephone Message Corporation*, http://www.ihearditonhold.com/statistics.html, September 13, 2003.
8. "Phone Calls Waste a Month Each Year," *Office Systems*, September 1989, p. 14.
9. "Managing Meetings: A Critical Role," *The Office*, November 1989, p. 20.
10. "Managing Meetings," p. 20.

Chapter 4

1. Julie Schmit, "Continental's $4 Million Typo," *USA Today*, May 25, 1993, p. B1.

Chapter 5

1. Marilyn vos Savant, "Ask Marilyn," *Parade Magazine*, November 3, 1996, p. 8.

Chapter 9

1. Theophilus B. A. Aldo, "The Effects of Dimensionality in Computer Graphics," *Journal of Business Communication*, Vol. 31, December 1994, pp. 253–265.
2. See, for example, "Tabling the Move to Computer Graphics," *Wall Street Journal*, January 30, 1991, p. B1; Jeremiah J. Sullivan, "Financial Presentation Format and Managerial Decision Making: Tables Versus Graphics," *Management Communication Quarterly*, Vol. 2, November 1988, pp. 194–216.
3. Edward Tufte, *The Visual Display of Quantitative Information*, Graphics Press, Cheshire, CT, 1983.

Chapter 11

1. Kerry L. Johnson, "You Were Saying," *Managers Magazine*, February 1989, p. 19.
2. Wharton Applied Research Center, "A Study of the Effects of the Use of Overhead Transparencies on Business Meetings, Final Report," Philadelphia: University of Pennsylvania, September 14, 1981; Tad Simons, "Study Shows Just How Much

Visuals Increase Persuasiveness," *Presentations Magazine,* March 1998, p. 20.

3. Betty A. Marton, "How to Construct a Winning Presentation," *Harvard Management Communication Letter,* April 2000, p. 5.

4. Albert Mehrabian, "Communicating Without Words," *Psychology Today,* September 1968, pp. 53–55.

5. David Wallechinsky, Irving Wallace, and Amy Wallace, *The Book of Lists,* William Morrow, New York, 1977, pp. 469–470.

6. Jolie Solomon, "Executives Who Dread Public Speaking Learn to Keep Their Cool in the Spotlight," *Wall Street Journal,* May 4, 1990, p. B1.

Chapter 12

1. U.S. Department of Labor, *Occupational Outlook Handbook,* 2005–2006 ed., Bureau of Labor Statistics, http://www.bls.gov/oco/ (accessed on May 19, 2005).

2. Sandra L. Latimer, "First Impressions," *Mt. Pleasant* (MI) *Morning Sun,* May 8, 1989, p. 6.

3. See, for example, Jules Harcourt and A. C. "Buddy" Krizan, "A Comparison of Résumé Content Preferences of *Fortune* 500 Personnel Administrators and Business Communication Instructors," *Journal of Business Communication,* Spring 1989, pp. 177–190; Rod Little, "Keep Your Résumé Short," *USA Today,* July 28, 1989, p. B1; Darlene C. Pibal, "Criteria for Effective Résumés as Perceived by Personnel Directors," *Personnel Administrator,* May 1985, pp. 119–123.

4. Elizabeth Blackburn-Brockman and Kelly Belanger, "One Page or Two? A National Study of CPA Recruiters' Preferences for Résumé Length," *Journal of Business Communication,* January 2001, pp. 29–57.

5. "Most Serious Résumé Gaffes," *Communication Briefings,* March 1991, p. 6.

6. "To Be or Not to Be," *The Secretary,* April 1991, p. 6.

7. Albert P. Karr, "Labor Letter," *Wall Street Journal,* September 1, 1992, p. A1.

8. Harcourt and Krizan, pp. 177–190.

9. Therese Droste, "Executive Résumés: The Ultimate Calling Card," *Hospitals,* March 5, 1989, p. 72.

10. Stephanie Armour, "Security Checks Worry Workers," *USA Today,* June 19, 2002, p. B1.

Chapter 13

1. Lynn Ulrich and Don Trumbo, "The Selection Interview Since 1949," *Psychological Bulletin,* Vol. 43, 1956, p. 100.

2. Shelly Liles, "Wrong Hire Might Prove Costly," *USA Today,* June 6, 1989, p. 6B.

3. Mary Bakeman et al., *Job-Seeking Skills Reference Manual,* 3rd., Minnesota Rehabilitation Center, Minneapolis, 1971, p. 57.

4. Jeff Fee, "Practicing Cubicle Courtesy," *Indianapolis Star,* August 11, 2002, p. F1.

CREDITS

Chapter 1   Pages 2, 4: Courtesy of Nissan North America/Debra Sanchez Fair; page 11: © Kevin Irby Photography.

Chapter 2   Page 18: © Joel W. Rogers/Corbis; page 20: Courtesy of The Nucon Group/Gilbert C. Morrell, Jr.; © Ki Ho Park/Kistone Photography; page 26: Photo by Tom Stoddart; page 30: Courtesy Texas Instruments.

Chapter 3   Page 44: © Royalty-Free/PhotoAlto/Getty Images; page 46: Courtesy of The Hilliard Marketing Group/Amy Hilliard; page 48: © AP Wide World Photos.

Chapter 4   Page 68: © Artiga Photo/Corbis; page 70: Courtesy of PricewaterhouseCoopers/Noel McCarthy; page 76: © Misha Gravenor.

Chapter 5   Pages 88, 90: Courtesy of World Wrestling Entertainment/Gary Davis; page 98: © Robert Houser; page 107: © Misha Gravenor.

Chapter 6   Pages 116, 118: Courtesy of Annie's Homegrown/Ann Withey; page 127: © David Strick/Redux; page 131: Courtesy of Sir Speedy, Inc.

Chapter 7   Page 140: © Howard Kingsnorth/zefa/Corbis; page 142: Courtesy of Wurzburg, Inc./Patrick Vijiarungam; page 153: Courtesy of National Multiple Sclerosis Society; page 159: Courtesy of The Home Depot.

Chapter 8   Page 168: Intel CEO with chip © UPI/Landov; page 170: Courtesy of Intel Corporation/Howard High; page 171: © AP Wide World Photos; page 185: Courtesy of General Mills.

Chapter 9   Pages 190, 192: Courtesy of Rock and Roll Hall of Fame/Todd Mesek; page 197: © Ezra Shaw/Getty Images.

Chapter 10   Pages 222, 224: Courtesy of Habitat for Humanity/Steve Messinetti; page 226: reprinted with permission from Weight Watchers International, Inc.

Chapter 11   Page 254: © Royalty-Free/Iconica/Getty Images; page 256: Courtesy of Georgia Hispanic Chamber of Commerce/Sara González; page 260: © AP Wide World Photos; page 266: Reuters/Corbis.

Chapter 12   Page 278: © Royalty-Free/Corbis; page 280: Courtesy of Computer Sciences Corporation/Paul Orvos; page 293: Copyright © 1994–2006 Eli Lilly and Company. Used with permission; page 296: Used by permission of Netscape Communications Corporation.

Chapter 13   Page 312: © Adrian Brown/Bloomberg News/Landov; page 314: Courtesy of Monster.com/Jeff Taylor.

ANSWERS TO TEST PREPPERS

Chapter 1
Test Prepper 1.1
1. F   2. F   3. T   4. T   5. F
6. Audience: The person with whom you're communicating—perhaps your roommate.
7. Communication: The process of sending and receiving messages—such as writing or speaking.
8. Feedback: The reaction to a message—such as sending a response.
9. Filter: A person's interpretation of a message—such as getting angry.
10. Medium: The form of the message—perhaps an e-mail.
11. Message: The information communicated, such as "That's a relief."
12. Stimulus: An event that creates a need to communicate—such as seeing a sad scene at the movies.
13. Answers will vary. Most will center on the idea that all forms are important.

Test Prepper 1.2
1. F   2. T   3. F   4. T   5. T
6. Answers will vary. Possible answers might include communicating negative, sensitive, or complex information.

Test Prepper 1.3
1. T   2. F   3. T   4. F   5. T
6. Abstract word: A word that calls up a symbol or feeling rather than a concrete object—such as *happiness*.
7. Concrete word: A word describing an object that can be perceived by the senses—such as *book*.
8. Connotation: The feelings a word generates, such as having negative feelings associated with the word *boss*.
9. Denotation: The direct meaning of a word. For example, the denotation of *boss* is a person who exercises control over workers.
10. Euphemism: The act of substituting a vague or mild term for one considered harsh or offensive, such as using *unmotivated* for *lazy*.
11. Jargon: The specialized language of a group, such as using the word *pica* as a unit of measurement in publishing.
12. Slang: An expression characteristic of a particular group, such as using the word *dis* for *disrespect*.
13. Answers will vary. Possible answers might include sensitive situations, such as delivering bad news the receiver may take personally.

Chapter 2
Test Prepper 2.1
1. F   2. T   3. F   4. T   5. T
6. Groupthink: The tendency for a group to encourage agreement and to discourage dissent.
7. Team: A group organized to work together to accomplish an objective.

Test Prepper 2.2
1. T   2. F   3. T   4. T   5. F
6. Ethnocentrism: The tendency to judge other cultures according to your own culture's standards—such as an American expecting an international colleague to speak English.
7. Answers will vary, but be careful not to make hasty value judgments about the gender differences identified in Table 2.1.

Test Prepper 2.3
1. F   2. T   3. T   4. T   5. F
6. Ethics: Values relating to the rightness or wrongness of an action.
7. Answers will vary.

Test Prepper 2.4
1. T   2. F   3. F   4. T   5. F
6. Answers will vary.

Chapter 3
Test Prepper 3.1
1. F   2. T   3. F   4. T   5. T
6. Answers will vary. Possible answers might include that many believe nonverbal messages because they are more spontaneous and more difficult to fake than verbal messages.

Test Prepper 3.2
1. F   2. T   3. T   4. T   5. F
6. Answers will vary.

Test Prepper 3.3
1. T   2. F   3. F   4. T   5. T

Test Prepper 3.4
1. T   2. F   3. F   4. T
5. Agenda: A list of topics to be considered at a meeting.
6. Minutes: An official record of the proceedings of a meeting.

Chapter 4
Test Prepper 4.1
1. F   2. T   3. F   4. T
5. Audience analysis: Learning everything you can about the receiver of your message.

Test Prepper 4.2
1. T   2. T   3. F
4. Brainstorming: Generating ideas to help solve a problem without paying attention to the ultimate quality of the ideas.
5. Organization: The order in which you discuss the topics in your message.

Test Prepper 4.3
1. F   2. F   3. F
4. Drafting: Composing a beginning version of your message.
5. Free writing: Writing without stopping for five to ten minutes.
6. Writer's block: The inability to produce a draft of your message.

Test Prepper 4.4
1. F   2. T   3. T
4. Editing: Revising a document to conform to standard English.
5. Revising: Modifying a message to make it more effective.
6. Answers will vary.

Test Prepper 4.5, 4.6
1. T   2. T   3. T
4. Answers will vary.

Chapter 5

Test Prepper 5.1
1. T   2. F   3. F
4. Dangling expression: A word or phrase that isn't logically connected to the rest of the sentence—such as "When three, my father took me to London."
5. Expletive: An expression such as "it is" that puts the real subject after the verb—such as "There is the report on the shelf."
6. Redundancy: Needless repetition—such as "and etc."
7. Answers will vary. Possible answers might include stressing the negative when an employee has failed to cooperate after positive language was already used, or using the negative for health or safety issues—such as "Do NOT touch this wire."

Test Prepper 5.2
1. F   2. F   3. T   4. F
5. Active voice: A sentence in which the subject is doing the action—such as "I ran the meeting."
6. Simple sentence: A sentence that contains one independent clause.
7. Compound sentence: One that contains two or more independent clauses and no dependent clauses—such as "Sardi's catered the event and The Embers provided the entertainment."
8. Compound-complex sentence: One that contains two or more independent clauses and one or more dependent clauses—such as "When Martha finally arrived, we took our seats, and Jose called the meeting to order."
9. Passive voice: A sentence in which the subject is acted upon—such as "The awards are being presented tomorrow."
10. Complex sentence: One that contains one independent clause and one or more dependent clauses—such as "Although I arrived late, I was present for the entire presentation."

Test Prepper 5.3
1. T   2. F   3. T   4. T
5. Parallelism: Presenting similar expressions in similar grammatical format—such as "adding, subtracting, and multiplying."
6. Answers will vary. Possible answers might include coherence/logic and parallel structure being important in both e-mails.

Test Prepper 5.4
1. F   2. T   3. T   4. F   5. T
6. Reader benefits: The advantage the reader or listener receives from the situation—such as "Completing this short questionnaire will ensure that your views are reflected in our research."

7. "You" attitude: The style of writing that makes the reader or listener the center of attention—such as "Your package should arrive within two days."
8. Answers will vary. Possible answers might include tone, volume of voice, visual aids, and body movement.

Chapter 6

Test Prepper 6.1, 6.2
1. T   2. F   3. F   4. T   5. T
6. Direct organizational plan: The sequence in which the major idea is presented first, followed by details.
7. Indirect organizational plan: The sequence in which the reasons are given first, followed by the major idea.
8. Answers will vary. Possible answers might include that a telephone call has the advantage of an immediate response, plus the possibility of clearing up any additional questions. E-mail has the advantages of allowing the reader to respond at his or her convenience and of providing a written record of the request.

Test Prepper 6.3, 6.4
1. F   2. T   3. F   4. T   5. T
6. Adjustment letter: A letter that responds to a claim letter.
7. Claim letter: A letter that informs the company about a problem with its product.
8. Resale: Information that attempts to reestablish the customer's faith in your product.
9. Answers will vary. Possible answers might include that while addressing the letter to the president will certainly get attention, customer service employees are more knowledgeable about specific company policies and procedures, product history, and warranty information.

Chapter 7

Test Prepper 7.1
1. T   2. T   3. F   4. F
5. Rhetorical question: A question asked to encourage the reader to think about the problem, such as "What would happen if all of our workers arrived 10 minutes late every day?"
6. Answers will vary.

Test Prepper 7.2, 7.3
1. T   2. T
3. Answers will vary.

Test Prepper 7.4
1. T   2. F   3. T   4. T   5. F
6. Central selling theme: The most important benefit from owning your product or using your service—for example, ease of use.
7. Answers will vary. Possible answers might include refusing to sell the product and even suggesting finding employment elsewhere.

Chapter 8

Test Prepper 8.1–8.4
1. F   2. F   3. T   4. F   5. T
6. Answers will vary.

Chapter 9
Test Prepper 9.1–9.3
1. T   2. F   3. T   4. T   5. F
6. Primary data: Data that you collect for your own specific purposes—such as administering a questionnaire to your fellow students.
7. Secondary data: Data collected by someone else for a different purpose—such as a student questionnaire administered by someone else for a different purpose.

Test Prepper 9.4–9.7
1. F   2. F   3. T   4. F   5. T
6. Bar chart: A chart with horizontal or vertical bars that represent the values.
7. Line chart: A chart with the vertical axis standing for values and the horizontal axis standing for time.
8. Pie chart: A circle chart with wedges representing each component.
9. Table: An arrangement of data in columns and rows.
10. Answers will vary. Possible answers might include the longer students spend in school, the fewer music CDs they purchase each week.

Chapter 10
Test Prepper 10.1
1. T   2. F   3. T   4. F
5. Generic headings: Report headings that simply identify the topic discussed in the section.
6. Talking headings: Report headings that both identify the topic discussed in the section and reveal the conclusion.
7. Answers will vary. Possible answers might include tradition, company policy, the formality of the reports prepared, and other factors.

Test Prepper 10.2–10.5
1. F   2. T   3. F   4. T   5. F
6. Direct quotation: Using the exact words of another person.
7. Documentation: Providing the source for words or ideas of another person used in your report.
8. Paraphrase: Summarizing or restating the words or ideas of another person in your own words.
9. Plagiarism: Using another person's words or ideas without giving proper credit to the original source.
10. Answers will vary. Possible answers might include there is no need to document commonly known facts than can be verified easily.

Chapter 11
Test Prepper 11.1, 11.2
1. T   2. T   3. F   4. T   5. F   6. F
7. Answers will vary. Possible answers might include extenuating circumstances such as the need to work long hours, or

the improving trend of the student's grades, or the benefits the institution might derive from the student's attendance and subsequent graduation.

Test Prepper 11.3, 11.4
1. T   2. T   3. F   4. T
5. Answers will vary.

Test Prepper 11.5
1. F   2. T   3. T   4. F
5. Answers will vary.

Chapter 12
Test Prepper 12.1
1. T   2. F   3. F   4. F   5. T
6. Answers will vary.

Test Prepper 12.2
1. F   2. T   3. T   4. F   5. T
6. Electronic résumé: A résumé that is stored in a computer database
7. Reference: Someone who has agreed to provide information to a prospective employer about a job applicant's fitness for a specific job
8. Résumé: A brief record of one's history and qualifications for a job.
9. Answers will vary.

Test Prepper 12.3
1. F   2. T   3. F   4. F   5. F
6. Application letter: A letter to a prospective employer indicating your interest in and qualifications for a position within the company.
7. Answers will vary. Possible answers might include that such gimmicks send a nonverbal message to the reader that the applicant may be trying to deflect attention from a weak résumé.

Chapter 13
Test Prepper 13.1–13.3
1. T   2. F   3. T   4. T   5. F
6. Answers will vary. Possible answers might include an aspect of the student's present job that he or she enjoys and that is directly related to the new position. For the least liked aspect, select an aspect of the present job that the new job does not involve.

Test Prepper 13.4
1. T   2. T
3. Business etiquette: Acting politely and appropriately in a business setting.
4. Answers will vary.

Index